The Social Impact of Computers

The Social Impact of Computers

Richard S. Rosenberg
The University of British Columbia

ACADEMIC PRESS, INC.
Harcourt Brace & Company, Publishers
Boston San Diego New York
London Sydney Tokyo Toronto

This book is printed on acid-free paper. ♾

ACADEMIC PRESS, INC.
A Division of Harcourt Brace & Company
525 B Street, Suite 1900, San Diego, California 92101-4495

United Kingdom Edition published by
ACADEMIC PRESS LIMITED
24–28 Oval Road, London NW1 7DX

Library of Congress Cataloging-in-Publication Data

Rosenberg, Richard S.
The social impact of computers / Richard S. Rosenberg.
p. cm.
Includes bibliographical references and index.
ISBN 0-12-597130-3 (alk. paper)
1. Computers—Social aspects. I. Title.
QA76.9.C66R64 1992
303.48'34—dc20 91-29660
CIP

PRINTED IN THE UNITED STATES OF AMERICA
96 97 9 8 7 6 5 4 3 2

. . . But not because I am out of sympathy with their feelings about technology. I just think that their flight from and hatred of technology is self-defeating. The Buddah, the Godhead, resides quite as comfortably in the circuits of a digital computer or the gears of a cycle transmission as he does at the top of a mountain or in the petals of a flower.

Robert M. Pirsig, *Zen and the Art of Motorcycle Maintainence,* copyright © 1974 by Robert Pirsig, reprinted by permission of William Morrow and Co., Inc.

In memory of my parents, Leibel and Malka, who planted the seed of social concern, helped it grow, but could not see it flower.

CONTENTS

11

BUSINESS AND GOVERNMENT 253

12

ROBOTICS AND INDUSTRIAL AUTOMATION 289

PREFACE

> ***It has been suggested by some of the reviewers of* NINETEEN EIGHTY-FOUR *that it is the author's view that this, or something like this, is what will happen in the next forty years in the Western world. This is not correct. I think that, allowing for the book being after all a parody, something like* NINETEEN-EIGHTY FOUR *could happen.***
>
> **From a press release by George Orwell's publisher, Frederic Warburg, from notes dictated by Orwell, author of *1984,* in 1949. Copyright, Bernard Crick, *George Orwell: A Life* (London: Martin Secker & Warburg, 1980, p. 395).**

This quotation describes one limit of a future that a rapidly evolving technology makes possible. Will we move towards a society in which government is all-powerful and, by virtue of its mandate to protect the country, assumes extraordinary powers to monitor the daily lives of its citizens, aided by multinational corporations interested in preserving their control and markets? Will technology free the members of advanced industrial (or postindustrial) societies from a scarcity of goods and pave the way for a new age of enlightenment and plenty?

No definitive answers to such questions will be provided here, even if it were possible to do so. Rather this book should be read as a guide to the social implications of current and future applications of computers. Among the basic themes presented are the following:

- The changing nature of work in response to technological innovation as well as the threat to jobs.
- Personal freedom in the machine age as manifested by challenges to privacy, dignity, and work.
- The relationship between advances in computer and communications technology and the possibility of increased centralization of authority.
- The emergence and influence of artificial intelligence and its role in decision-making, especially in military applications.

- The growing importance of information as both a means to improve productivity and as a commodity in its own right.
- The hidden influence of computers as microprocessors are embedded in a myriad of products.
- The diffusion of the personal computers at work, at home, in schools, and elsewhere.

More specifically, this book discusses a number of issues that no single source has treated in sufficient depth. These include the following:

- Popular attitudes towards computers, computers and the human imagination, and computers in the arts.
- Recent advances in robotics and industrial automation, including the "factory of the future" and the role of this technology in the improvement of industrial productivity.
- Military applications of computers, especially in "Star Wars," and the dangers of autonomous decision-making.
- Computers and the home, beyond games and toward useful applications.
- The emerging information society and the dangers of control of information sources and dissemination.
- Videotex systems, including the very successful French version, Minitel, the recent U.S. failures, as well as the current major attempt, Prodigy.
- Office automation and the concern about the lack of a real payoff after the expenditures of many billions of dollars.
- Computers and telecommunications as global phenomena.
- Computer impact on working conditions: video display terminals and job safety, monitoring, and deskilling.
- Patent and copyright issues with respect to computer hardware and software.
- Computer crime, including unauthorized entry, hacking, and viruses.
- Privacy issues, including transactional data collection, government privacy protection, communication protection, computer matching, and caller ID.
- Information technology in the political process: voter solicitation, vote counting, and outcome projections.
- The influence of the Department of Defense in computer science research and education.
- International competition and the challenges of Japan and Western Europe in high technology.
- Women and computing: jobs, academic opportunities, and status.
- Ethics and professionalism in computing: special challenges and responsibilities.

No field growing and changing as rapidly as computers and microelectronics can be easily captured within the confines of a single book. Inevitably there are many topics, some quite important, that have been treated in a limited fashion. Although there are some examples of computer applications in science presented in Chapter 1, these are few, and only suggestive of the enormous importance of computers.

Most people are becoming increasingly familiar with computers through exposure at home, school, and work. To spark attention and interest in the effects of computers on society, the book begins with a selection of diverse applications ranging from smart automobiles to smart homes. This technology, in many of its manifestations, presents an image of a changing world full of promise and hope but with a host of associated problems and dangers. Only a concerned and informed populace can recognize and deal with the issues identified in the book.

The fourteen chapters in this book can be grouped as follows:

Chapters 1–3:	Background and historical information on computers and technology.
Chapters 4–7:	Some major applications: business, medicine, education, government.
Chapters 8–10:	Major social issues, including crime, privacy, work.
Chapters 11–13:	New technologies and problems: industry regulation, electronic funds transfer systems, international competition, national industrial policies, robotics and industrial automation, productivity, the information society, videotex.
Chapter 14:	Ethics and professionalism.

Some major topics—such as privacy, videotex, artificial intelligence, electronic funds transfer systems, home and personal computers, and the impact on work—are discussed in more than one place. Because several social issues are associated with each computer application, a certain measure of redundancy is inevitable. Thus, each major application is treated in depth at one place but referred to whenever the relevant social issues are examined. For example, artificial intelligence is first introduced and discussed in Chapter 2. Subsequently, its contributions are recognized in applications in such areas as expert systems (Chapter 4), medicine (Chapter 5), education (Chapter 6), military (Chapter 7), law (Chapter 8), and robotics (Chapter 12). The table of contents, in text references, and the index will be useful in locating such distributed discussions.

To make full use of the material presented here, the Notes and Additional Readings given at the end of every chapter should be considered. In such a field undergoing continual change, it is necessary to refer on a regular basis to relevant journals, magazines, books, and even newspapers. A representative list of these, as well as of professional societies, is given in the Appendix.

The material presented here should be accessible to most university students who have had an introductory course in computer science. Self taught or sufficiently motivated individuals who have gained an understanding of how computers operate should also profit from this book. Especially useful are backgrounds in sociology, economics, history, political science, or philosophy. Although many topics are covered, nothing is said about the details of programming, in BASIC or any other language, or computer hardware. Such technical information is readily available elsewhere.

ACKNOWLEDGMENTS

Many people have helped in the writing of this book, either directly or indirectly; I therefore apologize in advance to anyone I may have omitted. Let me mention, in no particular order, Alice Peters, Sari Kalin, Mike Brady, Alan Mackworth, Marc Romanycia, David LeBlanc, Ron Anderson, C. Dianne Martin, Mary Culnan, Marc Rotenberg, Joe Smith, Cal Deedman, Bob Fransen, Cynthia Alexander, Kelly Gotlieb, Andrew Clements, Jay (Buck) Bloombecker, Tom Forester, David Flaherty, Theresa Fong, Grace Wolkosky, Evelyn Fong, Gale Arndt, Richard Bonacci, Barbara Simons, Abbe Mowshowitz, Rob Kling, Kerstin Teglof Delgado, Robert Ellis Smith, Janlori Goldman, Arek Shakarian, Jocelyn Godolphin, Henry Jay Becker, Starr Roxanne Hiltz, David Bellin, Harriet Rosenberg, Carol Whitehead, and Nou Dadoun, for his careful reading of the manuscript under "battlefield" conditions. The comments of anonymous reviewers were welcome and helpful. I also acknowledge the many students at the University of British Columbia, who have asked many of the right questions.

Of course, I take sole responsibility for the final version of this book. Nothing would have been possible without the constant support and encouragement of my wife, Sheryl, and my children, Aryeh, Rebecca, and Hannah.

1

COMPUTERS ARE EVERYWHERE

"Plastics," a well-meaning elder whispered to young Benjamin in The Graduate. *It was sound financial advice, but "silicon" would have been closer to the mark.*

Dirk Hanson, *The New Alchemists,* Little, Brown and Company, 1982

INTRODUCTION

You are about to begin the study of both computers themselves and how they have affected and will continue to affect society. In the long history of technological innovation, the computer in some sense is no more notable than such major inventions as the steam engine, the train, electricity and electronics, the telegraph and telephone, the automobile, the airplane, radio, motion pictures, and television. Yet there is something special about the computer that makes it more than just another machine. Its ability to be programmed to perform an incredible variety of tasks distinguishes it from all others.

The first electronic computers filled large rooms, weighed many tons, and generated vast quantities of heat. Now computers of equal or greater power sit comfortably on the tops of desks. Within the last few years, electronics engineers, physicists, and computer specialists have produced a powerful microprocessor that can slide easily through a paper clip. Such microprocessors are used in watches, cameras, microwave ovens, portable computers, automobiles, and assembly line robots. Other applications are sure to follow. Computers are now commonplace in schools, offices, and (more recently) the home. They generate our checks, our bills, and our receipts. They are used to store and retrieve enormous quantities of information for an incredible variety of purposes. Work and play are equally affected, as the following examples show.

• A two-page advertisement in *The York Times Magazine* shows one robot reading a newspaper and saying, "When I was your age, robots did what they were told," while another, with only its arms showing and holding a basketball, responds, "But Dad, my generation is different." The copy asks us to "imagine a generation of robots that can learn from their experiences and make their own decisions. It's happening—thanks to Neural Networks that enable computer systems to mimic the human brain."[1]

• In an advertisement for IBM, a worker reassures his fellow workers that although computers in the factory was once a scary idea, he now runs one:

> "I figured I'd get burned either way—computers show up and I get fired, or computers don't show up and the plant closes down. But what happened is, they retooled the plant and while that was going on they sent me to school, to an IBM-sponsored course at the community college."[2]

• *The New York Times* reports that in the information age, libraries are leading the way:

> In the vanguard of information technology, today's librarians are as likely to be experts in work stations, networking, communications protocols, electronic imaging and fiber optics as they are in books and manuscripts. . . . Information rather than oil or steel is likely to become the most precious commercial resource, and the company that can gather, evaluate and synthesize information ahead of its rivals will have a competitive advantage. Technology will also enable workers to collaborate on projects regardless of their physical locations, so the ability to exchange information on data networks is crucial. Libraries have addressed these issues for years.[3]

• Not only humans will benefit from developments in high technology. Some of their closest friends may have their lives saved.

> Novato, Calif.—Dolly is a protodog—specifically, dog No. 7F7E482105. She's one of the first pets in Northern California to partake in an international database aimed at retrieving lost animals and preventing euthanasia. . . . Dolly sports the latest in dog technology—a microchip tucked under her fur between her shoulder blades. . . . If for instance, Dolly jumped her fence and was picked up as a stray, shelter personnel would wave a scanner over her back. The scanner would activate the chip and pick up a 10-digit number that appears on a battery-powered display. That number would be called into Infopet's hot line.[4]

• The needs of computer programmers and hardware specialists do not consist entirely of computers and programs. Physical needs must also be met and in the heart of Silicon Valley, it is not surprising that stores, the most famous being Fry's Electronics, exist to satisfy all desires both technological and physical. There under one roof, the hungry computer "techie" can find computer chips and potato chips, "modems and Maalox," "Twinkies and cable connectors," Coca Cola and *Computerworld*.[5]

• The pun may be forced but the connection between "worms" and "Apples" strikes fear into the heart of the Macintosh user:

> A virus that can freeze files, distort printer fonts, crash applications and ultimately prevent computers from starting is rapidly spreading through Apple Computer, Inc. Macintoshes in the U.S. and Europe. . . . Norstad (an analyst at the academic computing center at Northwestern) said he has received "hundreds of reports" of the virus which infects the invisible Desktop files used by the Finder, which helps the Mac manage files and folders.[6]

- Cyberspace and artificial reality are terms used to describe,

> "an infinite, computer-generated world where humans experience an approximation of reality. There, geographic distance is irrelevant and participants can see, hear and even touch objects that exist only as computer data—pure information. The more romantic see cyberspace as a fantastic world that exists behind the computer screen. . . . The practical envision it as a new form of computer-user interface, in which users wear helmets and gloves to be able to see and manipulate data, or as a powerful communication tool for business and education."[7]

- What is real? Is there a human out there on the other end of this telephone? Increasingly, digitized voices are being used to respond to human requests in a wide range of situations.

> Telephone users looking for the human element in today's age of voice mail, interactive telephone systems and touch-tone billboards must look pretty hard. Rather than battling intransigent operators and antiquated switching equipment, callers encounter "automated attendants" dubbed Silicon Sally—often with little more luck than the frustrated caller in the comedy routine.[8]

- So much data is stored in computers that serious consequences may result from "inadvertent" actions resulting in the loss of important information. One such occurrence, in which the computer was blamed, is particularly memorable:

> Houston—A computer operator at Exxon headquarters here says he inadvertently destroyed computer copies of thousands of documents with potentially important information on the Alaska oil spill. Under a Federal court order, Exxon was required to preserve the computer records along with all other material concerning the grounding of the Exxon Valdez in Prince William Sound on March 24 and the subsequent cleanup effort.[9]

- New techniques in artificial intelligence are being used in consumer products such as washing machines, air conditioners, camcorders, and televisions. Not surprisingly, Japan is leading the way as companies implement developments in fuzzy logic, originally proposed by Lotfi Zadeh, a professor of computer science at the University of California at Berkeley. "Fuzzy logic can accommodate a more complex reality. It lets computers deal with shades of gray—concepts such as about, few, many, and almost."[10] One product is a washing machine that uses an optical sensor to detect the quality of impurities in the water just as the wash cycle begins. This information is used to limit excessive washing and thereby save water and electricity as well as reduce long term wear on clothes.

The range of concerns in this limited group of selections is indicative of the degree to which computers have made a major inroad into the national consciousness. It is difficult to avoid either reading about computers, encountering them directly, or having someone tell you about his or her most recent experience with them. Furthermore, it is possible to appreciate their impact without knowing how they work or how to program them, just as one may be able to appreciate the effects of traffic jams or automobile pollution without understanding the principles of the internal combustion engine or even how to operate a motor vehicle.

A VARIETY OF APPLICATIONS

> The new information technologies—telecommunications and computers—may change our lives more than any other fields of technological development.[11]

The number of applications reveals how pervasive computers have become. Many of these applications incorporate microprocessors, tiny computing elements that perform a decision-making function when supplied with information from a variety of sensors. As such, much computer-governed behavior is hidden from view, and thus the true extent of computer penetration into contemporary technology is probably unappreciated. It is important to recognize that while computers have opened up many new possibilities, society for the most part functioned in a quite similar manner prior to the onset of the "computer age." Checks were processed, taxes collected, students educated, products manufactured, airplanes flown, medicine practiced, people entertained, and wars fought all without the benefit of computers. Not to deny the many advantages that have accrued from the introduction of computers into all areas of life, some balanced perspective should be maintained. Computers are indeed marvelous inventions that are transforming the workings of society, but their diffusion brings a variety of real and potential problems.

The following applications, chosen from disparate areas, illustrate the flexibility and versatility of computer-mediated equipment. In some instances computers improve the efficiency of existing processes; in others, they make possible new and innovative ones. New industries have been created—home computers, for example—and others have disappeared—for example, slide rules.

Smart Automobiles

A major effort is underway to increase automobile performance in the areas of handling, fuel efficiency, riding comfort, informational aids, and entertainment. Microprocessors have been used for several years to control engine functions in order to improve fuel economy. New systems, controls, displays, and monitors continue to be introduced. Some concern has arisen about whether or not the average driver really benefits from an increasing array of dashboard gadgets. Voice systems have largely disappeared because of driver irritation, as have CRT (cathode-ray tube) displays. Nevertheless, automobile designers foresee an accelerating growth in the incorporation of microprocessors and sensors in automobiles. For example, Motorola, a major chip manufacturer, anticipates an automotive market of $10 billion in computer chips by 1993.[12] At present, most cars employ five or six microprocessors to perform such functions as the following:[13]

- control of the various activities of the digital radio;
- integration of such dashboard functions as theft alarm, LCD graphic displays, and other digital displays;
- HVAC functions—heater, ventilation, and air-conditioning;
- new, sophisticated automatic transmission;

- computer suspension control, just starting to appear;
- anti-lock braking systems; and
- "engine management system" for all engine functions, including memory to store malfunctions for subsequent analysis.

In somewhat more detail, we will examine several innovations in automobile computer applications. Consider the following:

Traction Control. Electronic traction control, which can compensate for different driving conditions, has extended the power of anti-lock braking systems. Such systems must reduce the torque of the engine when sensors detect skidding or the onset of brake locking. The Toyota Lexus LS 400 and the Cadillac Allanté, for 1990, employ traction control.[14]

Ride Control. Many new models have a system of sensors and controlled suspension, which, under microprocessor control, respond to road conditions that affect roll, pitch (nosing), bounce, and the actual load-based height of the car.[15]

Tire Pressure. High tire pressure can influence ride, and low pressure increases wear and decreases fuel consumption. Information from sensors in the tires and brakes together with that about speed and road conditions are processed to indicate to the driver that tire pressure may not be adequate. Research is currently underway, in a collaboration between Goodyear Tire & Rubber Company and Lotus Engineering of England, to inflate or deflate tires automatically based on the information gathered by sensors embedded in the tires.[16]

Smart Transmission. Porsche has introduced a new automatic transmission, Tiptronic, to provide much finer control. For example, Tiptronic uses "40 kinds of data" to select among five shift patterns stored in memory.[17]

Reducing Noise. By using the stereo system in combination with sensors for engine, tire, and exhaust noise, and feedback microphones inside the vehicle, a microprocessor computes a mirror image of the current noise profile. It then generates this image through the stereo system thereby cancelling much of the unwanted sound. Lotus Engineering in Britain has developed such a system, which when added to an existing quality stereo system may cost as little as $150.[18]

Among developments on the horizon are so-called drive-by-wire systems. These either augment or replace traditional mechanical linkages between the accelerator and the engine, as well as the steering wheel and the front wheels, with sensors that measure pedal depression or wheel rotation and cause an appropriate actuator to respond. In addition, fuzzy logic is being used to deal with situations in which inexact reasoning is required. Patents exist for both automatic transmission and anti-skid brake systems based on implementations of this particular strategy.[19] Of special importance is the use of satellites for onboard navigational systems.

One final areas of development is a technology for both smart cars and smart roads, called IVHS (intelligent vehicle/highway systems). This term includes such features as providing current information on accidents, detours, congestion, and services to central controllers and drivers. More advanced features would be systems to avoid collisions by warning drivers or even assuming direct control of the vehicle. Efforts in this direction are underway in Europe in two large projects that unite government and industry researchers as well as many smaller ones. Japan also has an extensive program that includes major government involvement while in the United States, government has so far not taken a role.[20]

A Sampler of Scientific Applications

The first applications requiring considerable computational speed arose from scientific questions, albeit mediated by military exigencies, namely computations associated with ballistic requirements, as well as the much more important Manhattan project, to produce nuclear weapons. It is not surprising therefore that computers, from supercomputers to personal computers, have become an integral component of scientific investigation, whether monitoring laboratory experiments, directing telescopes, counting particles, simulating complex ecological systems, or solving large systems of equations for weather prediction. We briefly describe a few applications in the following scientific areas:

Biology

Whereas medical research has developed many antibiotics that combat a wide variety of bacterial diseases, successes have been quite limited with respect to viruses. While vaccines exist for polio and smallpox, influenza, because of the large number of strains, HIV, because of its complexity, and others such as hepatitis and viral pneumonia have proven resistant. One promising approach, in what has been called computer-aided drug design, is the use of high-powered workstations and computer-aided design (CAD) systems to produce models of viruses based on current theory in chemistry, crystallography, and molecular biology. Models of candidate anti-viral agents can be constructed, studied and modified in hopes of obtaining effective drugs. While success has been limited, increased computational power offers hope for the future.[21]

From the very small to the very large, from the microbe to the ecological zone, scientists are beginning to employ satellite imagery and computers to designate geographical regions necessary to preserve the diversity of flora and fauna. The satellite images record topological information that is combined with data on land ownership to identify areas that are badly managed, in danger, and worth special protection. Several states, including Idaho, Utah, and Oregon are working on such state-wide detailed topographic maps.[22]

Astronomy

In April 1990, the $2 billion Hubble space telescope was launched after many years of delay. Its purpose is to provide astronomers with much clearer pictures than currently available on Earth because of atmospheric interference. Images sent back by the telescope will be processed by a computer program developed by Alias Research Inc. of Toronto. This program will produce three-dimensional color pictures, which NASA (National

Aeronautics and Space Administration) expects to use as a means of informing and educating the public about the findings of this project.[23] *

The search for interesting and important cosmic events has largely been dependent on direct human observation, but with the vastness of the universe and the faintness of light arriving from enormous distances, it has been necessary to develop tools to increase the probability of detecting rare events. Berkeley's Lawrence Laboratory has developed a computer program to guide a telescope autonomously all night long searching for one of 1300 pre-programmed galaxies. It then compares this new image with the previously saved one to detect any differences, which if discovered will serve to warn astronomers that this galaxy may have undergone a supernova.[24]

Physics

For many phenomena, the computer has come to serve as an experimental testbed, with computational power being used to simulate the real world. In fact, the needs of scientific computing have been a major motivating force in the development of larger and faster computers including, of course, supercomputers. The simulation of a complex physical phenomenon produces vast quantities of data, which necessitates the development of presentation methodologies such as high resolution graphics. More recently, with the increased computing power resulting from networks of workstations linked to a supercomputer, a new field has emerged: visualization in scientific computing (ViSC). To quote from a National Science Foundation Report on ViSC:[25]

> As a tool for applying computers to science, it offers a way to see the unseen. As a technology, Visualization in Scientific Computing promises radical improvements in the human–computer interface and may make human-in-the-loop problems approachable. . . . Major advances in Visualization in Scientific Computing and effective national diffusion of its techniques will drive techniques for understanding how models evolve computationally, for tightening design cycles, integrating hardware and software tools, and standardizing user interfaces.

Mathematics

Traditionally, mathematicians have required only a pencil and paper, or chalk and a blackboard to do their work, but more recently, the computer has assumed an important role and thereby changed the way mathematics is done. Consider the following:

- In 1976, Wolfgang Haken and Kenneth Appel used a computer to prove the Four Color Conjecture, which states that any map can be colored with at most four colors such that no two adjacent regions have the same color. They managed to "reduce" the problem to a large number of cases (1,482), each one of which could be examined by the computer program.[26]

* Interestingly enough, manufacturing problems in the telescope itself, not discovered until after it had been launched, resulted in a major investigation on earth and degraded images from space, a bitter disappointment after many years of delay.

• Late in 1988, a team of researchers led by Clement Lam of Concordia University in Montreal announced the proof of one example of a conjecture made almost 200 years ago by Carl Friedrich Gauss. The formal statement of this conjecture is that there are no finite projective planes of order 10, which in somewhat simpler terms corresponds to the impossibility of constructing a matrix with 111 rows and columns such that each row has exactly 11 positions filled with ones, and any two rows have only one filled position in common. This result required 3,000 hours of computation on a Cray-1, carried out over a two year period, during idle time. Note that checking such a result by hand is impossible.[27]

• In many cases mathematical results are implemented in a computer program to improve the efficiency of existing algorithms or to make possible previously intractable processes. One very famous example is the result achieved by Narendra K. Karmarkar, a mathematician at AT&T Bell Laboratories, in 1984. Without going into any details, we note that in the area of linear programming, a mathematical technique used to solve very large problems in scheduling, Karmarkar's result improves speeds by a factor of 50 to 100, so that for a difficult problem for which traditional methods would require weeks to solve, a solution can be obtained in less than an hour, resulting in considerable financial savings. It is interesting that a program incorporating Karmarkar's method was patented by AT&T.[28]

• Current methods in cryptography to ensure the security of transmission by governments, financial institutions, and others, depend on the expectation that very large numbers, used for encoding and decoding keys, are extremely difficult to factor, that is, to determine numbers whose product yields the original number. However, recent results suggest that the optimistic expectation is not warranted. For example, in 1971 a 40-digit number was factored to considerable acclaim. In October 1988, almost unbelievably, a 100-digit number was factored and in 1990 in an extraordinary achievement by several hundred researchers and about one thousand computers, a 150-digit number was factored into three irreducible factors. To indicate the magnitude of the computations required, consider that a brute force method that attempted to factor the number by trying to divide it by every smaller number would take 1,060 years even if each division could be performed in one billionth of a second. A new factoring method was developed and the problem was subdivided into many smaller pieces to achieve the final answer.[29]

High Definition Television (HDTV)

If ever a technology has been promoted as a test of a nation's determination to maintain economic dominance in the face of repeated and growing challenges, it is high definition television (HDTV). The term is rife with political, economic, and engineering overtones, however, and for a variety of reasons represents perhaps the most anticipated technology since the personal computer itself. In brief, HDTV would have about twice the horizontal and vertical resolution of current television, giving a significant increase in picture quality, achieved by a doubling of the number of lines transmitted, as well as an increase in the ratio of horizontal to vertical picture size, from 4 : 3 to 16 : 9, approximating that of a film screen.

The only U.S. world-class manufacturer of television sets is Zenith Electronics Corp., and it makes many of its sets in Mexico. Thus HDTV is viewed by many legislators as a last ditch effort to resume a previously dominant presence in this most important consumer industry, especially given the prediction, "that the television receiver of the year 2000 will contain a greater number and more sophisticated microchips than the personal computer of the year 1990."[30] Estimates vary but in the most optimistic scenario, presented in a report by the American Electronics Association, world semiconductor sales for U.S. firms would be $124 billion with a strong U.S. presence in HDTV (50% of the U.S. market controlled by U.S. firms), compared to $62 billion for a weak U.S. presence (only 10%).[31] The stakes are high, so high that considerable pressure has been generated by politicians, trade associations, and professional societies to encourage government spending to support research and development in the private sector.

There is, however, a lack of consensus on whether or not HDTV represents the true wave of the future or merely a consolidation of the past. Although, as previously noted, television receivers will have many microprocessors, the basic transmitted signal is still expected to be analog. Thus some critics of HDTV have argued that the United States should skip this technology altogether because of the lead currently held by Japan and Europe and move vigorously towards blanketing the country with a fiber-optic network over which signals can be transmitted digitally. As author George Gilder notes, "Replacing moribund TV technology will be digital telecomputers, connected to the world through a network of fiber optics. Telecomputer users will be able to dial up digital databases, programs, movies, classrooms, or news coverage anywhere on the continent, ultimately, all over the world."[32] Furthermore Senator Al Gore, chairman of the Subcommittee of Science, Technology and Space, made the following statement:[33]

> We can't just worry about HDTV, we need to pay attention to the next revolution in TV technology—digital TV. The technology being developed for visualization can be used to develop super-high-resolution digital television and the same fiber-optic network that links computers today could be used to carry digital TV signals in the future. The U.S. has a lead in visualization and networking, but we need to redouble our efforts in order to keep that lead and to leapfrog the Japanese. We can lead the digital TV revolution.

At the Second Annual Conference and Exhibition on HDTV, held in February 1990, conference speakers pointed out a number of misconceptions about the current level of achievements in HDTV development. Among the warnings issued are the following:[34]

There Is No HDTV Boom. Europe is not excited and there is no consumer market yet in Japan.

HDTV Will Not Be a Significant Factor in Semiconductors. Contrary to forecasts, HDTV will not drive the seminconductor industry.

HDTV is Not around the Corner. One expert predicts a U.S. standard will not appear before 1994, that sets will then sell for the price of an automobile, and that by 2002 or so only one percent of the population will have one.

Government Funding Is Not Required. No special HDTV legislation is needed but perhaps tax credits might be useful.

Going to Digital Transmission Directly Is No Solution. The basic problem is transmitting the vast number of bits necessary for both the picture and high fidelity sound. Thus an analog system might be operative before the problems of digital transmission are solved.

Video Games

There is certainly little need to describe video games to anyone living during the early 1980s, when they suddenly captured a large share of the entertainment market, and the late 1980s, when they made a successful comeback after a difficult period. Teenagers were the prime group to whom advertisers devoted their attention. A number of companies—Atari, Mattel, and Coleco, in the early days and Nintendo, Sega, NEC, more recently, and a newly arisen Atari—suddenly achieved prominence, attracting considerable attention on the stock market as well. As their popularity mounted, so did public criticism. Children seemed to be so mesmerized that they would use their food allowance on video games and even steal money to play. Video game arcades sprang up everywhere, especially in downtown commercial areas, shopping malls, and near schools. Individual machines appeared in many stores. Their appearance in the home has accompanied the popularity of home computers. In fact, many would suggest that the reason most families have purchased home computers is to play video games, other more frequent explanations such as financial management and education notwithstanding.[35]

As video games gained in popularity, voices were raised in concern, arguing that children were becoming "hooked," to the detriment of other responsibilities such as school. Furthermore, the games existed in an essentially dehumanizing environment that emphasized human-machine interaction at the expense of interpersonal relations. They were criticized for excluding girls by reinforcing the male-oriented nature of both the games themselves and the arcades. Occasionally even bounds on ordinary decency were exceeded as games appeared in which success involved violence against women.

Manufacturers are looking to new technological developments to rekindle the flame in the arcade market. The home market for video game cartridges and players continues to boom. In 1990, sales of Nintendo reached about $2.5 billion, making it the best selling toy in the United States; it controls about 90% of the home video-game market.[36] The basic Nintendo box is a special purpose computer, which is connected to a television set. Optional components are Zapper guns and specialized joy sticks and gloves, which permit more realistic interactions. But what is particularly profitable about this industry is the cost of game cartridges compared to the player itself. That is, once having bought a basic system for about $100, a parent faces on ongoing assault to purchase the cartridges at $40 to $50 each. To add to the mounting costs, Nintendo and a revitalized Atari have introduced portable game players about the size of a paperback book with a 2-1/2-inch diagonal screen and headphones. Atari has color graphics and a larger screen while Nintendo has faster graphics.

The future for video games holds such promising developments as 3-D effects on high resolution screens, a wide range of brighter colors, intelligent adaptation to an individual player's skills, the use of speech recognition as an additional communication channel, more powerful graphics (here already with 16-bit machines), and the use of videodisks to supply large amounts of memory. These improvements will result from faster microprocessors as well as sophisticated software. From their primitive origin as variations of the game of Pong to their current sophisticated level, video games have depended on developments in microelectronics. The games can be seen as a logical outgrowth of pinball machines and simultaneously as an introduction to a new age of advanced computers, graphics, and software.

As a final note, to illustrate that Nintendo may have educational benefits, we observe that early in 1990, Nintendo announced a gift of $3 million to the Media Lab at the Massachusetts Institute of Technology to determine how children can learn while they play (Super Mario Brothers, for example). It may be that new Nintendo games will be produced as part of the research project, yet another instance of a continuing partnership between business and institutions of higher education.[37]

SOCIETAL ISSUES

> While bringing many benefits to society, the revolution [computers and electronics] will also bring problems, tension, and disbenefits.[38]

Discussions about technological change and society generally take a form similar to the above quotation. That is, technology brings many important benefits—better communication, less dangerous work, faster transportation, and reduction in home labor, among others—but there are drawbacks. At one level, somewhat abstract, are the fears that we will become slaves to our own machines (this topic will be explored at some length in Chapter 3). An extreme form of this position is that in the long run machines will actually be able to solve problems and replace people in most of their jobs. The evolution of machine intelligence will be steady and inexorable until gradually people will literally serve machines. Although this theme is usually one for science fiction, recent work in artificial intelligence has suggested to some that with the arrival of the computer, especially in its current form, a serious beginning has been made on the road to producing intelligent robots.

Publicity about the Fifth Generation project in Japan has stimulated public and private support in the United States for a major research investment in a race with the Japanese to develop practical intelligent machines that can understand spoken language and the world around them (see Chapter 11). None can doubt that such machines will have a profound impact on society in more ways than can be imagined, but it is not necessary to wait for them—if indeed they ever arrive—to be concerned about how computers have already affected our lives. If we agree with the accepted view that the benefits of computers far outweigh any associated detrimental effects, it is still necessary to delineate these effects and to gauge their significance.

Issues and Problems

There are several ways to present and discuss social issues arising from the increasing use of computers. One method is by category; that is, each major area of application is studied and the particular problems recognized. Another method is to propose a list of areas of concern, or possible problems, and then study each application to see if it illustrates any of these problems. Both approaches can be combined by first listing and describing a number of application areas and a number of social issues and then constructing a diagram that depicts which social issues are relevant to which applications. The simple metaphor is to view society as a fabric woven with warp and woof threads. The *warp* consists of the lengthwise threads of a woven cloth through which *woof* threads are woven, and the *woof* consists of the crosswise threads carried back and forth by the shuttle and interwoven with the lengthwise threads of the *warp*. These definitions are interdependent just as the issues and applications are. For the purposes of this metaphor, societal issues are the warp, and computers, technology, and applications are the woof. The dividing lines are not always sharp, however.

Application areas and technological developments include the following:

Robotics and Industrial Automation. The integration of computers and movable electromechanical arms—to perform such tasks as assembling parts, welding, and spray painting—define industrial automation. Robots may also be used for jobs dangerous to humans in hazardous environments such as under the sea, mines, space, and nuclear reactors. Flexible manufacturing systems represent a new way of organizing production.

Office Automation. The integration of computers, mainframes and personal, local and long-distance communication networks, facsimile machines, and printers will transform the office. Word-processing, electronic filing and retrieving, electronic mail, automatic scheduling of meetings, management information systems, and remote data entry and programming are among the new possibilities.

Telecommunications. The interconnection of computers with communication networks opens up a wide range of possibilities for distributed computing, distributed work, and worldwide information networks for business and government use.

Electronic Money Systems. The use of automatic teller machines (ATMs), point-of-sale terminals (POSs), and computer communication systems results in electronic fund transfer systems, the so-called "cashless" society. A vast network linking financial institutions, retailers, wholesalers, and the public will change shopping and banking habits.

Personal Computers. The explosion of microcomputers available for use in the office, school, and home has brought computers out of the private preserve of data processing professionals into the hands of the general public. Marketed as just another consumer item, they may have been oversold but do provide an ever-expanding range of possibilities for the family, including games, financial programs, educational programs, and access to information systems.

Microprocessors. The miniaturization of computing power in the form of microprocessors has enabled the computer to be incorporated in an ever-increasing variety of consumer products. Among these are cameras, automobiles, television receivers, and microwave ovens. Improvements in efficiency and repair will change production practices and servicing procedures. Consumer products can be more energy-efficient and more flexible.

Service Professions. These include medicine, education, and law, among others. Computer-based devices will improve medical record keeping, diagnosis programs, medical imaging systems such as CAT scanners and, of course, billing systems. The computer in the school is being hailed as a major aid to education both in traditional instruction and as an exciting new subject in its own right. Legal information retrieval systems will help case preparation.

Home Information Systems. Teletext or videotex systems, which provide communication via television broadcast systems, cable, or telephone lines, are on the verge of reaching many Americans and Europeans. Services available over specially adapted television sets or personal computers include banking, shopping, reservations, educational material, electronic polling and opinion surveys, and solicitation of donations.

Electronic Mail and Teleconferencing. The use of computer terminals and communication networks will permit messages to be sent across the country and stored in computers or printed and delivered locally as ordinary mail. New networks will encourage a novel form of information sharing.

Government Regulation. The role of government in regulating communication systems is undergoing a change in emphasis. AT&T has separated from its regional companies, and more competition in the long-distance and data transmission market is being encouraged. Less concern with antitrust regulations is also apparent. The government suit against IBM was dropped, and a more aggressive posture resulted, evidenced by IBM's enormous success in the personal computer market. Other issues for government concern are its support of high technology developments, its control of high technology exports (technology transfer), and the free flow of research results.

The Arts. Artists are making use of computers in movies, graphics, and music. Digital computer-controlled synthesizers provide enormous possibilities for technically minded composers. High resolution graphics systems and recent developments in software permit the generation of sophisticated images.

Artificial Intelligence. From the halls of academia and private research laboratories to the market place, developments in artificial intelligence (AI) are achieving national importance. Whether in the design of expert systems, vision systems for robots, intelligent English interfaces for databases, or diagnosis system for doctors, AI has come to the fore.

Computers and the Law. Computers, because they are so necessary and are used for so many purposes, can be used for illegal activities such as, for example, embezzling money, accessing information without permission, and using computer time without payment.

How to legally safeguard software and hardware under patent, copyright, or trade secrets regulations is also a problem.

This list provides a sense of how important computers have become to the functioning of a modern society. It now remains to outline an accompanying list of social issues. For some of these, computers are only the next stage in technological development, and so the problems are only existing ones exacerbated. Others are unique to the computer and must be treated as directly associated phenomena. Among the social issues are the following:

Work. How do all these computer-related developments affect the employment of people? Will the number of available jobs increase or decrease? Will the skill requirements change? How will people accommodate to the increased use of computers on the job? What will happen to the traditional social organization of the office under office automation, sometimes called the "office of the future"?

Health. Is sitting in front of a video display terminal (VDT) dangerous to your health, both physically and psychologically? Are other computer-related activities problematic? For example, there is increased incidence of individuals becoming so infatuated with computers that they withdraw from human contact.

Privacy and Personal Freedom. Computers permit enormous amounts of information to be gathered, stored, processed, and linked. There is a concern about how these records are used, incorrect information, and the right to inspect one's own file. Can the collection of information inhibit individual action? Who has access to personal information? Under what conditions must the government reveal what it has collected (the freedom of information issue).

Centralization of Control. Will computers be used to extend the power of management over workers? Is it inevitable that increased amounts of more accurate information will shift power to the top, or will distributed computing lead to distributed responsibility and control? Will governments become more powerful and centralized as in Orwell's *1984?*

Responsibility. Will the widespread use of computers and communication systems fragment society? Will families cluster around their home information systems for entertainment, shopping, education, and even jobs, forsaking outside contacts? Will fewer and fewer people actually produce things and more and more people engage in service activities and information processing? How will this change society?

Human Self-Image. How does the computer affect our self-image? Is there a threat to human dignity as machines continue to perform more activities formerly the sole province of people? Is technology an irresistible force with its own imperative? Can one maintain human(e) qualities in a computer age?

Ethics and Professionalism. How responsible are computer professionals for their actions? Should they adopt codes of behavior similar to doctors and lawyers? Do computer-mediated situations present new problems for ethical behavior?

	Work	Health	Privacy and personal freedom	Centralization of control	Responsibility	The information society	Human self-image	Ethics and professionalism	National interests	Meritocracy
Robotics and industrial automation	X	X					X		X	X
Office automation	X	X		X	X		X	X		X
Telecommunications			X	X		X		X		
Electronic money systems	X		X	X	X			X		
Personal computers		X				X				X
Microprocessors	X		X			X				X
Service professions	X			X	X	X		X		X
Home information systems	X		X		X	X		X		X
Electronic mail and teleconferencing	X		X			X				
Government regulation		X	X	X					X	
The arts						X	X			
Artificial intelligence	X					X	X		X	
Computers and the law			X		X					

FIGURE 1-1 Social Issues and Computers.

National Interests. Does the future economic well-being of a society depend on its achievements in high technology? Will success for some countries mean failure for others?

Meritocracy. Will the use of computers accentuate the tensions between the educated and the untrained? Will the work of society be divided between challenging and interesting jobs and routine and boring jobs? Will the poor and uneducated view computers as yet another powerful tool in the hands of the rich, and will they be right?

Which issues apply to which technological areas? Figure 1-1 is not a precise formulation, because the definitions themselves are not precise. It should suggest the general patterns of interaction of social issues and technological innovations. As time goes on, the number of rows and columns will vary as new concerns emerge in response to new applications. It is important to be aware of the possible consequences of technological developments, but this awareness requires a familiarity with the technology itself as well as with the economic, political, social, and legal structures of society. Only a beginning is attempted here, but an old Chinese saying is appropriate: "A journey of a thousand miles begins with one step."

Public Opinion

We have articulated a selection of possible problems associated with computer use in today's society. Their severity is a matter of debate among computer specialists and social scientists—but how do nonexperts, ordinary people, feel about computers? It was not until the late 1950s that the computer emerged as an object of praise and fear. Cartoonists of the period depicted computers or robots as challenging the ability of humans at work and at play. Operators at consoles in front of floor-to-ceiling computers typed in queries that elicited humorous responses. The cartoons reflected such concerns as possible loss of jobs, threats to human problem-solving skills, personal liberty, and an increasing intrusion into all aspects of human life. Did the cartoonists and editorial writers truly capture the hopes and fears of the general population?

In 1971 *Time* magazine and the American Federation of Information Processing Societies, Inc. (AFIPS) conducted a major survey to determine the public's attitudes towards computers.[39] Over 1000 adults from a representative sample of the U.S. population were interviewed on a wide range of topics. The survey results are extensive and lengthy, but a few observations are revealing.

Almost half of the working public has some contact with computers.

About 90% felt that computers will provide much useful information and many kinds of services.

36% felt computers actually create more jobs than they eliminate; 51% believed the opposite.

84% wanted the government to regulate the use of computers.

With respect to privacy, 58% were concerned that computers will be used in the future for surveillance and 38% believed that they were a threat to privacy (but 54% disagreed).

Only 12% believed that computers could think for themselves but 23% expected that they might disobey their programmers in the future.

54% thought that computers were dehumanizing people and 33% believed that they were decreasing freedom; 59% disagreed.

On the whole, the general public displayed a reasonable attitude to the current ability of computers and the potential threats they posed. (Chapter 9 presents more detailed results about concerns with privacy.)

Some twelve years later (September 1983) Lou Harris and Associates, Inc. conducted a study for Southern New England Telephone entitled *The Road After 1984: The Impact of Technology on Society.*[40] Conducted well into the age of the home computer, this survey should reveal a more sophisticated public awareness. Some highlights follow:

Some 67% of the general public believes that personal information is being kept in files, somewhere, for purposes unknown to them.

45% acknowledges that they know how to use a computer, most at the beginner level.

88% believes that the computer will make the quality of life somewhat or a lot better.

85% agrees that computers can free up time for individuals to do creative and highly productive work.

55% feels that computers can make human robots out of workers by controlling every minute of their day.

In mid-1990, another major poll was released, again conducted by Lou Harris and Associates with Dr. Alan F. Westin, and sponsored by Equifax Inc. Its primary thrust was to evaluate attitudes of consumers towards the increasing use of personal information, stored in computers, by both the private sector and government. Equifax Inc. is a major supplier of consumer credit records and is understandably concerned about its public image. While more of the highlights of this poll will be presented in Chapter 9, it is of special interest to note that the public continues to be concerned about threats to their privacy: In 1990, 79% of the population felt that their privacy was being invaded compared with 34% in 1970.[41] Furthermore, by 79% to 19%, Americans agree that, "If we rewrote the Declaration of Independence today, we would probably add privacy to the list of "life, liberty, and the pursuit of happiness' as a fundamental right."

SUMMARY

Computers have become pervasive in contemporary society. They have been used to steal credit ratings, eliminate jobs, protect dogs, create a new reality, and improve the efficiency of washing machines. Other major applications include improved automobile performance, the design of anti-viral agents, the computer visualization of scientific phenomena, the proof of difficult mathematical theorems, the design of smart automobiles, the development of high definition television, and video games.

Associated with the benefits of computers are a number of real and potential problems. The many and varied applications of computers, including robotics, office automation, electronic money systems, personal computers, home information systems, and artificial intelligence, have given rise to social problems. Relevant issues include work, health, privacy, responsibility, self-image, and national interests.

From their earliest appearance computers have aroused feelings of fear, awe, and concern, as has been revealed in public opinion surveys. Despite increased familiarity, the public's perception of computers still seems to be conditioned more by media exaggerations than by reality.

NOTES

1. "Advertisement: Martin Marietta," *The New York Times Magazine*, February 26, 1989, pp. 46–47.
2. "Advertisement: IBM," *Harper's Magazine*, September, 1990, pp. 40–41.
3. Peter H. Lewis, "Where the Libraries Are Leading the Way," *The New York Times*, May 13, 1990, p. F 8. Copyright © 1990 by The New York Times Company. Reprinted by permission.
4. J. A. Savage, "Humane Society Collars a Chip off the Old Hound Dog," *Computerworld*, April 3, 1989, p. 10. Copyright 1989 by CW Publishing Inc., Framingham, MA 01701. Reprinted from Computerworld.
5. Katherine Bishop, "Store Serves All Needs of the Computer Crazed," *The New York Times*, July 25, 1989, p. A 6.
6. James Daly, "One Bad Worm Spoils Whole Bunch of Apple Macintoshes," *Computerworld*, January 15, 1990, p. 101. Copyright 1990 by CW Publishing Inc., Framingham, MA 01701. Reprinted from Computerworld.
7. Peter H. Lewis, "Put on Your Data Glove and Goggles and Step Inside," *The New York Times*, May 20, 1990, p. F 8.
8. Mary Gooderham, "Hello, Silicon Sally," *The Globe and Mail*, Toronto, Canada, October 24, 1989, p. A 1.
9. Robert Suro, "Tapes On Alaska's Oil Spill Erased by Exxon Technician," *The New York Times*, July 2, 1989, p. A 1. Copyright © 1989 by The New York Times. Reprinted by permission.
10. Larry Armstrong and Neil Gross, "Why 'Fuzzy Logic' Beats Black-Or-White Thinking," *Business Week*, May 21, 1990, pp. 92–93.
11. Edward Cornish, "The Coming of the Information Age," *The Futurist*, April 1981, p. 14.
12. William J. Hampton, Neil Gross, Deborah C. Wise, and Otis Port, "Smart Cars," *Business Week*, June 13, 1988, pp. 68–71, 74.
13. "Computers," *The New York Times Advertising Supplement*, May 21, 1989, pp. 64–65.
14. Ronald K. Jurgen, "Global '90 cars: Electronics-aided," *IEEE Spectrum*, December 1989, pp. 45–49.
15. *Ibid.*, p. 47.
16. "'Smart' Tires That Read the Road," *The New York Times*, February 25, 1990, p. F 11.
17. Lawrence M. Fisher, "A New Transmission for the 90's," *The New York Times*, March 7, 1990, p. C 7.
18. Lawrence M. Fisher, "Adding Noise to Cut a Car's Noise," *The New York Times*, January 10, 1990, p. C 3.
19. *Ibid.*, Jurgen, p. 49.
20. Karen Wright, "The Shape of Things to Go," *Scientific American*, May 1990, pp. 92–96B, 98, 100–101.
21. Joseph Alper, "The Microchip Microbe Hunters," *Science*, **247**, February 16, 1990, pp. 804–806.
22. Keith Schneider, "How to Map Out the Best Places for Rare Species," *The New York Times*, June 3, 1990, p. E 3.
23. Geoffrey Rowan, "Canadian Computer Program to Shape Space Pictures," *The Globe and Mail*, Toronto, Canada, April 30, 1990, p. B 6.
24. Malcolm W. Browne, "Devices Help Scientists Find Supernovas," *The New York Times*, April 3, 1990, p. B 5.
25. Karen A. Frenkel, "The Art and Science of Visualizing Data," *Communications of the ACM*, **31** (2), February 1988, pp. 110–121.
26. Paul Wallich, "Beyond Understanding," *Scientific American*, March 1989, p. 24.
27. *Ibid.*

28. William G. Wild Jr. and Otis Port, "The Startling Discovery Bell Labs Kept in the Shadows," *Business Week*, September 21, 1987, pp. 69, 72, 76.
29. Gina Kolata, "Giant Leap in Math: 155 Divided to 0," *The New York Times*, June 20, 1990, p. A 8.
30. Karen A. Frenkel, "HDTV and the Computer Industry," *Communications of the ACM* **32** (11), November 1989, pp. 1300–1312.
31. *Ibid.*, p. 1303.
32. George Gilder, *Microcosm: The Quantum Revolution in Economics and Technology*. New York: Simon & Schuster, 1989.
33. *Ibid.*, Frenkel, p. 1307.
34. Ronald K. Jurgen, "HDTV's Rough Road Ahead," *The Institute, A News Supplement to IEEE Spectrum*, April 1990, pp. 1, 3.
35. "How Our Readers Are Using Computers," *Consumer Reports*, September 1983, pp. 470–471. This report states that 69% of the respondents actually used their home computer for games, compared to 63% for learning about computers, 61% for learning to program, and 59% for word processing. The readership of *Consumer Reports* is particularly well-motivated, it should be noted.
36. Thane Patterson and Maria Shao, "'But I Don't Wanna Play Nintendo Anymore!" *Business Week*, November 19, 1990, pp. 52, 54.
37. Geoffrey Rowan, "Two Views of Nintendo: Educational Toy or Epileptic Danger?" *The Globe and Mail*, Toronto, Canada, May 19, 1990, p. B 5.
38. Philip H. Abelson, excerpt, "The Revolution in Computers and Education," *Science*, **215**, pp. 751–753, February 12, 1982. Copyright © 1982 by the AAAS.
39. *A National Survey of the Public's Attitudes Towards Computers* New York: Time, 1971.
40. Louis Harris and Associates, *The Road After 1984: The Impact of Technology on Society* (for Southern New England Telephone, 1983).
41. Louis Harris and Associates and Alan F. Westin, *The Equifax Report on Consumers in the Information Age* (Equifax Inc., 1990).

ADDITIONAL READINGS

A Variety of Applications

Alexander, M. "Going Down the Road Feeling Smart." *Computerworld*, March 5, 1990.

Beck, M., Meyer, M., Lewis, S. D., and Hager, M. "Smart Cars, Smart Streets." *Newsweek*, December 5, 1988, pp. 86–87.

Defanti, T. A. "The Mass Impact of Videogame Technology." In Marshall C. Yovits (ed.), *Advances in Computers, Vol. 23*. New York: Academic Press, 1984, pp. 93–140.

Gibson, W. *Neuromancer*. New York: Ace Science Fiction Books (Berkley Publishing) 1984.

Hayes, B. "Machine Dreams." *Discover*, October 1989, pp. 82–87.

Heppenheimer, T. A. "Taking the Crush Out of Rush Hour." *High Technology Business*, March 1989, pp. 26–30.

Jurgen, Ronald K. "Putting Electronics to Work in the 1991 Car Models." *IEEE Spectrum*, December 1990, pp. 72–75.

Jurgen, Ronald K. "Smart Cars and Highways Go Global." *IEEE Spectrum*, May 1991, pp. 26–36.

Loftus, G. R. and Loftus, E. F. *Mind at Play: The Psychology of Video Games*. New York: Basic Books, 1983.

Marbach, W. D., Seghers, F., Symonds, W. C., Gross, F., and Cole, P. "Super Television." *Business Week*, January 30, 1989, pp. 56–59, 62–63.

McWilliams, Gary, Gross, N., and Port, O. "A Whole New Way of Looking at the World," *Business Week*, November 12, 1990, pp. 77, 79, 81.

Neff, R. and Shao, M. "The Newest Nintendo Will Take a Slow Boat to America." *Business Week*, July 2, 1990 p. 46.
Port, O., Armstrong, L., and Gross, N. "High Definition TV Is Rallying a Digital Revolution." *Business Week*, January 30, 1989, pp. 64–66.

Societal Issues

Dertouzos, M. L. and Moses, J. (eds.). *The Computer Age: A Twenty Year View*. Cambridge, Massachusetts: MIT Press, 1980.
Dunlop, Charles and Kling, Rob (eds.). *Computerization and Controversy: Value Conflicts and Social Choices*. Boston: Academic Press, 1991.
Forester, T. (ed.). *The Information Technology Revolution*. Cambridge, Massachusetts: MIT Press, 1985.
Forester, T. (ed.). *Computers in the Human Context*. Cambridge, Massachusetts: MIT Press, 1989.
Florman, S. *Blaming Technology: The Irrational Search for Scapegoats*. New York: St. Martin's, 1981.
Friedrichs, G. and Schaff, A. (eds.). *Microelectronics and Society*. New York: New American Library (A Mentor Book), 1982.
Lewis Jr., A. O. (ed.). *Of Men and Machines*. New York: E. P. Dutton, 1963.
Mowshowitz, A. A. *The Conquest of Will: Information Processing in Human Affairs*. Reading, Massachusetts: Addison-Wesley, 1976.
Weizenbaum, J. *Computer Power and Human Reason*. San Francisco: W. H. Freeman, 1976.

2

COMPUTERS AND THE HUMAN IMAGINATION

A yet more complex form of interaction can be found in the processes of interaction that constitute a partnership of computer and artist, bent upon making art jointly.

Nicholas P. Negroponte, in *The Computer Age: A Twenty-Year View*, The MIT Press, 1980.

INTRODUCTION

Machines that can move, talk, play games, or mimic human behavior in some other way have held a considerable fascination for people in every era. It is not surprising these days to encounter at the newsstand one or more magazines that report yet another human ability recently achieved by a computer. The mechanisms used to produce such interesting behavior have ranged from steam, clockwork devices, and electromechanical systems to today's mainframes and micros.

Contemporary depiction of robots is generally favorable—witness the lovable robots of the *Star Wars* movies and their part in the series' phenomenal success. Only a few years earlier, however, one of the main protagonists in *2001: A space odyssey* was a malevolent computer called HAL. Robotic machines, such as Terminator (I and II) and Robocop (I and II), have been perceived as threats both to society in general and humans in particular and as tools or even partners in the process of civilization.

Contemporary artists in many fields have been eager to use computers as partners in the process of creating imaginative works. Music and the visual arts have been the primary beneficiaries (perhaps too strong a term in the opinion of many) of the advances in computer technology. Recently, computers and sophisticated graphics terminals have been used in movie animation to produce extraordinarily complex images. This development will permit directors to combine humans and computer-generated images without recourse to the construction of physical sets. Less interesting results have been achieved in the application of computers to the written or spoken arts. Except perhaps for free verse, where much of the art is in the ear and mind of the beholder, computers and language have not meshed successfully.

There has always been (or so it seems) a curious attraction to artifacts that resemble humans. In our own time, the digital computer has become the test bed for exploring the possibility of artificial intelligence (AI), that branch of computer science concerned with the attempt to develop programs that exhibit intelligent behavior. Indeed, AI has become not only a major branch of computer science but also a growing presence in the marketplace. AI is also an important factor in many of the computer applications discussed in this book.

THE INTELLIGENT MACHINE IN FACT AND FICTION

> Charlie had his way, and I was soon on the show. Charlie was right: Abdullah [a mechanical figure controlled internally by a hidden person] pulled them in because people cannot resist automata. There is something in humanity that is repelled and entranced by a machine that seems to have more than human powers. People love to frighten themselves. Look at the fuss nowadays about computers; however deft they may be they can't do anything a man isn't doing, through them; but you hear people giving themselves delicious shivers about a computer-dominated world. I've often thought of working up an illusion, using a computer, but it would be prohibitively expensive, and I can do anything the public would find amusing better and cheaper with clockwork and bits of string. But if I invented a computer-illusion I would take care to dress the computer up to look like a living creature of some sort—a Moon Man or a Venusian—because the public cannot resist clever dollies. Abdullah was a clever dolly of a simple kind and the Rubes couldn't get enough of him.[1]

Automata and Androids

In his interesting and informative book *Human Robots in Myth and Science,* John Cohen has traced the human fascination with the possibility of living and thinking artifacts.[2] He describes a variety of instances in antiquity of statues that were supposed to speak and offer advice and prophecies. Hephaestus, also known as Vulcan, god of fire, was accompanied by two female statues of pure gold that assisted him in his activities. In the fifteenth century B.C., the statue of King Memnon near Thebes, supposedly emitted a variety of sounds depending on the time of day. Hero of Alexandria (285–222 B.C.) built mechanical birds that apparently flew and sang.

There are many stories of devices originating in the East that moved and talked. Consider this tale of a robot of the third century B.C. in China.

> King Mu of Chou made a tour of inspection in the west . . . and on his return journey, before reaching China, a certain artificer, Yen Shih by name, was presented to him. The king received him and asked him what he could do. He replied that he would do anything which the king commanded, but that he had a piece of work already finished which he

> would like to show him. "Bring it with you tomorrow," said the king, "and we will look at it together." So next day Yen Shih appeared again and was admitted into the presence. "Who is that man accompanying you?" asked the king. "That, Sir," replied Yen Shih, "is my own handiwork. He can sing and he can act." The king stared at the figure in astonishment. It walked with rapid strides, moving its head up and down, so that anyone would have taken it for a live human being. The artificer touched its chin, and it began singing, perfectly in tune. He touched its hands, and it began posturing, keeping perfect time. It went through any number of movements that fancy might happen to dictate. The king, looking on with his favourite concubine and other beauties, could hardly persuade himself that it was not real. As the performance was drawing to an end, the robot winked its eye and made advances to the ladies in attendance, whereupon the king became incensed and would have had Yen Shih executed on the spot had not the latter, in mortal fear, instantly taken the robot to pieces to let him see what it really was. And, indeed, it turned out to be only a construction of leather, wood, glue and lacquer, variously coloured white, black, red and blue.[3]

The willingness of people to accept life in objects of stone, metal, or wood seems evidence of some deeply embedded need to believe in the power of either the gods or their specially chosen servants, to create life in any form. The effect is even stronger if the things that move or talk resemble humans. This need has not diminished over the centuries.

The illustrious figures Albertus Magnus (1204–1272) and Roger Bacon (1214–1294) are supposed to have created, respectively, a life-size automaton servant and a speaking head. At the end of the sixteenth century in Prague, Rabbi Loew produced a living being—the legendary Golem—out of a clay figure by inserting into its mouth a strip of paper with a magical formula. The creation of life from earth or other inanimate substances is a common theme in both history and literature that reached its apogee, in fiction at least, with Baron Frankenstein's monster some two centuries later.

The golden age of automata was perhaps in Europe in the eighteenth century. Skilled craftsmen built incredibly lifelike mechanisms that were exhibited to enormous crowds. The more lifelike the appearance, the greater the acclaim. Apparently the most impressive of these automata was a duck built by Jacques de Vaucanson (1709–1782) and exhibited in 1738. A rebuilt version of this automaton was displayed in Milan at La Scala in 1844 amid great excitement. A member of the audience wrote the following:

> It is the most admirable thing imaginable, an almost inexplicable human achievement. Each feather of the wings is mobile. . . . The artist touches a feather on the upper portion of the body, and the bird lifts its head, glances about, shakes its tail feathers, stretches itself, unfolds its wings, ruffles them and lets out a cry, absolutely natural, as if it were about to take flight. The effect is still more astonishing when the bird, leaning over its dish, begins to swallow the grain with incredibly realistic movement. As for its method of digestion, nobody can explain it.[4]

There is no question of such devices exhibiting free will or initiating independent action. However lifelike, the duck was no more than a complex clock mechanism of approximately 4000 parts, and from the moment it began to move, its actions were completely predetermined. We marvel at the incredible ingenuity of the inventor but at the same time we are aware of the limitations of the invention. Still, the skill of these inventors was mind-boggling. Especially impressive are the life-size androids built by Pierre Jacquet-Droz and his two sons near Neuchatel, Switzerland between 1768 and 1774. One, a "child" android called the Writer, can be mechanically programmed to write any 40 characters of text. Another, the Musician, which has the form of a woman, moved with a marvellous grace replete with subtle gestures that included head motions and a curtsy.

The so-called Chess Player of 1769, built by Baron Wolfgang von Kempelen (1734–1809) was a famous fraud. Costumed as a Turk, the automaton appeared to move the pieces on a chess board and to play quite a good game of chess. It is believed that, unknown to the audience, a person was concealed under the board, though this fact was not actually established during the automaton's lifetime. Edgar Allan Poe, one of those who argued for the hidden person hypothesis, exploited this theme when he wrote, in 1838, the short story called "Maelzel's Chess-Player."

The Theme of the Robot

> It is unreasonable . . . to think machines could become *nearly* as intelligent as we are and then stop, or to suppose we will always be able to compete with them in wit or wisdom. Whether or not we could retain some sort of control of the machines, assuming that we would want to, the nature of our activities and aspirations would be changed utterly by the presence on earth of intellectually superior beings.[5]

A robot can be thought of as a mobile computer with sensory, tactile, and motor abilities. Furthermore, it is an artifact made in the image of its human creator, who has endowed it with some form of lifelike behavior. It need not, at least in principle, be machine-like. One might argue that Frankenstein's monster was a robot created from a human corpse and given the spark of "life" by the power of lightning.

The relationship between the scientist or inventor and his or her creation has inspired many tales. Two basic plots have emerged. In one, the robot is a subordinate, a servant quick to obey but unable to initiate independent action. The other is concerned with self-motivated behavior, with the robot (or creation) as potential adversary or potential master. Creations of this type have caused trouble through willful disobedience, as exemplified by Frankenstein's monster, and through carrying out a request too zealously and too literally, as shown in the story of the sorcerer's apprentice and in *The Monkey's Paw* by W. W. Jacobs.[6]

Much of the literature in this area relates to the Greek myth of Prometheus, the hero who disobeyed Zeus, stole fire from heaven, and gave it to humankind. This gift permitted people to keep themselves warm, to illuminate the night, and to create tools and other objects. As punishment for this theft Prometheus was chained to a mountaintop and plagued for eternity by vultures picking at his liver—a torment one might recommend today for the designers of some particularly terrible computer programs. It is often forgotten that the full title of Mary Shelley's *Frankenstein,* published in 1818, is *Frankenstein: or, the Modern Prometheus.* (Remember also that Baron Frankenstein's monster has no name of its own. Thanks to Hollywood, it has become known simply as Frankenstein.)

In her study of robots and androids in science fiction, Patricia Warrick isolates four themes that emerge from Shelley's novel and recur in modern science fiction.

1. The Promethean theme: the acquisition of a hitherto forbidden skill that is now put to the supposed benefit of humankind.
2. The two-edged nature of technology: benefits are frequently offset by unanticipated problems.
3. The precipitous rejection of technology: the monster launches a campaign of terror only after Dr Frankenstein abandons him.
4. The uneasy relation between master and servant: what is created sometimes turns against the creator and becomes the master.[7]

This last point is perhaps best exemplified in *Erewhon* (1872), by Samuel Butler, which explores the relationship between humans and their machines. The narrator, discussing the reasons given by the society of Erewhon for banishing machines, notes that it is not existing machines that are to be feared, but the fact that they evolve so rapidly and in such unpredictable directions that they must be controlled, limited, and destroyed while they are still in a primitive form. Compare this fear with the sentiment expressed nearly a century later by one of the founders of artificial intelligence in the quotation that began this section. The following quotation from *Erewhon* may serve as a grim commentary on our age:

> True, from a low materialistic point of view it would seem that those thrive best who use machinery wherever its use is possible with profit; but this is the art of the machines: they serve that they may rule. . . . How many men at this hour are living in a state of bondage to the machines? How many spend their whole lives, from the cradle to the grave, in tending them by night and day? Is it not plain that the machines are gaining ground upon us. . . .[8]

Other Utopian novels, such as Aldous Huxley's *Brave New World*—written about 50 years later—and George Orwell's *1984,* are more concerned with general issues surrounding the organization of a future society. Nevertheless, the all-powerful computer plays an integral role in these societies, whether it regulates the birth process, as in *Brave New World,* or controls a vast two-way communications network by which Big Brother has access to every person, as in *1984*. (See the discussion on videotex in Chapter 13.) The title *1984* has itself become the shorthand term for the perfectly totalitarian society in which all efforts are devoted to maintaining the state against its enemies, both internal and external, real and imagined. "Big Brother is watching you" is the ultimate warning for a society in which there is complete absence of privacy and individual freedom.

In the twentieth century, perhaps *the* work of art that most successfully addresses the problem of people and their people-like machines is the play *R.U.R.* (1921) by Karel Capek.[9] In fact the word "robot" made its first appearance in this play, whose title is an abbreviation for "Rossum's Universal Robots." In *R.U.R.* humankind has become so dependent on robots that when the robots revolt, there is no hope. However, the robots do not know how to reproduce themselves, the formula having been lost in the general destruction accompanying their takeover. Thus, the people are ultimately destroyed by their creations, a bitter example of the fourth theme mentioned above.

At variance with the almost universal pessimism expressed so far has been the impact on science fiction of Isaac Asimov's robot stories. Asimov, one of the most prolific writers of our time, wrote a series of short stories dealing with robots and in the process introduced a substantial realignment into the imagined human-robot relationship. In his 1942 story "Runaround," Asimov described "the three fundamental Rules of Robotics—the three rules that are built most deeply into a robot's positronic brain." These govern robot behavior with respect to humans in order to prevent any harm coming to a human either through an action or lack of action by a robot. The three laws are as follows:

> First Law: A robot may not injure a human being, or, through inaction, allow a human being to come to harm. Second Law: A robot must obey the orders given it by human beings except where such orders would conflict with the First Law. Third Law: A robot must protect its own existence as long as such protection does not conflict with the First or Second Laws.[10]

The working out of implications inherent in these three laws informs the plots of many of the subsequent stories in Asimov's robot series.

The trend of reforming robots has probably reached its peak in the *Star Wars* movies, in which the two robots—R2D2, the chirpy fire hydrant, and C3PO, the prissy, gold-encased English butler—do not appear to have even one malevolent transistor between them. They exist only to serve their masters—humans. In real life another race of robots has appeared in the last few years: those indefatigable workers on the assembly line, the industrial robots (these will be discussed in Chapter 12). We can conclude with the observation that intelligence artifacts, whether in the form of humans or not, continue to exert a powerful influence on the human imagination. In some ways technology, the product of our minds and hands, is a mixed blessing. Writers have explored this ambivalence for many years, but the issues have sharpened with the appearance of that most marvelous of all inventions, the computer.

COMPUTERS AS A CREATIVE MEDIUM

> "The Eureka"
>
> Such is the name of a machine for composing hexameter Latin verses which is now exhibited at the Egyptian Hall, in Piccadilly. It was designed and constructed at Bridgewater, in Somersetshire; was begun in 1830, and completed in 1843; and it has lately been brought to the metropolis, to contribute to the "sights of the season. . . ."
>
> The rate of composition is about one verse per minute, or sixty an hour. Each verse remains stationary and visible a sufficient time for a copy of it to be taken; after which the machine gives an audible notice that the Line is about to be decomposed. Each Letter of the verse is then slowly and separately removed into its former alphabetical arrangement; on which the machine stops, until another verse be required. Or, by withdrawing the stop, it may be made to go on continually, producing in one day and night, or twenty-four hours, about 1440 Latin verses; or, in a whole week (Sundays included) about 10,000.

> During the composition of each line, a cylinder in the interior of the machine performs the National Anthem. (Anonymous, Illustrated London News, *1895*.)

What effects has the computer had either directly or indirectly on the arts? "Arts" here means music, drawing and graphics, movies, literature, and dance. We are concerned with the use of computers in the creative process as a tool or aid rather than as the subject matter of the work itself. In the best of all possible worlds you, the reader, would have access to a computer and be able to use it to produce music (with a synthesizer), art (with a graphics system), and perhaps poetry. Second best would be a tape of music, a portfolio of drawings, and a slim volume of computer-generated poetry. Unfortunately, we are in a position only to describe and comment, not to present and demonstrate.

There are a number of issues to keep in mind as we proceed. To what degree is the computer itself creative? This seems to be a question with which the artists themselves have little concern. For those interested in the computer as a tool, there is hardly any reason to attribute special powers of creativity to it. The artist wants to explore ways of creating under his or her initiative. The computer can give the artist a variety of means to extend and augment his or her abilities. Will anything significant emerge from the application of computers to art? The simple answer is "only time will tell." There may not appear to be any great artistic accomplishments up to now. The computer is a relatively new invention, and people will take time to learn how to use it.

Music

Music has probably been the art form in which the most interesting results have been achieved. This is not very surprising, because even before computers were invented, music could be represented by means of an electronic signal that is readily available for a computer to modify. The original signal itself can be generated by electronic equipment. That is, a complex piece of equipment incorporating signal generators, synthesizers, and microprocessors is like a giant "intelligent" organ that can be used by the contemporary composer.

In the 1950s, electronic music meant tape splicing and other manual rearrangements of sound. It was not until the 1960s that sound synthesizers, high-speed digital-to-analog converters, and sound generation programs appeared. One of the most famous early works was the "Illiac Suite for String Quartet" by Lejaren Hiller of the University of Illinois. This composition relied on the computer for the generation of random numbers. Music with a strong random component in its performance or composition is called aleatory music. For purposes of composition computers have proven invaluable because the composer is able to set the parameters of permissible variation, and the computer can select the actual path to be followed. Once the program has been designed the role of the composer is to modify, shape, and select.

However, quite a few discordant sounds have been made as well by critics and the general public. For example, Lars Gunnar Bodin of the Electronic Music Studio of Stockholm has written, "in spite of great efforts in time and money, relatively little of artistic significance has been produced in computer music".[11] The composition of music using mechanical and electronic aids has been subject to criticism similar to that once directed at the mechanical reproduction of music. The German writer E. T. A. Hoffman (about whose life and stories Jacques Offenbach composed the opera *Tales of Hoffman*) wrote the following in 1816:

> To set to work to make music by means of valves, springs, levers, cylinders, or whatever other apparatus you choose to employ, is a senseless attempt to make the means to an end accomplish what can result only when those means are animated and, in their minutest movements, controlled by the mind, the soul, and the heart. The gravest reproach you can make to a musician is that he plays without expression; because, by so doing, he is marring the whole essence of the matter. For it is impossible that any impulse whatever from the inner man shall not, even for a moment, animate his rendering; whereas, in the case of a machine, no such impulse can ever do so. The attempts of mechanicians to imitate, with more or less approximation to accuracy, the human organs in the production of musical sounds, or to substitute mechanical appliances for those organs, I consider tantamount to a declaration of war against the spiritual element in music; but the greater the forces they array against it, the more victorious it is. For this very reason, the more perfect that this sort of machinery is, the more I disapprove of it; and I infinitely prefer the commonest barrel-organ, in which the mechanism attempts nothing but to be mechanical, to Vaucanson's flute player, or the harmonica girl.[12]

Before concluding this discussion we should hear from some of the composers themselves. Composer Paul Lansky of Princeton describes himself as a sculptor of sound for whom the computer is an indispensible tool. The composer of computer music is both creator and performer. Composer Charles Dodge says that although 15 years ago there were no great works of computer music, there probably are now. According to him, the computer offers the composer a marvellous set of tools and opens up a "whole uncharted universe of sound."[13] Jan Morthenson of Sweden predicts that, "Electronic music, a child of the cathode-ray tube and transistor more than a Stravinsky and a Webern, may provoke a paradigm shift in the history and perception of music."[14] In a more cautionary vein, John Melby of the University of Illinois states the following:[15]

> [T]he aim of computer music is (or, at least, should be) the enhancement of the capability to produce significant works of music utilizing the digital computer as a medium. The production of sound per se is, of course, a part of the whole process, but it is a means to an end and not the end in itself.

Visual Arts

> Put simply, the computer is becoming a hot item in the art world.[16]

Turning to drawing, graphics, and video art, we find, up to fairly recently, considerable inventiveness but a certain sameness of technique. Facile use of a new and powerful tool may be the problem. As in music, we may have to look to the future for the emergence of real art and not just the obvious exploitation of an available technology. One of the early and important artists to use computers was A. Michael Noll. In an article written in 1967, he makes the point that even though the computer must be programmed to perform each action, its speed, decision-making ability, and large memory give it great power even to the point of appearing to produce the unexpected.[17] The computer permits the artist to explore many possibilities and, in some sense, demonstrates a measure of creativity.

In the interest of exploring this notion, Noll programmed a computer to generate a picture composed of pseudo-random elements resembling paintings done by Piet Mondrian, a well-known twentieth-century artist. The computer-generated picture was displayed, along with a Mondrian painting for the benefit of one hundred subjects, who were asked which they preferred and which was in fact the Mondrian. Fifty-nine percent preferred the computer picture and only 28% could identify the Mondrian picture. An interesting fact is that people found the Mondrian too precise and machine-like in its placement of the picture elements, whereas the randomness in the placement of the corresponding picture elements in the computer picture was found pleasing.[18]

The relationship between art and technology has always been uneasy. It has taken many years for photography to be recognized as art and the suspicion remains that the photographer achieves most by selection rather than by creation, since the camera seems to do most of the work. Thus, it is not surprising that acceptance of such a marvellous piece of equipment as a computer should be resisted by both the public at large and the artist as well. But change is inevitable, given the nature of our times. Ken Sofer, an artist himself has written as follows:

> By the mid '60's this spirit of experimentation and invention had become nothing less than a cultural imperative. How could a traditional painting or sculpture hope to shock, excite, stimulate, or even draw a glance from an audience weaned on neon billboards, movies, radio and tv? Large, colorful, sometimes kinetic images—plentiful, cheap, disposable—were now part of daily experience, made to be ingested in an instant while the viewer whizzed by on the freeway or flipped through a glossy magazine. The demands of high-speed experience rapidly transferred to art-viewing . . .[19]

Somehow these expectations have not been fulfilled. Too frequently the computer is used as an overpriced electronic paintbrush. Most of the results could hardly be termed "fine art": repetitious patterns, distorted images of human forms, and randomly placed patches of randomly generated lines. Sofer adds that, to complete the package, pretentious titles are used: "Combinatorial Cybernetic Still-Life #5000," for example. The situation is really not as grim as Sofer maintains, for many artists have used the computer in a creative and exciting way. One of these is Harold Cohen, who has designed a program called AARON in order to study the way people both produce and understand drawings. Not surprisingly, Cohen has discovered that much of the enjoyment and appreciation of a work of art is brought by the viewer. Many times he has been asked if what is being displayed is indeed art. Another well-known artist who has turned to the computer is Philip Pearlstein, famous for his super-realistic nudes. Mr. Pearlstein has described the computer "as another wonderful tool for the artist" and has become quite familiar with tablets, menus, and pixels.

The critic Cynthia Goodman, writing in the catalog accompanying the show of computer art, *Digital Visions,*[20] points out that artists have resisted computer technology because of, "their fear that the computer would usurp artistic creativity and control."[21] On the other hand, the artist Lillian Schwartz, reflecting the opinion of many, was concerned, "that remarkably repetitive images were being produced by those with access to the same program and equipment."[22] One final remark in support of the computer is from the artist Colette Bangert, who works with her husband:[23]

> I now think much more clearly about my handmade work and have much more control as a result of having made computer drawings. In addition, I recognize that our computer efforts have led to unique and unfamiliar images, which I might never have considered introducing into my drawings. On the other hand, I consider that our computer drawings are extensions of my handmade drawings.

One artist Hubert Hohn,[24] in reaction to the idea of the computer as a sophisticated tool, has decided to, "try to define a computer aesthetic based on the unique properties of the machine. . . . I want to see what happens when a computer is allowed to be itself—not forced to function as a paintbrush or a camera or a lump of charcoal."[25] Letting the computer be itself in this case involved writing a simple program to print out the current state of memory as a structured array of 0's and 1's and attaching titles such as, "SELF PORTRAIT," or, "THE MACHINE EXAMINES THE STATE OF ITS MEMORY IN THE ACT OF EXAMINING THE STATE OF ITS MEMORY," or, "THE MACHINE SEEKS THE ORIGIN OF ITS CONSCIOUSNESS." In some sense the titles have assumed an importance far beyond the work itself.

Film

Some would say that movies are *the* exciting domain of contemporary arts. They are another fairly recent art form. In their early years, movies were seen mainly as popular entertainment, and profits were the main motive for their production. Almost inadvertently, artists were attracted to this new medium and succeeded over time in producing important and serious artistic endeavors. However, there has always been an uneasy peace between the goals of profit and art. Many of the experimental efforts in film have emerged from a stream outside the so-called commercial film industry.

One of the earliest and most important filmmakers to use the computer as an integral part of the creative process is John Whitney. Fully aware of the potential of computers as early as the 1940s, Whitney observed that

> the best "computer art" did not compare well with lacework from Belgium made a century ago. But the computer possessed a unique capability of making very complex pattern flow. One could plan exacting and explicit patterns of action and distinctive motions as intricate as lace, but in a way no Belgian lacemaker would ever imagine.[26]

Whitney created a number of films, with music, generated by computer. They are characterized by the complex development of geometric themes in a rhythmic pattern accompanied by an original musical score. He has no illusions about the role of computers in the creation of art and very bluntly states his beliefs that computers will never create "meaningful" art. The crucial issue in creativity is judgment, not calculation.

It is altogether fitting that the real breakthrough in the application of computers to the making of films was made by Walt Disney Studios in *TRON* (1982). Long the world leader in animated feature films, Disney Studios recognized that the state of the art in computer animation was sufficiently well developed for computers to make a major contribution to filmmaking. The traditional Disney animation system required that many people work over long periods of time to produce thousands upon thousands of drawings. Developments in graphics, however, both in hardware and software, have permitted generation by computer of representational three-dimensional scenes. In all previous movies based on fantasy or science fiction, very complex models—usually quite small—were designed and built. Actors were positioned and cleverly photographed against these models to give the illusion of vast reaches of space, giant castles, enormous space ships and other constructs of the projected future or distant past. Of course many other techniques have been employed in the composition, photography, and editing of films, and computers have played an important role in these phases as well. As for *TRON,* although in its time it was a technological success, its artistic failure limited its influence.

In July 1984, *The Last Starfighter* was released. It included about 25 minutes of computer-generated film, compared to about 5 minutes in *TRON*. The computer scenes were generated by Digital Productions, using a Cray X-MP. This machine replaced the earlier Cray-1 (used in the making of TRON) and was needed in such prodigious computations as those for the hero's space ship *Gunstar,* which required 750,000 polygons and achieved an extraordinarily realistic effect. Interestingly enough, it is a more difficult challenge to represent soft objects such as flowers and people than spaceships and robots.

A Lucasfilm division called Pixar (founded by George Lucas, the creator of the enormously popular and successful *Star Wars* series), set up to carry out research and development in advanced computer graphics, was purchased in 1986 by Steven Jobs and is now an independent company. It has made a number of important contributions to such movies as *Star Trek II: The Wrath of Khan* and *Return of the Jedi,* as well as producing award-winning animated shorts such as *The Adventures of André* and *Wally B.*, and culminating with the 5-minute *Tin Toy,* the first computer-generated film to win an Academy award. Although the computational efforts to create even short films are prodigious, the fundamental creative act still resides in the human animators, who must design the original figures, environment, and of course, story line. The appearance of the very successful film *Roger Rabbit,* a full length movie integrating hand drawn animated characters with humans, serves as a reminder of how much is yet to be achieved by computer animation systems. The lengthy time involved in producing traditional animated movies, however, to say nothing of the associated high costs, certainly provides impetus for further research.

There is an area in which the application of current computer technology to films has aroused some controversy, namely the colorization of black and white movies. For a generation raised with color television and primarily color movies, black and white images do not seem to be attractive, or at least this is what Turner Entertainment, the current owner of such classic movies as *The Maltese Falcon, Casablanca, Miracle on 34th Street,* and *It's a Wonderful Life,* maintains.[27] Consider the following summary of two positions, keeping in mind that the owner of a work of art, or any property for that matter, has complete control over his or her possession:[28]

> The Directors Guild of America has protested colorization on the grounds that its members' works of art are being tampered with. [They] defended black-and-white films as an art form, meriting the preservation granted to historical films or national landmarks.
>
> The colorists' position is that they are simply offering the public an option; those who prefer the black-and-white can simply turn down the color control on their television set.

Multimedia

Whatever role the computer plays in traditional art forms and whatever contributions it makes, it will generally be viewed as a tool, albeit a sophisticated one. Recent technological developments combining video cassette recorders (VCRs), TVs, computers, and compact disk (CD) players suggest the possibility of a new art form, usually referred to as multimedia. The ability to represent digitally both sounds and images permits their manipulation by computer programs and their display using high resolution television and high fidelity amplifiers and loudspeakers. As with many other innovations in their early stages, there seems to be a lack of agreement on what multimedia actually is. Witness the following:[29]

> For some, it means simply choreographing text, sound, and animated graphics to create relatively crude cinematic effects. Others reserve the terms for PCs that also can control laser-disk players and VCRs and perhaps even display the contents on a PC screen. Still others look forward to sophisticated and expensive systems that would treat video information as just another type of digital data, thus permitting enormous flexibility in how it can be edited, manipulated, and displayed.

Given that some of the major players in computers and software such as IBM, Apple, Intel, Microsoft, NeXT, Fujitsu, and NEC are involved, one can expect a stream of products, advertisements, and testimonials to the virtues of multimedia. Apple has already launched a product, HyperCard, that integrates text and graphics in an information retrieval and display context and is a forerunner of a more advanced idea called hypermedia. The terms hypermedia and multimedia are frequently used interchangeably to suggest this mixing of electronic media to achieve new and startling effects. Currently multimedia exists primarily in educational software and in-house training programs, but its potential for art is apparent. What is also quite apparent is that multimedia means big bucks—estimates of over $11 billion by 1994, with approximately $2 billion in information retrieval,

$2 billion in education and training, $3.5 billion in business presentations, and $4 billion from consumer sales.[30] Where does art fit in?

CONTEMPORARY VIEWS OF THE MACHINE

We are living in an age of science and technology. The newsstand has exploded with *Omni, Macworld, PC World, Home Electronics, Technology Review, Discover,* and other magazines whose covers advertise stories on biotechnology, artificial life, new theories of the universe, and, inevitably, computers. In addition to the purely technological articles on how microprocessors will revolutionize our lives, stories on intelligent machines appear with regularity. We are told how computers will do the work of doctors, lawyers, and other professionals and that robots will soon be making regular appearances in our homes and in our places of work and play.

The public at large is infatuated with the robot. The immensely popular R2D2 and C3PO are totally dedicated to the well-being of their human masters. They are the complete antithesis, of, say, Frankenstein's monster and are, in fact, a realization of the kind of robot proposed by Isaac Asimov. We are now in the era of the robot as friend and servant. Some voices have been raised in warning about the possibility of massive unemployment resulting from the introduction of robots into the assembly line. The counter-argument is that robots will be engaged in boring and dangerous activities and thus free people to realize their full potential in other areas of life. In any case, robots are on the way. We are even being encouraged to attribute robotic qualities to household devices that incorporate electronics—manufacturers inform us in their advertisements that our televisions, microwave ovens, cameras, and other pieces of everyday equipment have an "electronic brain" that can think (for us) and therefore act for us.

Intelligent machines may not be an entirely unmixed blessing, as you will recall from that powerful motion picture, *2001: A space odyssey.* A computer called HAL (a name only one letter removed from IBM) begins acting unpredictably as it tries to ensure the success of the space mission, believing that it is in jeopardy because of the actions of the human crew. It causes the death of two men before it is dismantled by the one remaining human. As its circuits are progressively disconnected it appeals piteously to be allowed to continue functioning. It even promises to be good in the future. All this is to no avail, as it has in fact violated Asimov's First Law and must be punished.

This impressive film leaves us with the assured feeling that we humans will retain ultimate control because we can "pull the plug." The popular media generally present a favorable viewpoint toward robots or intelligent machines: They will secure more leisure time for everyone and liberate people from dangerous work; they will mine the seas, explore space, and bring prosperity to all. However, some nonscientific observers think that if machines become intelligent enough they will develop a sense (a strategy) of self-preservation that will cause them to defend their existence. The scientific approach to the development of intelligent machines is called artificial intelligence.

ARTIFICIAL INTELLIGENCE: A BRIEF INTRODUCTION

Machines and Living Things Compared

In a paper written in 1955, Anatol Rapoport points out the strong relationship between the level of technology and contemporaneous mechanical models of living things.[31] He first defines a technological "phylum," in comparison with a biological phylum, as characterized by a principle of operation. He then goes on to distinguish four technological phyla that came into being successively. The first phylum is the tool that serves primarily to transmit muscular forces; the second is clockworks that operate under the principle of stored mechanical energy, released subsequently and perhaps gradually; the third is heat engines that operate on supplied fuels; the fourth is machines that operate on the principle of storing and transmitting information.

Because tools do not operate independently, they have rarely been compared to living things, although weapons are often personified in mythology, for example, King Arthur's Excalibur and Siegfried's Nothung. The second phylum, however, has suggested living things, especially in such complex realizations as mechanical dolls and animals. (In fact, for Descartes, animals were equivalent to highly complicated automata that lacked only souls to differentiate them from humans). The main difficulty with clockworks is that their source of energy is too much unlike the source of energy of living things to allow for a strong comparison. The analogy to living things becomes much stronger when we turn to heat engines powered by such fuels as coal and oil. "It became apparent that machines could be constructed which did not need to be 'pushed' but only 'fed' in order to do work."

In the early twentieth century, the development of the telephone switchboard served as a technological model for the central nervous system. This model, together with the physiological research on the reflex arc, suggested—mainly to the early behaviorists—that "behavior was . . . a grand collection of units called reflexes," to use Rapoport's words.

It was with the arrival of the fourth phylum, however, best represented by the general purpose digital computer, that the possibilities of "thinking machines" became most likely, at least in the opinion of the most devoted practitioners of artificial intelligence (AI). Here is a machine of such structural and behavioral complexity that comparisons to the human brain invite serious analysis. Computers are applied to an incredibly wide variety of tasks including many that were formerly the sole province of humans. This gradual encroachment on a private domain has undoubtedly indicated to many people that it is only a matter of time until no exclusively human activities or skills remain. As has often been pointed out, whereas the first industrial revolution replaced man's muscle, the second is replacing his hand and brain.

Few disciplines can have their historical beginnings precisely determined as AI can. In the summer of 1956, a number of researchers met at Dartmouth College to discuss issues of mutual concern focussed on the central question of how to program machines (digital computers) to exhibit intelligent behavior. Among the attendees were Marvin Minksy,

John McCarthy (who is said to have suggested the term artificial intelligence), Alan Newell, and Herbert Simon (subsequently a Nobel laureate in economics). They gave impetus to, and shaped the direction of, research for years to come. The story of their motivations, how they attempted to realize them, and the major developments—a tale of almost epic dimensions—is recounted by Pamela McCorduck in her book *Machines Who Think*.[32] A shorter version will be presented here.

There are a number of reasons to introduce AI at this point. First, it represents the current best attempt, together with cognitive science, to understand the nature of intelligent behavior. Second, the computational models it has developed have had an impact on a variety of disciplines such as linguistics, psychology, education, and philosophy. Third, and probably most important, is its current visibility in the public eye as a developer of systems for providing "senses" for industrial robots, natural language interfaces for databases, expert systems for chemistry, medicine, prospecting, and so forth. Aside from the typical, sensational claims made for AI in the public media, there are some solid achievements and, more importantly, some hope for significant accomplishments in the future.

A Short History of Artificial Intelligence

A number of events coincided after the Second World War to give rise to the new discipline called AI. Most important, of course, was development of the digital computer, significantly accelerated by the needs of war research. A significant paper written in 1943 by Warren McCulloch and Walter Pitts, called, "A Logical Calculus of the Ideas Immanent in Nervous Activity,"[33] stimulated a number of people to explore the possibilities of achieving intelligent behavior from a machine. In 1948 Norbert Wiener's *Cybernetics* appeared. This book was subtitled "Control and Communication in the Animal and the Machine" and arose from Wiener's wartime research for designing mechanisms to control anti-aircraft guns.[34] Researchers interested in intelligent behavior were stimulated to apply the principles of feedback, whereby a system's desired goals are compared to its current situation in order to drive the system closer to where it should be.

Much of the early research could be characterized by its reference to such terms as *adaptive, learning,* or *self-organizing*. That is, what seemed to be required was the application of powerful and general learning principles to a system with very little built-in knowledge. There were hopes of simulating certain aspects of the neuronal structure of the brain, based both on the McCulloch and Pitts work and that of the psychologist Donald Hebb. However, by the early 1960s the directions for the next 20 years were firmly in place. Basically, work on learning systems was abandoned, especially in North America, and the effort turned toward determining how knowledge could be represented in a computer and furthermore how it could be used to solve problems, play games, "see" the world, communicate in natural language, and even infer new knowledge.

Right from the outset of this new direction two streams developed that were sometimes complementary and sometimes antagonistic. One arose from parallel developments in psychology that signalled a movement away from the then-dominant theoretical position of behaviorism toward the newly emerging field of information processing or cognitive psychology. Here the metaphor of information processing by computer was applied to the human system and the heretofore restricted domain of the human mind. Practitioners design models, construct programs, and carry out experiments in an attempt to answer questions about how humans think, solve problems, use language, and see the world.

The second stream is concerned with the building of computer programs to exhibit various aspects of human behavior. That is, to program a computer to solve problems, it is not obviously necessary that the methods used have anything, or much, in common with how people do it. Researchers in AI may be influenced in designing their programs by a variety of sources, of which perceived human methods is one and introspection, hardware architecture, available software, and computational limitations are others. It may turn out that the programs developed are suggestive of mechanisms underlying human performance, but this result is not the primary aim of the researchers.

In the early 1960s, programs were developed to play games such as checkers and chess, communicate in English, prove theorems in logic and geometry, and recognize simple patterns. Their level of performance was not very high in general but there were indications that a new enterprise had been launched that promised to make a major contribution to the study of intelligent behavior. In these early years, AI was sometimes viewed as a somewhat less than respectable branch of computer science. Since then, however, the founding fathers, as they are sometimes called—John McCarthy, Marvin Minsky, Alan Newell, and Herbert Simon—have all been awarded Turing Awards. The Turing Award is given annually to outstanding figures in computer science by the Association for Computing Machinery (ACM), the major association of computer scientists in the United States.

In the mid-1960s much of the research effort was devoted to robotics or integrated artificial intelligence. This work is discussed in Chapter 12. We can mention here that a number of hand-eye systems were built consisting of a computer-controlled mechanical arm and television camera, as well as one mobile robot called "Shaky." Out of this period came a renewed interest in the major components of intelligent behavior, namely vision or image understanding, natural language understanding, problem solving, game-playing and so forth. It became quite clear that the major issues underlying much of the research in AI could be characterized—but not solved, of course—by two words: representation and control. That is, it will be necessary to represent vast amounts of knowledge in the computer even to carry out rather simple tasks. Of course, knowledge is not enough; how and when to use it—control—is of paramount importance.

In pursuit of these goals, new programming languages have been developed. LISP, designed by John McCarthy, was among the earliest and clearly the most important. Some of the ideas incorporated in these languages have been adopted by other language designers. A history of ideas for AI would show that many formerly esoteric notions arising from AI research have become commonplace in other fields. This has become a major side effect of the research.

During the 1970s the earlier research areas continued to develop, with new branches emerging. Among the latter are expert systems, knowledge engineering, advanced question-answering interfaces to databases, and a variety of new applications. The work in expert systems involves the design and building of large programs to incorporate specialized knowledge and inference mechanisms in order to advise and assist users of the system. Several such systems have been developed in specific branches of medicine, chemistry, and even prospecting. Typically, teams of researchers, both computer scientists and experts, work together to extract and reformulate the specialized knowledge. Programs are written, tested, and modified until they achieve a satisfactory level of performance. For example, one of the earliest expert programs, called MYCIN, was designed to aid a physician in selecting an appropriate antibiotic to treat a blood infection.

The problem for the doctor is to prescribe one of the many available antibiotics before all the laboratory tests results are in. This situation usually requires the doctor to weigh the various known symptoms in order to narrow the range of possible infections, with an aim to selecting the antibiotic that best covers the spectrum of likely diseases. The program incorporates a reasoning system that tries to simulate that of a good diagnostician. (More detail will be given in Chapter 5.)

Artificial Intelligence Now

During the 1980s, AI evolved in several interesting directions. Expert systems (ES) have continued their diffusion into the business sector as the most visible evidence of the AI enterprise. Companies large and small set up groups to design and implement ES in the hopes of improving performance and maintaining corporate knowledge beyond the work life of individual employees. Most companies have used special high-level programming languages called shells for the implementation of ES and many seemed to be satisfied with the results.[35] More detail will be given in Chapter 4 on the applications of ES in business.

With respect to more technical aspects, a greater emphasis has been placed on putting AI on a firmer theoretical foundation through the increasing use of logic as both a representational language and a computational one. A range of human activities, such as common sense reasoning, reasoning in the face of uncertainty, diagnosis of faulty systems, and learning under a variety of conditions has been formalized and modeled using a variety of different logics and statistical theories. That favored language for implementing AI programs, LISP, has been superseded in many parts of the world by Prolog, a language with a built-in problem solver, based on formal theorem-proving in logic. Prolog is the most popular example of a programming approach called logic programming, an attempt to take traditional logic, a passive descriptive language, and to add a control structure to transform it into a problem solving language. Current research is focused on developing distributed, or parallel, implementations as well as incorporating a system of constraints in order to increase problem solving efficiency.

The 1980s have also witnessed a return, albeit in a modified form, to the neural networks of the 1950s and 1960s. In their current incarnation, such terms as connectionism and parallel distributed processing have also been applied to research in this area. Once again the goal is to design individual neurons, geometries, learning rules and training procedures to construct large networks to learn interesting and complex behaviors. The primary emphasis is on learning and the motivation derives in part from the availability of cheap microprocessors, which permit the construction of relatively large, fast networks. In addition, the behavior of such networks has attracted the attention of researchers from such disciplines as physics, mathematics, and psychology, in addition to AI. Some interesting results have been reported but connectionism remains controversial as some of these results have not been adequately explained. Furthermore, many in the AI community are familiar with the devastating criticism launched against the previous generation of neural networks, known as perceptrons, by the distinguished AI researchers Marvin Minsky and Seymour Papert.[36]

In a somewhat lighter vein, but probably more accessible to the public, have been reports of the remarkable progress in chess-playing programs. Particularly noteworthy is a program called Deep Thought, which, in late 1988, achieved the distinction of being the first program to defeat a grandmaster, Bent Larsen of Denmark. Subsequently it was defeated by current world champion Gary Kasparov and former world champion Anatoly Karpov. Nevertheless, its overall level of performance is now world caliber and improving. Deep Thought was developed at Carnegie-Mellon University by five graduate students and employs a special-purpose chip that permits it to examine about 750,000 moves per second. Thus success has been achieved not through the incorporation of explicit, deep chess knowledge but rather because of increases in brute force speed made possible by advances in computing technology. The next generation of Deep Thought will run 10 to 100 times faster, as improved chips are used. In spite of Deep Thought's successes, this result is rather disappointing in that most AI researchers felt improved chess knowledge would be necessary to improve performance. The implications for other domains of AI are not at all clear.

There are critics of the AI enterprise, and their arguments range from questioning the morality of doing research that can be used by government in surveillance activities to concern about the possibly false philosophical principles that underlie AI. The former position is held by Joseph Weizenbaum of the Massachusetts Institute of Technology. Much of the early research in AI, well into the 1970s in the U.S., was in fact funded by the Advanced Research Projects Agency (ARPA) of the Air Force and through the 1980s by its successor, DARPA (Defense ARPA). Additional funding came from the Strategic Defense Initiative (SDI, popularly known as "Stars Wars") as well as more traditional sources such as the National Science Foundation (NSF) and the National Aeronautics and Space Administration (NASA). This heavily defense-oriented association led some critics to suggest that the major beneficiary of the research would be the defense establishment. For example, an important research area in the early 1970s was speech recognition. In this process a computer, programmed to receive the electrical signal resulting from the transformation of the acoustic speech wave, produced first a representation in words and second a representation of the underlying meaning. It was Weizenbaum's claim that one of the goals of this research was to enable U.S. security agencies to monitor conversations automatically and determine whether or not they posed a risk to government. His argument was also broader, in that he criticized the entire AI enterprise for attempting to produce what he called an "alien intelligence." That is, while programs that could engage in a broad range of behavior might be possible, they would not be desirable because they would be fundamentally at odds with the human experience and spirit. Not surprisingly, this opinion was immediately and vigorously challenged by leading researchers in the field.

Criticism on the basis of philosophical principles was launched by Hubert Dreyfus, a philosopher at the University of California at Berkeley. He argued that the goals of AI were impossible in principle and that researchers were either misguided or were misleading the community at large. He and his brother Stuart, a distinguished applied mathematician, have criticized the extravagant claims made for expert systems, countering them with the contention that human expertise is too deep, too intuitive, too broad, and too open-ended to be captured by a computer program. The Dreyfusses (mainly Hubert) argue that because the dominant stream of Western philosophy, analytic philosophy, is bankrupt, any applied research based on it, such as AI, will not succeed. These criticisms are considerably weakened when applied to neural networks, about which the Dreyfusses have reserved judgment.[37] The charges have largely been ignored within the AI community and occasionally angrily denounced as being ill-informed. In recent years, other philosophers such as Daniel Dennett[38] and John Haugeland[39] have found useful ideas in AI.

When all is said and done, AI has become an important factor both in computer science and in society at large. It is clear that the development of intelligent or even pseudo-intelligent machines will have a significant impact on our future. The role of AI in the various areas investigated in this book will be assessed, for it has become much more than an academic discipline. Furthermore, note that it will not be necessary for sophisticated systems to be developed before their impact is felt. The premature use of pseudo-intelligent machines may introduce the unfortunate possibility of people being forced to adapt to machines that are not really very smart at all. As we shall see in the next chapter, the emergence of the "chip" will also significantly increase the impact of computers in general and "intelligent" ones in particular.

SUMMARY

The human fascination with artifacts that mimic human behavior is longstanding and has inspired tales and legends from many cultures. Particular noteworthy are the automata built by the Jacquet-Droz family of Switzerland between 1768 and 1774. The theme of robots and their ambiguous relation to their human creators has been expressed in such works as *Frankenstein, R.U.R.*, and *2001: A space odyssey*. In the twentieth century Isaac Asimov, in his robot stories, and George Lucas, in his *Star Wars* series of movies, have presented robots whose sole purpose has been to serve their human masters.

By many artists, musicians, and film makers the computer is seen as a new and powerful tool for the creation of art. Supercomputers are being used to generate extraordinarily realistic film images, doing away with the need for special models and special photographic effects.

In the mid-1950s a new scientific discipline made its appearance. Its goal was to develop computer programs to exhibit intelligent behavior. Its name is artificial intelligence and its contributions to technology will be significant. AI techniques are currently being used in vision systems for robots, natural language interfaces for databases, and expert systems for many applications.

NOTES

1. From *World of Wonders*, by Robertson Davies. © 1975. Reprinted by permission of Macmillan of Canada, a Division of Canada Publishing Corporation.
2. John Cohen, *Human Robots in Myth and Science* (London: Allen & Unwin, 1977).
3. Joseph Needham, *Science and Civilization in China, History of Scientific Thought, Vol. 2* (Cambridge, United Kingdom: Cambridge University Press, 1956), p. 53.
4. John Kobler, "The Strange World of M. Charliat," *Saturday Evening Post*, March 25, 1955, p. 70.
5. Marvin Minksy, *Information* (San Francisco: Scientific American, 1966), p. 210.
6. W. W. Jacobs, *The Monkey's Paw* (New Rochelle: Spoken Arts Records, SA1090, 1970).
7. Patricia S. Warrick, *The Cybernetic Imagination in Science Fiction* (Cambridge, Massachusetts: MIT Press, 1980).
8. Samuel Butler, *Erewhon* (New York: New American Library, 1960), p. 180.
9. Karel Capek, *R.U.R.* (London: Oxford University Press, 1923).
10. Isaac, Asimov, "Runaround," in *I, Robot* (London: Granada, 1968), pp. 33–51.
11. Lars Gunnar Boden, in Leopold Froehlich, "Give Tchaikovsky the News," *Datamation*, October 1981, p. 136.
12. E. T. A. Hoffman, "Automata," in E. F. Bleiler (ed.), *The Best Tales of Hoffman* (New York: Dover, 1967).
13. Charles Dodge, in Froehlich, "Give Tchaikovsky the News," p. 140.
14. Jan W. Morthenson, "Aesthetic Dilemmas in Electronic Music," in Robin Julian Heifitz (ed.), *On the Wires of Our Nerves* (London and Toronto: Associated University Presses, 1989), p. 67.
15. John Melby, "Computer *Music* or *Computer* Music?" in Heifitz, *On the Wires of Our Nerves*, pp. 95–96.
16. Joan Darragh, as quoted in Paul Gardner, "Think of Leonardo Wielding a Pixel and a Mouse," *The New York Times*, April 2, 1984, Section 2, p. 1. Copyright © 1984 by The New York Times Company. Reprinted by permission.
17. A. Michael Noll, "The Digital Computer as a Creative Medium," *IEEE Spectrum*, October 1967. Reprinted in Zenon W. Pylyshyn (ed.), *Perspectives on the Computer Revolution* (Englewood Cliffs, NJ: Prentice-Hall, 1970), pp. 349–358.
18. *Ibid.*, pp. 354–355.
19. Ken Sofer, "Art? Or Not Art?" *Datamation* (Cahners Publishing Co), October 1981, p. 120.
20. Cynthia Goodman, *Digital Visions: Computers and Art* (New York: Henry N. Abrams, Inc. and Everson Museum of Art, Syracuse, 1987).
21. *Ibid.*, p. 46.
22. *Ibid.*, p. 47.
23. *Ibid.*, p. 56.
24. Hubert Hohn, "The Art of a New Machine or Confessions of a Computer Artist," *Technology Review*, November–December 1988, pp. 64–73.
25. *Ibid.*, p. 67.
26. John Whitney, *Digital Harmony* (New York: McGraw-Hill/Byte Books, 1980), p. 30.
27. Mark A. Fischetti, "The Silver Screen Blossoms into Color," *IEEE Spectrum*, August 1987, pp. 50–55.
28. *Ibid.*, p. 50.
29. Maria Shao, Richard Brandt, Neil Gross, and John Verity, "It's a PC, It's a TV—Multimedia," *Business Week*, October 9, 1989, pp. 152–155, 158, 162, 166.
30. *Ibid.* p. 154.
31. Anatol Rapoport, "Technological Models of the Nervous System." Reprinted in K. M. Sayre and F. J. Crosson (eds.), *The Modelling of Mind* (New York: Simon & Schuster, 1968), pp. 25–38.
32. Pamela McCorduck, *Machines Who Think* (San Francisco: Freeman, 1979).
33. Warren McCulloch and Walter Pitts, "A Logical Calculus of the Ideas Immanent in Nervous Activity," *Bulletin of Mathematical Biophysics*, 5, 1943, pp. 115–133.
34. Norbert Wiener, *Cybernetics: Control and Communication in the Animal and the Machine, Second Edition* (New York: Wiley, 1961).

35. Edward Feigenbaum, Pamela McCorduck, and H. Penny Nii, *The Rise of the Expert Company* (New York: Times Books, 1988).
36. Marvin Minsky and Seymour Papert, *Perceptrons: An Introduction to Computational Geometry, (First Edition, 1969) Second Edition* (Cambridge, Massachusetts: MIT Press, 1988).
37. Hubert L. Dreyfus and Stuart E. Dreyfus, *Mind Over Machine: The Power of Human Intuition and Expertise in the Era of the Computer,* Paper ed. (New York: The Free Press, 1988).
38. Daniel Dennett, *Brainstorms* (Montgomery, Vermont: Bradford Books, 1978).
39. John Haugeland, *Artificial Intelligence: The Very Idea* (Cambridge, Massachusetts: MIT Press (A Bradford Book), 1985).

ADDITIONAL READINGS

Computers as a Creative Medium

Anderson, J. "Multimedia: About Interface." *Macuser,* March 1990, pp. 89–93, 96.
Brand, S. *The Media Lab: Inventing the Future at MIT.* New York: Viking Penguin, 1987.
Browne, M. W. "Secrets of the Concert Hall Yield to the Computer." *The New York Times,* September 19, 1989, p. B 1.
Browne, M. W. "Computers Help Fill in the Gaps of Pompeii's Past." *The New York Times,* July 13, 1990, p. B 6.
Lansdown, J. and Earnshaw, R. A. *Computers in Art, Design and Animation.* New York: Springer-Verlag, 1989.
Latham, W. "Sculptures in the Void." *New Scientist,* January 27, 1990. pp. 41–41, 44–45.
Mathews, M. and Pierce, J. R. (eds.). *Current Directions in Computer Music Research.* Cambridge, Massachusetts: MIT Press, 1989.
"Multimedia," (In Depth Section) *Byte,* February, 1990, p. 200 ff.
Panel Proceedings of SIGGRAPH '89, *Computer Graphics,* **23**(5), December 1989.
Rivlin, R. *The Algorithmic Image: Graphic Visions of the Computer Age.* Redmond, Washington: Microsoft Press, 1986.
Roads, C. (ed.). *Composers and the Computer.* Los Altos, California: William Kaufmann, 1985.
Roads, C. (ed.). *The Music Machine: Selected Readings from Computer Music Journal.* Cambridge, Massachusetts: MIT Press, 1989.
Thompson, T., Wolff, C., and Cook, D. "Music is Alive with the Sound of High Tech." *Business Week,* October 26, 1987, pp. 114–116.

Artificial Intelligence: A Brief Introduction

Barnden, J. A. and Pollack, J. B. (eds.). *Advances in Connectionist and Neural Computational Theory.* Norwood, New Jersey: Ablex, 1989.
Dreyfus, H. L. *What Computers Can't Do, Second Edition.* New York: Harper & Row, 1979.
Feigenbaum, E. A. and McCorduck, P. *The Fifth Generation.* Reading, Massachusetts: Addison-Wesley, 1983.
Graubard, S. T. (ed.). *The Artificial Debate: False Starts, Real Foundations.* Cambridge, Massachusetts: MIT Press (Daedalus Special Issue), 1988.
Hebb, D. *The Organization of Behavior.* New York: Wiley, 1949.
Johnson, G. *Machinery of the Mind.* Redmond, Washington: Microsoft Press (A Tempus Book), 1986.
Rosenberg, Richard S. "The Impact of Artificial Intelligence on Society." Technical Report 88-20, Department of Computer Science, University of British Columbia, September 1988.
Schank, R. *The Cognitive Computer.* Reading, Massachusetts: Addison-Wesley, 1984.

Searle, J. *Minds, Brains and Science.* Cambridge, Massachusetts: Harvard University Press, 1984.

Shrobe, H. and The American Association for Artificial Intelligence (eds.). *Exploring Artificial Intelligence: Survey Talks from the National Conferences on Artificial Intelligence.* San Mateo, California: Morgan Kaufmann, 1988.

"The Grandmaster's Nemesis." *The Economist,* December 23, 1989, pp. 95–96.

von Neumann, J. *The Computer and the Brain.* New Haven: Yale University Press, 1958.

Waterman, D. A. *A Guide to Expert Systems.* Reading, Massachusetts: Addison-Wesley, 1986.

Weizenbaum, J. *Computer Power and Human Reason.* San Francisco: Freeman, 1976.

Winograd, T. and Flores, F. *Understanding Computers and Cognition: A New Foundation for Design.* Norwood, New Jersey: Ablex, 1986.

3

CRITICISM AND HISTORY

The clock, not the steam engine, is the key-machine of the modern industrial age. For every phase of its development the clock is both the outstanding fact and the typical symbol of the machine: even today no other machine is so ubiquitous. . .

The clock, moreover, served as a model for many other kinds of mechanical works, and the analysis of motion that accompanied the perfection of the clock, with the various types of gearing and transmission that were elaborated, contributed to the success of quite different kinds of machines. . . .

The clock, moreover, is a piece of power-machinery whose "product" is seconds and minutes: by its essential nature it dissociated time from human events and helped create the belief in an independent world of mathematically measurable sequences: the special world of sciences.

INTRODUCTION

Computers did not suddenly appear. Technological innovation does not arise from thin air. There are strata of previous technological achievements and economic and human resources. We frequently assume that our times are unique and that only our particular genius could have brought forth such wonders. Many craftsmen, inventors, and scientists laid the necessary groundwork for the modern computer. Its history extends from the invention of the abacus to the designing of the Jacquard loom and beyond.

> There is a time when the operation of the machine becomes so odious, makes you so sick at heart that you can't take part; you can't even passively take part, and you've got to put your bodies upon the gears and upon the wheels, upon the levers, upon all the apparatus and you've got to indicate to the people who run it, to the people who own it, that unless you're free, the machine will be prevented from working at all. (Mario Savio, Berkeley, December 2, 1964.)

For many, the above quotation was the rallying cry of the protest movement of the 1960s and early 1970s in the United States. It seemed to express the feelings of many that the state was a powerful, oppressive machine grinding up its young to further its single-minded aims. The issue here is not politics, but this perception of technology in control. It is necessary and important to confront the criticisms raised, if not to answer them completely.

COMMENTS ON TECHNOLOGICAL CHANGE

The following two points of view—two caricatures, perhaps—define the conflicting poles of the debate.

> Computers are just tools. We as their inventors and employers decide what we shall do with them. They are more complex and have greater potential than other tools but you should never forget that ultimately that is what they are. All statements to the contrary are alarmist.
>
> A computer is not just another tool. Computers can perform activities that previously only people could do. Furthermore, by virtue of their enormous speed and capacity they can give unpredictable results when applied in new areas. They already endanger privacy, employment, even freedom. Although previous tools posed some of these difficulties, the computer represents not just more of the same but an obvious quantum jump.

You may not have yet formed an opinion on this issue. In fact it may be premature to expect it. Even if you agree with the first viewpoint, you might in daily life be expected to defend that view again and again as the computerization of society proceeds and new issues crop up. Computers are here and now. Can we still shape our own destiny?

Computers are in a real sense a natural continuation of technological development, and there exists a large body of commentary on the effects and dangers of technology itself. Important scholars have provided a number of incisive insights and warnings.

Machine analogies can be readily perceived in human situations. For Lewis Mumford, the slave population involved in building the pyramids can be seen as a mega-machine, the individual humans analogous to cogs and gears, each performing a limited repeatable task. Siegfried Giedion views the assembly line in a similar manner. In one of his most damning criticisms of modern technology he shows how bread has evolved from nourishing food to convenient, well-packaged, food product. The claim that technology is neutral and merely a tool that can be used for good or ill is subjected to a major critique by Jacques Ellul. The association of technology with totalitarianism in the advanced industrial state is a subject for study by Herbert Marcuse. Norbert Wiener points out that just by virtue of its size and speed the computer can go beyond being a tool and in some sense create a new reality.

In an important article published in 1969, John McDermott describes technology as "the opiate of the educated public, or at least its favorite authors."[1] He gives a representative list of the fruits of the cornucopia as seen by a number of the so-called prophets of technology.

> An end to poverty and the inauguration of permanent prosperity (Leon Keyserling), universal equality of opportunity (Zbigniew Brzezinski), a radical increase in individual freedom (Edward Shils), the replacement of work by leisure for most of mankind (Robert Theobald), fresh water for desert dwellers (Lyndon Johnson), permanent but harmless social revolution [and] the final come-uppance of Mao-Tse-tung and all his ilk (Walt Rostow), and, lest we forget, the end of ideology (Daniel Bell).[2]

This brief characterization of points of view should be fleshed out. In all the uproar over the wonders of technology, there should be place for a few wise voices with a message of caution and concern. This book explores the impact of recent computer developments. Beyond the initial, obvious benefits, future problems may lurk. It is worth listening to the group of critics, historians, and commentators that includes Mumford, Giedion, Ellul, Marcuse and Wiener—the old, but honorable, guard.

Lewis Mumford

A major social critic and the grand old man of the environmental movement, Mumford is also a distinguished historian of technology. In a long series of books beginning in 1922, he has been especially concerned to establish the continuity of craftsmanship and technology down through the ages. Furthermore, he has attempted to catalog and analyze the variety of forces technology brings to bear against the maintenance of humanity in everyday life. Power, centralization, autocracy, mechanization, and control are a few of the key words that only begin to suggest the many issues that have exercised him for so many years. It is difficult to do justice to a lifetime of scholarship in so brief a space.

We will here be concerned with Mumford's analysis of the impact of computers and automation. He is disturbed not so much by the physical replacement of workers as by the elimination of the human mind and spirit from the process of production. The spirit suffers because of the elevation of computer decision-making and the parallel subordination of individual initiative. The system or organization becomes all-knowing and all-powerful. The individual—both as scientist, engineer, or manager and as consumer—must abide by the established rules even if there is a loss of a human way of life.

For Mumford, the computer itself and its role in automation is just one more step along a road of constrained human choice. He has traced the enslavement of people from the building of the pyramids, under an organizational scheme that he likens to a machine, to the development and refinement of the modern assembly line. It is not inevitable that technology be used to enslave society (even assuming that we feel enslaved), because decisions as to its use must frequently be consciously made. If we have the knowledge and the will, we can structure society so that spontaneity and choice are encouraged and even rewarded. But if computers are left to make what are fundamentally human decisions the consequences may be indeed serious, because computers may be programmed to return only those results desired by the leaders and managers.

In contrast to these perceived limitations in computers, strenuously challenged of course by most computer enthusiasts, Mumford offers a paean to the human brain.

> Unfortunately, computer knowledge, because it must be processed and programmed, cannot remain constantly in touch, like the human brain, with the unceasing flow of reality; for only a small part of experience can be arrested for extraction and expression in abstract symbols. Changes that cannot be quantitatively measured or objectively observed, such changes as take place constantly all the way from the atom to the living organism, are outside the scope of the computer. For all its fantastic rapidity of operation, its components remain incapable of making qualitative responses to constant organic changes.[3]

Siegfried Giedion

The major work of the architectural and social critic Siegfried Giedion, *Mechanization Takes Command,* appeared in 1948, before computers had achieved a significant presence.[4] He is concerned with the process by which traditional human activities have gradually been assumed by machines to the obvious detriment of the final product. He is interested in "the elimination of the complicated handicraft."[5] An important example is the making of bread, long a central enterprise of human existence. From the beginnings of agriculture and the cultivation of wheat, the preparation of bread has been a necessary and honorable activity. The connection of humans with the organic is well exemplified through bread, its manufacturing (i.e., making by hand), distribution, and consumption. Riots have been provoked by scarcity of bread or slight increases in its price. The images conjured up by the simple phrase "the breaking of bread" are suggestive of basic human relations: sharing, participating, a sense of community, a willingness to understand, and a desire to reaffirm historical continuity.

The problem is, the quality of bread today is highly suspect. For the most part in North America, it looks and tastes like cardboard. Few remember, or even care, what a treat real bread can be. The story begins with the mechanization of kneading, clearly a strenuous activity requiring pulling and pushing and the use of feet as well as hands. In the late eighteenth century, the French pharmacologist Antoine Augustin Pametier described kneading as a process in which flour, yeast, water, and air are sufficiently well mixed to produce a new substance. It is clear that kneading is physically difficult and an obvious candidate for mechanization. Mechanical rotary kneaders were developed as far back as the Romans, and experiments continued through the Renaissance into the industrial era. Surprisingly, however, complete mechanization did not take place until after 1925, with the introduction of the high-speed mixer in the United States. Whereas early machines simulated the action of human hands, the high-speed mixer has an agitator that "usually consists of two arms attached to simple steel bars, which perform sixty to eighty revolutions a minute."[6] In explaining why they have not been widely adopted in Europe, Giedion notes that the more delicate European wheats cannot accommodate to the tremendous speed and shocks produced by these mixers. Beyond the efficiency of using the mixers, there was a stronger motivation: "the main reason seems to have been that the energetic mixing made possible the manufacture of a bread even whiter than before."[7]

The final stage in the process is baking. Again, over time a satisfactory form of oven evolved. It resembled an egg, a shape that proved economical and advantageous for uniform heat distribution. However, there were limitations involved in the method of heating, the means for sweeping out embers, and the problems of dealing with large quantities of bread. And so the shape, size, and method of heating evolved: steel plates replaced brick and gas heaters replaced coal. Still, mechanization was not complete because what was needed was an assembly line process to measure and allocate the ingredients, to mix them into dough, and to cut, weigh, mold, and position the individual portions on a conveyor belt ready for the oven. As early as 1840, the French had achieved the mass production of bread.

Other aspects of the mechanization process should be mentioned. Two basic ferments were used to make the dough rise, yeast and leaven. These underwent a number of chemical transformations to speed up the fermentation process, increasing the weight of the bread. For example, carbonic acid increased the speed of fermentation and human labor was thereby reduced. Additional chemicals were added to make bread look whiter. These additives were used as long ago as the mid-eighteenth century. Even the milling process to produce the flour was altered to produce a whiter, cleaner product. At the beginning of the nineteenth century artificial bleaching was introduced to decrease the aging process and improve the whiteness. More recently, vitamins have been added to replace the nourishment lost through the actions of the previous processes.

As a result of all these innovations, in North America the bread factory has largely replaced the bakery. The small egg-shaped oven has become the 100-foot tunnel oven. The complete process has been mechanized, from the mixing, in several stages, to the dividing, the rounding into balls, the moulding, the placing into pans, and the high-speed fermentation to, finally, the baking of the bread in the oven on an endless conveyor belt. The cooling process is accelerated by artificial means, and the bread is sliced, packaged, and distributed.[8] One question remains. What has happened to the bread?

The technological process has certainly produced a bread of uniform quality, which, it is argued, the public demands.

> The bread of full mechanization has the resiliency of rubber sponge. When squeezed it returns to its former shape. The loaf becomes constantly whiter, more elastic, and frothier. . . . Since mechanization, it has often been pointed out, white bread has become much richer in fats, milk, and sugar. But these are added largely to stimulate sales by heightening the loaf's eye-appeal. The shortenings used in bread, a leading authority states, are "primarily for the purpose of imparting desirable tender eating or chewing qualities to the finished product." They produce the "soft velvet crumb," a cakelike structure, so that the bread is half-masticated, as it were, before reaching the mouth.[9]

The story of bread teaches that in the face of increased mechanization there is a strong tendency for the natural to suffer. But is it inevitable? Visitors to San Francisco rave about its sourdough bread, which is mass-produced. French bread is world famous for its taste, texture, and smell and is usually sold by small, family-owned bakeries. Thus, technology is inextricably woven into the social fabric of a culture. If it is important to maintain the quality of bread, independent of issues of mass production and distribution, it will be maintained. Therefore, to understand how technology affects the quality of life it is necessary, at the very least, to understand how public opinion is formed and shaped and how it manifests itself in the accommodation of the new. However, there is one critic of technology who argues that we don't have a real choice.

Jacques Ellul

A French sociologist, Jacques Ellul has become one of the world's foremost critics of technology. His major work, published in France in 1954, appeared in the United States in 1964 under the title *The Technological Society*.[10] He presents a very grim picture, indeed. He views technology as an irresistible, mysterious force, far more menacing than either Mumford or Giedion have supposed. It has an ability to change every aspect of life that it encounters. First, it is necessary to understand what Ellul means by *technique*. It is similar to Giedion's *mechanization* but much stronger.

> The term *technique*, as I use it, does not mean machines, technology, or this or that procedure for attaining an end. In our technological society, *technique* is the *totality of methods rationally arrived at and having absolute efficiency* (for a given stage of development) in *every field of human activity*. Its characteristics are new; the technique of the present has no common measure with that of the past. (Emphasis added.)[11]

The sense of the term will become clearer as we continue.

Ellul argues that although techniques derive from crafts and methods prior to the eighteenth century, there has been a quantitative change, and technique has taken on a life of its own with its own internal logic. Initiated by the labors of past generations, it has somehow become a separate force with potentially terrible consequences.

Ellul presents four explanations of why technique was constrained until the eighteenth century.

1. Only certain constrained areas were amenable to technique.
2. Other areas of life such as leisure, social intercourse, sleep, prayer, and play were more predominant.
3. Technique was local and spread slowly.
4. The geographical and historical isolation of societies permitted, indeed required, the flourishing of many different types of techniques.

The situation is different now—we face the new and terrible power of technique and its unremitting campaign against human individuality. Progress still depends on the individual, but only within the terms defined by technique. Thus, efficiency is of prime concern, and aesthetics and ethics are sacrificed. Progress is a concept inherent in the system and is largely unrelated to the desires or wishes of the people.

It almost seems as if technique is some kind of living, breathing monster out of control, our control at least, with its own aims and its own means of achieving them. What are some of the features of this monster?

> [Technique] has been extended to all spheres and encompasses every activity, including human activities. It has led to a multiplication of means without limit. It has perfected indefinitely the instruments available to man, and put at his disposal an almost limitless variety of intermediaries and auxiliaries. Technique has been extended geographically so that it covers the whole earth. It is evolving with a rapidity disconcerting not only to the man in the street but to the technician himself. It poses problems which recur endlessly and ever more acutely in human social groups. Moreover, technique has become objective and is transmitted like a physical thing; it leads thereby to a certain unity of civilization, regardless of the environment or the country in which it operates.[12]

Here, in brief, are some of the characteristics of technique as it operates currently:

Rationality. Aspects of management such as standardization, division of labor, and quality control.

Artificiality. Technique creates an artificial world, denying and eliminating the natural world.

Automatism of Technical Choice. The human has no role to play. Technique acts and people observe.

Self-augmentation. Technique changes and evolves with no help or direct intervention by people.

Monism. Technique forms a single whole and its various components are self-reinforcing.

The Necessary Linking Together of Techniques. There seems to be a historical necessity operating in which the technique at one stage must follow the one at a previous stage.

Technical Universalism. Geographic—technique has been spread by commerce, war, and the export of technicians. Qualitative—technique has taken over the whole of civilization.

The Autonomy of Technique. A good example is the functioning of an industrial plant as a closed system that is independent of the goals and needs of the society in which it exists.

Since it is not really made clear how technique has evolved, it is certainly not clear what, if anything, can be done. In contradistinction to Ellul's unrelieved pessimism, evidence can be offered of how much life has improved over the years. The obvious decreases in hunger and sickness, the lengthening of the life span, and the increase in literacy are proof of the fruits of technology. Ellul's critics would grant that all is not roses but on balance the good brought by technology far outweighs the ills.

Herbert Marcuse

A social philosopher and political theorist, Marcuse has written on Freud and Marx. In his political writings he is very much concerned with the relation between political power and the quality of life. He analyzes the growth of technology, especially under capitalism, and its impact on people's lives. Marcuse believes that there is a strong connection between political power and technology and that, furthermore, the state maintains itself through its control of industrial productivity. This power reaches out through all aspects of life, and transfers traces of the machine ethic to them. In *One-Dimensional Man* Marcuse describes the relation between people and their things (to which may be added, in a natural extension, the computer).

> We are again confronted with one of the most vexing aspects of advanced industrial civilization: the rational character of its irrationality. Its productivity and efficiency, its capacity to increase and spread comforts, to turn waste into need, and destruction into construction, the extent to which the civilization transforms the object world into an extension of man's mind and body makes the very notion of alienation questionable. The people recognize themselves in their commodities; they find their soul in their automobile, hi-fi set, split-level home, kitchen equipment. The very mechanism which ties the individual to his society has changed, and social control is anchored in the new needs which it has produced.[13]

From his political perspective, Marcuse argues that automation will ultimately lead to a socialist state after the capitalist industrial machine has done its worst. Presumably, when the workers assume control of the means of production, they will humanize the work place, freeing themselves from boring and dangerous jobs. Their goal will be not to maximize profits but to liberate the human spirit. In Marcuse's opinion, true freedom will ultimately emerge from automation. This view contrasts sharply with that of Ellul.

Norbert Wiener

Called the father of cybernetics, Norbert Wiener was an important mathematician who had a deep concern about the possible social impact of his work. Cybernetics and automation are intimately related, as engineering is related to mathematics and physics. In fact, the subtitle of Wiener's very influential book, *Cybernetics,* is *Control and Communication in the Animal and Machine.*[14] The central notion in cybernetics is feedback. In this process, an action is maintained by continuously reducing the monitored difference between the current state and the desired state. This principle underlies much of industrial automation, hence Wiener's anguish over the fruits of his labor. He views automatic equipment as equivalent to slave labor, which means that humans in competition with the mechanical slaves must accept economic conditions equivalent to theirs. That is, employers will not pay their human workers more than the costs associated with robots performing equivalent work. He prophecied a period of serious unemployment when the new technology becomes pervasive.

Wiener was much less pessimistic about the future in the second edition of this book, which appeared some 13 years after the first. He felt that many of his concerns were starting to be accepted by the business world. The relation between technological change and unemployment is perhaps the central issue in assessing the impact of technology. There appears to be a general consensus that, initially, technological innovation may result in the loss of jobs but eventually more jobs are created than lost. (We will return to this question in Chapter 10.)

Wiener was also troubled by the ability of computers to produce unintended and unanticipated results. The problem results from a combination of factors, including the speed of the computer, the inadvisability of interfering with it during its computation, the narrowness of the program's scope and the limitations of the data. Note that none of these elements has anything to do with whether a computer can exhibit intelligent behavior. The fundamental point is that computers operate so much faster than do humans that there is a basic mismatch in their interaction. One had better be very sure that the computer is doing what is desired and intended.

Wiener offers a strategy much easier stated than carried out.

> Render unto man the things which are man's and unto the computer the things which are the computer's. This would seem the intelligent policy to adopt when we employ men and computers together in common undertakings. It is a policy as far removed from that of the gadget worshipper as it is from the man who sees only blasphemy and degradation of man in the use of any mechanical adjuvants whatever to thoughts.[15]

Wiener feels that computers can ultimately be controlled for the benefit of society. But this sentiment seems to be expressed more as a caution—against the possibility of a terrible future if computers are not used wisely—than as a realistic expectation.

The views of the social critics given above range from apprehension to horror. The easy response to them is, yes there have always been problems, yes there will be more problems, but we are in control of our own destiny. The debate will continue and will probably increase in intensity as the presence of computers is more strongly felt. In all likelihood, the discussion will turn on whether or not the computer in its most prevalent form—the microprocessor—represents a quantitative change in technology. The final word in this section, reminding us that technology is not a recent concern, goes to the nineteenth-century social philosopher John Stuart Mill.

> Suppose that it were possible to get houses built, corn grown, battles fought, causes tried, and even churches erected and prayers said by machinery—by automatons in human form—it would be a considerable loss to exchange for these automatons even the men and women who at present inhabit the more civilized parts of the world, and who assuredly are but starved specimens of what nature can and will produce. Human nature is not a machine to be built after a model, and set to do exactly the work prescribed for it, but a tree, which requires to grow and develop itself on all sides, according to the tendency of the inward forces which make it a living thing.[16]

A Measure of Optimism

> The fact is, that civilization requires slaves. The Greeks were quite right there. Unless there are slaves to do the ugly, horrible, uninteresting work, culture and contemplation become

> almost impossible. Human slavery is wrong, insecure, and demoralizing. On mechanical slavery, on the slavery of the machine, the future of the world depends.[17]

As most of this book is a study in success of the computer in its incredibly wide variety of forms and applications, we need hardly pause to praise it. Nevertheless, the few words of cheer above should be welcome, as a clear statement of technology as the servant of the people who invent it, develop it, and employ it to serve the needs of everyone. About one hundred years later, this view was reinforced by Herbert Simon, winner of the Nobel prize in economics in 1978 and one of the fathers of artificial intelligence. Simon views technological change from the unique combined vantage point of economist, computer scientist, and cognitive psychologist. In a ringing challenge, Simon presents probably one of the most optimistic and encouraging statements of the technological vision.

> It is to realize, perhaps for the first time in human history, that we are a part of the world; that we are a part of this vast machinery; that man is not outside nature, that man is not above nature, but that man is a part of nature.
>
> If we can make peace with ourselves on those terms, it will have at least one desirable byproduct: As we design new technology, as we make use of our knowledge about the world and the knowledge that we are gaining about ourselves, about our thinking processes, through research in AI and cognitive simulation, we will realize that we have to apply our technology in a way that keeps man's peace with the universe in which he lives, instead of conceiving our technology as a weapon with which man can wage war on the rest of nature.[18]

One can almost hear the trumpets.

A BRIEF HISTORY OF COMPUTERS

The next few pages will sparkle with such catchy names as ENIAC, EDVAC, UNIVAC, EDSAC, MARK 1, and others. They are the names of the earliest real computers, developed about forty years ago. How they came to be is a fascinating, long, and involved story. There is a problem inherent in an abbreviated history—it may appear to be a series of inventions that were historically inevitable. The social forces, the burgeoning requirements of applied mathematics, and the demands made during times of war and peace—including the computation of ballistic tables, navigational aids, and census statistics—are discussed in the Additional Readings.

Before the Twentieth Century

Computing probably began with counting, and counting began with fingers and sticks and stones. The abacus, one of the oldest calculating devices, was known to the Egyptians as early as 460 B.C. and is still used today in many parts of the world. There are two classes of computing machines—*analog* and *digital*. An abacus is a digital device in which the positions of individual beads on wires represent numbers. In analog machines, the instantaneous value of a continuously varying physical quantity such as a length, voltage, or angular position represents a number. Before it was rendered obsolete by the pocket calculator, the slide rule was probably the most commonly used analog computing device. Its operation makes use of the fact that the product of two numbers is equivalent to the sum of their logarithms. By using a length on a stick to represent the logarithm of a number, multiplication is carried out by positioning two sticks appropriately. A traditional watch with face and hands is analog (no matter what process is used for positioning the hands), whereas one with only numbers, which change in discrete jumps, is digital. In this history the analog computer is a minor player.

Brian Randell, editor of *The Origins of Digital Computers,* divides their history into two streams: mechanical digital calculation and sequence control mechanisms.[19] These are the two major concerns of computation—how to actually perform a calculation and how to control sequences of calculations. Counting, the former, was of primary concern historically.

For centuries wheels with teeth or cogs in a linked train have been used to deal with addition that involves carries. The complete story includes the development of number systems, leading to the use of the decimal system in Europe. John Napier (1550–1617), best known as the inventor of logarithms, probably was the first person to use the decimal point in arithmetic operations. Until quite recently the credit for inventing the first calculator was given to the famous French philosopher Blaise Pascal (1623–1662). It is supposed that his impetus was to aid his father in performing calculations. In any case, at age nineteen he designed his first machine and by 1645 he had achieved a patent on it. The currently recognized first inventor, however, is Wilhelm Schickard of Tubingen (1592–1635), who apparently sent a set of drawings of a calculating machine to Kepler, the famous astronomer, in 1623. Who was first is not particularly important, since the idea and the necessary technology were in the air. The historical record is probably incomplete. The real importance of a new invention is heavily dependent on the social environment in which it occurs.

Some thirty years after Pascal's invention Gottfried Leibniz (1646–1716), a great mathematician and universal thinker, designed the Leibniz wheel, a crucial component of mechanical calculators. His machine, which was not constructed until 1694, permitted multiplication and division as well as addition and subtraction and was much more efficient than previous devices. As useful calculating devices were developed, the impetus grew to refine and improve them in order to carry out even more complicated computations. Leibniz himself raised the banner for the relief of drudgery through technology.

> Also the astronomers surely will not have to continue to exercise the patience which is required for computation. It is this that deters them from computing or correcting tables, from the construction of Ephemerides, from working on hypotheses, and from discussions of observations with each other. *For it is unworthy of excellent men to lose hours like slaves in the labor or calculation which could safely be relegated to anyone else if machines were used.* (Emphasis added.)[20]

Charles Babbage: The Difference Engine and the Analytical Engine

Over the next century a number of refinements took place in the basic calculator, but it was not until the mid-nineteenth century that a generally successful calculator became available. Charles Babbage (1792–1871), a most remarkable man—mathematician, inventor, and initiator of scientific management—flourished in this period. Undoubtedly, he deserves the title father of the computer. Ironically, his story is one of generally unfulfilled ambition. In 1821, he became interested in building a "Difference Engine" to automate the calculation of algebraic functions by using successive differences. A story describes the moment of its inception. Apparently Babbage was checking some calculations with John Herschel (the son of Sir William Herschel, the discoverer of Uranus) when Babbage remarked, "I wish to God these calculations had been executed by steam." Herschel simply replied, "It is quite possible." (Steam was the major power source of Babbage's time.)

In 1836, before his Difference Engine was completed, Babbage conceived of a much more powerful, general purpose computer that he called the Analytical Engine. In the end, neither machine was completed, for a variety of reasons—lack of sufficient financial resources, technical requirements beyond the skill available, and a design that underwent too-frequent change. There is little doubt, however, that Babbage at this early date envisioned a machine of such scope that its power would not be realized for more than a hundred years. His design included a memory store, an arithmetic unit, punched card input and output, and a mechanism that provided enough power of control to do iteration and branching. Following his death, others tried to build similar machines with little success. When successful machines were finally built, some of their designers were aware of his work; others were not. In the final analysis, Babbage appears to have been a cranky genius with ideas impossible to realize—for both economical and technical reasons—in his time.

No history of this period would be complete without mention of Augusta Ada, Countess of Lovelace (1816–1852), the only child of the poet Lord Byron, and a person of some mathematical ability. In 1840, when Babbage presented a series of lectures in Italy on his machine, they were attended by a young engineer, L. F. Menabrea. Ada translated his notes on the lectures and added comments of her own. Her work is the major account of the Analytic Engine. She may also have been the first programmer—she included a program to compute Bernoulli numbers, an important task for many physical problems. Her description of the engine is quite lyrical, not surprising for the daughter of a poet.

> We may say most aptly that the Analytical Engine weaves *algebraic patterns* just as the Jacquard loom weaves flowers and leaves. Here, it seems to us, resides more originality than the Difference Engine can be fairly entitled to claim.[25]

It appears that even the idea of a computer provoked in her mind the possibility that people might readily believe in the creative powers of such machines. She was at pains to disabuse the public of such a thought.

> The Analytical Engine has no pretensions whatever to *originate* anything. It can do whatever we *know how to order it* to perform. It can *follow* analysis; but it has no power of

> *anticipating* any analytical relations or truths. Its province is to assist us in making *available* what we are already acquainted with.[26]

What did Babbage achieve in the end? He did not build his Analytical Engine, but he did anticipate much of what would follow. He failed to realize his vision, probably because of his restless mind, the limitations of contemporary technology, and the lack of an obvious need for the projected computing power. He continually designed more advanced machines while the struggle was still on to realize his earlier designs. Still, his intellectual achievement was monumental.

Control of Computation

Ada's reference to the Jacquard loom relates to the second theme in our history of computers—sequence control mechanisms. The problem is twofold: (a) how to represent numbers and develop a mechanism for performing arithmetical operations on them, and (b) how to carry out sequences of calculations without human intervention, which could only restrict operational speeds. The automata discussed in Chapter 2 were generally controlled by a rotating pegged cylinder or a disc with holes, much as contemporary music boxes are. The problem of how to actually control a process by a mechanism essentially external to that process first arose in the weaving industry.

It was probably a man called Basile Bouchon who in 1725 used a perforated tape to control the weaving of ornamental patterns in silk. This idea was refined over the years by a number of inventors, including Jacques Vaucanson, the creator of the remarkable mechanical duck. The most important contribution was made by Joseph Marie Jacquard (1752–1834). Building on the work of Vaucanson, Bouchon, and others, he designed a system of control that used a connected sequence of punched cards. The holes in the card determined whether or not vertical hooks controlling the warp threads were used in the pattern being woven. By the end of the nineteenth century looms with 400 or 600 hooks were quite common. As early as 1812, there were approximately 11,000 Jacquard looms in France.

In 1836, Babbage adopted the Jacquard card mechanism not only for entering numbers into the machine but most importantly for controlling the sequence of operations necessary to carry out the calculations. It was easier to punch up a set of cards, he reasoned, than to make changes directly within the central core of the computer. Once the cards were made they could be used again whenever the particular computation was desired. Clearly this is much easier than physically altering the computer itself. Babbage anticipated the notion of a fixed machine performing computations under the direction of a program. It is interesting that a technological advance in one area turned out to be influential in quite another one. The story resumes in the United States, where for the most part the electronic computer was first invented and subsequently refined.

Near the end of the nineteenth century in the United States, the demands made on the Census Office became quite burdensome. The 1870 census was the first to make use of mechanical equipment of a rather simple kind. The key figures were John Shaw Billings, who was in charge of the 1880 census, and Herman Hollerith, (1860–1929) who worked for the Census Office from 1879 to 1883 and later supplied the tabulating equipment for the 1890 census. There is some controversy over who should be given credit for the tabulating machine concept. It seems that Billings suggested the idea of using punched cards to represent information but Hollerith actually built the machine. Billings apparently mentioned that he was inspired by the Jacquard loom principle. In any case the machines, patented by Hollerith in 1889, won a competition and were used in the 1890 census to punch and process approximately 56 million cards. Hollerith's machines, in an improved version, were also used in the 1900 census. However, relations between his company and the Census Bureau (the name was changed in 1903) deteriorated so much that for the 1910 census the Bureau used its own machines, which were developed by James Powers.

After Hollerith left the Census Office, he formed a company in 1896 called the Tabulating Machine Company. In 1911 it merged with two other companies to form the Computer-Tabulating-Recording Company. Thomas J. Watson, Sr., formerly with National Cash Register, became president in 1914. Ten years later he changed the company's name to International Business Machines (IBM). In the same year in which Hollerith's company merged, James Powers formed his own company, Powers Tabulating Machine Company, on the basis of patents received while he was employed by the Census Bureau. This company eventually merged with Remington Rand in 1927. Thus, the rivalry of Powers and Hollerith at the turn of the century gave rise to two companies that were rivals in the development of the electronic computer.

Birth of the Modern Computer

Babbage's machine did not die with him—his son attempted to raise money to complete it. (All that remains is a number of incomplete sections.) Others were influenced. Percy Ludgate, an Irish accountant, attempted to build his own Analytical Engine in 1903. He died in 1922 leaving only a 1909 sketch describing his design. The Spaniard Leonardo Tores Y Quevedo (1852–1936) wrote in 1914 an interesting paper outlining a program-controlled device in the spirit of Babbage's Analytical Engine. He was also well known for his endgame chess playing automata. As we move into the 1930s, the story starts to become rather complicated. Historians are still uncovering and evaluating claims for machines and devices. Furthermore, secret work done during World War II, especially work on the Colossus project undertaken in England, is gradually being declassified only now. It was a very exciting and interesting time—social conditions were ripe for the building of the first computer.

Before the first digital computer was developed there were a variety of analog computers in operation designed to solve specific problems. The most important of these, called the differential analyzer, was built at the Massachusetts Institute of Technology (MIT) by Vannevar Bush in 1931. Its purpose was to solve differential equations arising from several areas of mathematics. More important, perhaps, was its influence on computational endeavors elsewhere. For example, a version of the differential analyzer was built at the Moore School of Electrical Engineering at the University of Pennsylvania between 1933 and 1935. This effort provided the crucial experience from which the first electronic computer emerged some ten years later. As a side effect, MIT's commitment to analog computers, at the expense of digital ones, probably began at that time.

Electromechanical Computers

It is generally agreed that the first electronic computer was built at the Moore School under the direction of John Mauchly (1907–1980) and John Presper Eckert, Jr. (b. 1919). Called ENIAC (Electronic Numerical Integrator and Computer), it was built between 1943 and 1946. There were others who claimed to be the first. The common factor of such claims was that the device was not electronic but electromechanical; that is, it relied on a mixture of electrical and mechanical components.

Unfortunately, the first of those had very little impact on the development of computers in general. In fact, it was not until after World War II that the important work of Konrad Zuse (b. 1910) became known. He began in Germany to design electromechanical calculating aids in 1934; by 1938 he had produced the Z1, a somewhat unrealiable mechanical computer. With the help of Helmut Schreyer he succeeded in building the Z3, "a floating point binary machine with a 64 word store. This machine, since it was operational in 1941, is believed to have been the world's first general purpose program-controlled computer."[23] Zuse continued his work during the war, but resources were not made available to extend his design. He made another important contribution with the design (in 1945) of a programming language called Plankalkul. This work also was not as influential as it should have been because it was unknown at the time.

In the United States, important work on digital computers was initiated at the Bell Telephone Laboratories in New Jersey under the direction of George Stibitz. It is not surprising that Bell would be interested in computers, nor that they would be based on the relay circuit technology already in place in the telephone system. Stibitz and his associates began their research in 1937 and produced the first model, called the Complex Number Computer, in 1940. This so-called Model I was followed by a number of computers over the years: Model II, the Relay Interpolator, Model III, a relay calculator, the Ballistic Computer, and finally Model V in 1946. This model was a general purpose computer under program control. Even though it was slow, it did permit programs to be changed easily and was quite reliable as well.

Another important early development in computer technology was the work of Howard Aiken (1900–1973). In 1937, while an instructor at Harvard, he convinced IBM to begin the design of a computer. Together with three IBM employees—C. D. Lake, F. E. Hamilton, and B. M. Durfee—Aiken built the Harvard Mark 1, or Automatic Sequence-Controlled Calculator, in 1944. Basically a mechanical computer, it was more than 50 feet long, perhaps the largest ever built. More important than the machine itself, probably, was the fact that it was an entry point for IBM into the world of computers. After this machine, Aiken went on to build a series of machines at Harvard based on mechanical components. When questioned many years later about his reluctance to use electronic components, he replied that he knew that electronics were the way to go but that they were unreliable at first and he preferred the dependability of mechanical systems. At IBM the development of machines continued with the Pluggable Sequence Relay Calculator, installed in 1949, and the SSEC (Selective Sequence Electronic Calculator), completed in 1948 under the direction of Wallace Eckert. The series of computers that followed launched IBM into world leadership.

ENIAC: The First Electronic Computer

The work of Aiken and Stibitz was well known to the designers of the ENIAC, as was that of John V. Atanasoff, who had built a special purpose computer to solve systems of simultaneous linear equations. In fact, Mauchly visited Atanasoff at Iowa State University in 1941 to see his computer and invited him to come to the Moore School. There has been much controversy about how much ENIAC owed to Atanasoff. Mauchly in later years called Atanasoff's computer a "little gizmo." A court ruling in 1973, resulting from litigation between Honeywell and Sperry Rand over the ENIAC patent, was not clear-cut. The ruling, issued in October of 1973, stated, "Eckert and Mauchly did not themselves first invent the automatic electronic digital computer but instead derived the subject matter from one Dr. John Vincent Atanasoff."[24] Nevertheless, the judge acknowledged Eckert and Mauchly as the inventors of ENIAC, and Atanasoff's work did not change the ENIAC patent claims.

Two of the participants have written books about the development of this first electronic computer.[25] Herman Lukoff, an engineer, and Herman Goldstine, a mathematician together with Arthur Burks and John von Neumann, were involved in the development of the ENIAC and successor machines. The Moore School had gotten involved with computers—albeit analog ones—in 1933, with the construction of a differential analyzer. John Mauchly, a physicist interested in the possibilities of electronic means of computation, joined the Moore School in the fall of 1941. Eckert, an electrical engineer employed as an instructor at the Moore School, was supportive of Mauchly's interests. In August 1942 Mauchly wrote a memo, "The Use of High Speed Vacuum Tube Devices for Calculating," which has been called one of the most important documents in the history of computers.[26] The Moore School had by this time become involved with the Ballistics Research Laboratory of the U.S. Army Ordnance Department. Captain Herman Goldstine, acting as liaison officer, helped convince the U.S. government to sign a contract with the Moore School in 1943 to develop an electronic calculating machine for computing ballistic tables. The machine was completed in the fall of 1945. It was a monster. Incorporating over 18,000 vacuum tubes, 70,000 resistors, and 10,000 capacitors, 100 feet long, 10 feet high, and 3 feet deep, it consumed 140 kilowatts in operation.

The Stored Program Concept

The next major step was to control the computer's actions by means of a program stored in its memory. If this could be done, programs could be manipulated just like data. Even more important, the computer could become involved in the preparation of programs themselves through the development of assemblers, compilers, and operating systems. (The latter are themselves programs that reside in the computer and permit the running of user-written programs.) As in many other areas of computer invention, the question of who was responsible for the stored program concept is somewhat unclear. Currently, there is general agreement that John von Neumann is the person to whom most of the credit belongs. Some facts are clear: The idea did emerge in the ENIAC group and it was expressed in print in a draft report dated June 30, 1945, written by von Neumann on the proposed EDVAC. Von Neumann (1903–1957) was one of the supreme genuises of the twentieth century. He made major contributions to such diverse areas as the foundations of mathematics, quantum mechanics, game theory, hydrodynamics, and the foundations of computer organization and software. Contemporary computers have been described as von Neumann machines. However, there is some question about the origin of the ideas in the 1945 report.

Apparently, the stored program concept emerged in group discussions during the ENIAC project. Von Neumann first became involved with work at the Moore School when taken there by Goldstine in August of 1944. It is his opinion that von Neumann did make the major contribution. It is unfortunate, though, that the draft report did not acknowledge the work of others, and thus became known as the von Neumann report. Goldstine claims that von Neumann did not expect it to be widely circulated before he produced a revised version. Others have not been so agreeable.

Mauchly himself tried to set the history straight. In late 1979 he stated that as early as April of 1944 he and Eckert had planned to include both programs and data in the same memory. Furthermore, they discussed these plans with von Neumann in September of that year when he first came to the Moore School.

> We started with our basic ideas: there would be only *one* storage device (with addressable locations) for the *entire* EDVAC, and this would hold both data and instructions. All necessary arithmetic operations would be performed in just *one* arithmetic unit. All control functions would be centralized.[27]

Von Neumann quickly understood the nature of these ideas and reformulated them in his own terms, using such biological terms as organs and neurons. Mauchly insists that von Neumann was merely rephrasing ideas developed by himself and Eckert. In any case, the von Neumann report does contain the first known program for a stored program digital computer; it happens to be a sorting program.

The Moore School went on to complete the EDVAC and delivered it to the Ballistics Research Laboratory near the end of 1951. Mauchly and Eckert left to form their own company, the Electronic Control Company, in late 1946. (The name was changed to Eckert-Mauchly Computer Corporation in 1947.) Problems with patent disputes and the constraints of the university environment had led to this separation. They conceived UNIVAC (a Universal Automatic Computer) but its development required continued research supported by contracts. For the Northrup Aircraft Company they completed in 1949 a computer called BINAC—the first operational stored-program electronic computer that used mag [sic] tapes rather than punch cards. In 1950 Eckert and Mauchly sold their company to Remington Rand because of monetary problems. The following year the UNIVAC I was completed and used for the computation of the 1950 U.S. census. In 1955 Remington Rand merged with the Sperry Corporation and continued to manufacture the UNIVAC series. (The UNIVAC name was discontinued in 1983.)

Developments in England

In 1946, Von Neumann and Goldstine went to the Institute of Advanced Studies at Princeton University and began to work on a new computer, the IAS. The early 1950s saw the beginnings of the computer explosion, as computers developed at a number of research institutions in the United States and elsewhere.

The MARK 1, developed at Manchester under F. C. Williams and T. Kilburn, was probably the first stored program computer to be operational. It was a rather primitive machine and is important mainly for the concept it embodied and for the fact that its development was fairly independent of the Moore School effort.

Another significant project in England was the computer built at Cambridge University under the direction of Maurice Wilkes, called EDSAC (Electronic Delay Storage Automatic Calculator). This machine was based on the EDVAC principles—Wilkes had attended an important series of lectures at the Moore School in 1946. The EDSAC has been called the first practical stored program computer to be completed. It executed its first program in May 1949.[28] Finally, the classified work done at Bletchley Park during World War II has recently been disclosed. A computer called COLOSSUS was developed there under the leadership of Professor Newman and Mr. Flowers, with a major contribution by Alan Turing (1912–1954). Turing was later involved with the ACE computers built at the National Physical Laboratories at Teddington.

No history of computing would be complete without mention of Alan Turing. His name has primarily been associated with a theoretical construct called the Turing machine, which he created to explore general issues of computation. More recently his contributions to the design of actual computers, especially his work on a highly secret coding machine called Enigma, have been made public. From a theoretical and a practical perspective Turing is certainly one of the fathers of the modern computer.

The Rise of IBM

The age of the computer had arrived and growth was explosive. IBM quickly established its dominance and its name became synonymous with the computer. How this happened has been debated, but no one disputes the fact that IBM is the major company in the field, both in the United States and worldwide. Of all the factors contributing to its success, the most important was probably its organizational structure, which was highlighted by a large, well-motivated, and dedicated sales staff. The company stressed a well-trained and responsive sales and service division. Its availability and concern did much to carry its customers through the early uncertainties of the commercial computer age. In the 1960s the industry was described as IBM and the Seven Dwarfs. The dwarfs in 1967 were Sperry

Rand (later Sperry Corporation), Control Data Corporation, Honeywell, RCA (Radio Corporation of America), NCR (National Cash Register), General Electric, and Burroughs. In 1971, General Electric sold its computer hardware operation to Honeywell but maintained its computer services division and has recently shown strength in specialized computer equipment. RCA sold its computer operations to Sperry in 1971. Consolidation continued into the 1980s and 1990s, as in 1986 Sperry merged its computer operations with Burroughs' to form UNISYS, Honeywell sold its computer business to Groupe Bull (France), with a share to Japan's NEC, and on May 6, 1991 AT&T acquired NCR for $7.4 billion.

As the 1980s ended, the number two company in the world was Digital Equipment Corporation, far behind IBM as can be seen in Figure 3-1, which shows the growth curves of some of the leading computer companies over the past few years. It should be noted that among the ten leading companies in data processing revenue four are American—IBM (1), Digital (2), UNISYS (5), and Hewlett-Packard (7)—three are Japanese—NEC (3), Fujitsu (4), and Hitachi (6)—and there are one each, French—Groupe Bull (8), German—Siemens (9), and Italian—Olivetti (10). A number of U.S. companies, among the most prominent names in the computer industry, seem to be in serious decline. For example Control Data, once second only to IBM , has now dropped to number 35 worldwide with revenues of $1.69 billion. Other companies which have lost significant market share are NCR, Wang, Data General, and Texas Instruments (all United States). Among companies whose revenues in data processing have grown substantially during the 1980s are Apple (United States), Toshiba, Canon, Matushita, (Japan), Compaq (United States), and Philips (Holland).

Computers are usually categorized by size and power. Supercomputers are at the top, then mainframes, followed by minicomputers, workstations, and personal computers at the bottom. There are no precise dividing lines, and as the power of workstations continues to increase they exert an upward pressure on the minicomputer market, as minicomputers once did to mainframes. Sun, the leading company in the workstation market, has challenged both Digital and IBM by producing computers that are smaller, faster, and cheaper. Indeed in the fourth quarter of its fiscal year ending in June 1990, Digital announced its first loss in 33 years. IBM remains the dominating force in the computer industry and, in spite of various setbacks, is likely to hold its position into the foreseeable future. For example, IBM was number one in 1989 in most of the sub-markets of the computer industry. Table 3-1 illustrates IBM's domination over its leading challengers. In the workstation market ($6.8 billion), IBM is currently in fifth place with 8.7% while the leader Sun has 21.3%, although in early 1990 IBM announced a new series of RISC (Reduced Instruction Set Computers) computers that will probably improve its position. Finally, in the information services area ($22.5 billion), IBM is in seventh place with 5.3% compared to the leader EDS at 11.0%.

Questions have been raised about the effect of such a powerful force on other companies in the industry and, more importantly, on the development of the field itself. Indeed, many of IBM's practices have become *de facto* standards. We will discuss some of these issues in Chapter 11.

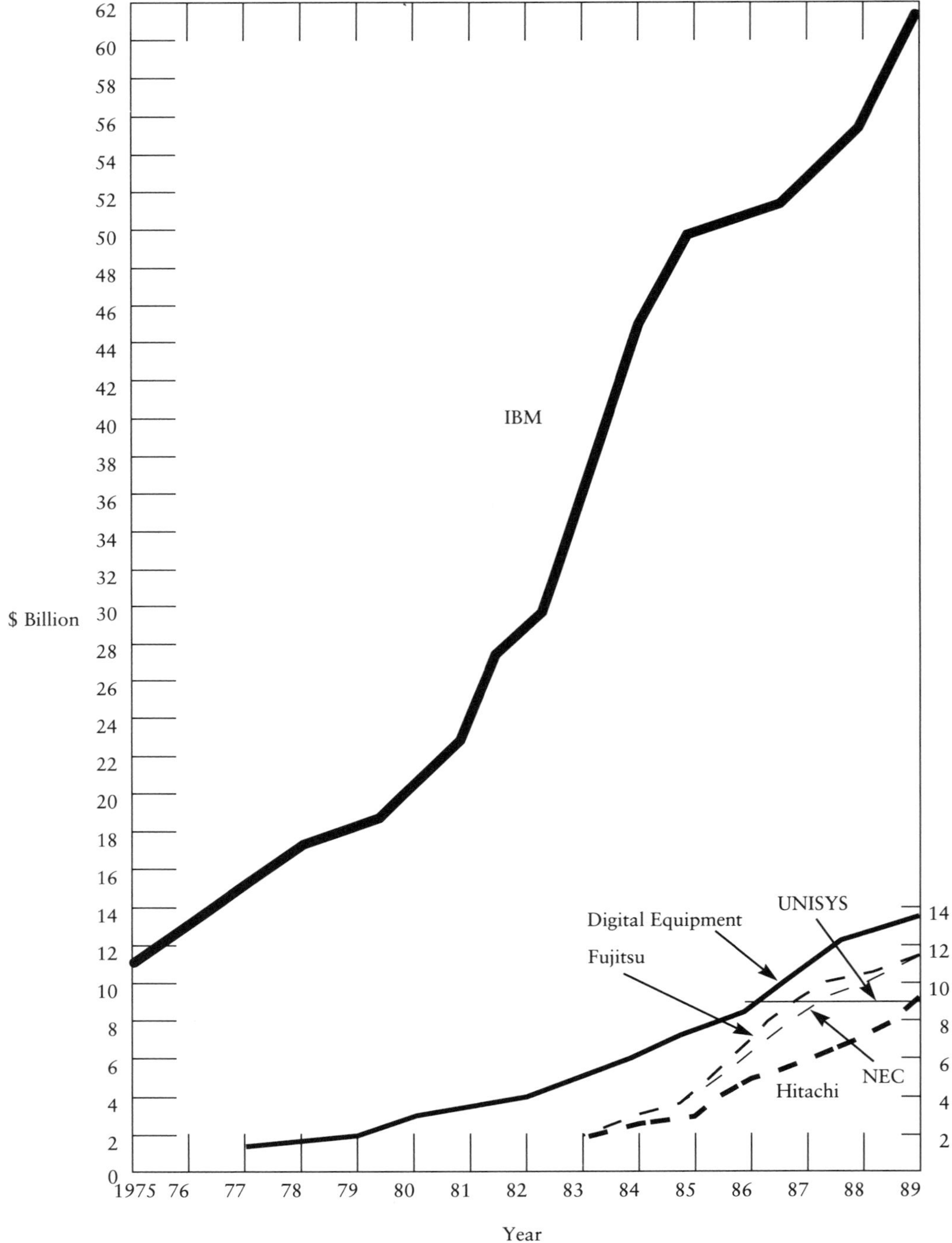

FIGURE 3-1 Data Processing Revenue of IBM and its Competitors. Adapted from *Datamation* (Cahners Publishing Co.), June issues, 1976–1990.

TABLE 3-1

IBM AND ITS LEADING COMPETITORS IN SELECTED MARKETS. DATA TAKEN FROM *DATAMATION* (CAHNERS PUBLISHING CO.) JUNE 15, 1990, PP. 183–201.

	IBM's share	Leading challenger	Total world market ($billion)
Mainframe	44.4%	Fujitsu (11.6%)	28.2
Software	34.3%	Fujitsu (5.9%)	24.6
Midrange	29.4%	Digital (11.6%)	23
Maintenance	24.0%	Digital (11.3%)	29.3
PCs	22.3%	Apple (9.6%)	37.4
Peripherals	18.0%	Digital (5.7%)	56
Communications	15.7%	AT&T (7.6%)	19.1

THE EMERGENCE OF THE CHIP

If the aircraft industry had evolved as spectacularly as the computer industry over the past 25 years, a Boeing 767 would cost $500 today, and it would circle the globe in 20 minutes on five gallons of fuel.[29]

If the automobile business had developed like the computer business, a Rolls-Royce would now cost $2.75 and run 3 million miles on a gallon of gas.[30]

The History

The modern computer developed from a mechanical calculator into an immense electronic machine with thousands of vacuum tubes that occupied a large room. The power requirements were enormous and the issue of reliability was of paramount concern. When ENIAC was completed in 1946, it was generally believed that only a very few computers would be necessary to serve the computational needs of the nation. Developments were already underway, however, to change the basic structure of computers. As early as 1945, Bell Laboratories began research to develop electronic devices useful for telecommunications. Leading this research team were William Shockley, John Bardeen, and Walter H. Brattain. They were awarded the Nobel prize for physics for their invention, in 1947, of the point contact transistor. This device was not an instant success, because it operated over a limited range of frequencies, could amplify only to a limited degree, had limited stability, and was expensive to manufacture. It would have been difficult to predict at this point the shape of things to come.

As an electronic component, the vacuum tube generates a great deal of heat in operation, requires considerable power, and occupies a relatively large space. The advantages of the semiconductor are striking: low power requirements, minimal heat generation, and above all microscopic size. The semiconductor, as its name suggests, has conductive properties between those of a conductive material such as a copper and an insulating material such as plastic or rubber. The first transistor was made of germanium, as was the second, called the junction transistor. Both were developed by Bell in 1951. Eventually silicon came into wide use, first for transistors and later for integrated circuits, or chips.

Over the next few years developments were rapid, and prices fell correspondingly. The basic motivation for miniaturization, however, did not derive from the requirements of computer engineers. It was the basic need of the space and missile programs for compact, durable, and light components that motivated the drive for miniaturization. Developments were further accelerated by a combination of advances in scientific knowledge and the growth of scientific entrepreneurship.

Transistors were first used in hearing aids in the early 1950s. It was not until 1955 that the first all-transistor radios appeared. Much more importantly, in that same year IBM introduced a computer in which over 1000 tubes had been replaced by more than 2000 transistors. In addition to the virtues of the transistor already noted, there is one additional important point that had great implications for the future.

> The great advantage of the transistor, an advantage scarcely appreciated at the time, was that it enabled one to do away with the separate materials—carbon, ceramics, tungsten and so on—traditionally used in fabricating components. At the same time the transistor raised the ceiling that sheer complexity of interconnections was beginning to place on system design. . . . The transistor was the first electronic component in which materials with different electrical characteristics were not interconnected but were physically joined in one structure.[31]

The next natural step was to include more than one transistor in the same physical structure. Once this idea was articulated, developments took place very rapidly. The integrated circuit includes—on a single chip of silicon—transistors, diodes, resistors, and capacitors, all connected in a functional circuit.

Once it was introduced, the integrated circuit business grew rapidly worldwide, with nearly $1 billion in sales in 1970 and $3.6 billion in 1976. These figures are dramatic in more ways than one since there has been a corresponding reduction in prices over these years and an increased number of active elements per circuit. For example, the cost per bit (binary digit) of random-access memory has declined an average of 35 percent per year since 1970.[32] Furthermore, from a single bit per circuit in 1959, the growth curve has been from 1K (1024) in 1970, to 4K in the mid-1970s, to 16K in the late 1970s, to 32K shortly after, followed by 64K in the early 1980s to the 256K bit memory in 1983, to the 1 megabit DRAM in the late 1980s, the 4 megabit DRAM in the early 1990s, and the 16 megabit DRAM in the mid-1900s. (The letter K is an abbreviation for 1024 but is typically used as 1000; a megabit is one million bits; DRAM means Dynamic Random Access Memory.) The benefits of integrated circuits are as follows:

They are cheaper.

Labor and materials are saved by not having to make large numbers of connections.

The integrated connections are more secure; hence, less maintenance is required.

Power and space requirements are drastically reduced, resulting also in savings on cooling fans and transformers.

Quality control is improved.

In 1964 Gordon Moore, one of Robert Noyce's colleagues at Fairchild, suggested that the complexity of integrated circuits would continue to double every year. Moore's law is apparently still in effect and augurs well for improvements into the 1990s.

The Microprocessor

So far we have discussed the development of circuits that have either been preprogrammed to carry out well-defined functions or are available for memory purposes. One of the most significant technological innovations of our time took place in 1971 at Intel, a semiconductor company founded two years earlier by Robert Noyce and others in Santa Clara, California.

M. E. Hoff, Jr., a young engineer, invented an integrated circuit that is essentially equivalent to the central processing unit of a computer. Consider the following description:

> Hoff's CPU [Central Processing Unit] on a chip became known as a microprocessor. To the microprocessor, he attached two memory chips, one to move data in and out of the CPU and one to provide the program to drive the CPU. Hoff now had in hand a rudimentary general-purpose computer that not only could run a complex calculator but could also control an elevator or a set of traffic lights, and perform any other tasks, depending on its program.[33]

Intel brought out its first microprocessor chip, the 4004, in 1971. A larger model, the 8008, followed in 1972. Near the end of 1973 came the second generation 8080 chip, more than twenty times faster than the 4004. This last chip formed the basis for the personal computer bonanza that followed. Other companies—such as Rockwell International, National Semiconductor, Texas Instruments, and Motorola—soon entered the microprocessor derby.

In early 1989, Intel introduced its new mocroprocessor, the i486, successor to the 386 (technically the 80386) and two to four times faster. At that time, Intel sold a less advanced version of the 386, the 386SX, to computer manufacturers for $89 while the new i486 sold for $950. 386SX-based computers could be bought for $1500, a remarkable price given their power, and yet another indication of the rapid pace of development. One more startling indication is that while the 386 contained 375,000 transistors, the i486 had over one million. Less than one year later, TRW and Motorola (which makes the 6800 series of chips for the Apple Macintosh and Sun computers, among others) announced a "superchip" with about four million transistors:[34]

> Two hundred million operations per second mean the (chip) is the computational equivalent of some supercomputers that fill an entire room, require elaborate refrigeration sys-

> tems and weigh several tons. . . . Commercial successors of the superchip could find use in a wide variety of applications where high speed, small size and great computing power and reliability are needed. Among these are computer-aided design, medical diagnosis, plant process control and complex imaging.

In fact such powerful computers are required to help design, build, and verify the increasingly complex chips under development. Such incredible increases in power and decreases in size seem to occur with such regularity in the computer industry that we tend to forget how remarkable these achievements are and how great an impact they continue to have on our lives.

The Semiconductor Business

The semiconductor business is perhaps the crowning jewel of the American industrial system. Its important early growth period was fostered by the U.S. Department of Defense, which subsidized developmental costs. As it coincided with the emergence of scientific entrepreneurship, the U.S. lead was ensured. The semiconductor industry has an economic impact far beyond its own domain, because of the multiplier effect. That is, a piece of equipment depending on semiconductors is likely to cost many times more than the integrated circuit itself.

Ian Mackintosh, of the British Consultants Mackintosh International, wrote an important paper in 1978 in which he predicted that U.S. domination of the semiconductor market would be increasingly challenged by Japan.[35] This prediction has come true, in that Japan has achieved dominance in the production of DRAMs. As of early 1989, Japan controlled 77% of the world market, with the U.S. having a 15% share, Korea 5%, and West Germany about 3%.[36] Remember these are memory chips, not sophisticated microprocessors, of which the U.S. is still the world leader in the design and production. Nevertheless, Japan is expected to control about 90% of the 4 megabit chip market.[37] Furthermore, Mackintosh analyzed the origins of the industry in the U.S. with a view to determining future directions. The following strategic factors have been crucial, in his estimation.

The Role of Governments. The federal government, especially the Department of Defense and the space program, have underwritten a good portion of the development costs—an estimate of almost $1 billion between 1958 and 1974 alone.

The Benefits of Industrial Synergism. The U.S. integrated circuit industry grew very rapidly because of a receptive computer market eager to make use of the new technology.

The Impact of Technological Innovation. The American entrepreneurial system puts a premium on development and marketing.

Market Factors. The U.S. market is large enough to support the growth of a new and dynamic industry.

Industrial Structure. Except for certain very large companies (such as IBM), most semiconductor companies depend almost entirely on this single product.

Management and People. The management of most successful companies is flexible and responsive to new technological developments.

Availability of Venture Capital in Substantial Amounts.

Large, Capable Research Laboratories.

Skill Clusters. For example, Silicon Valley.

That almost mythical community, Silicon Valley (named for the basic material of semiconductors) is a region running from Palo Alto south to San Jose along San Francisco Bay. It is the home of a number of chip manufacturers, personal computer companies, and peripheral-device companies. It has achieved worldwide fame as a source of innovation and expertise in the incredible explosion of microelectronics technology. Its achievements have been so overwhelming that other regions of the United States and the world have sought to plant seeds for their own Silicon Valleys.

The tradition of scientific entrepreneurship in the Valley is not new. As far back as 1939, David Packard and William Hewlett formed an electronics company, Hewlett-Packard, which in 1990 had total revenues of over $13 billion. The initial impetus of the phenomenal postwar growth of Silicon Valley came from William Shockley, one of the inventors of the transistor. He left Bell Laboratories and moved to Mountain View, California to set up Shockley Semiconductor Laboratory in 1955 and it attracted a number of young, ambitious engineers and physicists. One of these was Robert Noyce, who (with seven others) left Shockley two years later to form Fairchild Camera and Instrument. The Silicon Valley syndrome of old companies spawning new ones was well under way.

After a few years the next generation of offspring were born: National Semiconductor in 1967, Intel—founded by Noyce—in 1968, and Advanced Micro Devices in 1969. These are among the "Fairchildren" of Fairchild alumni. Not only the semiconductor has flourished in Silicon Valley; a whole range of computer-related companies have found the atmosphere congenial. Such large mainframe corporations as Tandem Computers and Amdahl were founded there.

In the personal computer market, Apple has been an outstanding success story, with sales increasing from $165 million in 1980 to $5.74 billion in 1990. Other micro manufacturers such as Atari and Commodore have their home in Silicon Valley, as well as the leader in workstations, Sun, whose sales increased from $115 million in 1985 to $2.76 billion in 1990. Many disk drive manufacturers such as Seagate, Conner, Quantum, and Tandon are also neighbors. Although Silicon Valley has become a metaphor for "high tech" success, there are other important areas in the United States with similar achievements. On the east coast, Route 128 near Boston is the home of Digital Equipment, Wang, Prime, and Data General, all computer companies, as well as Lotus, a leading software house. The St. Paul–Minneapolis area is the home of Control Data, Cray, and 3M. In Texas one finds Compaq, another success story in the personal computer market and a major competitor of IBM. Compaq's revenues have increased from $239 million in 1984 to almost $3.6 billion in 1990. In the Dallas–Fort Worth area are EDS (the U.S. leader in computer services), Tandy, and Texas Instruments.

The success of all these regions depends on a number of factors, including a critical mass of nearby scientific expertise: Stanford University and the University of California at Berkeley for Silicon Valley, Harvard and MIT for Route 128, and the University of Minnesota for the St. Paul–Minneapolis area. In addition, other important factors are an existing base of technological skills, managerial skills, and venture capital resources, all of which have made Silicon Valley, especially, a much envied world center of microelectronics. There is, however, the downside to paradise, such as pollution, job alienation, a roller-coaster economy, unaffordable housing, and minimal job security and job loyalty.

The Personal Computer

Almost exactly 30 years after the first electronic computer made its appearance, the first personal computer was marketed. Since then, sales have been phenomenal. In the United States, sales for 1981 (excluding software and peripherals) reached $1.4 billion; they were up to $2.6 billion in 1983, and approximately $6 billion in 1985. Worldwide sales were $6.1 billion in 1982 and soared to $37.4 billion in 1989. All this has been made possible by the microprocessor, but the idea of making a computer at a price low enough to sell to an individual, coupled with the belief that the computer would have sufficient appeal for that individual, is a product of American scientific and business genius.

As mentioned previously the major success story of the personal computer, discounting IBM's achievements and Compaq's success in riding on IBM's coattails, is Apple, founded in Silicon Valley by Steven Wosniak and Steven Jobs, then in their early twenties. In the by now familiar Valley legend, Wosniak built the first machine in his parent's garage. (Interestingly, Jobs left Apple (or was pushed) in 1985 and in 1987 announced a new computer from his company, NeXT, Inc.) The first Apple machine was marketed in 1976 and by 1983 its sales had exceeded $1 billion, reaching well over $5 billion by 1989 and propelling it to eleventh place in the worldwide computer market. Other players in the personal computer game are the Tandy Corporation (maker of Radio Shack and Tandy computers), Atari, Commodore (the PET, the Commodore 20 and 64, and the Amiga series), Unisys, and Zenith; from Japan, NEC, Toshiba, and Fujitsu; and from Europe, Groupe Bull and Olivetti. It is significant that Digital Equipment has very little presence in the PC market. As previously noted, IBM waited until 1981 to enter the market but did so with a splash.

We are living in a time when computers are numbered in the millions. They are no longer the private preserve of the government, large businesses, and research institutions. Extraordinary power is becoming available to a wide segment of society. How that power will be distributed and used, and to what ends, is a question yet to be answered.

SUMMARY

There is a rather simple dichotomy between the view that technology is neutral, just a tool, and the view that it can create serious problems independent of the intentions of the developers. Critics of the unrestricted use of technology include Lewis Mumford, who is very concerned about the dehumanizing aspects of automation; Siegfried Giedion, who argues that technology in the pursuit of efficiency may be achieved at the loss of quality and traditional human skills; and Jacques Ellul, who presents an enormously pessimistic view of technology (or *technique*) as an all-powerful force independent of human control.

Charles Babbage, an irascible genius of nineteenth-century England, essentially invented the modern computer. He was unable to build it because of limitations in the technology of the time and his continual changes of the conception.

The modern electronic computer is generally acknowledged to have been invented at the Moore School of Electrical Engineering, at the University of Pennsylvania, by John Mauchly and John Presper Eckert in 1945. Called ENIAC, it was funded by the Department of Defense and motivated by the computational needs of wartime research and development. Other contributions were made in the United States, England, and Germany, and their history is only now becoming clear. IBM (a name synonymous with the computer) has had phenomenal growth and impact on the industry.

The major triumph of technology in the third quarter of the twentieth century may well be the integrated circuit, usually called the chip. Another phenomenon of our times is the personal computer, which provides enormous computing power at relatively low cost and small size. The impact of this machine on society is impossible to predict, but the opportunities it opens will probably have a significant impact on society.

NOTES

1. John McDermott, "Technology: The Opiate of the Intellectuals," *New York Review of Books*, July 31, 1969, p. 25.
2. *Ibid.*
3. Excerpt from *The Myth of the Machine: The Pentagon of Power*, copyright © 1970 by Lewis Mumford, reprinted by permission of Harcourt Brace Jovanovich, Inc. (p. 273).
4. Siegfried Giedion, *Mechanization Takes Command* (New York: Oxford University Press, 1948).
5. *Ibid.*, p. 5.
6. *Ibid.*, p. 172.
7. *Ibid.*
8. For a detailed description, see Samuel A. Matz, "Modern Baking Technology," *Scientific American*, November 1984, pp. 122–6, 131–4.
9. Giedion, *Mechanization Takes Command*, p. 198.
10. Jacques Ellul, *The Technological Society* (1964; reprint ed., New York: Vintage, division of Random House, 1967).
11. *Ibid.*, p. xxv.
12. *Ibid.*, p. 78.
13. Herbert Marcuse, *One-Dimensional Man* (Boston: Beacon, 1966), p. 9.
14. Norbert Wiener, *Cybernetics: Control and Communication in the Animal and Machine, Second Edition.* (New York: MIT Press and Wiley, 1961).
15. Norbert Wiener, *God and Golem* (Cambridge, Massachusetts: MIT Press, 1966), p. 73.
16. John Stuart Mill, *On Liberty* (Boston: Ticknor and Fields, 1863), p. 114.

17. Oscar Wilde, *The Soul of Man under Socialism and Other Essays* (New York: Harper Collins, 1970), p. 245.
18. Herbert A. Simon, "Prometheus or Pandora: The Influence of Automation on Society," *Computer*, November 1981, p. 91. Copyright © 1981 IEEE.
19. Brian Randell, ed., *The Origins of Digital Computers, Selected Papers* (New York: Springer-Verlag, 1973), p. 1.
20. Gottfried Liebniz, as quoted in Herman H. Goldstine, *The Computer from Pascal to von Neumann* (Princeton: Princeton University Press, 1972), p. 8.
21. Augusta Ada, Countess of Lovelace, notes to L. F. Menabrea, "Sketch of the Analytical Engine invented by Charles Babbage, Esq.," in B. V. Bowden, ed., *Faster Than Thought* (London: Pitman, 1971), p. 368.
22. Ibid., p. 398.
23. Randell, *Ibid.*, p. 156.
24. As quoted in Nancy Stern, *From Eniac to Univac* (Bedford, Massachusetts: Digital, 1981), p. 4.
25. Goldstine, *The Computer from Pascal to von Neumann*. Herman Lukoff, *From Dits to Bits: A Personal History of the Electronic Computer* (Portland, Oregon: Robotics, 1979).
26. Randell, *Origins of Digital Computers*, p. 289.
27. John Mauchly, contribution to "Readers' Forum," *Datamation*, October 1979, p. 217.
28. Randell, *Origins of Digital Computers*, p. 353.
29. Hoo-min D. Toong and Amar Gupta, "Personal Computers," *Scientific American*, December 1982, p. 87.
30. "The Computer Moves In," *Time*, January 3, 1983, p. 10. Copyright 1983 Time Warner Inc. Reprinted by permission.
31. F. G. Heath, "Large Scale Integration in Electronics," *Scientific American*, February 1970, p. 22.
32. Robert N. Noyce, "Microelectronics," *Scientific American*, September 1977, p. 67. This influential paper presents important reasons for the success of the integrated circuit.
33. Gene Bylinsky, "Here Comes the Second Computer Revolution," *Fortune*, November 1975. Copyright © 1975 Time Inc. All rights reserved. Reprinted in Tom Forester (ed.), *The Microelectronics Revolution* (Cambridge, Massachusetts: MIT Press, 1981), p. 6.
34. "Computer Superchip 'Impressive'," *The Vancouver Sun*, January 4, 1990, p. B 4.
35. Ian M. Mackintosh, "Micros: The Coming World War," *Microelectronics Journal*, **9**, (2) (1978). Reprinted in Tom Forester (ed.) *The Microelectronics Revolution* (Cambridge, Massachusetts: MIT Press, 1981), pp. 83–102.
36. Mel Mandell, "U.S. Chips Are Down," *High Technology Business*, March 1989, p. 12.
37. David E. Sanger, "Contrasts on Chips," *The New York Times*, January 18, 1990, p. C 1.

ADDITIONAL READINGS

Comments on Technological Change

Bell, Daniel. *The Coming of the Post-Industrial Society*. New York: Basic Books, 1983.
Frankel, Boris. *The Post-Industrial Utopians*. Cambridge, United Kingdom: Polity Press, 1987.
Kuhns, William. *The Post-Industrial Prophets*. New York: Harper & Row, 1971.
Masuda, Yoneji. *The Information Society as Post Industrial Society*. Bethesda, Maryland: World Future Society, 1981.
Nora, Simon and Minc, Alain. *The Computerization of Society*. Cambridge, Massachusetts: MIT Press, 1981.
Reinecke, Ian. *Electronic Illusions: A Skeptic's View of Our High-Tech Future*. New York: Penguin, 1984.
Shallis, Michael. *The Silicon Idol: The Micro Revolution and Its Social Implications*. New York: Oxford University Press, 1984.

Winner, Langdon. *Autonomous Technology: Technics-out-of-Control as a Theme in Political Thought*. Cambridge, Massachusetts: MIT Press, 1977.

Winner, Langdon. *The Whale and the Reactor: A Search for Limits in an Age of High Technology*. Chicago: University of Chicago Press, 1986.

A Brief History of Computers

Augarten, Stan. *Bit by Bit: An Illustrated History of Computers*. New York: Ticknor & Fields, 1984.

Blohm, Hans, Beer, Stafford, and Suzuki, David. *Pebbles to Computers: The Thread*. Toronto, Canada: Oxford University Press, 1986.

Burks, Alice R. and Burks, Arthur W. *The First Electronic Computer: The Atanasoff Story*. Ann Arbor: The University of Michigan Press, 1988.

Flamm, Kenneth. *Creating the Computer: Government, Industry, and High Technology*. Washington, D.C.: The Brookings Institution, 1988.

Lavington, Simon. *Early British Computers*. Bedford, Massachusetts: Digital Press, 1980.

Lundstrom, David. E. *A Few Good Men from Univac*. Cambridge, Massachusetts: MIT Press, 1987.

Metropolis, N., Howlett J., and Rota, Gian-Carlo. *The History of Computing in the Twentieth Century*. New York: Academic Press, 1976.

Mollenhoff, Clark R. *Atanasoff: Forgotten Father of the Computer*. Ames, Iowa: Iowa State University Press, 1988.

Williams, Michael R. *A History of Computing*. Englewood Cliffs, New Jersey: Prentice-Hall, 1985.

The Emergence of the Chip

Braun, Ernest and MacDonald, Stuart. *Revolution in Miniature: The History and Impact of Semiconductor Electronics*. Cambridge, United Kingdom: Cambridge University Press, 1978.

Hanson, Dirk. *The New Alchemists: Silicon Valley Fever and the Micro-Electronics Revolution*. New York: Avon, 1983.

Hayes, Dennis. *Behind the Silicon Curtain: The Seductions of Work in a Lonely Era*. Boston: South End Press, 1989.

Rogers, Everett M. and Larsen, Judith K. *Silicon Valley Fever: Growth of High-Technology Culture*. New York: Basic Books, 1984.

Siegel, Lenny and Markoff, John. *The High Cost of High Tech: The Dark Side of the Chip*. New York: Harper & Row, 1985.

4

THE BUSINESS WORLD

American business has a voracious appetite for more and better information.

Mark Klein, "Information Politics," *Datamation* (Cahners Publishing Co.), August 1, 1985.

INTRODUCTION

A major part of the June 5, 1971 issue of *Business Week* was devoted to a serious overview of computers in business.[1] The underlying sentiment was that computers are wonderful tools but they must satisfy traditional business principles, they must be used wisely, and they tend to generate their own special problems. Technology is changing rapidly, prices are falling, machines are getting faster and smaller, and software to deal with many of the pressing problems of business will soon be available. Minicomputers (minis) were the big news, much cheaper than mainframes but with more computing power for the dollar. And computers were being used everywhere.

Process Control and Manufacturing. Steel plants, automobile factories, the aerospace industry.

Education. Business schools, high schools and elementary schools.

Financial Institutions. Banks, credit card systems, the stock market.

Government. Social security administration, research, defense department (3200 computers, and the electronic battle field), economic modeling.

A list for today would be similar but much longer, as would be the list of concerns and claims. Our purpose in this chapter is to trace the evolution of data processing systems—their problems, their uses, and their future. The term data processing has evolved into the more ambitious concept, information processing, and industry managers need management information systems. These systems will provide instant information, decision-making models, forecasts, statistics, graphs, and tables. With a terminal on the desk, the manager can directly access all these forms of business information, or so the story goes.

Among the potential future benefits of computers, none has been as acclaimed as the automated office. There has been a call for the office to be transformed by computers and communication networks in order to decrease paperwork and increase productivity. The personal computer, which has slipped into every nook and cranny of the company, will play an important role. Up-and-coming aids to interaction with computers are an emerging application of artificial intelligence—natural language communication—and graphics. The impact of computerization on the organizational structure of companies is an issue, as are the fears of some office workers about the potential industrialization of the office.

DATA PROCESSING SYSTEMS

The computer is almost synonymous with business. After use in military applications, the first computer sales were to business. Since then (more than thirty years ago) business, in all its multifarious interests, has become the major user of computers. Some of the uses are obvious: payroll, accounts receivable, sales records, inventory control—management of all the basic records and computations needed to operate a business. As computer technology evolved and was in fact actively spurred on by the rising expectations of the business community, the range of uses expanded rapidly to meet both perceived and anticipated needs.

The Evolution of Data Processing

Cyrus Gibson and Richard Nolan described the goals of managers in introducing computer facilities and the resulting organizational problems that have arisen.[2] They were interested in methods and techniques for improving these facilities in response to the changing requirements of a company. In 1974, they argued that there are four stages of electronic data processing (EDP) growth and that it follows the classic S-curve from an initial to a mature phase. The first stage, accounting applications, reflects the replacement of manual methods by the computer with the primary goal of cost savings. Succeeding stages are characterized by a flowering of new possibilities that exploit the power and speed of computers. Stage 2 shows a "proliferation of applications in all functional areas" such as cash flow, budgeting, inventory, and sales. Stage 3 is consolidation, as the applications of Stage 2 are accommodated and control is emphasized. In Stage 4 more sophisticated software appears, focussed on the database with a variety of on-line activities, as well as financial and simulation models.

It is instructive to remember that not too many years ago when the population was not much smaller than it is today, bills were received, payments were acknowledged, payrolls were computed and disbursed, and society functioned more or less as it does currently, without computers. The arrival of the computer, however, meant that management had the potential system capacity to engage in an enormous variety of new activities. This power would translate into quicker, more, and possibly better service for the customer, more (not always better) controls, better forecasts, and new ways of evaluating information. A new version has arisen of Parkinson's Law that work expands to fill the time available: Applications expand to fill the computer power available. (A corollary might be that ambition expands even faster.) For example, simulation and financial models represent complex applications made possible only by computers.

Simulation models are used to study complex systems for which exact mathematical analysis is too difficult. Companies trying to gauge market trends or determine crucial factors in the production process may decide to develop computer programs that simulate the situation of interest. Such programs are designed to simulate relevant features of the real world and study their interaction, because the world is too complex and cannot usually be modified to serve desired purposes. Care must be taken that important and relevant variables are recognized and properly interrelated. The underlying model must be carefully constructed and subsequently evaluated to ensure that the results produced are meaningful and significant.

Simulation is a powerful tool for science, government, and industry, but it must be carefully used. In the early 1970s, a considerable controversy arose in the wake of the publication of *The Limits to Growth,* a report that warned of a coming breakdown of the industrial world due to shortages in fuels and raw materials.[3] The report, based on a simulation model, was criticized for ignoring certain information, badly estimating the importance of some of the parameters, and ignoring crucial relations among selected variables. Currently a similar debate rages over the greenhouse effect and the concern that unless we curtail the production of carbon dioxide, a byproduct of industry and automobiles, we will have to confront the effects of higher temperatures around the world. If company policy is to be based on the results of simulations, management must be convinced of their accuracy—a non-trivial requirement. Even so, the use of simulations has become another important weapon in management's operational and planning arsenal.

Financial planning models depend on sophisticated mathematical models that have been designed to predict medium- and long-term events. Such models have become quite useful and important and would not be possible without computers. Their construction requires mathematical, financial, and programming skills. As computer systems have become more powerful these models have taken on a new significance. They can be responsive to changing world conditions and permit managers to make quick decisions. It is interesting to consider a world in which the major financial institutions all depend on sophisticated financial models to carry out their activities. To the best program go the spoils.

One of the major advances of the 1970s was the development of on-line systems. An on-line system permits almost instantaneous access to, and response from, the system. For example, a banking system permits on-line access when the teller can update an account directly from a terminal. Prior to such a development it was necessary to enter a day's activities off-line—that is, into intermediate storage—and then enter them later into the system. With on-line systems management can have rapid access to personnel information, customer information, and sales information. It should be noted that an on-line system typically permits access to several hundred users. This requires a large mainframe computer, considerable auxiliary storage in the form of disks and drums, communications networks, many video display terminals (VDTs), and printers.

Gibson and Nolan pointed out a number of the problems associated with the growth of EDP systems in general. One of the earliest was the location of the data processing division within company organization and the implications of this decision. A data processing center could be a branch of the financial division, a service center accommodating a number of departments, or an autonomous division with its own vice-president. Each of these has its own advantages and disadvantages for the company, for middle management, and for the employees. Not uncommonly, the first computer appeared in the finance department, since there were immediate applications in accounting. Soon other departments such as sales, marketing, production, and research saw in the computer an important and necessary instrument. In some cases the large investment in computing resources was jealously guarded by the financial department, and part-time release to other departments may not have been sufficient. Pressure arose for either a central independent computer facility or center to which all divisions or departments would have equal access, or a computing facility directly responsible to other users. In the former case, the center would be just another company division responsible to the president and in competition for resources in its own right. In the latter, the center would be a service department expected to provide whatever might be required and dependent on its clients for its budget. Clearly, different organizational roles imply differing degrees of responsibility. Computer professionals may be either technicians or part of the executive hierarchy.

Five Generations of Computers

One of the best overviews of the evolution of computer systems has been provided by Frederic G. Withington, a vice-president at Arthur D. Little Incorporated and a long-time student of data processing systems.[4] He outlines five generations of computers, the first being 1953–1958 and the last 1982–? (see Table 4-1.). (The first three generations run from 1953 to 1974, the year the article was written. The last two represent predictions whose accuracy can be better determined at present.) The names of Withington's generations are instructive.

The first three periods represent the initiation and consolidation phase—new hardware, new software, traditional applications, changing organizational structure, and consolidation of the new technology. Withington predicted that the fourth generation, information custodians, would be characterized by very large file stores, general purpose data manipulators, and centralized control with logistic decisions moving to headquarters and tactical decisions moving out. The forecast was actually quite accurate, with a couple of exceptions. The software did not evolve as rapidly as expected, although time-sharing systems did predominate. In the area of hardware, Withington did not anticipate the microcomputer explosion.

The last generation, action aids (beginning about 1982), he supposed would make use of new hardware such as magnetic bubble or laser-holographic technology. This last does not seem likely in the foreseeable future. Most computer companies have given up on magnetic bubble memories, and laser-holographic technology has yet to appear. Less centralized computing was anticipated, but the overwhelming integration of computing and communications could hardly have been expected. Furthermore, rapidly expanding devel-

TABLE 4-1

FIVE GENERATIONS OF COMPUTERS.*

Name	Period	New Hardware	New Software	New Functions	Organizational Location	Effect on Organization
Gee whiz	1953–1958	Vacuum tubes, magnetic records	None	Initial experimental batch applications	Controller's department	First appearance of technicians (with salary, responsibility, and behavior problems); automation fears among employees
Paper pushers	1958–1966	Transistors, magnetic cores	Compilers, input/output control systems	Full range of applications, inquiry systems	Proliferation in operating departments	EDP group proliferation; some workers and supervisors alienated or displaced; introduction of new rigidity but also new opportunities
Communicators	1966–1974	Large-scale integrated circuits, interactive terminals	Multifunction operating systems, communications controllers	Network data collection, remote batch processing	Consolidation into centrally controlled regional or corporate centers with remote terminals	Centralization of EDP organization; division data visible to central management; some division managers alienated; times shortened response
Information custodians	1974–c. 1982	Very large file stores, satellite computers	General-purpose data manipulators, virtual machines	Integration of files, operational dispatching, full transaction processing	Versatile satellites instead of terminals, with control still centralized	Redistribution of management functions, with logistic decisions moving to headquarters and tactical decisions moving out; resulting reorganization; field personnel pleased
Action aids	c. 1982–?	Magnetic bubble and/or laser-holographic technology, distributed systems	Interactive languages, convenient simulators	Private information and simulation systems, intercompany linkages	Systems capabilities projected to all parts of organization; networks of different organizations interconnected	Semiautomatic operating decisions; plans initiated by many individuals, leading toward flickering authority and management by consensus; greater involvement of people at all levels; central EDP group shrinkage

* *Source:* Reprinted by permission of the *Harvard Business Review.* An exhibit from "Five Generations of Computers" by Frederic G. Withington (July/August 1974).

opments in office automation promise to revolutionize the basic operation of business. Another important achievement will be in management information and decision analysis systems.

Guidelines for Growth

The transition from computer management to data resource management is an important step. Clearly, the situation changes as the range of applications grows, access diversifies via remote terminals, and more and more activities depend on data processing. In a natural way, the computer is thus transformed into a multi-functional data resource that is no longer the preserve of a designated division but is far-reaching and integrated into all the operations of the organization. Information in a variety of forms is now accessible—on modern systems, by all levels of management, whether or not they are near the computer, technically sophisticated, or have financial, managerial, marketing, or sales expertise.

In 1979 Richard Nolan extended the stages of data processing growth from four to six.[5] He considered the growth in knowledge and technology, organizational control, and the shift from computer management to data resource management—a necessary broadening of computer applications. It is obvious that the growth of knowledge exerts an important influence on the direction and nature of further developments. In terms of organizational control, management must determine a balance between tight and so-called slack control. In fact, this balance will vary depending on the stage of growth. For example, to facilitate growth the control should be low and the slack should be high, but as the system matures both should be high. Nolan bases his results on a study during the 1970s of many companies that passed through all the stages except the last one.

And what of the predictions for the 1990s? The previous decade has been witness to enormous technological and organizational changes, as companies struggle to accommodate an endless flow of new hardware and software. Arguments have raged about centralization versus decentralization, fulfilling user needs or management's directives, control, massive investment in technology with little obvious payoff, aging and fragile software investment, and an unpredictable and rapidly changing world economy. Given the basic and continuing importance of management and information, it is worth paying attention to the words of Peter Drucker, one of the world's foremost experts on management theory and practice. In a 1988 paper,[9] Drucker notes that computers are still being used for the most part to facilitate traditional computational efforts, i.e. to "crunch conventional numbers," but that as a company, especially a large one, moves from "data to information, its decision processes, management structure, and even the way its work gets done begin to be transformed." Consider Drucker's definitions: [10]

> Information is data endowed with relevance and purpose. Converting data into information thus requires knowledge. And knowledge, by definition, is specialized. . . . The information-based organization requires for more specialists overall than the command-and-control companies we are accustomed to.

And Drucker argues that competition demands that companies "will have to convert themselves into organizations of knowledge specialists."

If it sounds a bit too theoretical so far, perhaps we should turn to the industry practitioners themselves:[11]

> As the companies reorganize for the '90s they are also exploding some myths. Chief among these is the notion that decentralization, the theme of the 1980s, will be the favored organizational approach to the emerging global marketplace. The pundits couldn't be more wrong, the executives reveal. Centralized control will increase, new centralized functions and entrepreneurial teams will arise.

A sampler of opinions follows:

> Willem Roelandts, vice president and general manager of Hewlett-Packard Co.'s Computer System's Group in Cupertino, California:
> *People will still be decentralizing but with more limited degrees of freedom. HP is simultaneously shifting to an organizational structure of smaller groups often geographically dispersed but with increased centralized control and coordination of activities.*
>
> Glenn Miller, Businessland, Inc. director of strategic planning, San Jose, California:
> *[A]fter a decade of allowing independent business units (IBUs) to call their own IS [Information Systems] shots, many companies are realizing that they are stuck with a variety of inconsistent technologies and no way to forge enterprisewide applications.*
>
> Norman Lewis, director of Ford Motor Co.'s North American Systems Group, Dearborn, Michigan:
> *Multinationals develop products in each market for each market. Global companies start by looking at the marketplace as a whole and finding what is common. They then find ways to address the needs of individual markets with a global product[.] The global approach requires common business procedures, common products and unifying standards, both IT-based and cultural.*[12]
>
> John Shirley, president and chief operating officer of Microsoft Corp.:[13]
> *Companies will have to be centralized to satisfy users. Microsoft customers, like the West Coast aerospace companies, are examples of decentralized firms, where decisions are often made at the departmental level. That will have to change if you hook them up to network servers. . . . By the end of the 1990s, most corporations will have the vast majority of their PCs hooked to corporatewide networks. Electronic mail will be ubiquitous by the end of the decade, available to everybody on a network.*
>
> Tom Cato, vice president of the Information Services Inc. subsidiary of Hospital Corporation of America:[14]
> *We will continue to decentralize our computer operation by further extending the role of computers inside the hospital operation, and each department will be further automated. Distributed processing is the way we're tackling our DP [Data Processing] opportunities.*

There seems to be a considerable difference of opinion about the directions that business organizational structures will move in response to developments in information systems. Interestingly enough, when 50 U.S. information systems executives were asked to rate 18 issues in order of importance they chose the following (in descending order of importance):[15]

- rapport and credibility with senior management,
- knowledge of the business,
- strategic systems opportunities,
- long-range vision and plan, and
- skills mix and motivation of IS personnel.

In recognition of significant difficulties associated with the automation of the office, *Fortune* devoted the cover of its May 16 1986 issue to the provocative claim, "The Puny Payoff from Office Computers."[16]

> Have the millions of computers purchased by U.S. businesses brought any overall improvement in productivity? Surprisingly, the best information available says no. . . . [O]n a national scale, business's investment of hundreds of billions of dollars in computers has failed to bring about a discernible improvement in productivity.

A number of reasons have been proposed to support this claim. These include the argument that computerization involves a long learning curve, that it may require a reorganization of the work process to realize significant gain, and simply that computers have been oversold so that they are misapplied in many applications. From another point of view, only the massive adoption of computers has prevented businesses from hiring many more people to maintain the same productivity levels.

Almost five years later the problem had not gone away, as a survey by the consultants Index Group reports ". . . the problem looming largest in the minds of corporate computer jockeys is convincing their colleagues to change their business practices to take advantage of office automation."[17] The startling statistic is that between the years 1980 and 1989, while the share of office equipment as a percentage of capital equipment rose from 3% to 18%, the productivity of office workers remained essentially unchanged. Over the same period the productivity of blue collar workers has increased substantially. We will have more to say about the difficult subject of productivity measurement later, but one final observation from the Index Group is particularly relevant: ". . . only about one-third of projects alter business practices. Most of the rest merely turn paper shufflers into computer-printout shufflers."[18]

The final words in this section will go to Richard Walton, distinguished and informed scholar of information system design and implementation. In a recent book, Walton makes the obvious but profound claim that the effective implementation of advanced information technology (IT) in organizations "is a function of integrating the technical aspects of IT systems *and* [emphasis added] the social aspects of the organization."[19] To elaborate, we include a few additional comments, recognizing that they barely do justice to this important book, which proposes a detailed framework for the implementation of advanced IT.[20]

He notes that certain principles have been recognized early on in the implementation of IT:

- project champions,
- top management support,
- good relationships between developers and user departments,
- user involvement,
- adequate organizational resources,
- communication, and
- supportive organizational climate.

But more recently, these principles have been extended in the following ways:

- Top management should do more than merely support projects it approves. IT should develop and promulgate a broad version of IT, a vision capable of inspiring and guiding specific IT projects.
- Users are increasingly viewed as legitimately influencing design as well as installation activities.
- Advanced IT has "dual potentialities." For example, IT "can either routinize work or it can widen the discretion of users; it can strengthen hierarchical control or facilitate self-management and learning by users."

MANAGEMENT INFORMATION SYSTEMS: A PROMISE UNREALIZED?

Definitions and Characteristics

What is a management information system (MIS)? There are many conceptions and definitions depending on who is doing the defining and to what purpose. One of the foremost figures in the development of MIS, Gordon B. Davis, has supplied a definition of what MIS should be:[21]

> . . . an integrated man/machine system for providing information to support the operations, management and decision-making functions in an organization. The system utilizes computer hardware and software, manual procedures, management and decision models, and a database.

In 1985, some eleven years after the definition given above, Davis and co-author Margrethe Olson provided the following updated definition of MIS:[22]

> . . . an integrated, user-machine system for providing information to support operations, management, analysis and decision-making functions in an organization. The system utilizes computer hardware and software; manual procedures; models for analysis, planning, control and decision making; and a database.

It is fairly clear that, at least in the view of Davis and Olson, not much had changed in eleven years, a somewhat surprising situation given such enormous technological developments as PCs, networking, workstations, spreadsheets, word processing, laser printers, fiber optics, Fax, cellular phones, and more. In any case, MIS is not easily characterized. An MIS must incorporate expertise from a variety of areas such as organizational theory, economics, accounting, statistics, and mathematical modeling, to say nothing of computer hardware and software. It sounds incredibly ambitious and it is. In the view of many, the open-ended expectation engendered by such descriptions is one of the major reasons why any working system is felt somehow to be short of the mark, no matter what it actually accomplishes.

What are the components of such systems and what functions do they (or are they supposed to) perform? One way of viewing an MIS is as a pyramid structure. At the bottom is the routine transaction processing that occupies a good deal of the computer power of the system (recall that such activities as payroll and accounting were the first application of computers, beginning in the mid-1950s). The next level is concerned with supporting day-to-day activities at the operational level, whereas the third level represents a jump to tactical planning and decision-making. At the top level the MIS concept is fully expressed, with a wide array of resources for strategic planning and management decision-making.

The pyramid—transactions, inquiries, planning, and decision-making—sits on top of the data. Where do the data reside? The problems of representation, structure, organization, and integrity of data have occupied much attention in both the research and business communities. Gradually the notion of a database management system (DBMS) has evolved and this concept is fundamental to MIS. The DBMS must be responsible for manipulating data, on demand, by the variety of application subsystems supported by MIS. DBMS theory is currently a very active research and development area, with relational databases the most commonly used.

The decision-assisting models at the top level of the pyramid have evolved into a major component of MIS usually referred to as decision support systems (DSS). These will be discussed in the next sub-section. In general, models may be used to deal with such areas as inventory, personnel selection, new product pricing, and budgetary control. Four major areas have contributed heavily to the conception and evolution of MIS:[23]

Managerial Accounting. This area deals with such issues as cost analysis, assignment of responsibility, the provision of reports at a variety of levels, and budgetary information.

Operations Research. This discipline is concerned with determining optimal decisions by using mathematical models and procedures in a systematic and specific way. Some of these mathematical techniques are linear programming, queuing theory, game theory, decision theory, and statistics.

Management and Organization Theory. This research area is concerned with reaching satisfactory solutions, constrained by the human limitations on the search for solutions. The behavioral and motivational consequences of organizational structure and systems within organizations are also a concern.

TABLE 4-2

THE MAJOR FUNCTIONAL SUBSYSTEMS OF AN MIS.*

Functional Subsystem	Some Typical Uses
Marketing	Sales forecasting, sales planning, customer and sales analysis
Manufacturing	Production planning and scheduling, cost control, cost analysis
Logistics	Planning and control of purchasing, inventories, distribution
Personnel	Planning personnel requirements, analyzing performance, salary administration
Finance and accounting	Financial analysis, cost analysis, capital requirements planning, income measurement
Information processing	Information system planning, cost effectiveness analysis
Top management	Strategic planning, resource allocation

* *Source:* Gordon B. Davis and Margrethe H. Olson, *Management Information Systems: Conceptual Foundations, Structure and Development, Second Edition,* 1985. Reprinted by permission of McGraw-Hill, Inc., New York.

Computer Science. Advances in hardware, software, algorithms, networks, and distributed processing have an impact on the realization and power of MIS.

The major functional subsystems and activity subsystems of an MIS are shown in Tables 4-2 and 4-3. They are, of course, intimately related. Clearly, an MIS can be a very comprehensive system designed to serve an incredibly wide range of needs.

As might be expected, a number of criticisms have also surfaced. Many of these revolve around the issue of centralization versus decentralization of the information resources, of the computer facilities, and of the analysis and modeling systems. In a sense, certain of these problems have become academic in the age of distributed computing that was brought in by advances in computer technology and communications. But the organizational issues remain—of access, and of smaller specialized databases versus larger uniform ones. Recent proposals have suggested that the time may be fast approaching when most executives sitting at their own desks will be able to call up any data they desire, in any form the wish, from personal computers that are part of a large, complex computer network. However, until that time arrives, a number of issues still need to be considered.

TABLE 4-3

THE MAJOR ACTIVITY SUBSYSTEMS OF AN MIS.**

Activity Subsystem	Some Typical Uses
Transaction processing	Processing of orders, shipments, receipts
Operational control	Scheduling of activities and performance reports
Management control	Formulation of budgets and resource allocation
Strategic planning	Formulation of objectives and strategic plans

** *Source:* Gordon B. Davis and Margarethe H. Olson, *Management Information Systems: Conceptual Foundations, Structure and Development, Second Edition,* 1985. Reprinted by permission of McGraw-Hill, Inc., New York.

Decision Support Systems and Executive Support Systems

A direction MIS has taken recently is toward decision support systems (DSS). One early definition of DSS follows:

> Decision Support Systems . . . represent a point of view on the role of the computer in the management decision making process. Decision support implies the use of the computer to:
> 1. Assist managers in their decision processes in semistructured tasks.
> 2. Support rather than replace, managerial judgment.
> 3. Improve the effectiveness of decision making rather than its efficiency.[6]

More recently Rockart and De Long have written a book with the title *Executive Support Systems*[25], and the designation ESS has become more commonly used. Whatever the name, the idea of executives having hands-on access to information via PCs or terminals is not yet generally acceptable, but gradually more and more upper management executives are demanding to see the data prior to massaging by their support staffs. There are good reasons for this growth, as Rockart and de Long note:[26]

> 1. Use of information technology to support executives makes good managerial sense. Despite the complex, unstructured, and unpredictable nature of their work, there are many logical applications of IT which can effectively support executive tasks.
> 2. The technology, both hardware and software, is rapidly improving. . . . Applications for managers that were technically impractical and too costly only a few years ago have now become significantly easier to implement.
> 3. More and more top managers have become computer literate . . . many middle managers who have come to rely heavily on computers in their jobs are now being promoted to the executive ranks.

Of course there are a number of reasons against the adoption of ESS, including the following: as currently structured, ESS do not fit today's management styles or needs; further they cannot provide the type of information needed most by executives—verbal, anecdotal, non-formal and therefore difficult, if not impossible, to capture in a program; there are perhaps negative properties associated with the new technology—manipulating numbers via spreadsheets and simulations may mislead as to what is actually being accomplished, and communication facilities are useless unless there exists a desire to communicate; more concretely, many attempts to implement working ESS have failed.[27]

Rockart and De Long define ESS as follows:[28]

> The routine use of a computer-based system, most often through direct access to a terminal or personal computer, for any business function. The users are either the CEO [chief executive officer] or a member of the senior management team reporting directly to him or her. Executive support systems can be implemented at the corporate or divisional level.

This definition seems to be surprisingly weak, permitting even mundane systems to qualify as ESS. However, from the description of the design, development, and implementation of an EIS (executive information system) at the North American Aircraft Division of Rockwell International Corp.,[29] it is clear that a working system is a major enterprise and goes far beyond the scope suggested in the above definition. Indeed, beyond the "two fundamental goals . . . [to] make the system simple enough so the executives can *use* their machines, and [to] convert the cost performance reports from paper to electronic displays so that executives *have* to use their machines," the following guidelines were used in developing the system:[30]

> *Derived Information.* Mechanisms must be present to provide information that not only tells what is wrong but why.
>
> *Anticipating Questions.* The EIS must be more than just a page-turner. It must have database access, drill-down functions—the ability to navigate through a hierarchy of increasingly finer levels of detail in the database, and what-if-capabilities—tools for trend analysis and answering ad hoc queries.
>
> *Soft Data.* To make effective decisions, executives need explanations and analysis information.
>
> *Standards and Procedures.* The EIS database should become the single source of information for executives so that they no longer receive conflicting reports.
>
> *Accuracy.* The data must be accurate, timely, comprehensive and useful.
>
> *Responsiveness.* EIS development must be fast enough to deliver an application while it is still useful.
>
> *Benefits.* The bottom line on EIS is truly the fiscal bottom line.

Expert Systems

Probably the greatest commercial impact of artificial intelligence (AI) has been in the area of expert systems (ES). In the past few years, ES have become the most visible and highly publicized product of the entire AI enterprise. Indeed, they can be characterized as an almost independent discipline. They have been applied in a wide and growing number of domains including medicine, education, finance, industry, and the military. In their simplest form, they consist of a body of knowledge, typically quite narrow but necessarily deep, and a reasoning apparatus, or engine, that is able to use this knowledge to perform a range of activities including answering questions, predicting events, offering warnings, or identifying meaningful patterns.

Beyond this rather limited overview, work in ES can be divided into two broad categories: implementation of specific expert systems employing so-called shells, and research in diverse areas associated with basic problems in AI such as knowledge representation, reasoning in general and reasoning with respect to uncertainty, knowledge acquisition among domain-specific experts, programmers, and others operating within the constraints of a commercially available ES shell. The emphasis on knowledge acquisition dominates because of the need to translate informal expertise into the requirements of the shell's knowledge representation formalism. The inference strategy and problems of uncertain information are predetermined within a given shell and therefore must be accepted by the user.

The availability of shells of varying degrees of complexity has resulted in an explosion of ES. Many companies, from the very small to the very large, have built ES to capture some part of their corporate expertise. Systems abound, as described by Feigenbaum, McCorduck and Nii,[31] in such major companies as IBM, Digital Equipment, Toyota, American Express, Sears, Frito-Lay, and Texas Instruments, and are increasing at a rapid rate. Probably the most well-known and the most successful are the systems XCON (eXpert CONfigurator) and XSEL (eXpert SELector), developed at Digital Equipment to configure computer systems automatically and to assist interactively in the selection of saleable parts, respectively.[32] One testimonial comes from David Wise, a senior system analyst at Frito-Lay, Inc.: ". . . although expert systems software is not yet mature and can't do everything you want it to do, it does enough. We've been very satisfied; our payback has been millions of dollars and the ability to make better decisions."[33] The applications are seemingly endless but the following are representative: medical diagnosis, computer configuration, mineral prospecting, oil well analysis, stock market decision-making, financial analysis and planning, insurance analysis, electromechanical fault-finding and repair, and military analysis and decision-making.

Expert systems are also referred to as knowledge-based systems (KBS), with the subtle implication that other business software is somehow devoid of, or seriously impoverished with respect to, basic business knowledge. Of course, all software must incorporate "knowledge" in a variety of forms to perform adequately. The claim for ES must be regarded as a claim for an approach that explicitly separates knowledge from how it is used so that incremental growth can take place in a coherent fashion. In addition, the acquisition of knowledge as an ongoing joint enterprise of specialists and programmers is a unique contribution. Of particular significance to executives is the growth of sophisticated ES in financial planning. Such systems represent yet another important component in the gradually growing tool kit of computing resources for executives.

Managers and Data Processing

A number of questions have arisen about the role and responsibilities of data processing managers within the company. These go beyond the issues of computing and include problems of response to developing needs, worker management, organizational mobility, and of course, planning. Bob King, manager of Mobil Oil's corporate applications services department, was asked, "Bob, you have a well-run operation. Where are your best DP people going? Where do they move within your company?" He replied as follows:

> Generally, nowhere outside the dp function. Unfortunately, with very few exceptions, they're not going anywhere at all.
>
> In spite of possessing latent talents which could be very effectively used in other areas of the company, computer people are not generally seen as movers. DP people are locked in—

due to their own desires, their relatively high pay scales, and their image as technicians with limited business knowledge. DPers certainly aren't ascending to the top management ranks of other functions as was forecast a decade ago.[34]

The achievements of these managers, such as providing instantaneous access to information, both raw and processed, to company executives, have led to better decision-making. Ironically, this development has not benefitted the data processing professional, who seems to be more comfortable with and more committed to machines than people. Other factors beginning to limit the role of the data processing manager are the increasing sophistication of the user, aided by the widespread use of minicomputers and micros, and the growing importance of distributed computing. A more demanding user community is forcing computer managers to be more responsive and accommodating and perhaps less able to rise in the company hierarchy.

All the same, information systems or information technology managers have continued to look upward in the corporation. Indeed, "In the world of business computing, the 1980s has been the decade of the chief information officer [CIO]. Company after company has named a senior executive, reporting to the CEO, to preside over its strategic information agenda and data-processing operations."[35] There have been problems, however, that do cast doubt on the long-term viability of the CIO concept. In a 1988 survey of 400 top IS executives across the country, "59% of respondents thought of themselves as CIOs, yet only 27% reported directly to the top of the company."[36] In early 1990, *Business Week* reported the results of another survey of 300 CIOs showing that only 2% were on the corporate board, only 7.7% reported to the CEO or president, and only 40% were on a senior management committee.[37] A basic problem is that most senior executives view CIOs or information managers as too narrow in their interests and perhaps lacking in credibility. In more detail, the following reasons are given for upper management's less than positive view of information processing managers:[38]

- IS executives think and speak in terms of technology, not business.
- IS hasn't delivered on competitive advantage promises.
- Management focuses on short-term financial goals.
- Management doesn't understand IS costs.
- Strategic planning is inadequate at the corporate level.
- IT is not embedded in the product, so it's not considered strategic.

THE OFFICE OF THE FUTURE

Office automation will change the way all office workers function. With more than 50 million workers currently employed in American offices, this means we will be profoundly affecting our entire society. But we could not take on the task of training this many workers in new work techniques with our present office systems. We'll need systems that are intu-

> itive and tutorial, to minimize and ease the training process. To the extent that we succeed in building friendly systems we will greatly increase the speed and scope of office automation's impact.[39]

Office Automation

What is sometimes called the "electronic office" will be brought about by "office automation" or by the use of "office information systems." It will eliminate paper, promote electronic communication, isolate workers and break down social interaction, reproduce industrial automation in the office, decrease waste of time in preparing documents, and generally improve productivity. Such are the claims made by proponents and the critics.

What is included under the general term "office automation?" The definition to be used, taken from Mowshowitz,[40] is given below:

> Office automation is the use of information technology in an office environment to create, process, store, retrieve, use, and communicate information in the performance of managerial, professional, technical, administrative, and clerical tasks.

Although not part of the definition, the usually understood reason for introducing office automation is to *improve* performance, but there are other reasons, such as to facilitate a new service that would be impossible without the technology, or to reinforce management's control. In any case, this definition does capture a general overview of office automation. More specifically, some of the office functions made possible by computers and associated technology follow, but first let's look at a spectrum of traditional office activities:

Answering the telephone and handling messages.
Typing written and dictated material.
Filing and retrieving material.
Copying letters and reports.
Opening and handling mail.
Scheduling meetings and conferences.
Billing and accounting.
Processing internal memoranda.
Miscellaneous—organizing parties, selecting gifts, buying take-out lunches.

In addition, higher level functions include the following:

Carrying out research.
Monitoring market changes.
Drafting original documents.
Utilizing resource people.
Dealing with middle and upper management.

What are the current and proposed functions of the electronic, or automated, office? They are many and diverse, but a number have been mentioned by most observers. Consider the following categories:

Word Processing. This application involves the use of computer-aided facilities to enter, manipulate, and edit text, typically via a personal computer, either stand-alone or in a network.

Electronic Mail. This is a system for transmitting messages in text, Fax, or voice. There are four different delivery systems:

1. Common carrier-based systems and public postal systems.
2. Fax.
3. Personalized computer-based message systems.
4. Communicating word processing systems.

Database Management/Information Retrieval. The ability to store and retrieve large amounts of information under a variety of conditions has made computers irreplaceable in the office and has created a new industry—the marketing of information.

Spreadsheets. No single application, with the exception of word processing, has had as great an impact in companies. Employees from all levels of the organization are able to model cash flow, expenses, accounts receivable, and other economic factors in order to explore a variety of what-if scenarios. Thousands of variables can be included. The demands of spreadsheet users for ever more powerful personal computers has become a driving force in the PC industry.

Desktop Publishing. The ability to produce sophisticated in-house brochures, newsletters, advertising material, and reports has saved businesses considerable amounts of money, driven the development of low-cost laser printers, challenged traditional composition and printing methods, and facilitated grassroots publishing.

Computer-Aided Design/Computer-Aided Manufacturing (CAD/CAM). Economical tools have been developed to permit engineers and draftsmen to design and manufacture new products using desktop computers. These are programs that facilitate the drawing and manipulation, in 3-D and color on high-resolution monitors, of precise and detailed diagrams.

Experts Systems and Decision Support. As discussed previously, these systems are assuming increasing importance to management and the ability to run them on PCs and workstations will accelerate this process.

Graphics. The development of special programs, high-speed processors, and high-resolution color monitors and laser printers has resulted in the widespread use of graphics in design, documents, and video.

Teleconferencing. The use of telecommunication systems permits communication over long distances via audio, computers, video, or combinations of these.

Activity Management. This category includes systems such as electronic tickler (reminder) files and automated task-project management to track, screen, or expedite schedules, tasks, and information.

Other possibilities include the following:

- electronic blackboards for broadcasting messages;
- electronic calendars for scheduling;
- computerized training to provide employees with up-to-date information and introduce new skills via CD-ROM, VCRs, and interactive systems;
- the portable office, including communication links—modems, FAX, and cellular telephones—portable computers, computers with pen-based entry rather than keyboards, and paging devices; and
- the home office as a means for increasing the flexibility of work arrangements.

If all this sounds rather overwhelming, it should, because one of the major components of the so-called information revolution is the electronic office. Much of the work force is currently engaged in white-collar jobs, and what happens in the office matters a great deal.

Currently most white-collar workers use computers, and the Institute of the Future, in California, forecasts that by 1995, 90% will sit in front of a screen.[41] The market for information technology is enormous and growing. Worldwide sales of information systems and services by the top 100 suppliers in 1989 totalled $256 billion, up 5.2% over 1988. Although not all these sales are to businesses, a substantial number are. Some interesting figures are $56 billion for peripherals (including printers, terminals, storage devices, keyboards, monitors, and scanners), $37.4 billion for PCs, and $19.1 billion for data communications. Predictions are that worldwide sales of computer and business equipment will grow to over $385 billion in 1993 and telecommunications equipment and services will reach $250 billion.[42] Perhaps these numbers are just too large to be meaningful and a couple of concrete examples will prove more informative.

In 1963, American Airlines introduced its computerized reservation system called SABRE. In that year, "it processed data related to 85,000 phone calls, 40,000 confirmed reservations, and 20,000 ticket sales. Today [mid-1990] there are 45 *million* fares in the database, with up to 40 million changes entered every *month*. During peak usage, SABRE handles nearly 2,000 messages per *second* and creates more than 500,000 passenger name records every day."[43] In fact, SABRE is so successful that American Airlines has begun marketing the software to other airlines.

Wells Fargo is the nation's eleventh largest bank in an industry that "accounts for 35% of information technology purchases in the United States though they [financial institutions] employ only 5% of workers."[44] Electronic mail was introduced in 1984 and it currently links 6,600 employees who send 15,000 to 20,000 messages daily. One important by-product of the growing use of electronic mail is the apparent loosening of the management hierarchy, in that senior executives seem to be willing to interact with a wider and more diverse segment of employees.

The Personal Computer in the Office

Sometimes the pace of technological development confounds the best-laid plans of management for an orderly progression in the evolution of data processing facilities. Such is the case with the personal computer, which more and more has been finding a home in the office. Originally designed for hobbyists, the market for the personal computer exploded in the early 1980s and reached into schools, homes, small businesses, and executive offices. Early versions of microcomputers were quite limited and were used primarily to do simple accounting, maintain customer lists, and keep records of correspondence. But the machines and the associated software quickly became much more sophisticated and were soon performing such functions as budgeting, inventory management, word processing, and spread-sheet calculations. In small businesses the role of the microcomputer was relatively straightforward, namely, to automate many of the functions previously executed by secretaries. In the medium-to-large company the issue was much more complicated.

As the number of PCs has grown rapidly, a variety of problems has emerged. The basic concerns are with who controls purchases, and keeps track of them, and who decides when to lease instead of buy, when to sell, and what software to use. These decisions are especially important when PCs and PC software represent a substantial capital investment. There are a variety of strategies in operation including the following:[45]

Technological Committee. To coordinate technical needs and standards.

Task Force. Made up of IS and business unit members to oversee data management, technology management, and information management.

Senior Management. A senior IS executive with staff formulates technology investment decisions.

With the arrival of laptop computers, additional problems have arisen, with respect to communications, maintenance, and security. Probably of most importance is availability—who gets them and for how long. These problems are significant given the growing popularity of laptops: U.S. sales were about 1.1 million in 1989 and are expected to rise to 3.5 million in 1993, with a market value over $11 billion.[46] One interesting aspect of laptop use is that while some companies have permitted access from the field to electronic mail and other non-sensitive services, they have restricted access to the mainframe "for practical reasons—including security."

Probably of greater importance than laptops is the movement of workstations from the research environment into the commercial world. Although it is difficult to define the distinction between workstations and PCs, especially those at the top of the line, it can be said that they are faster, with high resolution monitors, and typically run under the UNIX operating system. The current leaders are Sun Microsystems, Hewlett-Packard, Digital Equipment, MIPS, and looming as always, IBM. Estimates are that the worldwide workstation market will grow from $6.8 billion in 1989 to $16.2 billion in 1993, with growth in the commercial market from $900 million to $4.1 billion over this period.[47] Workstations will be important in distributed computing applications grounded in the client/server model as opposed to the more common host-based model used in mainframes or large minicomputers.

On the Road to Better Communications

In the early days, computers were locked away in antiseptic rooms guarded by a cadre of initiates who were the sole custodians of programming, data preparation, and result reporting. As the number of people who had direct access to the computer increased, greater demands were made on the managers of computer facilities to provide easier access and better, more readable output. The development of time-sharing systems gave many people better access, but it has been certain improvements in hardware and especially in software that have, in fact, opened up computers.

Graphics and Imaging

Since the business of management is to make decisions based on all the available information, it is important to reduce the effort of gathering, processing, and displaying that information. Recently, technology and software developments have combined to make graphics facilities widely available to both information processing professionals and executives. For most managers, graphics presentation is a needed relief from pages of texts and tables. As someone remarked, a computer graphics picture is worth a thousand printouts. The benefits claimed for computer graphics are straightforward: saving of time in the production, interpretation, and communication of data, and assistance in management decision-making provided by visual information that is much easier to assimilate. Interactive graphics systems also encourage managers to explore the available information more extensively. Graphs, charts, and bar diagrams are readily available.

We should distinguish between graphics, the creation and manipulation of computer-generated images, and imaging, the representation of paper documents as special computer files. An important early instance of imaging began in 1988 when American Express included with its billing statements "laser-printed, reduced facsimiles of the original receipts, including signatures. The reproduced forms were not photocopies, but rather digitized electronic images printed in the billing statements."[48] Scanners are used to convert documents directly into computer files that can then be manipulated—printed, included in other documents, retrieved, and mailed electronically. Within a rather short time the market for information and image managing is expected to grow rapidly, the micrographics market from $1.4 billion in 1988 to $2.28 billion in 1993, and the electronic imaging market from $800 million to $6.8 billion in this period. The major markets in 1988 were health care (18%), government, manufacturing, financial services (each 15%), wholesale and retail (13%), and insurance (10%).[49]

Computer graphics is already a major segment of the computer industry. The 1989 worldwide market totaled $26.3 billion, expected to grow to $44.3 billion by 1993.[50] This growth has paralleled the growth in the PC market as more than half the processing power for computer graphics is carried out by PCs and workstations. Some of the components of this growth are the following:[51]

CAD/CAM. Clearly, high quality images are a necessity.

Architectural Design. Graphics is used to produce high quality designs and as a major component of "walk-through" systems.

Visual Communications. This includes presentation, multimedia, training, entertainment, and video production and involves optical disks and scanners.

Graphic Arts. Included under this heading are electronic, or desktop publishing, prepress, illustration, design, and fine arts. The Macintosh has been highly successful in this market.

Mapping. Graphics are heavily involved in GIS (Geographical Information Systems), geophysics, and cartography.

Science and Medicine. Such activities as visualization, imaging, and analysis occur under this heading.

HDTV (High Definition Television). Discussed in Chapter 1.

Many of these applications serve the important purpose of condensing and distilling large amounts of data in order to improve the decision-making process. By employing a distributed system with either a large mainframe to store data and several linked graphics terminals to display it or a network of graphic workstations and servers, management can reduce costs and increase convenience. Therefore, graphics is rapidly becoming an important component of the automated office as well as an important management tool and thus a means to improve productivity. Decreasing costs and improved power are also significant factors in the widespread use of graphics equipment.

EDI (Electronic Data Interchange)

As more companies have computerized their internal operations, it has become inevitable that inter-company communications would move from paper (mail) and telephone to the computer. This process is encouraged by the globalization of industry and the growth of worldwide communications networks. It seems to make good business sense that companies that depend upon one another should be able to facilitate this interaction by computer networks, i.e., electronic data interchange (EDI). As in many other areas, EDI growth is fueled by the need to obtain a competitive advantage and to respond to customer needs. For example, IBM is in the process of requiring that all its suppliers and customers use EDI.[52] A formal definition of EDI is provided by Phyllis Sokol, a pioneer in EDI standards:[53]

> Electronic data interchange (EDI) is the INTER-COMPANY COMPUTER-TO-COMPUTER communication of STANDARD BUSINESS TRANSACTIONS in a STANDARD FORMAT that permits the receiver to perform the intended transaction.

Instead of generating a transaction on paper and then mailing it to a receiver, who then enters the data into a computer and runs an application program, the sender generates the transaction by computer, transmits it via a computer network, and the receiver simply has to run the application program on this transmitted data. By the above definition, the data must be transmitted both in a standard form and for standard business transactions. Thus electronic mail would not be considered as part of EDI.

Other Developments

To minimize keyboard interaction by building in a variety of useful facilities, accessible by alternative means, is thought by many to be a way to encourage computer use. This idea, in part, is the strategy behind Apple's introduction of the Macintosh computer. It provides a variety of commands, displays, and computations that the nonexpert may access by pointing to a location on the screen with a "mouse." This menu of resources eliminates the need for programming skills, at least for simple tasks, and reduces the necessity of typing long lists of commands. The user can do financial computations and integrate the results into a report simultaneously. The screen is meant to capture the feel of a desk top from which layers of paper are lifted to reveal what lies beneath. The "lifted" papers can then be recalled and used. This development probably represents the wave of the future—in 1990, some 6 years after the introduction of the Macintosh, Microsoft released Windows 3.0, which transformed IBM compatible PCs into Macintosh-like computers.

Much more experimental and considerably less developed is the possibility of interacting with computers in ordinary language, as opposed to programming languages or special purpose database query languages. A growing problem in the use of computers is the proliferation of such specialized languages and systems, which pose a serious obstacle to the casual user who is unwilling to invest in the necessary effort to acquire a modicum of expertise. As a result of research in artificial intelligence, a few companies have developed and marketed natural language interfaces to databases. These permit the user to type in such queries as, "Who are the top five salesmen in the first six months of 1990?" and, "Correlate salary to years of service for all supervisors over the age 55." Some systems currently available are INTELLECT (Artificial Intelligence Corp.), Themis (Frey and Associates), and RAMIS II English (Mathematica Products Group).

Beyond typing questions into a computer in ordinary language, the next significant development would be direct voice communication. The ability to issue commands or request information by voice would be the ultimate in office automation. Presumably the computer would also be able to respond by voice, when appropriate. Speech understanding, not recognition, however, is an enormously difficult problem, especially if subject matter, range of speakers, and environmental conditions are unconstrained. For very specialized purposes and under severe constraints, a few simple commands can currently be recognized. For example, telephone companies are developing programs to recognize variants of yes or no in response to automated questions. Speech production, a much easier task, is now routinely available on some personal computers, telephone directory systems, and answering machines. Years ago, Texas Instruments introduced *Speak-and-Spell,* a toy that produced digitized speech instead of playing back previously recorded words and phrases. When speech understanding of some quality finally arrives, it will have an incredible impact in the office and elsewhere. One final way to facilitate communication with computers is to improve systems to read handwritten data; considerable progress is being made in this area after many years of stagnation.

ORGANIZATIONAL AND SOCIAL ISSUES

We have discussed the major impact of computers on business but have not said very much about how computers will affect the managerial structure or office workers. It is obvious that the introduction of computational facilities has altered both the structure and nature of work.

The Changing Role of Middle Management

From the discussion of the representation of management information systems as a pyramid, it might be inferred that the top of the pyramid represented higher-level management, the bottom lower-level management and the middle, middle management. This rather simple picture is instructive, for it does show a small group of top management supported by an ever increasing number of middle and lower-level managers. Furthermore, middle management is obviously situated to serve as a buffer between the top and the bottom. Traditionally its role has been to transform the high-level policy decisions of top management into actions to be carried out by lower-level management, to monitor the execution of the policies, and to report and interpret the results to the top. In the age of the computer and the availability of vast quantities of information, the role of middle management is undergoing a fundamental change. In 1983 *Business Week* attempted to characterize this transformation.[54]

Simply stated, much of middle management's function has been made redundant as a result of information being made directly available to top managers. Stored, processed, and displayed in a variety of forms in computers, this information obviates the need, in many cases, for human intervention. In a real sense, the applications programs have captured some of the expertise of the middle managers once and for all.

> The Bureau of Labor Statistics places unemployment among managers and administrators in nonfarm industries at its highest levels since World War II. And that does not include the thousands of managers who accepted early retirement or opened their own businesses.[55]

Changes are beginning to appear in a number of ways.[56]

Information can now flow directly from the factory to the top managers without intervention by middle managers.

Surviving middle managers must broaden their viewpoint to deal with inter-disciplinary problems.

Career advancement patterns in the corporations have changed, and there are fewer possibilities for upward movement.

First-line managers have assumed increased responsibility for running the plant with less intervention from middle managers.

There will be an increased emphasis on product-related activities such as manufacturing, marketing, and computing and less concern with financial matters and analysis.

The economic recession of the late 1970s resulted in the dismissal of many middle managers as companies sought to reduce costs. Cuts were also made in companies and industries not seriously damaged by the recession, as senior management took the opportunity to reduce managerial overhead with the help of new computer systems. Even with the recovery of recent years, middle managers have not been rehired in significant numbers.

In a famous cover story, which appeared some five and one-half years later, *Business Week* re-examined the plight of middle managers.[57] Although computers are hardly mentioned, their role surely underlies the structural changes in management over the past ten years to the degree that, "The classic pyramid form of the large corporation is crumbling. Corporate structure is taking on a flatter shape, with fewer layers and fewer people." And as management professor Warren Bennis of the University of Southern California business school predicts, "tomorrow's corporate structure will look like an hourglass—with the fewest managers in the middle."[58] In early 1990, concern with the general well-being of middle management continued, as one consultant observed, "Unlike the blue-collar employment bloodbath that hit old-line industries at the beginning of the 1980s, this one is striking hardest at middle managers in advanced technology companies."[59]

There is the danger, in management's eyes, that the data processing staff could come to substantially replace the middle managers it has eliminated. But by preventing each department or division from developing its own computational facility, through the use of central mainframes or distributed workstations, this possibility should be no problem. All in all, the trend is toward a flatter organizational structure, leaner staffs, more decision-making at lower management levels, increased computer training, and more effective information flow. Managers who wish to survive and prosper must increase their computer sophistication.

Groupware and Cooperative Computing

In terms of the organization of work, the computer and associated communication networks have opened up new possibilities for cooperative work among individuals. Such terms as groupware, coordination theory, and computer-supported cooperative work have become popular as ways of describing these attempts to use technology to facilitate productive efforts among teams of workers. For example, one definition of groupware is that, "in the broadest terms, [it] describes software, systems and services that help groups of workers do their jobs better. . . . Groupware operates basically in two main ways, by regulating work content or by controlling workflows."[60] Since it is necessary that work be shared, it is important that it be available on demand, in whatever form is useful for the job at hand, and that it be straightforward to convert it into alternative forms. There are many software products currently available that are advertised as groupware, their function being to aid group work.

Coordination theory seems to have originated at the Massachusetts Institute of Technology as the description of a new academic discipline with the goal "to develop a scientific theory that would explain how the activities of separate players, both individuals and machines can be coordinated. . . . An important area for coordination will be developing and using computer and communication systems to help people work together in small or large groups."[61] For example, the technology is certainly available for the communication of large amounts of information over distributed networks. What is needed, however, are systems that can coordinate distributed multiple processors, servers, and databases to the advantage of work teams for both system development and ongoing system management.

Office Work

Significant changes are occurring in the organizational structure of companies as a result of information technology. It is also affecting the nature of office work. The actual role of the technology is not always easy to identify, however. The crucial factor in evaluating the office environment is the attitude of management, its goals, its methods, and its expectations for the new equipment. Ostensibly, the primary reason for introducing, and continuing the introduction of, computers and communications systems is to increase productivity. More machines should mean fewer people doing the same work and therefore an increase in individual productivity. As sales expand, additional people may be necessary or even more equipment. The very presence of the computer creates the real possibility of providing a wide range of new services to the public and new tools to management. Thus productivity may not increase as rapidly as expected and staff reductions may not take place. Nevertheless, management may succeed in implementing, by means of the technology, a number of its tactical as well strategic goals.

From one point of view, management's long term goal is to control every aspect of the production process, whether in the factory or the office. Of course, this position derives from an analysis of factory work, in which things are the end result of the process. In the office, it is not so easy to measure either productivity or control but several issues have arisen that indicate to some that control is the foremost concern. Among these are electronic monitoring, health, and deskilling. These issues will be extensively discussed in the section *The Changing Nature of Work,* in Chapter 10.

SUMMARY

The history of computers is very much intertwined with their role in business. From their earliest use in payroll and accounting to more recent applications in knowledge-based decision making, computers have become an integral component of the business community. Some of the business applications are in financial planning, processing orders, billing, simulations, and real-time computing.

Information processing has taken several organizational forms, both in response to technological developments and management structures. There have been many attempts to provide models to characterize the growth of data processing, with varying degrees of success. With the arrival of PCs and workstations, a certain measure of chaos has occasionally entered the picture.

Management information systems (MIS) have been advertised and anticipated for several years. They are supposed to support a variety of management and decision-making functions and they have succeeded in part, although not perhaps as the integrated systems envisioned by the data processing pioneers. More recently, MIS has evolved into decision support systems, executive information, or support, systems, and expert systems, the last being an application of work in artificial intelligence.

Opening up more ways of serving computing needs is the growth in distributed computing. From large mainframes, to networks of minicomputers linked to mainframes, to PCs linked to minis linked to mainframes, to PCs linked to workstations in host-server systems, the opportunities are open-ended, but there are many associated difficulties. Of paramount consideration is the communications hardware and software necessary to make such systems work.

As noted, PCs and workstations have appeared on the scene in large numbers, bringing computing power to everyone's desk (and home), but usually with little planning and overall control, at least until recently.

The so-called office of the future features electronic mail, word processing, database management, spreadsheets, desktop publishing, CAD/CAM, scheduling, and occasionally teleconferencing. The impact on employment and work structure has yet to be understood. A number of other technological advances are entering the world of business. Among these are graphics (for generating images and presenting data in novel and informative ways) and electronic data interchange to facilitate communication among companies. Progress has also been made in natural language interfaces to databases as well as voice communication and speech synthesis.

One of the major casualties of the growing use of computers in companies is middle management. It is being squeezed out as a result of the expanded role of line managers and the increasing direct availability of information to upper management. Within the office there is a growing concern about the disruption of the traditional social organization.

NOTES

1. "Business Takes a Second Look at Computers," *Business Week*, June 5, 1971, p. 59.
2. Cyrus F. Gibson and Richard L. Nolan, "Managing the Four Stages of EDP Growth," *Harvard Business Review*, January–February 1974, pp. 76–88.
3. D. H. Meadows, D. L. Meadows, J. Randers, and W. W. Behrens III, *The Limits to Growth* (New York: Universe, 1972.)
4. Frederic G. Withington, "Five Generations of Computers," *Harvard Business Review*, July–August 1974, pp. 99–102.

5. Richard L. Nolan, "Managing the Crisis in Data Processing," *Harvard Business Review*, March–April 1979, pp. 115–126.
6. *Ibid.*, p. 124ff.
7. John Leslie King and Kenneth L. Kraemer, "Evolution and Organizational Information Systems: An Assessment of Nolan's Stage Model," *Communications of the ACM*, May 1984, pp. 466–475.
8. Izak Benbasat, Albert S. Dexter, Donald H. Drury, and Robert C. Goldstein, "A Critique of the Stage Hypothesis: Theory and Empirical Evidence," *Communications of the ACM*, May 1984, pp. 476–485.
9. Peter F. Drucker, "The Coming of the New Organization," *Harvard Business Review*, January–February 1988, p. 46.
10. Reprinted by permission of *Harvard Business Review*. An excerpt from "The Coming of the New Organization," by Peter F. Drucker, January–February 1988, pp. 46–47. Copyright © 1988 by the President and Fellows of Harvard College; all rights reserved.
11. Ralph Carlyle, "The Tomorrow Organization," *Datamation* (Cahners Publishing Co.), February 1, 1990, pp. 22, 23.
12. *Ibid.*, p. 23, 24.
13. Parker Hodges, "The Application Decade Begins," *Datamation* (Cahners Publishing Co.), January 15, 1990, p. 25.
14. *Ibid.*, p. 30.
15. Clinton Wilder, "Foreign and U.S. Execs See Eye-To-Eye on Top IS Issues," *Computerworld*, May 22, 1989, p. 63.
16. William Bowen, "The Puny Payoff from Office Computers," *Fortune*, May 26, 1986, pp. 20–24. Copyright © Time Inc. All rights reserved.
17. "Managing Computers, A Lot to Learn," *The Economist*, March 3, 1990, pp. 64–65.
18. *Ibid.*, p. 65.
19. An excerpt from Richard E. Walton, *Up and Running: Integrating Information Technology and the Organization* (Boston: Harvard Business School Press, 1989).
20. *Ibid.*, pp. 1–2.
21. Gordon B. Davis, *Management Information Systems: Conceptual Foundations, Structure, and Development* (New York: McGraw-Hill, 1974), p. 5.
22. Gordon B. Davis and Margrethe H. Olson, *Management Information Systems: Conceptual Foundations, Structure, and Development, Second Edition*, (New York: McGraw-Hill, 1985).
23. *Ibid.*, pp. 13–14.
24. P. G. Keen and M. S. Scott Morton, *Decision Support Systems: An Organizational Perspective* (Reading, Massachusetts: Addison-Wesley, 1978), p. 13.
25. John F. Rockart and David W. De Long, *Executive Support Systems: The Emergence of Top Management Computer Use* (Homewood, Illinois: Dow Jones-Irwin, 1989).
26. *Ibid.*, pp. 6–7.
27. *Ibid.*, pp. 7–9.
28. *Ibid.*, p. 16.
29. David A. Armstrong, "How Rockwell Launched its EIS," Part One, *Datamation* (Cahners Publishing Co.), March 1, 1990, pp. 69–72, and the follow-up, Part Two, "The People Factor in EIS Success," *Datamation* (Cahners Publishing Co.) April 1, 1990, pp. 73–75, 78–79.
30. *Ibid.*, Part One, p. 70.
31. Edward Feigenbaum, Pamela McCorduck, and H. Penny Nii, *The Rise of the Expert Company* (New York: Times Books, 1988).
32. Virginia E. Barker and Dennis E. O'Conner, "Expert Systems for Configuration at Digital: XCON and Beyond," *Communications of the ACM*, **32**(3), March 1989, pp. 298–318.
33. Johanna Ambrosio, "Expert Systems Make Their Mark in Corporations," *Computerworld*, August 6, 1990, p. 10.
34. Janet Crane, "The Changing Role of the DP Manager," *Datamation* (Cahners Publishing Co.), January 1982, pp. 96ff.

35. John J. Donovan, "Beyond Chief Information Officer to Network Manager," *Harvard Business Review*, September–October 1988, p. 135.
36. Ralph Emmett Carlyle, "CIO: Misfit or Misnomer?" *Datamation*, August 1, 1988, p. 50.
37. Jeffrey Rothfelder with Lisa Driscoll, "CIO is Starting to Stand for 'Career is Over'," *Business Week*, February 26, 1990, pp. 78–80.
38. Jeff Moad, "Why You Should be making IS Allies," *Datamation* (Cahners Publishing Co.), May 1, 1990, pp. 26–29, 32, 34.
39. Amy Wohl, president of Advanced Office Concepts, as quoted in Kenneth Klee, "Wanna Bet," *Datamation* (Cahners Publishing Co.), September 1982, p. 65.
40. Abbe Mowshowitz, "Social Dimensions of Office Automation," in Marshall C. Yovits (ed.), *Advances in Computers, Vol. 25* (New York: Academic Press, 1986), p. 336.
41. "A Survey of Information Technology," *The Economist*, June 16, 1990, p. 5.
42. "The Datamation 100," *Datamation*, June 15, 1990, pp. 22–214, and "Industry Outlook," *Computerworld*, December 24, 1990, p. 72.
43. Max D. Hopper, "Rattling SABRE—New Ways to Compete on Information," *Harvard Business Review*, May–June 1990, p. 120.
44. Barnaby J. Feder, "Getting the Electronics Just Right," *The New York Times*, June 4, 1989, pp. F1, F8.
45. Janette Martin, "What's Your Strategy for Buying PCs?" *Datamation*, July 15, 1990, pp. 69–70.
46. Steve Ditlea, "In Support of Laptops," *Datamation*, July 1, 1990, p. 71.
47. Michael R. Liebowitz, "UNIX Workstations Arrive!" *Datamation*, June 1, 1990, p. 24.
48. "Imaging: Changing the Way the World Works," Special Advertising Section, *Business Week*, April 2, 1990, p. 105.
49. *Ibid.*, p. 106.
50. John Gantz, "The Market at Large," *Computer Graphics World*, March 1990, p. 33.
51. *Ibid.*, pp. 36–37.
52. Patricia Keefe, "Electronic Data Interchange," *Computerworld*, May 15, 1989, p. 110.
53. Phyllis K. Sokol, *EDI: The Competitive Edge* (New York: Intertext Publications/Multiscience Press (McGraw-Hill), 1989).
54. "A New Era for Management," *Business Week*, April 25, 1983, pp. 50ff.
55. *Ibid.*, p. 50.
56. *Ibid.*
57. John A. Byrne, Wendy Zellner, and Scott Ticer, "Middle Managers: Are They an Endangered Species?" *Business Week*, September 12, 1988, pp. 80–85, 88.
58. *Ibid.*, p. 88.
59. Dan Lacey as quoted in Elizabeth M. Fowler, "Job Outlook for Middle Managers," *The New York Times*, February 6, 1990, p. C 15.
60. Esther Dyson, "Why Groupware is Gaining Ground," *Datamation*, March 1, 1990, p. 52.
61. Daniel Williams, "New Technologies for Coordinating Work," *Datamation*, May 15, 1990, p. 92.

ADDITIONAL READINGS

Data Processing

Allen, Brandt. "Make Information Services Pay Its Way," *Harvard Business Review*, January–February 1987, pp. 57–63.

Dearden, John. "Measuring Profit Center Managers," *Harvard Business Review*, September-October 1987, pp. 84–88.

Drucker, Peter. *The New Realities*. New York: Harper & Row, 1989.

Vincent, David R. *The Information-Based Corporation*. Homewood, Illinois: Dow Jones-Irwin, 1990.
Verity, John W. "Rethinking the Computer," *Business Week,* November 26, 1990, pp. 116–119, 122, 124.

Management Information Systems: A Promise Unrealized?

Applegate, Lynda, Cash, Jr., James I., and Mills, D. Quinn. "Information Technology and Tomorrow's Manager," *Harvard Business Review,* November–December 1988, pp. 128–136.
Carlyle, Ralph. "The Out of Touch CIO," *Datamation,* August 15, 1990, pp. 30–32, 34.
De Salvo, Daniel A. and Liebowitz, Jay (eds.) *Managing Artificial Intelligence & Expert Systems*. Englewood, New Jersey: Yourdon Press (Prentice-Hall), 1989.
Gauthier, Michael R. "Executives Go High Tech," *Business Month,* July 1989, pp. 44–47.
Kerr, Susan. "The Applications Wave Behind ISDN," *Datamation,* February 1, 1990, pp. 64–66.
Leonard-Barton, Dorothy and Sviokla, John J. "Putting Expert Systems to Work," *Harvard Business Review,* March–April 1988, pp. 91–98.
Main, Jeremy. "At Last, Software CEOs Can Use," *Fortune,* March 13, 1989, pp. 77–78, 80–82.
Mumford, Enid and MacDonald, W. Bruce. *XSEL's Progress: The Continuing Journey of an Expert System*. New York: John Wiley & Sons, 1989.
Umbaugh, Robert E. (ed.). *The Handbook of MIS Management*. Boston: Auerbach Publishers, 1985.
Umbaugh, Robert E. (ed.). *The Handbook of MIS Management, Supplement IT*. Boston: Auerbach Publishers, 1986.

The Office of the Future

Buell, Barbara and Brandt, Richard. "The Pen: Computing's Next Big Leap," *Business Week,* May 14, 1990, pp. 128–129.
Brandt, Richard. "Why Everyone is Gaping at Microsoft's Windows," *Business Week,* May 21, 1990, pp. 150–151, 154.
Kamel, Ragui (ed.). "Special Issue: Voice in Computing," *Computer,* **23**(8), August, 1990.
Francis, Bob. "A Corporate Vision for Publishing," *Datamation,* January 15, 1990, pp. 64–67.
Lewis, Geoff, Rothfelder, J., King, R. W., Maremont, M., and Peterson, T. "The Portable Executive," *Business Week,* October 10, 1988, pp. 102–106, 110, 112.
Mackowski, Maura J. "People Power Mail," *Compuserve Magazine,* March 1990, pp. 14–18.
Markoff, John. "For PCs, the Mouse Will Reign," *The New York Times,* October 12, 1988, pp. 1, 35.
Schatz, Willie. "EDI: Putting the Muscle in Commerce & Industry," *Datamation,* March 15, 1988, pp. 56–59, 62, 64.
Verity, John W. and Brown, Corie. "The Graphics Revolution," *Business Week,* November 28, 1989, pp. 142–145, 148, 153.

Organizational and Social Issues

Hirschheim, R. A. "Understanding the Office: A Social-Analytic Perspective," *ACM Transactions on Office Information Systems,* **4**(4), October 1986, pp. 331–344.
Kraut, Robert E. (ed.), *Technology and the Transformation of White-Collar Work*. Hillsdale, New Jersey: Lawrence Erlbaum Associates, 1987.
Olson, Margrethe H. (ed.). *Technological Support for Work Group Collaboration*. Hillsdale, New Jersey: Lawrence Erlbaum Associates, 1989.
Winograd, Terry. "Can Office Technology Support Dialogues?" In G. X. Ritter (ed.), *Information Processing 89*. New York: Elsevier Science Publishers (North-Holland), 1989.

5

MEDICINE AND COMPUTERS

. . . medicine's second revolution, which is transforming the profession from an art into a powerful and highly effective applied science.

Lewis Thomas, "Medicine's Second Revolution," *Science 84*, November, 1984. Copyright 1984 by the AAAS.

INTRODUCTION

Medicine is, at its root, people helping people. Doctors skilled at diagnosis and treatment are expected, in our society, to recognize the health problems of their patients, recommend the best ways to treat them, monitor this treatment, and adjust it if necessary until full health returns or a stable condition is achieved. In the course of this process it may be necessary to prescribe changes in diet, administer drugs, use equipment to monitor various body functions, or perform surgery—in short, to apply any necessary technology to meet the perceived needs of the patient. This model for health care in the United States stresses treatment rather than preventive methods and is eager to employ expensive and sophisticated technology. Examples of the latter are open-heart surgery, dialysis machines, and computer-aided tomography (CAT) scanners.

The computer has been used in this system in a variety of ways. It has found a natural home in the health delivery system and has supported a kind of medical practice that emphasizes and depends upon high technology. These computers have responded to the deeply felt concerns of hundreds of thousands of health care professionals working within the current system. On the other hand, some are concerned that loss of humanity and increase in alienation might result from the growing dependence on machines.

The most natural and earliest use of computers in medicine was in record-keeping, billing, and payroll, as in other areas of society. In medicine, however, record-keeping serves a function beyond its immediate use. The ability to access medical records in an information system can serve a research as well as a directly medical function. Some important application areas for computers are cross-sectional image analysis systems, psychiatry, and medical education. Attempts are being made to automate the decision-making process of physicians and to supplement the available knowledge needed in medical practice. Potentially important applications of artificial intelligence are being made in those areas.

People with a variety of disabilities, such as blindness, deafness, and paralysis, have been important beneficiaries of technological developments. The computer and (even better) the microprocessor have opened up a number of possibilities otherwise beyond their reach. There are now automatic devices for communication and for answering the telephone or the door. Other devices can monitor the ill and alert doctors or nurses if help is needed. Besides these uses, computer programming itself is an occupation that can liberate the homebound because it can be practiced in the home. Video games are being used in therapy for patients suffering from brain disorders as a result of strokes, tumors, and degenerative diseases. The games help improve hand-eye coordination, patient alertness, attention, concentration, memory and perceptual motor skill. A variety of Atari programs have been used as "verbal/mathematical skill reinforcers, memory drills, perceptual motor skill practices, and table games."[1] Patients seem to be much more amenable to and even enthusiastic about a session with a video game than with a traditional therapist. There are plans to tailor software more specifically for rehabilitation purposes in the video game context. All in all, it sounds like a marriage made in heaven.

MEDICAL INFORMATION SYSTEMS

On the surface, medical information systems appear to include just computer databases that store information, programs to process user queries, and more programs to present the results in a variety of forms. However, special demands on medicine have resulted in the development of information systems with appropriate properties. It may literally be a matter of life and death that medical records be accurate, complete, and current. This requirement is the most basic, but there are a number of subsidiary ones beyond patient care, namely administration, accounting, monitoring and evaluation of service, research, and resource allocation. Figure 5-1 represents an idealized information system. On the left are the various sources of the medical record. The information must be represented in a well-structured, unambiguous, and readily accessible form. On the right are some of the uses to which the medical records can be put. Obvious uses are diagnosis, therapeutic decisions, and accounting and administration. Important indirect applications include teaching, clinical research, and epidemiological studies. Finally, access is available to attending physicians, consultants, nurses, paramedics, and—in the future—the patient, as an active participant in the health care process.

No existing system exhibits all these features, but a number capture many of them. Donald Lindberg, Director of the National Library of Medicine, has pointed out the following salient aspects of medical information systems:[2]

Admissions Office.

Ambulatory Care Department. Outpatient scheduling and testing.

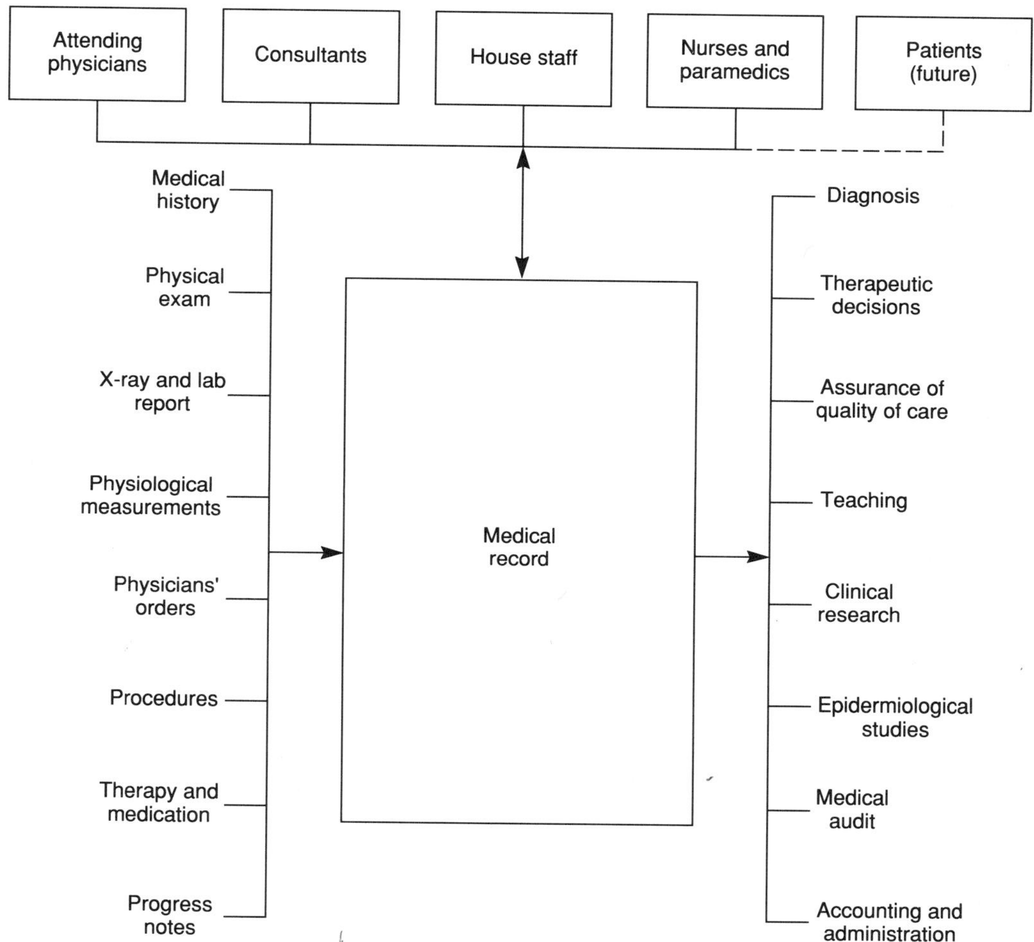

FIGURE 5-1 The Computerized Medical Information System. From Thelma Estrin and Robert C. Uzgalis, "Information Systems for Patient Care," November 1979. Copyright © 1979 IEEE, all rights reserved. Reprinted by permission of *Computer*.

Business Office. All financial matters similar to any other business.

Clinical Laboratory. Enormous amounts of test data must be dealt with.

Dietetics Department. Interrelating meal scheduling with doctor's wishes, patient's preferences, food availability, and so on.

EKG Units. The collection and examination of tapes from many different units must be coordinated.

Intensive Care Units. Collection of data, monitoring, warnings.

Medical Records Department. Everything is collected here, from multiple sources, into the patient record, the most important hospital file.

Mental Health Center. Psychological tests and interpretations.

Operating Room. Scheduling, maintenance of resources.

Pharmacy. Deals with prescriptions, drug supplies.

Radiology. Scheduling, collection and interpretation of X-ray film.

Education. Educational applications of medical records.

Research. Epidemiological studies, evaluation of experimental procedures, and planning.

Although this list appears to be lengthy, there are other areas of the hospital that will certainly benefit from the increased use of computers:[3] services for the hearing impaired, imaging and diagnosis (including ultrasound and nuclear magnetic resonance), patient interviewing by computer, local area networks, nursing aids (e.g. on-line access), and dispatching of emergency medical services. It is clear that computers have become indispensable to the modern health care system. A discussion of two well-known hospital medical information systems will help reveal some of the issues associated with their implementation and day-to-day use.

In 1976, in a cooperative endeavour with the Harvard Medical School, Boston's Beth Israel Hospital began development of an integrated clinical computing system with the following goals:[4]

1. Information should be captured at distributed terminals.
2. Information should be available at every terminal.
3. Response time should be rapid.
4. The system must be highly reliable.
5. Confidentiality should be protected; only authorized persons should have access to data.
6. The system should be user-friendly, with no need for user manuals.
7. There should be a common registry, with a single set of data for each patient.

As of 1984, there was a network of Data General Eclipse computers in place, supporting 300 terminals and 100 printers. Beth Israel, a teaching hospital of the Harvard Medical School, has 452 beds and 54 bassinets and in 1984 recorded 19,000 admissions and 160,000 outpatient visits. The system stores information on each of 539,000 patients that have been cared for since 1966. The various components include registration, clinical laboratories, radiology, surgical pathology, printed reports (produced every evening for each patient), pharmacy, and financial operations. To gain some sense of the use of this system, we note that in one week of 1984, 44,579 references were made to the common database, about 6654 per day. Most departmental and laboratory personnel were impressed by the ease of use: 87% agreed it was probably or definitely better, faster (83%), and more accurate (81%), but somewhat fewer found their work more interesting (71%). Staff physicians, house staff, medical students, and nurses found the system either moderately helpful or very helpful in looking up laboratory information (97%), as compared with a response of 71% for printed reports. Overall the system has been heavily used and highly valued.

The second system to be discussed is called PROMIS (the PRoblem-Oriented Medical Information System).[5] PROMIS represents a radical departure from mainstream information systems. Its design does not focus solely on the centrality of the medical record in patient care and teaching, but also manifests a demanding, even a coercive, tone in the working environment it presents to doctors. PROMIS enforces a strict input regimen employing a touch sensitive screen, offering a limited number of choices. It takes into account such factors as the current and past medical history of the patient, including treatment and progress reports; personal and social values, such as willingness to undergo certain treatments and various costs of health services; and specific knowledge about medical decision making—how doctors solve health problems. This is a very active system in that it attempts to aid physicians, not just maintain records.

The following results are derived from a long term experiment at the Medical Center Hospital of Vermont. House staff felt that at least one to two weeks were necessary to accommodate to the system and that the introductory educational program was seriously deficient. Doctors were most vocal in their unhappiness with the system, while nurses were considerably more positive, perhaps because they were the heaviest users and therefore received the most benefits, not the least of which was the deference they received as the local experts.

PROMIS was linked to three ancillary services: pharmacy, radiology, and clinical laboratories. The pharmacists were strong supporters of PROMIS because they felt that their role in health care, the provision of drugs, could now be carefully monitored, thus safeguarding patients to a degree not previously possible. For radiologists, having direct access to patient records improved their diagnoses by providing a context of complete clinical data in which to review the radiological data. The results from the clinical laboratories were not as positive, because for the demonstrations upon which all these reports are based, little effort was made to train laboratory staff properly. In addition, the existing hospital computer system had been well-designed for laboratory use, leaving PROMIS in an inferior position. The simple results of the experiment are that to be acceptable to a broad range of intended users, the system design must be adaptive and flexible. It must be able to respond in a coherent way to the requirements of users over an extended period.

These two systems were designed for small and large hospitals, for both treatment and research. On the other hand, the arrival of the inexpensive personal computer has made it possible for every doctor's office to have a system for maintaining medical records. Individual doctors are most likely to use the computer strictly as a billing and accounting system. The storage of medical records may not be of the highest priority, given the costs of software, memory, and the ongoing expense of data entry. Nevertheless, by now most medical and dental practices depend upon computers for office management.

Recently, the U.S. Department of Defense (DOD) announced the Composite Health Care System (CHCS), to be installed at 754 locations worldwide ranging from large military hospitals to small clinics.[6] The system will automate patient administration, patient scheduling, nursing, order entry, clinical dietetics, laboratory, radiology, and pharmacy. Each facility will have communications, maintenance, and operations support. Furthermore, it will be able to interact with other DOD systems, such as the National Disaster Medical System and VA System, food service, medical logistics, and tactical automation system.

As we have seen, many reasons have been given for the importance and usefulness of medical information systems, but perhaps one additional reason might be offered: Medicare. In 1968, Medicare was introduced to help the elderly pay their medical bills. Medicare payments have become a crucial factor in hospital finances and the entire health care system, accounting for about 40% of hospital billings in 1987. Tight restrictions on Medicare payments, however, because of the federal government's decision to limit hospital payments to a fixed amount to treat each illness, as well as pressure by major corporations to limit the costs of large insurance carriers, have forced the health care system to tighten its operations. Thus, hospitals are encouraged to treat illnesses as quickly and cheaply as possible in order to recover a greater proportion of their costs. This situation has motivated the development and implementation of medical information systems to help reduce costs and at the same time improve the quality of care.

Medical Databases

The National Library of Medicine (NLM) is the "principal resource for the collection, organization, and retrieval of scientific literature in the health and biomedical fields."[7] The library has long been concerned with the application of computers to information retrieval and in 1964 introduced MEDLARS (Medical Literature Analysis and Retrieval System), its computerized retrieval and technical processing system. This system maintains data files, provides on-line retrieval services, and produces computer-photocomposed publications. In 1971, MEDLINE (MEDLARS on-line) came into service to provide an on-line capability. The MEDLINE database includes citations from 1,000 to 1,200 journals for the current years and the previous three years. Currently, the term MEDLINE is used to describe the database, not the on-line service, and in fact is the largest and most extensively used of all the Library's databases. Other databases contain information on ethical topics, cancer, chemical substances, epilepsy, health planning and administration, history of medicine, and toxicology. As of 1988, MEDLARS databases contained over 10 million journal article references and abstracts. The online network consists of over 14,000 institutions and individuals in the United States. The NLM is clearly an invaluable resource and conducts millions of searches annually both in the United States and around the world.

The arrival of the PC has meant, among other things, that health science researchers can now access databases directly. To facilitate this interaction, the NLM has developed PC-based software (which in this context means IBM compatible) called GRATEFUL MED[8]. Version 3.0, released early in 1988, permits the search of almost the entire MEDLARS database via a user-friendly interface. One important feature is the ability to include the GRATEFUL MED search capability in customized information systems.

As a final point, we might mention that medical databases have proved valuable resources in epidemiology and in tracing dangerous drug side effects and interaction. In the former situation, accurate records can be used to trace the spread of previously unsuspected diseases. In the latter, the widespread use of new drugs can be monitored to uncover adverse reactions.[9]

MEDICAL APPLICATIONS

The computer has found a welcome home in medical diagnosis, treatment, and aid to the disabled or physically disadvantaged. Powerful tools have become available for exploring parts of the body previously accessible only through surgery. For patients in intensive care or on life-support systems, the availability of microprocessors has relieved nurses of the responsibility of constant surveillance. In such applications, the computer is indispensable both as a high speed arithmetic processor and in its ability to make decisions by comparing observed data to previously stored criteria.

Body Imaging

Until recently there were two basic methods for identifying and investigating problems within the human body: X-rays—with or without the use of ingested or inserted dyes or radioactive tracers—and surgery. Both methods have obvious drawbacks. Surgery is a traumatic invasion of the body and should be reserved for situations that demand the actual removal of diseased or damaged organs or tissues or the correction of problems. Its use as an exploratory tool should be minimized. Over the past ten years a number of methods for producing images of various parts of the body have been developed, employing both invasive and noninvasive means. Probably the best-known is the computerized axial tomography or computer-assisted tomography (CAT) scanner.

CAT Scanners

The term *tomography* refers to "any of several techniques for making X-ray pictures of a predetermined plane section of a solid object, by blurring out the images of other planes."[10] In an ordinary X-ray picture, the X-ray source produces a diverging beam that passes through the body and falls on a photographic plate. Although it has proven to be an invaluable tool, conventional X-ray does have limitations in that there is little sense of depth, and soft tissues show up somewhat blurred. The CAT scanner uses X-rays to produce sharp, cross-sectional images of the human body. The patient lies horizontally on a table and is placed in the center of the apparatus, which consists of an X-ray source and collimator (a device to focus the beam) on one side, a detector and data acquisition system on the other. The body is kept stationary in the scanner, while the apparatus rotates around a given section, generating X-rays that are registered by the detectors as they pass through the body. There is attenuation of the beams as they pass through body structures of varying densities. The actual cross-sectional image is produced by using a computer to carry out a complex summation of the various measurements made. Although various algorithms for producing cross-sectional images have been known for years, it is only when using a computer that the computation becomes feasible.

The CAT scanner has been hailed as a major, almost revolutionary advance in medical diagnosis. It is important that the X-ray exposure necessary to produce a cross-sectional image is no greater than that for a conventional X-ray. Most major hospitals have acquired CAT scanners even though the price is of the order of $1 million. In fact it has become something of a controversial item, as there has been criticism of the unseemly haste with which hospitals have competed to purchase the latest and most expensive equipment. However, there is no denying that it has proven to be an important diagnostic tool.

Positron-Emission Tomography (PET) Scanners

As is often the case, new technology follows rapidly on the heels of the old. The use of a PET scanner requires the subject to ingest, or by injected with, a radioactive isotope, typically of oxygen, carbon, and nitrogen. The system detects the radioactive decay by means of special scintillation counters. These isotopes are called positron emitters, because as they decay they release positively charged particles that after collision with electrons are annihilated. Gamma rays result whose direction of travel can be detected very precisely, thereby revealing a great deal about the relevant body tissue. The patient is placed inside a ring structure containing an array of gamma ray detectors. The directions are identified and the computer comes into play to construct a cross-sectional image of the distribution of the positron emitter. The PET scanner has an advantage over the CAT scanner in that it is able to reveal the functioning of organs and tissues, not just their outline.

The PET scanner can be used to (a) monitor blood flow in certain areas of the heart, (b) assess the intake of sugar in cancer tumors or the brain, and (c) study chemical reactions that may suggest schizophrenia or Alzheimer's disease. There are many fewer PET scanners than CAT scanners in use, and many of the results obtained so far are still experimental.

There are some problems associated with the widespread use of PET scanners. Short-lived isotopes are necessary to prevent the patient from receiving too large a dose of radiation while the scan is in progress. Isotopes with such short half-lives (between 2 and 110 minutes) must be produced on-site by a cyclotron. The need to have a cyclotron on hand increases the costs enormously, on the order of $2 million for a PET installation. Furthermore, at the present stage of development the interpretation of the data is a very complex process. It still requires the efforts of specially trained chemists, mathematicians, physicists, computer scientists, and doctors. Both PET and CAT scanners are subject to the criticism that they expose the body to excessive radiation from either gamma rays or X-rays. A new and apparently safer method, the NMR, is currently being developed.

Nuclear Magnetic Resonance (NMR) or Magnetic Resonance Imaging (MRI)

NMR (also known as Magnetic Resonance Imaging, MRI) produces images similar to those obtained by CAT scanners but also permits the actual observation of certain internal processes such as the movement of blood, the reaction of cancerous tumors to a particular therapy, and the status of bypass grafts.[11] All these observations can be accomplished without X-rays, the injection of hazardous dyes, or the use of radioactive isotopes. Nuclear magnetic resonance has been used for many years by chemists to analyze uniform solids and liquids. In its medical application, the patient is placed inside a large cylindrical magnet. In the plane of radiation, the magnetic field can vary between 1500 and 15,000 gauss (more than 15,000 times the magnetic field of the earth). Under the influence of the large magnetic field, the atomic nuclei of hydrogen, phosphorous, and other elements act as tiny bar magnets and align themselves in the direction of the field. When the radio frequency (RF) is removed, the tiny magnets return to their original positions and in the process emit characteristic RF signals. An antenna in the cylinder detects the radio waves and transmits them to a computer to be analyzed and presented as an image. Further information is available, because the computer can also determine the rate at which the nuclei return to their original positions. It is possible to obtain a sequence of images of the human heart with the valves opening and closing.

There are some disadvantages. Among these are cost—an NMR system sells for about \$1.5 million, about 50% more than a CAT scanner. The system must be isolated from extraneous electromagnetic signals and magnetic substances. There may be a hazard to people with artificial joints and pacemakers. The long-term effect of high magnetic fields on the body is unknown. Pregnant women are currently being excluded from examination by NMR. It is being introduced more slowly than the CAT scanner, but the future holds much promise for its use.

Storage of Images

As a variety of techniques have emerged for producing images of the body, an interesting problem has arisen. Large numbers of images must be stored, cataloged, and made readily available for future reference. For example, "A 300-bed hospital generates about 1 gigabyte (8×10^9 bits) of picture information every day and is legally bound to hold it for three to seven years—30 years in the case of silicosis or black lung disease, illnesses that may have relevance to future lawsuits."[12] Diagnostic imagers could have been designed to produce digital output, which would have facilitated the storage of the images and their transmission over networks, but for commercial reasons this was not done; in addition, when scanners were first introduced, high resolution monitors were not generally available and film processing techniques and handling were. More recently a number of hospital and medical research centers in the U.S., Japan, and Europe have begun to implement and routinely use picture-archiving and communication systems (PACS). In more detail, a definition follows:[13]

> PACS accepts pictures or images, with associated text, in digital form and then distributes them over a network. The components of a PACS include control computers and a communication network, interfaces to imaging devices, storage media, display stations, and printers.

Some of the problems impeding the rapid growth of PACS are the quality of the resolution of digital images compared to film, the ability to view multiple films rapidly, and the low cost of film equipment compared to display stations of requisite quality. To deal with these issues, radiologists will have to accept digital images even though they are concerned about the possibility of extraneous details being introduced during computation. Another looming problem is the vast number of images that must be stored. One strategy is solid state memory for immediate use, magnetic disks for short-term, and optical disks for long-term.

The real payoff for PACS is the ability to transmit quality images over varying distances: local-area networks (LANS) linking scanners, data storage devices, and display stations in one department; wide-area networks for linking LANs within hospitals and medical centers; and teleradiology networks for national and worldwide distribution.

Electronic Monitoring

For the patient in the intensive care unit of a hospital, the immediate world is full of electronic hums and beeps, flashing lights, and video monitors. Many activities performed by nurses in the past are now being carried out by a combination of sophisticated electronics, microprocessors, and software. Many body functions can be monitored automatically and compared to desired (or dangerous) levels by specialized equipment that emits signals to warn the nurse if an emergency arises. This system relieves nurses of the stressful and tedious work of sitting at the bedside of critically ill patients. The patient can be assured of constant monitoring and the nurse can apply him or herself to patients who are conscious of nursing efforts.

Is the practice of medicine becoming increasingly dehumanized? How far have we moved away from the image of the doctor or nurse hovering near the patient, deep in thought, full of compassion? Perhaps this image is overly romantic and has little to do with the actual quality of care.

Computers in Medical Education

Aside from the use of computer-aided instruction in medical schools (the importance of which should not be overlooked), a significant and interesting application has been medical robots. These devices are shaped like humans, covered with synthetic skin, and chock full of electronics that simulate a variety of human functions. Controlled by computers, they are used to provide students with an opportunity to perform diagnostic tests before they are experienced enough to interact usefully with human subjects. As advances are made in robotics, these robots will become more sophisticated and more challenging for students.

ARTIFICIAL INTELLIGENCE IN MEDICINE

At the heart of medical practice is the diagnosis, that somewhat mysterious process by which a doctor assimilates medical evidence—in the form of family history, symptoms, the results of tests, and direct verbal reports—and determines a course of treatment along with further tests to ascertain whether the patient is in fact suffering a particular ailment. Although there have been significant advances in medicine, the determination of the nature, cause, and treatment of disease and disability is still often more art than science. The process depends heavily on the experience, knowledge, and skill of the attending physicians and sometimes on just plain luck. The educational process depends on teaching diagnostic skills by example, occasionally in stressful situations, with the hope that the novice will learn from the experienced.

As medicine becomes more specialized and more complex, the average doctor finds it increasingly difficult to keep up with recent developments. It is important, therefore, that doctors—especially in isolated and rural areas—have access to medical information systems. Such systems can serve as easily accessible, user-friendly medical libraries available at all hours over long-distance telephone lines. The next stage would be a system to provide medical advice or consultation. In this domain, artificial intelligence techniques can make a real contribution. One of the major research areas in AI is the modeling of human problem-solving and decision making abilities. In the last few years there has been a considerable effort to apply AI techniques to the problem of medical decision making. There are several components to this research: the acquisition of medical knowledge, the problem-solving system, a decision making strategy that captures the abilities of the best doctors, a means of adding new knowledge and modifying old, and finally, a facility for natural communication.[14]

MYCIN

One of the earliest and most influential systems for medical advice is called MYCIN, designed to recommend the appropriate antibiotics to treat bacterial infections. (MYCIN is a typical suffix for the names of antibiotics, for example, streptomycin and aureomycin.) Why not wait until all the laboratory tests are in and then produce a positive identification instead of prescribing with uncertainty? Frequently, a physician must make a decision before all the results of tests are available, in order to alleviate the suffering of the patient. This action requires making the best use of what is known, taking advantage of the ranges of coverage of different antibiotics. A doctor can make the right decisions on most occasions, but can a program? Of course there are no programs currently available that replace doctors, even if that were desirable; so in a real sense, the question is academic (with no pun intended), even though sophisticated programs of this kind, usually called expert systems (as discussed in Chapter 4), do operate autonomously in many other situations. At the very least, such programs can be used in parallel with a physician, as a backup and to ensure that nothing is overlooked.

Artificial Intelligence and Psychiatry

What of the use of computers, assisted by AI, to treat the mind? Can only psychotherapists, psychologists, and psychiatrists minister to the health needs of the human psyche?

For more than 25 years, Kenneth Colby and his colleagues have been developing computer programs to simulate mental disorders.[15] It was hoped that successful simulations would provide some insight into the identification, nature, and treatment of such disorders. For example, one program, called PARRY, was designed to model paranoid behavior. The program is able to communicate with an interviewer via a computer terminal. The program plays the role of an interviewer (or therapist) posing questions and responding to answers. It is guided by the particular theory being simulated and the power of the natural language analysis and generation components.

In 1965, Joseph Weizenbaum wrote a program called ELIZA (or DOCTOR) to carry out a kind of therapeutic conversation. Weizenbaum is highly incensed by the idea that a machine could ever act like a human.[16] Note that Colby himself was influenced by Weizenbaum's work: "If the [ELIZA] method proves beneficial, then it would provide a therapeutic tool which can be made widely available to mental hospitals and psychiatric centers suffering a shortage of therapists . . . several hundred patients an hour could be handled by a computer system."[17] Weizenbaum expresses his disgust in the following manner:[18]

> I would put all projects that propose to substitute a computer system for a human function that involves interpersonal respect, understanding, and love in the same category [that I would simply call obscene]. I therefore reject Colby's proposal that computers be installed as psychotherapists, not on the grounds that such a project might be technically infeasible, but on the grounds that it is immoral.

This controversy has existed for several years, but the research goes on. Whether or not humans will feel comfortable confiding in computers, only time will tell, but research continues under the assumption that they will. Furthermore, no longer do research programs depend upon developments in AI. For example, a system was developed at the University of Wisconsin to carry out computer-administered cognitive-behavioral therapy to a randomly selected group of twelve appropriate patients. The results were to be compared with another randomly chosen group of twelve who received cognitive-behavioral treatment from a therapist. The following results were reported:[19] ". . . six (50%) of the computer-administered therapy group and five (42%) of the therapist-administered therapy group were improved after treatment compared with two (17%) of the control subjects [who received no therapy]." In their discussion of the results, the authors note that,[20]

> . . . the computer cognitive-behavioral treatment program as used appears to be as effective as a human therapist in relieving mild to moderate depression. Although we want to emphasize that computer treatments must be used in the context of careful professional assessment and comprehensive management of patient problems, they may have a role to play in providing parts of effective, efficient, and economical treatment. Further development of direct patient-computer treatment programs, subject to rigorous evaluations is warranted. Implementations of such programs in clinical setting should await the results of further research.

This is a rather cautious statement about the potential role of computers in therapy, but it is interesting that part of the justification is based on efficiency and economy. While there is always a shortage of qualified people and funds to provide treatment, are computers, however carefully used, a significant part of the solution? For Weizenbaum, the answer is obviously no. For some therapists, the answer is a qualified yes.

COMPUTERS AND THE DISABLED

It sometimes seems as if the microprocessor was developed just to help the paralyzed, the paraplegic, and the bedridden. The impact is likely to be so revolutionary that science fiction will overlap with fact. Among the wonders that will come to pass: the blind will be helped to see (albeit dimly), the physically disabled to walk (albeit slowly and with difficulty), and the paralyzed to communicate with the world.

Paraplegics

A woman had suffered from *dystonia musculorum deformans* from the age of seven. This disease, spreading from her legs to her upper body, resulted in a loss of control over her legs, loss of bladder control, the necessity to live in a wheelchair with arm, leg, and back braces and dependence on a catheter and medication for pain and muscle spasms. In September 1982, at age 29, she received treatment from Dr. Joseph M. Waltz, director of neurological surgery at St. Barnabas Hospital in the Bronx, N.Y. After four weeks she could walk and no longer required the catheter or the braces. A miracle? Perhaps. It is a miracle of modern technology.[21]

Dr. Waltz has developed a spinal-cord stimulation system consisting of tiny platinum electrodes implanted along the upper spinal cord, connected to a receiver implanted beneath the skin, at the side, and a microprocessor hanging from a belt. The microprocessor generates low power radio frequency (RF) signals that are picked up by the receiver and then emitted by the electrodes to stimulate the spinal cord. After a period of fine tuning, the emitted signals will either augment or inhibit the brain's own impulses in an appropriate fashion. The system can help improve a number of other disorders such as cerebral palsy and epilepsy.

More recently, research was reported on attempts to grow nerve fibers through holes drilled in silicon chips that would subsequently be implanted to "redirect nerve impulses cut off because of injuries."[22] The hope is that such *switches,* combinations of the artificial and the natural, will direct nerve impulses from regrown fibers to the organs they are supposed to enervate. Of course, the payoff is years away.

The Visually Impaired

Most advances in the treatment of blindness are still experimental. For the blind, help comes in two forms: technology to improve access to information, and a means for providing a crude form of vision, not further discussed. In the former case, the important development is the Kurzweil Reading Machine.[23] The person places a book or printed page on its glass top. A scanning mechanism converts the print images to electrical signals that are processed by a computer program whose output device is a voice synthesizer. The program incorporates a large number of English phonological rules (over 1,000) and exceptions (over 1,500). The voice itself is somewhat difficult to understand, but users report that in a very short time they become quite comfortable with it. In addition, controls allow the user to vary the pitch, spell out the letters in words that have not been understood, repeat previous words, and increase the number of words scanned per minute. The Kurzweil machine has become an important element in the resources available to blind people, but because of its cost—about $25,000—it will, for the foreseeable future, be used primarily at reading centers and libraries for the visually impaired.

The Bedridden

Microprocessors are being used to control various parts of the environment of bedridden people by translating spoken or other commands into actions. One such individual, Rob Marince, who is paralyzed in his arms and legs, must lie on his back and until 1982 would have been condemned to the prison of the mind within the body.[24] Thanks to his brother and a friend, he now is at the center of a wondrous communication network. Through voice control he can summon television from around the world by requesting the satellite dish in the yard to be pointed in any given direction. With a vocabulary of about 300 words, he can play video games, participate in a conference type telephone system, use a video recorder, dictate letters, dim the lights, and even program a computer. In the future a robotic arm will be hooked up to the system. All this was quite expensive, even though Gary Marince, the ingenious brother, managed to acquire about $60,000 in free components from manufacturers.

Such systems have gotten cheaper, since the heart of the system, the microprocessor, has become relatively inexpensive. Witness Larry Boden, a quadraplegic, who uses a voice-activated IBM PC to perform a range of household activities, including answering and dialing a telephone, opening and closing drapes, turning lights on and off, and controlling an entertainment console and other appliances.[25] He will also be able to use a video camera to screen visitors and open the front door. The automation system, developed with funding from the Canadian government, should be available to other householders, disabled and non-disabled, for about $2500. Once the "smart home" becomes more common, such facilities will be available for everyone.

The computer itself has enabled a number of physically disadvantaged people to express themselves in ways not previously possible. Cerebral palsy has prevented many people from speaking understandably or from controlling their arms and hands to write. Typing requires less motor coordination, particularly on specially designed oversize keyboards connected to personal computers. With special programming languages and software, such people can communicate more readily, and minds locked in uncooperative bodies can emerge. A number of children with disabilities have found the computer to be a liberating force that returns much for the little effort required to press a few buttons. For those unable to speak clearly, a computer can display their words as they are keyed in and through a speech synthesizer make them heard. The applications are growing daily as the physically disadvantaged become aware of the potentialities of the computer.[26]

The Disabled at Work

In 1990 a comprehensive law was passed in the U.S. (The Americans with Disabilities Act), requiring employers, public institutions, and private companies to provide facilities sufficient to enable people with disabilities to enjoy all the benefits that the rest of society currently enjoys and usually takes for granted. Although the ramifications of this law are likely to be far-reaching and surely unpredictable, it is clear that the computer, or at least the microprocessor, and associated input/output devices will play an important role. What will also be important is that equipment, produced for the general public, be well-designed so that the physically disabled will also benefit from their use. This requirement receives added urgency given that almost 40 million Americans have disabilities. Specially designed computers with oversized keyboards and large monitors, and communication networks will permit the severely disabled to work and be educated at home. Speech synthesizers have been improved and their price lowered so that screen displays can be spoken for the benefit of people with visual impairments, software is available to translate from English to Braille for printing, light pens and joy sticks can replace or augment keyboards although adequate software is still in short supply, and speech recognition is an active research area for people with and without disabilities.[27]

Other applications of microprocessors to aid the disabled include their use in wheelchairs to improve control, and electronic mail or specialized telephone equipment to permit the deaf to communicate. Part of the motivation for a revitalized concern for the disabled was the reauthorization by Congress in 1986 of the 1973 Rehabilitation Act, with the addition of section 508, "to insure that handicapped individuals may use electronic office equipment with or without special peripherals." The implication is that disabled government employees, including federal, state, and local, should have "access to the same databases, operating systems, and applications programs as anyone else in his or her department."[28]

One very significant example of the power of the computer to increase independence, if not necessarily productivity, is Stephen W. Hawking, the world famous Cambridge physicist, who suffers from amyotropic lateral sclerosis. Also known as Lou Gehrig's disease, it is a progressive motor neuron disorder that profoundly affects the muscular system and has forced Hawking into a wheelchair at an early age as well as reduced his speech to unintelligibility and finally silence because of an emergency tracheotomy. By using a computerized speech synthesizer that he controls with a hand switch, he is able to produce speech, albeit with an American accent.[29]

A final comment from Dr. Frank Bowe, a former executive director of the American Coalition of Citizens with Disabilities, who is deaf: "When society makes a commitment to making new technologies accessible to everyone, the focus will no longer be on what people cannot do, but rather on what skills and interests they bring to their work. That will be as it always should have been."[30]

A Very Personal Computer

The first cardiac pacemaker was implanted in a human in 1958, in Sweden, and the second a year later in the United States. These early devices emitted pulses in a fixed, regular pattern to overcome the condition known as heart block, in which the body's method for stimulating the heart operates intermittently. Unfortunately, this fixed-rate system of stimulation could occasionally cause the heart to beat too rapidly (tachycardia), resulting in death. Advances in design resulted in pacemakers that operated only on demand, when the body's natural stimulation failed. Eventually, pacemaker technology benefitted from developments in microelectronics, and programmable microprocessors are currently being implanted. Physicians can vary such features as sensor-amplifier sensitivity, energy output per pulse, pulse width, pulse frequency, and delay between chamber pulses. In addition, system diagnostics are available over telephone lines to permit doctors to check the behavior of the pacemaker. Another innovation is a pacemaker that adjusts its rate in response to the patient's physical activity. One model determines this activity by measuring body motion while another is triggered by changes in blood temperature.[31]

There is a heart disorder called fibrillation, in which the heart suddenly goes into a chaotic state that restricts or stops circulation and can lead to death within a few minutes. Since action must be taken quickly, implantable defibrillators could save many lives by automatically detecting the onset of an attack. One current drawback is that they must be implanted during open-chest surgery, a traumatic and expensive operation. Under test is a procedure for implanting the electrodes into the heart transvenously, similarly to the way pacemaker leads are implanted.[32] The next important step under investigation would be a single device to combine a pacemaker, a device to control arrhythmia, or irregular beat, and a defibrillator.

Another implantable device is a programmable insulin-delivery system, first placed in a patient in November 1986. It contains a pump with an externally-refillable reservoir with enough insulin for about three months. The patient must measure the blood sugar level on a regular basis and then issue one of ten commands to the pump using an inductive-link transmitter. Finally, implantable cochlear devices that permit some hearing impaired people to hear noises and others to carry on telephone conversations are currently being tested by the U.S. Veterans Administration.[33]

SOCIAL ISSUES

Perhaps the most serious charge against the use of computers in medical care, or in the health delivery system, is that they tend to dehumanize the patient-physician relationship. This argument suggests that doctors will shunt patients towards computers in order to increase their income by treating more patients. For the foreseeable future, computers will not be treating people directly; they will be an adjunct to doctors, complementing their knowledge. But what about large information systems, in which the patient is just a record to be scanned, modified and, of course, billed. It is certainly possible for patients to be treated in a dehumanizing way in a large medical center. The question is whether or not the use of computers aggravates this situation. Critics of computers in medical care argue that by their very nature the machines, and the organizational structure in which they are embedded, tend to centralize control, diminish individual responsibility, and inevitably will decrease the human quality in the relationship. On the other hand, computers that assume much of the routine clerical work in hospitals and offices should free conscientious physicians to spend more time with their patients.

Hardly anyone could disagree with the important applications made feasible by computers in body imagery, education, and devices for the disabled. Surely the ability to diagnose internal problems by relatively noninvasive means is an incalculable benefit. But even here, the haste with which hospitals rushed to acquire million-dollar machines made many uncomfortable. The motivation seemed to be a concern with status and prestige rather than the therapeutic benefits. CAT scanners seemed to typify a large-machine mentality at the heart of the U.S. medical system. It was easier to purchase a large machine than to provide preventive medical care for the less fortunate members of the community. In the case of microprocessor-based equipment for the disabled, there should be no argument against the significant and beneficial changes made in the lives of such people. However, there seems to be an imbalance in that relatively large amounts of money have been made available for treatment and equipment for a relatively few individuals. On the other side it is argued that costs are high in the initial experimental phases, but in the long run many will benefit.

Let us explore these issues a bit further, given their importance and impact on the health care of the American public. The medical technology discussed above seems miraculous and all-powerful but it is certainly not cheap. In addition to costs of $1 million to $2.5 million for a NMR (or MRI) machine, the annual operating cost is about $640,000. CAT scanners sell for about $1 million, and shortly after being introduced in 1973 they became the fastest selling modern medical equipment in the United States. There are more than 4,000 CAT scanners in the United States and approximately 1,300 MRI machines. Note that MRI machines now cost up to $2.5 million and require an additional $2 million for site preparation. In comparison, for a population of 58 million, approximately 23% of the U.S. population, Great Britain has 19 MRI machines.[34] The very availability of all this technology, and the fear of malpractice suits, encourages physicians to employ all the tests—a CAT scan, an MRI scan, and even ultrasound, thereby substantially increasing the costs of medical care.

Even the (excessive) use of pacemakers can cause problems. A 1988 study of pacemakers implanted in 1983, in Philadelphia, showed that 20% were not necessary and an additional 36% were of questionable benefit.[35] The implantable defibrillator raises even more questions: it saves lives but costs are high, $50,000 initially and $18,000 for a minor replacement operation. Doctors have a tendency to over-prescribe this treatment and under-prescribe alternative effective control by drugs. Also, some patients suffer anxiety over when the defibrillator will kick in with a palpable thump and annoyance when it doesn't.

Some basic questions have emerged about the U.S. medical care system itself as compared with alternative systems in Canada and Great Britain: [36]

> Some authorities believe that the greatest promise for controlling and managing the deployment of medical technology in the United States lies in changing the health care payment system to one like Canada's, which draws on a fixed, rather than open-ended budget. . . . In countries with national health care, like Great Britain [and Canada], costs and technology are controlled through Government management of hospital budgets.

Under Canada's health plan, administered by the provinces, visits to doctors and hospital stays (except for a nominal per diem), including operations, are paid for by the government. Individuals and families contribute a basic monthly payment (about $60 per month per family). However, David Berkowitz, vice-president of consulting for ECRI, a non-profit group providing hospitals information on medical devices, cautions that, "In Great Britain and Canada people wait for weeks or months for an MRI scan. I don't think Americans would stand for that." [37]

The fundamental question to be addressed is whether or not computers will improve the health delivery system both in terms of the quality of the care itself and the numbers of people involved.

> The reliance on technology to solve what is essentially a complex social issue is not peculiar to medicine. Failure to recognize the interplay of social forces underlying a problem makes for inappropriate and wasteful uses of scarce resources.[38]

Surely, many people have been helped and will be helped by medical technology, but will society as a whole be improved? Another way to focus on the use of computers in medical care is to ask if money spent on computers might better be spent on nurses. Are large amounts of money being used to help a relatively small number of people with expensive technology, to the detriment of the health care services available to many others? Given the rising costs of health care, computers are seen by many administrators as a way to control expenditures while maintaining a high level of service. These decisions about the welfare of citizens must be made by society at large. To enable that process, the role and impact of computers in medicine must be regularly monitored and assessed.

SUMMARY

The practice of medicine is slowly being affected by the use of computers in record-keeping, diagnosis, treatment, and research.

Beyond the direct application of storing patient records, medical information can serve a variety of needs, including medical research. Computer databases, which can be searched more easily than manual ones, can uncover trends and access individual records at a distance. Systems vary in range of functions, ease of use, and ability to accommodate new data processing responsibilities. In medical diagnosis, computers play a vital role in the new area of body imaging, which includes such systems as CAT scanners, PET scanners, and NMR systems. Other important computer applications are the automated electronic monitoring of patients and the use of medical robots for teaching purposes.

AI has come to play a useful role. Diagnostic systems incorporate expert knowledge that is derived from physicians and implemented in programs that can perform limited medical reasoning. There have been tentative attempts to model psychologically deviant behavior.

The linking of computers to communication systems and to physical manipulators has provided new opportunities for disabled people to escape the boundaries of their beds and homes. The Kurzweil Reading Machine helps visually impaired people to access material not available in Braille automatically and quickly. Other aids for people with disabilities are still in the experimental stage.

New microprocessor-driven pacemakers are being used to deal with various cardiac problems. In addition, they facilitate long-distance patient monitoring and treatment.

Some commentators have expressed concern that an increasing use of technology in the medical delivery system will lead to dehumanization of the doctor-patient relationship. Large expenditures for medical technology have also been criticized as an allocation of resources away from preventive care.

NOTES

1. Susan L. Westphal, "Video Games Aren't All Play," *High Technology,* May 1983, p. 78.
2. Donald A. B. Lindberg. *Growth of Medical Information Systems in the United States* (Lexington, Massachusetts: Lexington Books, 1979).
3. Kevin C. O'Kane, "Computers in the Health Care Sciences," in Marshall C. Yovitts (ed.), *Advances in Computers, Vol. 27* (Boston: Academic Press, 1988), pp. 211–263.
4. Howard L. Bleich, Robert F. Beckley, Gary L. Horowitz, Jerome D. Jackson, Edna S. Moody, Caryn Franklin, Sandra R. Goodman, Michael W. McKay, Richard A. Pope, Timothy Walden, Saul M. Bloom, and Warren V. Slack, "Clinical Computing in a Teaching Hospital," in James G. Anderson and Stephen J. Jay (eds.), *Use and Impact of Computers in Clinical Medicine* (New York: Springer-Verlag, 1987), pp. 205–223. Originally appeared in *The New England Journal of Medicine,* **312,** March 21, 1985, pp. 756–764.
5. Pamela J. Fischer, William C. Stratmann, Henry P. Lundsgaarde, and David J. Steile, "User Reaction to PROMIS: Issues Related to Acceptability of Medical Innovations," in Anderson and Jay, *Use and Impact of Computers in Clinical Medicine,* pp. 284–301. Originally appeared in *Proceedings of the Fourth Annual Symposium on Computer Applications in Medical Care, SCAMC '80,* November 2–5, 1980, Washington, D.C., pp. 1722–1730.
6. "DOD's New Health Care System," *SIGBIO Newsletter,* **10**(3) September 1988, p. 81.
7. *MEDLARS and Health Information Policy* (Washington, D.C: U.S. Congress, Office of Technology Assessment, OTA-TM-H-11, September 1982).
8. "GRATEFUL MED Version 3.0," *SIGBIO Newsletter,* **10**(1), March 1988, pp. 7–8. Note that this name is a takeoff on the name of the well-known rock group, the Grateful Dead.

9. Susan Kerr, "IS: The Best Medicine for Drug Monitoring," *Datamation,* August 1, 1988, pp. 41–42, 44, 46.
10. Richard Gordon, Gabor T. Herman, and Steven A. Johnson, "Image Reconstruction from Projections," *Scientific American,* October 1975, pp. 56–61, 64–68.
11. Franklin H. Portugal, "NMR: Promises to Keep," *High Technology,* August 1984, pp. 66–69, 72–73.
12. William J. Dallas, "A Digital Prescription for X-Ray Overload," *IEEE Spectrum,* April 1990, pp. 33–36.
13. *Ibid.,* p. 33.
14. Bruce G. Buchanan and Edward H. Shortliffe (eds.), *Rule-Based Expert Systems: The MYCIN Experiments of the Stanford Heuristic Programming Project* (Reading, Massachusetts: Addison-Wesley, 1984).
15. Kenneth M. Colby, *Artificial Paranoia* (New York: Pergamon, 1976).
16. Joseph Weizenbaum, *Computer Power and Human Reason* (New York: Penguin Books, 1984). First published by W. H. Freeman and Company, 1976.
17. Kenneth M. Colby, J. B. Watt, and J. P. Gilbert, "A Computer Method of Psychotherapy: Preliminary Communication," *Journal of Nervous and Mental Disease,* **142**(2), 1966, pp. 148–152.
18. *Ibid.,* Weizenbaum, p. 269.
19. Paulette M. Selmi, Marjorie H. Klein, John H. Greist, Steven P. Sorrell, and Harold P. Erdman, "Computer-Administered Cognitive-Behavioral Therapy for Depression," *American Journal of Psychiatry,* **147**(1), January 1990, pp. 51–56.
20. *Ibid.,* pp. 55–56.
21. Mark A. Fischetti, "Probing the Human Body," *IEEE Spectrum,* January 1983, pp. 77–78.
22. John Mattill, "Chip Nerves," *Technology Review,* October 1987, p. 15.
23. E. Cantarow, "Raymond Kurzweil, Giving 'Sight' to the Blind," *SciQuest,* February 1981, pp. 21–23.
24. Philip Faflick, "Power to the Disabled," *Time,* December 13, 1982, pp. 66, 68, 70.
25. Richard Skelly, "Electronic Butlers," *The Vancouver Sun* (Canada), September 9, 1989, pp. G1, G4.
26. Sylvia Weir, Susan Jo Russell, and Jose A. Valente, "Logo: An Approach to Educating Disabled Children," *Byte,* September 1982, pp. 342 ff.
27. Frank Bowe, "Making Computers Accessible to Disabled People," *Technology Review,* January 1987, pp. 52–59, 72.
28. Susan Kerr, "For People with Handicaps, Computers = Independence," *Datamation,* May 1, 1988, pp. 39–40, 42, 44.
29. Peter H. Lewis, "A Great Equalizer for the Disabled," *The New York Times, Education Life,* November 6, 1988, pp. EDUC 61, 63.
30. *Ibid.,* Bowe, p. 72.
31. Elizabeth Corcoran, "Medical Electronics," *IEEE Spectrum,* January 1987, pp. 66–68.
32. Karen Fitzgerald, "Medical Electronics," *IEEE Spectrum,* January 1989, pp. 67–69.
33. *Ibid.,* Corcoran, p. 67.
34. Karen Fitzgerald, "Technology in Medicine: Too Much Too Soon?" *IEEE Spectrum,* December 1989, pp. 24–29.
35. *Ibid.,* p. 27.
36. *Ibid.,* p. 29.
37. *Ibid.*
38. Abbe A. Mowshowitz, *The Conquest of Will: Information Processing in Human Affairs* (Reading, Massachusetts: Addison-Wesley, 1976), p. 140.

ADDITIONAL READINGS

Medical Information Systems

Anbar, Michael (ed.). *Computers in Medicine.* Rockville, Maryland: Computer Science Press, 1987.

Casatelli, Christine. "Emergency Care Gets a Shot in the Arm." *Computerworld,* January 28, 1991, pp. 53–55.

Coleridge Smith, P. D. and Scurr, J. H. (eds.). *Microcomputers in Medicine.* New York: Springer-Verlag, 1988.

Hansen, R., Solheim, B. G., O'Moore, R. R., and Rogers, F. H. (eds.), *Medical Informatics Europe '88.* New York: Springer-Verlag, 1988.

The Human Body. By the Editors of Time-Life Books, *Understanding Computers Series.* Alexandria, Virginia, 1988.

Medical Applications

D'Alessandro, Michael. "Computers in Radiology: The Totally Digital Radiology Department of the Future." *SIGBIO Newsletter,* **10**(4), December 1988, pp. 2–6.

Fisher, Lawrence M. "Ultrasound Enters New Frontiers." *The New York Times,* November 28, 1990, p. C 7.

Freudenheim, Milt. "Will Hospitals Buy Yet Another Costly Technology?" *The New York Times,* September 9, 1990, p. F 5.

Rosenthal, Elizabeth. "Reshaping the Delicate Art of Skull Surgery with Computer." *The New York Times,* February 19, 1991, pp. B 5, B 8.

Scott, P. D. "The Computer at the Bedside: Current Use of Dedicated Systems in Patient Care." Chapter 7 in Anbar, Michael (ed.). *Computers in Medicine.* Rockville, Maryland: Computer Science Press, 1987, pp. 151–173.

Spangler, R. A. "A Picture is Worth One Million Words—Computed Diagnostic Images." Chapter 6 in Anbar, Michael (ed.). *Computers in: Medicine.* Rockville, Maryland: Computer Science Press, 1987, pp. 105–150.

Artificial Intelligence

Clancey, William J. and Shortliffe, Edward H. (eds.). *Readings in Medical Artificial Intelligence: The First Decade.* Reading, Massachusetts: Addison-Wesley, 1984.

Gibson, Richard. "The Computer Is In: More Doctors Use High-Tech Help for Diagnosis." *The Wall Street Journal,* July 8, 1987, p. 23, Section 2.

Hand, D. J. *Artificial Intelligence and Psychiatry.* Cambridge, United Kingdom: Cambridge University Press, 1985.

Miller, Perry L. *Selected Topics in Medical Artificial Intelligence.* New York: Springer-Verlag, 1988.

Patil, Ramesh S. "A Case Study on Evolution of System Building Expertise: Medical Diagnosis." In W. Eric Grimson and Ramesh S. Patil (eds.). *AI in the 1980s and Beyond.* Cambridge, Massachusetts: MIT Press, 1987.

Ticer, Scott. "Therapy on a Disk: The Computerized Road to Mental Health." *Business Week,* August 19, 1985, pp. 75–77.

Turkle, Sherry. "Artificial Intelligence and Psychoanalysis: A New Alliance." *Proceedings of the American Academy of Arts and Sciences,* **117**(1), Winter 1988, pp. 241–267.

Computers and the Disabled

"Computers and the Disabled." *Special Issue. Byte,* September 1982.

Holmes, Steven A. "U.S. Issues Proposed Rules on the Employment of Disabled Workers." *The New York Times,* March 12, 1991, p. A 11.

Ladner, Richard E. "Computer Accessibility for Federal Workers with Disabilities: It's the Law." *Communications of the Association for Computing Machinery,* **32**(8), August 1989, pp. 952–956.

Life-Sustaining Technologies and the Elderly. Washington, D.C. U.S. Congress, Office of Technology Assessment, OTA-BA-306, July 1987.

Pear, Robert. "U.S. Proposes Rules to Bar Obstacles for the Disabled." *The New York Times,* January 22, 1991, p. A 1.

Solomon, Barbara and Wagel, William H. "Spreading the Word on New Technologies for People with Disabilities." *Personnel,* July 1988, pp. 14–15, 17–18.
Technology and Handicapped People. Washington, D.C. U.S. Congress, Office of Technology Assessment, OTA-H-179, May 1982.

Social Issues

"The Future of Medicine." *The Economist,* October 20, 1990, pp. 17–18, 20.
Gibbs, Nancy. "Love and Let Die." *Time,* March 19, 1990, pp. 52–58.
Maké, Valerie. "Saving Money and Improving Health by Evaluating Medical Technology." *Technology Review,* April 1987, pp. 22, 24–25.
Mortimer, Hope. "Computer-Aided Medicine: Present and Future Issues of Liability." *Computer/Law Journal,* **IX**(2), Spring 1989, pp. 177–203.
Sidel, Victor W. "Medical Technology and the Poor." *Technology Review,* May–June 1987, pp. 24–25.

6

COMPUTERS AND EDUCATION

. . . [A]lthough new interactive technologies cannot alone solve the problems of American education, they have already contributed to important improvements in learning. These tools can play an even greater role in advancing the substance and process of education, both by helping children acquire basic skills and by endowing them with more sophisticated skills so that they can acquire and apply knowledge over their lifetimes.

U.S. Congress Office of Technology Assessment, *Power On! New Tools for Teaching and Learning,* 1988.

INTRODUCTION

In 1866, the blackboard was hailed as a revolutionary device certain to have a significant impact on the educational process. Since then, "revolutionary" changes have appeared more frequently: radio in the 1920s, film in the 1930s and 1940s, language laboratories and television in the 1950s, and beginning in the 1960s, the computer. Claims for the latter have been mounting ever since. It will allow students to learn at their own pace. It will not be judgmental, impatient, or unsympathetic. Appearance, social class, and race are irrelevant to it. The teacher will be free to devote quality time to those with real need while others acquire information, review material, take tests, or even play games. The computer will keep track of the student's progress, produce grades and averages, suggest additional material, and alert the teacher to any potential or actual problem. More and more material will be made available in an ever-increasing number of subjects. The computer itself will excite students, igniting their native curiosity and natural desire to learn. New programming languages and systems will appear, opening up innovative and challenging environments. In short, it is claimed, teaching and learning will never be the same.

The growth of computers in the schools during the 1980s has been significant. From 1981 to 1987, the percentage of schools with at least one computer grew as follows: Elementary schools, from 10% to 95%, Junior high schools, from 25% to 97%, Senior high schools, from 43% to 98%.[1] The total number of computers in public schools as of 1989 is estimated at 2.5 million, or about 1 for every 20 students, up from 250,000 in 1983.[2] There is, however, considerable variance in these figures, ranging from wealthy private schools to poor inner city ones. Although nearly $2 billion was spent on hardware during the 1980s, this figure represented less than 0.2% of the total public school budget.[3] The educational software market is approaching $300 million per year. In order to substantially increase the installed base of hardware and software to improve the above ratio to one computer for every three children would require an expenditure of over $4 billion.

The major manufacturers of microcomputers for the kindergarten to grade 12 education market, such as Apple, Commodore, IBM, and Tandy (Radio Shack), are competing strenuously. For example, Apple has a variety of programs including the Education Purchase Program, which provides special pricing to qualified schools for both pupils and teachers as well as discount repair, service, and upgrades.[4] Apple has the largest installed base of computers, mainly Apple II's (77% of all computers in grades K to 6 and 47% in high school). Even with increasing numbers of MS-DOS computers (8-bit machines), and Macintoshes, Apple has the largest number of software packages.

As companies rapidly introduce and expand their computer systems, it becomes a matter of survival for employees, including management, to acquire computer skills. In response to such needs a number of institutes and schools have appeared to serve this market. At the top of the line is the School of Management and Strategic Studies run by the Western Behavioral Sciences Institute in California. It caters to potential chief executives and provides some unique benefits, at a cost, of course. For example, each student receives a microcomputer to keep after the course is over. Much of the instruction, assignments, and consultation is carried out over a computer network. The result is a flexible, asynchronous system of instruction and communication, an important consideration for busy executives. They can pursue their education at their desks, at home, and in their free time. Though currently expensive, home education over computer networks may be a significant part of future education systems.[5]

Computer-assisted instruction is a well-known term, but what does it include and how well is it working? A well-publicized, much acclaimed computer learning environment is provided by the language LOGO. It arose out of research carried out by artificial intelligence researchers. The LOGO environment is supposed to liberate the young from the constraints of traditional educational methods. From the elementary school to the university, computers are playing an ever-increasing role both as part of traditional education and as a new focus for investigation. Finally, the impact of computers on the educational process has been criticized, and needs to be evaluated.

COMPUTER-ASSISTED INSTRUCTION (CAI)

> CAI is not just another computer application; it has the potential to shake up the entire school system and revolutionize education.[6]

Any discussion of computers in education is inevitably sprinkled with an alphabet soup of names: CBE, CAI, CAL, and CML. CBE is a very general term standing for computer-based education and includes all the others as subcategories. The basic division is along instructional and non-instructional lines. The major component of non-instructional uses is data processing, including record keeping, inventory control, and attendance and employment records. Some of the non-instructional applications are described as follows:

Computer-Assisted Testing (CAT). The computer is used solely as a testing medium. It is possible to take advantage of the computer's abilities to provide imaginative tests or merely to use it as a substitute for manual testing.

Computer-Assisted Guidance (CAG). The computer is used as an information retrieval system to provide career guidance for graduating students. It does not add to students' skills or knowledge but may encourage them to take certain courses to help with their future career plans.[7]

Computer-Managed Instruction (CMI). The teacher uses the computer to plan a course of study, tailored for the student, that consists of computer sessions, readings, and testings. The computer will keep track of the student's performance and provide regular reports, highlighting problems and accomplishments. (In Great Britain, this application is called computer-managed learning, CML.) In somewhat more detail, CMI is based upon a set of well-defined learning objectives, often tied in with a particular set of textbooks. The computer is used to test mastery of these objectives and provide learning prescriptions for each child based upon individual placement within the objectives. After each prescription is followed, the child is retested and a new set of learning prescriptions is generated based upon the test results.

These applications are useful and important, but the most interesting and potentially far-reaching work is being done in the areas of CAI and CAL (computer-assisted learning). Before launching into a detailed examination of some of the important work in this area, it may be helpful to first present a brief overview. In a historical survey of computer applications in education, Kurland and Kurland define the following phases in the development of educational computing:[8]

CAI Delivery Systems. As computers moved from the office to the classroom, the earliest of the major CAI systems was begun in 1959. The underlying intellectual foundation was behavioral learning theory, and these systems had the flavor of programmed learning, that is, a bit of new material, a few questions, a review, and then more of the same. The technology was based on large time-sharing systems with centralized software development.

The Micro Invasion and the Decentralization of Computers. The major systems such as PLATO had little market penetration when microcomputers made their appearance in the early 1980s. At first the style of software followed the previous systems but then diversification rapidly took place and new styles emerged.

LOGO and the Emergence of the Computer as a Tool to Think with. The computer and appropriate software to facilitate new ways of thinking was the next development, led by Seymour Papert of the Massachusetts Institute of Technology (MIT). LOGO was first implemented on mainframes and later, in the early 1980s, on microcomputers.

The Computer Literacy Movement—Schools Attempt to Regain Control. The movement was towards awareness of computers (history, components, applications, and some social issues) and computer programming (LOGO, Basic, and Pascal). There was a growing concern, however, with the superficiality of the approach.

The Computer as Tool—Word Processing and Personal Productivity. The emphasis on programming was decreasing and more attention was directed, in the mid-1980s, toward application programs to assist productivity in writing, business, and general education through word processing, databases, and spreadsheets.

Incorporation of Computers into the Mainstream Curriculum. Microcomputer software was being introduced at an enormous rate and two conflicting views were in competition: to strengthen the existing curriculum or to change it in response to the new technology, including video and CD-ROMs as well as very powerful microcomputers and networks.

Now we can return to a somewhat more leisurely examination of the dimensions and scope of CAI, still an important component of computer applications in education.

Varieties of CAI

Simply put, CAI is the use of the computer directly in the instructional process as either a replacement for or complement to books and teachers. CAI has been a factor in education for a long time—since the 1960s at least—as a much-heralded but never quite perfected educational system. Because of the premature introduction of CAI software, many educators have become quite cautious about the claims for such systems. However, with the pervasiveness of microcomputers, the demand to install CAI systems in schools has become overwhelming. An overwhelming amount of software is also available.

There are several varieties of CAI. In the basic mode of drill and practice, the computer asks a question, receives the answer and provides an appropriate response. If the student's answer is correct, positive feedback is provided, usually in the form of an affirming comment to the student. If the answer is incorrect but belongs in a class of expected answers, a variety of responses may be selected. Finally, if the answer is incorrect and the system cannot deal with it, it must repeat the original question, and supply the answer, or go on to a new but similar question. In the second case, the question may be repeated with an encouraging remark, or a new question is posed based on the student's perceived difficulty. Because the computer can be programmed to keep track of each student's individual performance over a long period of time, at any given session it can work on those areas that need special attention and also boost the student's ego by reinforcing performance in areas of past success. Clearly, drill and practice are helpful when simple facts are to be learned in a structured context.

Tutorial systems for CAI are much more complex, since in this context new information is being delivered. At each stage the program can supply some general piece of information, a fact, an example, or a question to test the student's comprehension. As the major purpose of tutorial programs is to teach, they must have some way of determining what the student probably knows, what his or her difficulties are, and how the material can best be presented. In such programs, the knowledge typically is represented in a tree structure, and the presentation involves following the branches exhaustively. By precisely defining a local context, this tree organization helps identify the problems that the student may be having.[9]

There are other aspects of this approach to CAI. For instance, more than one answer to a question may be acceptable, and the program must be prepared to deal appropriately with different responses. Furthermore, it must be able to produce sequences of questions that explore some area in detail, and such sequences may depend on the nature of the intervening questions. Clearly, the preparation, design, and realization of tutorial programs is a complex task, and it is not surprising that the overall quality of such programs could be better. As the material to be presented becomes more difficult, the problem of presenting it also becomes more of a challenge. Tutorial programs are increasingly useful as they allow more flexible input by the student. This input may include the ability to ask limited questions. Once again the influence of artificial intelligence will become increasingly important, as programs become able to communicate more readily with users. In addition to facility in natural language, the more advanced programs will need abilities in problem solving, knowledge representation, and inferencing.

Simulations are useful for studying processes so complex that it is difficult to determine the specific impact of individual variables. For example, suppose we are interested in studying traffic flow at a busy intersection. A computer program can be written to capture the important features of the intersection—the traffic light sequence, and estimates of traffic density in each direction—defined by the average expected occurrence of a vehicle in a given small time interval. How is the backup of traffic related to the arrival rates and the traffic light patterns? To facilitate this investigation, a simulation program will accept values for the input numbers and then display the resulting behavior as it unfolds over time, preferably using graphics. In more advanced applications, students will be able to construct the simulation domain themselves out of a building block set of components, to study not only the system behavior but how well it has been modeled. As the simulation unfolds, the system may ask the student about decisions involved in selecting values and about expectations that the student has about its behavior. Simulations are designed for more than the acquisition of factual knowledge. They encourage students to discover for themselves how something works. They have been used extensively in the physical and biological sciences as a substitute for and supplement to actual laboratory experiments, as well as in the social sciences to model such processes as presidential elections.

As video games established an incredible appeal and excitement outside the educational establishment, it was inevitable that the schools would begin using them to teach children. Games minimize any fears children may have about sitting in front of a terminal. They can be tailored to young children and to teenagers, who are enormously fascinated with them. They are challenging, almost hypnotic, and—if properly handled—can be an open door to most other forms of CAI. Some games can be combined with a question-and-answer feature to reinforce certain concepts. Others can be presented as a kind of puzzle for which the student must figure out the rules. How significant an impact games will have on education is still an open question.

Cognitive diagnostics is a fairly recent development still in the research stage, but is having some influence on educational methodology. The goal is to determine the kinds of errors the student is making with a view towards helping improve overall performance by suggesting new problem-solving strategies. Much of this work has been carried out at the Xerox Palo Alto Research Center under the direction of John Seely Brown, in the domain of simple arithmetic skills. The student answers a number of arithmetic problems, such as subtraction. The program analyzes the answers and supplies the teacher with the information necessary to help the student. Notice that this help does not just inform the student about rights and wrongs but describes in a systematic way how errors are being made. Work in this area is giving new impetus to theories of skill execution.

A 1987 survey of the distribution of educational software by type, with 7,325 programs included out of more than 10,000 available, showed that 51% were skills practice, 33% tutorial, 19% educational games, 15% rote skill, and 11% tool programs (for example, word processors and databases).[10] The sum is greater than 100% because some programs have been assigned to more than one category. The more advanced and potentially important applications, such as conceptual demonstration and development, hypothesis testing, and simulation totalled only 17%, with simulation itself at 9%. Thus, it appears that the major contribution of the computer to education is to facilitate traditional skills practice and rote drill in a flashier style than that provided by textbooks.

Major CAI Systems

A large number of companies are competing in the educational software market. They include the computer manufacturers themselves, such as IBM and Digital Equipment Corp. One of the most important systems, PLATO, was developed by Control Data Corp. in its heyday, but has since become independent as Control Data has reduced its scope of operations. Another important contribution was made by the MITRE Corp. with its TICCIT system.

PLATO

The PLATO system has been in existence, one way or another, at the University of Illinois since 1959.[11] It has been funded by the National Science Foundation, the Office of Education, and a combination of companies and organizations. In the early 1980s, Control Data Corp. (CDC) launched an extensive advertising campaign to market PLATO software for such microcomputers as the IBM PC, Apple II Plus, the ATARI 800, and the Texas Instruments TI 99/4A, the last two no longer produced. This campaign, an attempt to bypass the schools and go directly into the home with educational software in such areas as French, German, Spanish, simple arithmetic, and physics, was not very successful. PLATO systems have been used in the employee training programs of many large companies, including United Airlines. The U.S. Navy has also used it to train recruits.

TICCIT

TICCIT is a clever acronym for Time-shared Interactive, Computer-Controlled Information Television. Begun in 1971 at the MITRE Corporation, the development of hardware and software was funded by the National Science Foundation.[12] A number of features are unique to TICCIT. It (a) incorporates a design strategy into which all software must fit, (b) is designed to implement the tutorial mode of CAI rather than drill and practice, and (c) allows the user more initiative than do many other systems. Furthermore, it combines computers and television in an interesting and novel way. Each TICCIT station is a study carrel, containing what is apparently a color television set, a special keyboard, earphones, and a place to take notes. The displays on the screen are in color and quite sophisticated. A set of 15 "learner control" keys is used by students to select which instructional display to view next, which segment of material to study next, and how to accomplish this task.

COMPUTER-ASSISTED LEARNING (CAL)

> In my vision, the child programs the computer and in so doing, both acquires a sense of mastery over a piece of the most modern and powerful technology and establishes an intimate contact with some of the deepest ideas from science, from mathematics, and from the art of intellectual model building.[13]

CAL promotes a vision of the computer as a learning resource and as a stimulus for the imagination of the child, a powerful friend able to follow commands and respond to requests. The major figure in CAL is Seymour Papert, professor of mathematics and of education at the Massachusetts Institute of Technology. He has made major contributions in cognitive psychology and artificial intelligence. Earlier in his career, he worked with Jean Piaget, the eminent child psychologist. From these experiences have emerged some important ideas on how children might learn by using a computer—an ideal instrument, given its power to stimulate and to be whatever the child desires. The programming language Papert designed permits even young children to do very inventive things.

LOGO: A New Way of Learning?

The development of LOGO (or Logo) emerged from research in three areas: AI, psychology (based on the important work of Jean Piaget), and computer science in general. Seymour Papert and his colleagues at MIT began to put their ideas about education into effect. They are concerned with such issues as helping people (a) to build various computational models as a method of learning, (b) to interact with these models as a means to improve performance, (c) and to develop a sense of wanting to learn how instead of bemoaning one's deficiencies. One can learn in several ways: by being told directly, by reading, by being helped, and by discovering things oneself. Traditional teaching methods are based on the first two; the LOGO approach is based on the last two, together with the notion of the model, which is derived from research in AI.

It is important in the design of intelligent systems to develop appropriate models of both the problem and the solver. The model of the solver must include a representation of the problem-solving strategy, a representation of the problem domain, a means of evaluating the performance of the solver, and finally a strategy for improving (or in computer talk, debugging) the solver. As systems have been developed within this framework, a new appreciation has been gained—about learning, about the importance of adequate models, and about what a computer language must be able to do in order to represent problems and provide procedures for solving them.

In the area of education, especially that of children, the principles embodied in the LOGO concept include such important features as ease and simplicity of expression, explicit representation of fundamental programming ideas, and immediate feedback. Programs can be written very simply by children, but this in no way limits the power of these programs. As children grow in sophistication and become more experienced, the language permits them to extend and build on their previous work in a natural way.

Perhaps the most important aspect of LOGO's success has been the immediate response it provides to the student. The most popular LOGO environment is turtle graphics. (LOGO programs can be written to drive music synthesizers and physical mechanical devices also called turtles, but graphics is the most common output form). The screen may be visualized as a field on which a small, triangular object, a turtle, can move under program control. The turtle can be given a heading, a number of unit steps to take, and directed whether or not to leave a track. (LOGOs designed for different computers may have additional different properties.) By suitably directing the turtle—and this is, of course, what a program does—it can be made to produce a pattern on the screen.

One very important aspect of the use of LOGO in schools is its impact on the social environment. The traditional classroom has one teacher and many learners, and the flow of knowledge is directed from the teacher to the students. In an environment rich in self-discovery, new and interesting possibilities arise. For example, students can help one another to learn by sharing individual knowledge, by asking interesting questions, and by working together in common pursuits. Papert speaks to this issue in *Mindstorms*.

> By building LOGO in such a way that structured thinking becomes powerful thinking, we convey a cognitive style one aspect of which is to facilitate talking about the process of thinking. LOGO's emphasis on debugging goes in the same direction. Students' bugs become topics of conversation; as a result they develop an articulate and focused language to use in asking for help when it is needed. And when the need for help can be articulated clearly, the helper does not necessarily have to be a specially trained professional in order to give it. In this way the LOGO culture enriches and facilitates the interaction between all participants and offers opportunities for more articulate, effective, and honest teaching relationships.[14]

The notion of a "LOGO culture" is quite interesting, for it suggests a shared language, common interests, and common goals. This LOGO culture may more properly be spoken of as a subculture of the rapidly growing computer culture, in which children can share ideas and enthusiasms.

Intelligent Computer-Assisted Learning (ICAL)

In the last few years, the application of artificial intelligence to education has spawned a new field called ICAL. The idea is that developments in AI can improve traditional CAI programs by making them smarter and better able to deal with students, in less rigid formats. Work in AI in knowledge representation, planning, user modeling, natural language understanding, diagnosis, and qualitative reasoning is all relevant to the problem of determining, at any given stage in the interaction with a student, what he or she knows, or doesn't know, and how to plan the next stage. It should be recognized that currently there is a great deal of theorizing because these problems are very difficult. What is desired is nothing less than a system that will accommodate to unpredictable input by the student, use its current estimation of what the student should know in its planning, understand the domain knowledge sufficiently well, and have considerable linguistic knowledge to decipher the student's input. The ultimate aim is a system able to produce an appropriate response at every turn of the typically convoluted interaction between student and instructor. Current CAI is far removed from this scenario and is often accused of using computers as automatic page turners.

COMPUTERS IN HIGHER EDUCATION

Computers first made their presence in education felt at universities, both as research tools and as objects of study. Not long after the first electronic computer, ENIAC, was built at the Moore School of the University of Pennsylvania, students were being instructed in the intricacies of computer design and programming. Electrical engineering departments turned their attention to transistors, semiconductors, integrated circuits, and communications. New departments of computer science were founded, to instruct students in the care and feeding of computers—that is, programming—and to carry out research in such areas as operating systems, the theory of computation, numerical analysis, and artificial intelligence. Many important innovations have come from the universities—time-sharing systems, programming languages (such as LISP, Pascal, and Basic), graphics devices (SKETCHPAD), numerical packages, and a variety of intelligent systems. The universities have filled an important function in training large numbers of computer professionals and in introducing several generations of other students to computers long before computer use became fashionable in the wider society. This role was recognized quite early by computer companies. Among these, IBM was the most prominent in recognizing the fact that early exposure to a given computer system would be a major influence in subsequent choices made by the students when they established themselves in the outside world. This realization produced a strategy that worked exceedingly well and contributed to IBM's dominance in the computer industry.

More recently, computer companies including IBM, Apple, Digital Equipment Corp. (DEC), Hewlett-Packard (H-P), and Sun have again begun to respond to opportunities at the universities. These range from special purchase plans for students and faculty, and outright gifts of hardware, software, and maintenance to joint development projects including software and operating systems for existing machines, and the design and development of new machines and networks. A number of universities require their students, upon beginning their studies, to purchase computers under very favorable financial arrangements.

These include Carnegie-Mellon University (which for years has had very close relations with DEC), MIT, Dartmouth, Drexel University in Philadelphia, Clarkson College in Potsdam, New York, and Rensselaer Polytechnic Institute in Troy, New York.

The intention is clearly that every student be able to use a computer in a variety of interesting ways beyond straight programming: to check for assignments in a course, to prepare and submit assignments (via a file accessible only to the instructor), to browse the circulation file of the library and even reserve books, to take tests and exams, and to exchange messages, via electronic mail, with fellow students and professors. All this can be done from a computer, or terminal, in the student's own room or from one of the many work stations distributed around campus. Hard copies are available from fast printers near the work stations. Such systems require extensive and sophisticated computer networks permitting thousands of users to simultaneously access computers ranging from work stations to mainframes.

Universities who have forged research and development contracts with computer vendors often argue that, "Receiving free equipment is secondary to us. . . . [g]etting to know the vendors and shaping the computer market is most important. We let them know what higher education needs and if it is good for higher education it will be good for the commercial marketplace too."[15] M. Stuart Lynn, Cornell University's vice president for information technologies puts it this way: "Today's gifts only benefit us today. Having input into product development benefits us tomorrow."[16] In 1983, IBM, DEC, and other suppliers entered into an agreement with MIT to provide $50 million initially, now up to double that amount, in equipment and personnel for the development of software to enable programs to move easily among equipment manufactured by different companies as well as to meet other educational needs. Project Athena, as it is known, has resulted in more than one hundred projects, but apparently none of these represents a breakthrough in educational software.

The growing relationship between universities and big business raises serious questions about autonomy, ethics, and responsibility. Can a university researcher simultaneously be responsible to his or her university, discipline, students, and corporate sponsor? What about the free and open circulation of research results when industry has proprietary interests? Going one step further, a number of university researchers have themselves formed companies, to develop commercial applications of their own research efforts and to consult with industry in their areas of expertise. This development is not new and there are arguments in favor of cooperation between academia and business, but there are potential dangers. Researchers must be careful not to exploit their students' work for financial gain or use results achieved with the help of government funds for private profit. Computer science, especially artificial intelligence, is quite a lucrative field and there is considerable temptation for university researchers with these backgrounds to jump into the marketplace.

There is another important player in the university computing research environment, namely the federal government, in two major guises, the National Science Foundation (NSF) and the Department of Defense's (DOD) Defense Advanced Research Projects

Agency (DARPA). NSF funds basic research in the sciences but its level of funding is considerably below that provided by DOD. For example, more than 80% of the federal funding for computer science at the most prestigious universities, the University of California at Berkeley, Carnegie-Mellon, MIT, and Stanford comes from DOD.[17] Furthermore, the military tends to support applied research related to various mission-oriented projects. Thus, to a significant degree the goals of the defense establishment shape the nature of research undertaken at the major universities of the country and hence the academic curriculum. Some researchers bemoan this state of affairs, but most recognize the political realities to the degree that there is considerable concern about the impact of cutbacks in military research budgets as a result of the easing of international tensions. At MIT, the Artificial Intelligence Laboratory is in such a potentially difficult situation, given that more than three-quarters of its budget comes from DOD.[18] Of course, given the unpredictability of world politics and the internal imperative for growth and innovation, the possibility of a peace dividend may not be realized and research funds may not be threatened.

COMPUTER LITERACY

The idea that people should be knowledgable about computers in today's society hardly seems controversial. However, the details of various proposals to implement this idea have aroused some disagreement. The term commonly used to characterize a heightened awareness about computers and their role in society is computer literacy. Comparisons with the notion of general language literacy are unavoidable and frequently misleading.

Various definitions of the term have been proposed, some of which draw parallels to literacy as it refers to language skills and a minimal level of competence in some domain. Ronald Anderson and Daniel Klasson of the Minnesota Education Computing Consortium (MECC) define computer literacy as "whatever understanding, skills, and attributes one needs to function effectively within a given social role that directly or indirectly involves computers."[19] The given social role is meant to encompass general well-being as well as specific achievements.

In the schools, at all levels, the debate continues over the definition, importance, and relevance of computer literacy. Critics are wary of pandering to the newest, flashiest technology. In a delightful parody, Bill Lacy, the president of Cooper Union, has described the repercussions of the introduction of the pencil (later in colors and with eraser) into medieval Europe. Its introduction in schools met with the following responses:

> "Just because they have a pencil doesn't mean they have a lot of education going on."
> "I don't know why my kid needs a pencil to learn French. We *are* French."

Evaluating the claims made for computer literacy in the midst of the widespread publicity surrounding computers is not an easy task. Schools are under pressure by parents to provide their children with the best chance for a prosperous life, and that certainly includes computers.

Many universities and colleges are requiring as a condition of graduation that students take at least one course in what is sometimes called computer appreciation. Typically, this course includes an introduction to computer programming, a survey of computer applications, and a familiarization with the associated social issues. It is felt that every person, to be a functioning and responsible citizen, must be aware of the role of computers in contemporary society. The debate about the usefulness of computers in the curriculum turns on such issues as the intellectual content of computer literacy courses, the benefits of computer programming for the average student, the supposed transferability of computer skills, and improved job prospects. Definitive answers are not yet available, but a number of voices have been raised against the uncritical acceptance of the concept of computer literacy for everyone. Other issues arise at the primary and secondary school level, in relation to computer programming, computer-assisted instruction, and computer games.

Many commentators have argued that for most people, learning to program is neither necessary nor beneficial. The long term-trend is toward sophisticated, user-friendly software as in word-processing and financial planning programs. Programming is not a skill easy to acquire or practice. It is unlikely that very many people, besides professionals and eager hobbyists, will program on their own. Thus, for every student to learn how to program skillfully should not be the major aim of the computer literacy movement.

The primary emphasis in computer literacy should be in the historical, economic, legal, and philosophical areas. Computers must be seen in their historical context—as part of an ongoing technological process. The economic and legal implications of their use are a rich source of material for exploring many important social issues. It would be a mistake to focus on the computer itself, because treating even such a marvelous machine in isolation can only result in superficial understanding. This is real danger, if computer literacy courses are taught by programmers with little experience in other areas. The pressure to offer such courses may result in ill-conceived projects. Public pressure is a reality, however, and many schools have responded with such courses, and even programs, in computer literacy.

ISSUES AND PROBLEMS

A basic question, not easy to answer, is, does computer-assisted instruction improve learning? On the other hand, does it dehumanize the learning process? The mere use of new technology—whether blackboards, television, or computers—does not in itself guarantee better learning. One of the fundamental criticisms levelled against CAI is that an infatuation with hardware has minimized the concern about the educational merits of the courses. Critic after critic has bemoaned the poor quality of the material. As the market has grown, the rush to produce software has resulted in a lowering of quality. Perhaps there also exist some serious problems with educational theory itself, and it is unreasonable to expect CAI to produce wondrous results. Another problem frequently ignored is the difficulty of obtaining qualified teachers who know how to use available hardware and software to their best advantage.

Other important issues include the impact of computers and computer use on the social organization of the classroom, as a byproduct of such aids to computer learning as LOGO, and, of growing importance, the tendency of the new technology to exclude girls and women.

Impact of CAI

In a survey of the impact of computer-based instruction on achievement, Kurland and Kurland report on a number of studies done in the early 1980s.[21] Most have focussed on the issue of whether or not drill-and-practice CAI programs have improved student performance, as measured by test scores, in the given domain. Note that the concern with test scores narrows the interest in overall impact of CAI from the learning process as a whole to the easily quantifiable measurements of standardized tests. The simplest conclusion from many studies is that in such areas as basic arithmetic, vocabulary, and simple science facts, drill programs do indeed improve test results. Such results have been achieved for students in grades one to six as well as college students. For language arts and reading, however, the improvements are smaller. It is noteworthy that overall improvements resulting from CAI programs were no more effective than other, non-computer related remedial education.

Major studies were undertaken to evaluate the effectiveness of the large early CAI efforts, TICCIT and PLATO. After a five year study of PLATO involving thousands of students and a wide variety of materials, ". . . the researchers found no strong evidence that PLATO either helped or hindered students." This study, however, did have some methodological problems in terms of a lack of appropriate control groups and a wide variation in the quality of course materials. Nevertheless, the fact that hundreds of millions of dollars have been spent on the development of PLATO to achieve such non-results provides ample evidence for critics of the waste associated with computers in education and hampers the possible allotment of funds for future projects. Other studies reported some improvement in the rate at which new material was acquired, but cost-effectiveness has not been shown for CAI compared with other methods.

Because of the above reports, efforts in large-scale CAI have declined substantially and attention has turned towards the use of computers as tools and as important factors in the social organization of the classroom. What has been learned from this era of computer applications in the classroom? Large expenditures in time and money to produce educational software do not guarantee success, especially when there is no serious and meaningful methodology for the creation of educational software. This problem is not the direct fault of the technology but reflects the lack of an existing theoretical, psychological, and educational base. There has been a considerable trial-and-error component in many systems that are supposed to be well-established. Because the cost of producing quality courseware is so great, there is pressure to recover costs as quickly as possible through volume sales.

LOGO and the Classroom

The claims for the virtues of LOGO have been loud, insistent, and consistent since the late 1970s when it was first introduced. For example, two strong supporters, Maddux and Johnson, make the following claims for teaching children to program in LOGO:[22]

- Logo can provide a success [sic] experience for children who are accustomed to failure.
- Interesting things can be done with Logo by children who have received only a brief orientation to the language.
- The self-correcting nature of programming eliminates the need for adult correction for students who are sensitive to such correction.
- Logo may help promote social interaction and peer acceptance among children who are deficient in these important characteristics.

But perhaps the most controversial claim is that LOGO will improve general problem solving abilities, that there will be a transference from programming skills to conceptual skills in other disciplines, and that LOGO will unlock the natural curiosity and desire to learn inherent in all children, independent of their social and economic backgrounds—a sweeping claim, to say the least. Is there any evidence in support of all these claims?

An important early study of LOGO was carried out in two classrooms in an independent school in Manhattan by researchers from Bank Street College's Center for Children and Technology, between September 1981 and February 1984. One classroom included eight and nine year olds, and the other, eleven and twelve year olds, all of mixed socioeconomic backgrounds and achievement levels. Space does not permit a discussion of the experiments and methodology of this lengthy and careful study, so we will limit our presentation to a report of the most salient results.[23]

1. Teachers had a great deal of difficulty deciding on their approach to the use of LOGO in the classroom, between a structured environment and an environment to promote self-discovery.
2. Over the course of two years, students varied greatly in their interests and accomplishments. Teachers had difficulty in reaching those students who did not naturally take to the language.
3. Many students found the underlying logical structure of LOGO formidable and were unable to overcome their difficulties to the point that they could write even simple programs.
4. Teachers had difficulty rationalizing the role of LOGO into the ongoing classroom work. "Is Logo a legitimate part of the curriculum? And, if so, does it fit in as programming or math, or does it belong elsewhere? What can students be expected to learn from their efforts involving Logo: specific programming or math concepts, general problem-solving skills, or both?"

This final point is crucial and the fact that it still remains unanswered after such a lengthy study casts serious doubts on the validity of the strong, optimistic claims made for LOGO such as those of Maddux and Johnson. One other result from this study pertaining to this issue is reported in a paper by Pea, Kurland, and Hawkins. It is particularly clear cut and unequivocal:[24]

> On the basis of these results, we concluded that students who had spent a year programming did not differ on various developmental comparisons of the effectiveness of their plans and their processes of planning from same-age controls who had not learned to program.

They offer a number of suggestions to explain their results and are still enthusiastic about LOGO but caution that considerably more effort is required in curriculum planning, teacher training, and other areas before the hopes of the LOGO community can be realized. Other LOGO enthusiasts argue that these results do not *prove* that the strong claims are not valid.[25] Short of analyzing the concept of proof in empirical educational studies, it is impossible to deal with this criticism. Suffice it to say that the idea of LOGO remains appealing and the story is still being written.

One hopes that the computer, properly used, can be a liberating force, fostering what Ivan Illich, a well-known critic of technological fixes, calls conviviality.[26] Illich does not mention computers explicitly, but they have the potential to be tools for conviviality par excellence through the growing use of electronic mail, multimedia, teleconferencing, and other information and communication resources.

Gender Issues

Prior to the arrival of the computer, girls were not expected to do well in science and mathematics, and these expectations were often self-fulfilling, as the educational system did not encourage their participation in these areas. The current evidence is that the computer, in the classroom or as an extracurricular activity, has been largely monopolized by boys in the elementary schools and later by young men in the senior high schools. There seems to be a certain inevitability about this situation, given the general atmosphere pervasive in society at large about the "proper" role of women. Consider some of the results reported in the Second National Survey of Instructional Uses of School Computers, commissioned by the U.S. Department of Education in 1985. On the positive side, girls constituted about half of the students using computers in word processing and half overall, including elective computer programming classes and computer-game playing, across all grades from kindergarten to grade twelve. In playing computer games in middle and high schools, however, the number of boys did exceed the number of girls. In extracurricular activities, either before or after regular classes, boys outnumbered girls by a three to one margin; that is, boys seem to control computer clubs. Finally, the following results reveal some built-in biases of teachers who use computers in the classroom:[27]

> Individual computer-using teachers were asked to indicate the sex of the three students most affected by their experience with computers in school. About 62% of the students identified by elementary school teachers were boys; at the secondary school level, about

> 67% of those mentioned were boys. Moreover, the first person named by each teacher was overwhelmingly likely to be a boy—74% of the first mentioned at the elementary level and 78% at the secondary level.

Furthermore, when girls were mentioned it was typically because computers helped them academically, whereas boys were likely affected by becoming more confident, more disciplined, and more motivated. Surely female students of all ages need to be encouraged to participate and to excel in mathematics, science, and computer science.

The Technological Fix

Computers are a valuable and undoubtedly useful tool. They have an important role to play in the educational system, as they do in the rest of society. But they are only one part of the educational process. As Joseph Weizenbaum has said, "Children may not be motivated in school because they're hungry or they've been abused at home or for any number of reasons. Simply introducing computers avoids the question of why children may not be motivated in school. It converts a social problem into a technological problem and then tries to solve it by technical means."[28]

The limitations of technology in providing the answer to educational problems are revealed in a simple insight underlying what has come to be called the Comer process, after Dr. James Comer, a Yale University psychiatrist: ". . . a child's home life affects his performance in school, and . . . if schools pay attention to all the influences on a child, most problems can be solved before they get out of control. The Comer process . . . encourages a flexible, almost custom-tailored approach to each child."[29] These observations seem so obvious and so unglamorous compared to high technology that it is not surprising that it has taken so long for adequate attention to be paid to them.

SUMMARY

Computers are rapidly becoming a pervasive feature of the educational scene. Will they transform education or are they just one more educational novelty, as were radio, film, and television?

Almost all the schools in America have computers. They are used to teach programming and such subjects as arithmetic, geography, history, and so forth. They are also used to play games. The market for hardware and software is large and growing. Apple is currently leading, followed by Commodore and (Tandy) Radio Shack. Television and magazine advertisements by these manufacturers and others suggest to parents that their children will suffer if computers are not made available to them at school and at home.

Computer-based education can be divided into a number of categories. The major areas are computer-assisted instruction (CAI) and computer-aided learning (CAL).

CAI includes such activities as drill and practice, tutorial (in which new material is presented), simulation (a means to explore the behavior of complex systems), and games.

Among the major efforts in early CAI were PLATO, originally developed at the University of Illinois and later a collaborative effort with Control Data Corp., and TICCIT, developed by the MITRE Corp. These large systems have been succeeded by thousands of programs designed for use on microcomputers.

CAL puts the computer itself at the center of the learning experience, not as a tool to acquire knowledge in other areas. It is argued by CAL's foremost proponent Seymour Papert, one of the creators of the programming language LOGO, that an understanding of some of the important principles associated with programming can improve a child's performance in other areas of the curriculum. Some reported experiments have not supported this claim.

At universities, computers are being used in almost every area of instruction. Some universities are requiring that incoming students purchase or lease their own microcomputers. They will be used for word processing, assignments, library searches, and communicating with fellow students and professors. Comprehensive communication systems to support the growing number of computers have been initiated at most universities. The growing relation between universities and the Department of Defense is of some concern given the amount of military funding received by computer science researchers. Also of concern is the degree to which industry is cooperating in joint research efforts with faculty members and the impact of such efforts, as well as the military influence, on the academic program.

Computer literacy is a controversial area with many opinions about whether or not it constitutes a legitimate discipline. Other areas of computer applications in education have not yet proven their value. They seem to improve the rate of acquisition of knowledge in certain fact-driven areas, but even here they seem to be no more cost effective than other methods of instruction or remediation.

There is a basic concern that computers will be viewed as a technological fix to educational problems that are rooted in socioeconomic difficulties.

NOTES

1. Summary, *Power On! New Tools for Teaching and Learning* (Washington, D.C.: United States Congress, Office of Technology Assessment, OTA-SET-380, September 1988), p. 36.
2. Joseph Berger, "Computers Proliferating in Classrooms," *The New York Times,* August 9, 1989, p. B 8.
3. Maria Shao, John Carey, and Elizabeth Ehrlich, "Computers in School: A Loser? Or a Lost Opportunity?" *Business Week,* July 17, 1989, pp. 108–110.
4. Theresa Barry, "PCs in Education: Reading, Writing, and Algorithms," *Datamation,* December 15, 1987, pp. 43–46, 48.
5. Mark Ivey, "Long-Distance Learning Gets an 'A' at Last," *Business Week,* May 9, 1989, pp. 108–110.
6. David Moursand, as quoted in Deborah Soijka, "CAI Catches On," *Datamation* (Cahners Publishing Co.), March, 1981, p. 188.
7. Peter H. Lewis, "Navigating through a Job Hunt," *The New York Times,* September 18, 1988, p. F 13.
8. D. Midian Kurland and Laura C. Kurland, "Computer Applications in Education: A Historical Overview," in Joseph F. Traub, Barbara J. Grosz, Butler W. Lampson, and Nils J. Nilsson, *Annual Review of Computer Science, Vol. 2* (Palo Alto, California: Annual Reviews Inc., 1987), pp. 317–358.
9. For more information, see David Godfrey and Sharon Sterling, *The Elements of CAL* (Victoria, British Columbia, Canada: Press Porcepic, 1982).

10. *Ibid., Power On!*, p. 20.
11. Harold F. Rahmlow, Robert C. Fratini, and James R. Ghesquiere, *PLATO, The Instructional Design Library, Vol. 30* (Englewood Cliffs, New Jersey: Educational Technology, 1980).
12. M. David Merrill, Edward W. Schneider, and Kathie A. Fletcher, *TICCIT, The Instructional Design Library, Vol. 40* (Englewood Cliffs, New Jersey: Educational Technology, 1980).
13. From *Mindstorms: Children, Computers and Wonderful Ideas*, by Seymour Papert. Copyright © 1980 by Basic Books, Inc., p. 5. Reprinted by permission of Basic Books, a division of Harper-Collins Publishers. This book is perhaps the best source for learning more about LOGO, especially its principles and long-term goals.
14. *Ibid.*, p. 180.
15. Brian Hawkins, vice president of computing and information services at Brown University, as quoted in Leila Davis, "The University Connection," *Datamation*, September 15, 1989, p. 69.
16. *Ibid.*
17. Willie Schatz, "U.S. Computer Research's Basic Dilemma," *Datamation*, December 1, 1989, p. 45.
18. Seth Shulman, "Scrambling for Research Dollars," *Technology Review*, January 1990, pp. 14–15.
19. Ronald E. Anderson and Daniel L. Klasson, "A Conceptual Framework for Developing Computer Literacy Instruction," (St. Paul: Minnesota Educational Computing Consortium, November 5, 1980), p. 7.
20. Bill N. Lacy, "The Pencil Revolution," *Newsweek*, March 19, 1984, p. 17.
21. Kurland and Kurland, "Computer Applications in Education," pp. 336–338.
22. Cleborne D. Maddux and D. LaMont Johnson, *Logo: Methods and Curriculum for Teachers* (Binghamton, New York: The Haworth Press, 1988), p. 13.
23. Jan Hawkins, "The Interpretation of Logo in Practice," in Roy D. Pea and Karen Sheingold (eds.), *Mirrors of Kinds: Patterns of Experience in Educational Computing* (Norwood, New Jersey: Ablex Publishing Corp., 1987), pp. 3–34.
24. Roy D. Pea, D. Midian Kurland, and Jan Hawkins, "Logo and the Development of Thinking Skills," In Pea and Sheingold, *Mirrors of Minds*, pp. 178–197.
25. Maddux and Johnson, *Logo*, pp. 78–87.
26. Ivan Illich, *Tools for Conviviality* (New York: Harper & Row/Perennial Library, 1973).
27. Henry Jay Becker, "Using Computers for Instruction," *Byte*, February 1987, pp. 149 ff. Reprinted from BYTE magazine, February 1987, © McGraw-Hill, Inc., New York.
28. Joseph Weizenbaum as quoted in Alison B. Bass, "Computers in the Classroom," *Technology Review*, April 1987, p. 61.
29. Michel Marriott, "A New Road to Learning: Teaching the Whole Child," *The New York Times*, June 13, 1990, pp. A 1, B 8.

ADDITIONAL READINGS

Introduction

Becker, Henry Jay. "Computer Use in United States Schools, 1989: An Initial Report of U.S. Participation in the I.E.A. Computers in Education Survey." Paper presented at the 1990 meeting of the American Educational Research Association.

Costanzo, William V. *The Electronic Text: Learning to Write, Read, and Reason with Computers:* Englewood Cliffs, New Jersey: Educational Technology Publications, 1989.

"Educational Computing." Special Section, *Byte*, February 1987.

"The Technology Revolution Comes to Education." Special Advertising Section, *Business Week*, November 12, 1990.

Computer-Assisted Instruction

Bork, Alfred. *Learning with Computers*. Bedford, Massachusetts: Digital Equipment, 1981.
Burton, Richard. "Diagnosing Bugs in a Simple Procedural Skill." In Sleeman, D. and Brown, J. S. (eds.). *Intelligent Tutoring Systems*. New York: Academic Press, 1982.
Langhorne, Mary Jo, Danham, Jean O., Gross, June F., and Rehmke, Denise, *Teaching with Computers: A New Menu for the '90s*. Phoenix, Arizona: Oryx Press, 1989.
Lovis, Frank and Tagg, E. D. (eds.). *Computers in Education: Proceedings of the First European Conference on Computers in Education*. Amsterdam: North-Holland, 1988.
Taylor, Robert (ed.). *The Computer in the School: Tutor, Tool, Tutee*. New York: Teachers College Press (Columbia University), 1980.

Computer-Assisted Learning

Byte, Special Issue on LOGO, August 1982.
Goldberg, Adele. "Educational Uses of Dynabook." *Computers & Education*, 3(4), 1979, pp. 247–266.
Lawler, Robert W. and Yazdani, Masoud (eds.). *Artificial Intelligence and Education, Volume One*. Norwood, New Jersey: Ablex Publishing, 1987.
Maurer, H. (ed.). *Computer Assisted Learning: 2nd International Conference, ICCAL '90*. New York: Springer-Verlag, 1989.
Schostak, John (ed.). *Breaking into the Curriculum: The Impact of Information Technology on Schooling*. New York: Methuen, 1988.

Computers in Higher Education

Alexander, Michael. "Colleges Seek Corporate Money." *Computerworld*, February 18, 1991, p. 80.
Broad, William J. "As Science Moves Into Commerce, Openness is Lost." *The New York Times*, May 24, 1988, pp. 21–26.
Chen, Katherine T. "Education: Trouble Waiting in the Wings." *IEEE Spectrum*, November 1989, pp. 60–64.
Deutsch, Claudia H. "Corporate Takeovers." *The New York Times, Education Life*, Section 4A, August 6, 1989, pp. EDUC 42–44.
Kiesler, Sara and Sproull, Lee (eds.). *Computing and Change on Campus*. New York: Cambridge University Press, 1987.
Leinfuss, Emily. "R&D Without the Fee." *Datamation*, May 1, 1990, pp. 93–95.
Minksy, Leonard and Noble, David. "Corporate Takeover on Campus." *The Nation*, October 30, 1989, front cover, pp. 494–496.
Noble, Douglas D. "Cockpit Cognition: Education, the Military and Cognitive Engineering." *Artificial Intelligence & Society*, 3(4), October–December 1989, pp. 271–296.
Pastore, Richard. "PCs Take Command on Campus." *Computerworld*, March 4, 1991, p. 40.

Computer Literacy

Van Dyke, Carolynn. "Taking 'Computer Literacy' Literally." *Communications of the ACM*, 30(5), May 1987, pp. 366–374.
Wells, Ian. "Teaching Computer Literacy." *Impact* (The Newsletter of the Social Impact Group of the Boston Computer Society), Winter 1990, pp. 4–5.

Issues and Problems

Moonen, Jef. "Impact of Computer Technologies on Education." Invited paper for G. X. Ritter (ed.), *Information Processing 89*. Amsterdam: Elsevier Science Publishers (North-Holland), 1989, pp. 553–559.

Nathan, Joe. *Micro-Myths: Exploring the Limits of Learning with Computers*. Minneapolis: Winston Press, 1985.

Robins, Kevin and Webster, Frank. *The Technical Fix: Education, Computers and Industry*. New York: St. Martin's Press, 1989.

"Symposium: Visions for the Use of Computers in Classroom Instruction." *Harvard Educational Review*, 59(1), February 1989, pp. 50–86, and "Responses to 'Visions for the Use of Computers in Classroom Instruction'." *Harvard Educational Review*, 59(2), May 1989, pp. 206–225.

7

GOVERNMENT AND COMPUTERS

All government, indeed every human benefit and enjoyment, every virtue, and every prudent act, is founded on compromise and barter. We balance inconveniences; we give and take — we remit some rights that we may enjoy others. . . . Man acts from motives relative to his interests; and not on metaphysical speculations.

Edmund Burke, *Speech on Conciliation with America,* March 22, 1775

INTRODUCTION

Governments exist to serve their citizens, and presumably computers are playing a role in this endeavor. How, and for what purposes, do governments use computers? Their primary activity is record-keeping—the gathering, entering, maintenance, processing, and updating of files on individual, families, organizations, and companies. The government might actually be thought of as *the* great record-keeper, whose insatiable appetite for information arises from the belief that the continual accumulation of information inevitably leads to the provision of better services. The U.S. government is the single largest user of computers. Many of the applications are well known—taxation, social security, census, health, education and welfare, agriculture, and so forth. Other areas are national security and defense, and research.

Clearly, the government is more than simply a user of computers. By virtue of being such a major purchaser of computer technology, the government tends to set standards and shape the form of future developments. The needs of the Census Bureau played an important role in the early development of the computer. In carrying out its responsibility for the nation's security, the Department of Defense (DOD) has spurred research and development in integrated circuits, programming languages, operating systems, security methods, and fault-tolerant designs. The National Aeronautics and Space Administration (NASA) is concerned with such issues as miniaturization, low power consumption, high reliability, and resistance to the effects of vibration and weightlessness.

Another area of growing importance is the increasing involvement of computers in the political process. This new development in the use of computer technology makes it possible to produce detailed mailing lists of voters who will respond as desired to specific issues. The use of computer models to predict voter behavior is also increasing in popularity. Computer applications in war include the computerized battlefield, the use of computers in war games, and the increasing reliance on computers to make nuclear launch decisions.

Many other areas of activity that involve computer applications and the role of government will be dealt with in further chapters. Because government is intricately involved in so many phases of society, it is inevitable that government-related issues turn up in many areas. In relation to computers and the law, such issues as the legal protection of software, the use of computers by law enforcement agencies, and computer crime, are paramount. The federal government is being called upon to take an active role in directing the future of American industry. In the communications industry, steps in regulation will have significant repercussions with respect to the computer networks spanning the country. And how is international data flow to be supervised and controlled? Finally, one of the major concerns of the public is the question of privacy of computer records. This extremely important issue (discussed in Chapter 9) includes problems of government legislation and such related issues as freedom of information.

INFORMATION PROCESSING: ISSUES AND PROBLEMS

Background

The General Services Administration (GSA) produces a semiannual survey of computers and peripheral equipment in the federal government. Computers, or central processing units (CPUs) as they are referred to in this survey, are counted only if they exceed a few thousand dollars, and thus personal computers, of which there are several hundred thousand, are not included in the count. Halfway through fiscal year (FY) 1988, the total number of CPUs (given the above restriction) in the federal government was 36,236, and the total dollar value of CPUs and peripheral equipment was about $7.4 billion.[1] These numbers and those that follow show how the major computing resources are distributed in the federal government, as an indication of which departments and agencies have benefitted most from the technology, or needed to. Consider Table 7-1, which provides figures on the distribution of computers in the major departments and agencies.

Not surprisingly the three branches of the armed forces have 7,583 of the 12,933 largest computers in the government, or over 58%, a clear reflection of the importance of the defense establishment and its heavy dependence on high technology. In fact, over 40% of the entire dollar value of data processing equipment in the government resides in the three military services. Three years previously, the total number of CPUs was 18,183 (compared to the 36,236 mentioned above); thus in three years the number almost doubled, a very high growth rate indeed, to say nothing of significant increases in PCs as well. The entire

TABLE 7-1

DISTRIBUTION OF CPUs BY SIZE IN SELECTED DEPARTMENTS
OF THE U.S. FEDERAL GOVERNMENT HALFWAY THROUGH FY 1988.[2]

	Federal Government Departments[a b]							
CPU Size	Army	Airforce	Navy	Energy	Treasury	State	NASA	Total
Very Large[c]	41	31	73	64	—	—	—	297
Large[d]	55	43	119	10	64	—	—	338
Medium[e]	626	752	607	481	121	481	—	3,067
Small[f]	2,028	1,151	2,057	1,212	—	—	1,098	9,231
Totals	2,750	1,977	2,856	1,767				12,933

a. There are many other departments and agencies not shown.
b. Dashes indicate relatively small numbers.
c. $4 million and over.
d. $1–4 million.
e. $500 thousand–$1 million.
f. $50–500 thousand.

federal information systems budget has increased from $9.1 billion in 1982 to $17.4 billion in 1988 (or $14.1 billion in 1982 dollars), a faster growth rate than the rest of the federal budget.[3] One is tempted to wonder about this continual and rapid growth in expenditures on computer technology. The business of government seems to grow much faster than the population it is supposed to serve.

Granted, new needs are recognized, new methods of identifying problems are developed, new data is gathered, and new statistics are computed. But somehow the growth in computing power exceeds these requirements; it almost seems to be obeying some natural law of unrestricted expansion, driven perhaps by the ambition of managers and administrators. This view is not necessarily a criticism of the beneficial aspects of computer use, but is the expression of a concern about growth for growth's sake.

Automated Bureaucracy

Even before computer systems became prevalent, governments were regularly subject to the criticism that they were too bureaucratic. The most straightforward interpretation of this charge is that bureaucracies frequently are so concerned with rules and procedures that they forget that their purpose is to deal with people and their problems. Thus, it is feared that computer systems will serve bureaucratic interests, not the public's, by further shielding government workers from direct responsibility. Furthermore, how do such systems affect the quality of decisions? Are citizens still assured of due process when computers are part of the decision-making process? Can the high-level policymakers in Congress and the executive branch be sure that the bureaucracy is accountable?

It may be useful to provide more detail on the activities of the Office of Management of the Budget (OMB), given authority over federal information functions under the Paperwork Reduction Act of 1980. Within OMB, the Office of Information and Regulatory Affairs (OIRA) was established with specific authority over "general information policy, reduction of paperwork burden, federal statistical activity, records management activities, the privacy and security of records, agency sharing and dissemination of records, and the acquisition and use of automatic data processing and telecommunications and other information technology for managing information resources."[4] With respect to information policies for the federal government, the 1980 Act specified the following:[5]

> 1. The development, implementation, and oversight of uniform information resources management policies and guidelines.
> 2. The initiation and review of proposals for legislation, regulations, and agency procedures to improve information management.
> 3. The coordination, through budget review and other means, of agency information practices.
> 4. The promotion of greater information sharing among agencies through the federal information locator system (FILS), the review of budget proposals, and other means.
> 5. The evaluation of agency information practices.
> 6. The oversight of planning and research regarding the federal collection, processing, storage, transmission, and use of information.

These information policies are meant to accomplish the main purpose of the Paperwork Act—to reduce the amount of paper the government handles. Just transforming paper into computer memory is not the answer. More computers do not necessarily mean less information is handled; in fact, quite the opposite may be the case. Thus, OMB is obliged by the Act to determine, "whether the collection of information by an agency is necessary for the proper performance of the functions of the agency, including whether the information will have practical utility for the agency." Beyond its responsibility for paperwork clearance, OMB must

- prepare an inventory of all information collection activities,
- assign agencies as the primary collectors for other agencies,
- determine the goals for the reduction of information collection,
- monitor compliance with the recommendations of the Commission on Federal Paperwork,
- design and operate FILS, and
- report to Congress on an annual basis.

A major thrust of the Act is to reduce the paperwork burden on the general public by minimizing the government's requirements for information. In 1986, the Act was amended by the Paperwork Reduction Reauthorization Act, which called for additional reductions in the collection burden:[6]

> 1. [OMB was] directed to establish goals for agencies to reduce Federal paperwork burdens by five percent for each of the next four consecutive years beginning with FY 1987,
> 2. [the Act] clarified the treatment of paperwork requirements contained in regulations as being similar to other information collections, and

3. expanded the opportunities for meaningful public comments on agency information collection.

Interestingly, in 1988 OMB had to review 2,860 requests from agencies to approve new or existing information collections. Of these, 2,727, or 95%, were approved. The disapproval rate has been declining steadily since 1981 as collections not worthy of approval have been discontinued and as agencies have become increasingly familiar with the standards of OMB.

Problems at the Internal Revenue Service (IRS)

The activities of the IRS affect every taxpayer in the country, a rather large number given that some 110 million individual returns were filed in 1989. Reports of problems at the IRS appear with some regularity—witness 1985 when problems with the computer system threatened to bring operations to a halt. The IRS is currently in the midst of a massive $10.7 billion program to "design and acquire a new network of computer equipment and software to process returns during the next decade."[7] As the IRS itself has reported, however, all is not going well because of some very common failings in the design and implementation processes of very large information systems, such as "a lack of technical expertise, an inability to keep track of costs and a failure to develop a unified plan describing how the agency's thousands of computers—mainframe, desktop and portable—would work together under the new structure."[8]

Reports prepared by the agency's Internal Audit Division between November 1987 and January 1990 voice a number of criticisms expanding on the points made above. For example, one of the problems is that the IRS seems unable to carry out negotiations to prevent industry from overbilling, a somewhat surprising situation for the nation's tax collectors. Of special concern is that despite the fact that the new system will provide increased access for large numbers of employees to the vast amount of highly sensitive data held by the IRS, the IRS's risk management program "does not provide adequate evaluation of the security and integrity of service computer-based information systems."[9] All these issues assume considerable weight given the fact that the computing resources of the IRS are second only to those of the Pentagon in the federal government.

Information Systems in the Department of Defense (DOD)

In 1982, DOD undertook the long and expensive process of modernizing its 1960s system for planning and monitoring military activities, World Wide Military Command and Control System (WWMCCS). In 1989, after expenditures of nearly $500 million, "the users are outraged, the system is unfinished, responsibility for the project has been transferred, its name has been changed twice and no one is entirely sure what will happen now."[10] It seems to be a classic case of how not to design a large, complex information system: "poor communications with users, improperly designed specifications, missed deadlines, budget cuts. . . ."[11] The history is quite convoluted, but under the plan to modernize information systems, WWMCCS Information Systems (WIS) was created in 1982, under the control of the Air Force, to provide, among other things, an electronic message handling component with automated recognition of security level clearance, local and global networks, a coherent software development, maintenance, and expansion system, and a system for planning and executing operations.

In 1987, the government accounting office (GAO) reported that a major component was more than one year behind schedule, and the Air Force itself admitted that another was also delayed by a year. In 1989, WIS was transferred from the Electronics System Division of the U.S. Air Force Systems Command to the Data Support Center of the Defense Communications Agency, within the Pentagon itself, and renamed WAM (WWMCCS Automatic Data Processing Modernization Program). However interesting the military's penchant for building acronyms upon acronyms, it is clear that much has been spent and much needs to be spent before an adequate system is in place. Impatient users even began buying their own equipment and building their own systems. The security requirements were never met and new attempts are in place to establish them, albeit with reduced turnaround time and reduced system capabilities. Uniformity of equipment has been abandoned and more realistic goals have been set. A very expensive project has yet to be realized and the consequences on the day-to-day operation of this most sensitive branch of government are impossible to determine.

Applications in Congress

Up to this point, our discussion has been focussed on information technology in the federal government, meaning the executive branch and departments, but for years Congress and other legislative bodies have been developing information systems to aid in their work. Robert Lee Chartrand of the Congressional Research Office, in reviewing the progress made over the past several years, has noted that most of the recommendations made in 1966 for improved applications have indeed been implemented. Among these are the following: status of pending legislation, direct access to legislative research, current information on issues up for vote, current schedule of committee meetings and hearings, histories of committee action, selected readings of interest to each congressman, and constituent information.[12] More recently and not surprisingly, Congress has witnessed the appearance of microcomputers, electronic mail, Fax, telecommunication facilities, and graphics equipment.

It is expected that both houses of Congress would gradually acquire all the technology necessary to keep up with the growth in activities and the demands on available time. What is of particular interest is how the technology has permitted, and indeed encouraged, aggressive moves into new practices that were not previously possible. Consider the following applications and the impact that they have both on the operation of Congress, as a whole, and the performance of individual Representatives and Senators:[13]

Legislative Analysis Applications. These include straightforward information retrieval—bibliographic citations as well as full text—and the use of advanced models to delineate consequences of proposed legislation. Note that such systems tend to move Congress towards more equity with the executive branch, especially with respect to information matters.

Record-Keeping Applications. Among these are electronic voting in the House of Representatives, which by facilitating the voting process has resulted in an increased number of votes and has enabled the closer monitoring of voting behavior, permitting the exercise of party discipline.

Congressional Communication. Members of Congress receive large amounts of communication from their constituents and other interest groups, from their colleagues, and from their staffs. One aim of the communication application is to serve Congressional members' self-interest by promoting their images to maintain or to further their political ambitions. One example is the use of computers and laser printers to produce typewriter-quality letters in vast numbers, individually targeted to voters, in response to the rapidly increasing volume of congressional mail. Another is the use of electronic mail to facilitate communication from Washington with distant congressional districts.

Presumably, the technology should also improve the quality of work by providing up-to-the-minute information necessary in the drafting of effective legislation. Such improvements, if they have actually occurred, are not readily obvious. What does seem obvious is that the advantage of incumbents in the electoral process has been increased by the use of information technology. Those attempting to unseat current officeholders also face a publicly supported technological network at the service of the current Representative or Senator.

THE POLITICAL PROCESS

Computers are used to register voters prior to elections and to tabulate the results on election night. As a consequence of the nation-wide census held every ten years, election boundaries must be redrawn to reflect the new population distribution. Computers play an important role in this process of reapportionment and have aroused considerable controversy for their alleged technological contribution to gerrymandering. They are also employed to sample public opinion, predict the outcome of elections, and maintain detailed lists of supporters. Already fears have been voiced that the political party with sufficient financial resources to afford the best programmers and computers will have a major advantage in the electoral process.

Getting Elected

It requires a great deal of money to get elected to political office. The role of fundraiser has been assuming increasing importance. Traditionally, supporters have been identified and then canvassed for contributions during the campaign. But increasingly sophisticated fundraising methods have been developed that take advantage of the computer's abilities.

Mailing lists of supporters are carefully organized in terms of ethnic background, income, education, age, sex, and opinion on a number of issues. Also stored in the computer are texts of fundraising letters, each focussing on a particular issue. Such systems are maintained by the political parties and by corporate political-action committees (PACs), legislated by Congress to collect money for political candidates. Whenever a political issue surfaces, the appropriate letter form is selected, and "personally" addressed by the computer to those supporters with an appropriate profile. The rate of successful return has increased dramatically.

These techniques have also been used to mobilize support for political causes, in which case letters and telegrams are solicited rather than money. A system for this purpose requires a moderately-sized computer, considerable storage, a high-speed printer, folding-sealing-stamping equipment, and people to do data entry. The ability to target voters along ethnic, regional, religious, or any other lines results in more efficient fundraising and more effective pressure tactics. But the public should be aware of what lies behind current solicitation practices.

The low price of personal computers means that they are now readily available for almost every political campaign in the land. Something like 50,000 individuals are elected in each election cycle.[14] Besides the important fundraising activities, computers are also used to plan the candidate's schedule, organize press releases, plan questionnaires, and schedule volunteer workers. Basic financial programs can be used to monitor donations and expenditures in order to ensure that sufficient funds are available for the entire duration of the campaign. A number of software packages have been developed exclusively for use in election campaigns to analyze previous election results, keep track of supporters, and perform financial analysis.

What Does the Voter Want?

Nowadays, people are asked their opinion about everything: their favorite soap, television show, and politician. There are public polls such as Gallup, Harris, and Roper, and many private ones are done for elected officials as well as candidates. The computer is now used to store survey results and to perform sophisticated statistical analysis and projections. Over the years, models have been constructed that can predict with reasonable accuracy, on the basis of a careful sampling of voter preferences, the outcome of elections on the local, state, or federal level. A danger of such models is that both elected officials and candidates for political office will begin to tailor their opinions in the directions determined by the models. A basic conflict for elected officials will be heightened—to vote their conscience or to represent the political views of their constituency, when these are in opposition.

There may be more computer polling methods in the future. In Columbus, Ohio, about 30,000 homes, under an experimental system called QUBE, now terminated, were wired up to a central computer by a two-way communication system. QUBE has been used to sample public opinion in a quick and painless fashion. A question put to the subscribers appears on their television set. Viewers press either the yes or no button on their handsets when the vote is being taken. Each home on the network is briefly scanned, the votes are accumulated, and the results appear on the screen in a few seconds. Could (or should) such a polling method be used within the current political system? With this method in operation, a well-publicized issue would be presented to the voters. Advocates pro and con would be given air time to present their views in a variety of formats. Finally, a vote would be taken, and then what? Should a vote of this kind be binding? Is it similar to a plebiscite?

Many questions must be answered before so-called instantaneous or electronic polling can become part of the democratic process. The fundamental issue turns on whether or not democracy can function as an extended Athenian marketplace. Supposedly, democracy began in Athens, where the citizens of that city state (not the women or the slaves) decided issues of concern in open debate and public vote. Perhaps modern communication networks and computers can recreate the best features of that noble experiment. As might be expected, there would be a number of problems. How is a question to be formulated? How is the voting process itself to be monitored to ensure that only legitimate voters actually vote? How is the security of the central computers to be guaranteed? All these questions may be beside the main point—what benefits will actually accrue by integrating electronic polling into the current system?

How Are the Votes Counted?

> During the past quarter of a century, with hardly anyone noticing, the inner workings of democracy have been computerized. All our elections, from mayor to President, are counted locally, in about ten thousand five hundred political jurisdictions, and gradually, since 1964, different kinds of computer-based voting systems have been installed in town after town, city after city, county after county.[15]

On the face of it, computerized voting and counting would seem to promise efficient, quick, and error-free reporting of election results, and for the most part it does. But there are a number of worrisome cases that suggest that program errors and manipulation may be more endemic than previously realized. In an ongoing study since 1984, the State of Illinois has reported finding errors in the counting instructions of one fifth of all computer programs examined. Apparently the local testing programs, which typically use only about fifty votes, had not uncovered these errors. Thus, a piece of program code that *kicks in* after a few hundred votes could be inserted into a counting program to produce whatever results are desired. Instead of paying people to vote a certain way, as has been done, programs could be altered to steal elections, unless adequate safeguards are in place.

In the summary to his study of computer voting, Roy Saltman offered the following cautionary remarks:[16]

> While vote-tallying using telephones or stations similar to automatic teller machines is technologically feasible, the decision to implement such a system must be based on more fundamental factors. Any installed system must meet political and economic requirements, as well as technical requirements of accuracy and reliability. Political needs include equal access by individuals, the ability to verify registration, and the ability of the voters to vote in secret without intimidation. Internal controls must be implementable to demonstrate the correctness of the reported results.

Who Won?

For many people, the most exciting and interesting part of the election process is election night, as the returns are presented to the nation over the three television networks. In reporting the 1984 election, the networks for the first time used real-time computer graphics to display the results. Certain graphic information such as the candidates' pictures, maps of the states, and the forms of charts and graphs were prepared in advance. As the returns flooded in, the existing graphic information was combined with the new information and presented in a variety of colors and forms. A spokesman for CBS news noted, "In 1984, for the first time, we will be able to do true real-time, data-dependent images and animation."[17] (High resolution, three-dimensional animation in a wide range of colors must await another election.)

Computer models for predicting election outcomes on the basis of interviews with selected early voters have come under some criticism. In 1984 the landslide for President Reagan was anticipated quite early, but there was little surprise as most polls had predicted such a result. In the 1980 presidential election, however, many voters in the western part of the country apparently did not bother voting because the television networks declared President Reagan an early winner. While these lost votes probably did not affect the presidential election, they did have an effect on local and state elections. It has been suggested that early computer predictions should not be announced until the polls have closed everywhere. Staggered hours might be a solution. In any event, the power of computer models to affect the electoral process must be recognized and steps must be taken to remedy the situation.

THE NATION'S DEFENSE

A major responsibility of the federal government is to defend the nation from both internal and external enemies. This is certainly reflected in the fact that the defense budget is the major component of the total budget. The Department of Defense (DOD), with its vast resources, has taken a lead in the development of both computer hardware and software. Much of the early research in integrated circuits was funded by DOD for military purposes. Given the sheer size of the military establishment, problems of organization are serious. There is enormous difficulty in coordinating a world-wide enterprise consisting of millions of soldiers and civilian personnel and billions of dollars of equipment, while maintaining a high degree of military preparedness.

To maintain its large investment in advanced systems and to support new and risky projects, the Pentagon, in 1958, established an agency, DARPA (Defense Advanced Research Projects Agency), originally called ARPA, to fund research and development. This agency has had a major impact on semiconductors, computers, communication systems, applications, and artificial intelligence developments over the past thirty years. It has also exerted an enormous influence over the kind of research funded at U.S. universities and has thereby shaped the growth of computer science departments from their very inception.

The Computerized Battlefield

In the 1982 conflict between Britain and Argentina over the Faulkland Islands, a single $200,000 computer-guided missile, the French Exocet, demolished the British destroyer Sheffield, a $50 million warship. The power of computer-age weapons was frighteningly revealed. The general class of weapons with microprocessors are called precision-guided munitions (PGMs). Probably the most publicized and sophisticated of the PGMs is the cruise missile. It is programmed to fly a ground-hugging route to its target to avoid most radar, and has a microcomputer aboard with detailed topographic information about its route. During flight this computer can compare information received from its sensors with its programmed knowledge to keep the missile on course. Future versions are expected to be able to recognize their designated targets when they arrive, to reduce the possibility of being deceived by camouflage. After a 1,500-mile trip the cruise missile can hit a ten-foot-square target.

With weapons this smart, how necessary are people? Perhaps the goal of the next stage of warfare planning will be to remove people from the battlefield. Wars of the future might be fought with computer-controlled aircraft in the sky and robots on the land. Robots with radio receivers and transmitters could lead troops into battle or into dangerous forays where the risk of death is high. Would this make the threat of launching a war less frightening?

In October 1983, DARPA announced the Strategic Computing Initiative (not to be confused with the Strategic Defense Initiative, popularly known as "Star Wars"), "to provide the United States with a broad line of machine intelligence technology and to demonstrate applications of the technology to critical problems of defense."[18] Claims have been made that AI can contribute in such areas as the representation of knowledge, complex pattern-matching, and general problem-solving. In 1985, among the areas of research funded by DARPA, the following were judged likely to produce the best payoff in military applications in each of the services:

Autonomous Vehicles. The goal is to develop an autonomous land vehicle, or robot truck, able to operate over rough terrain, up to thirty miles from its home base, at speeds of about forty miles per hour, with the ability to report acquired information. As research progresses, the vehicle may be able to operate for periods as long as a few weeks.

Pilot's Associate. DARPA director, Robert Cooper reported in his 1983 testimony to the House Armed Services Committee that the pilot's associate would, "respond to spoken commands by a pilot and carry them out without error. . . . [It could] activate surveillance sensors, interpret radar, optical and electronic intelligence and prepare appropriate weapons systems to counter hostile aircraft or missiles."[19]

Battle Management and Battle Assessment. The focus is on aircraft carriers in combat. The problem is to facilitate decision-making under uncertainty and the resolution of multiple, conflicting goals. Again, Cooper notes that, "revolutionary improvements in computing technology are required to provide more capable machine assistance in unanticipated combat situations."[20]

Some of the social issues associated with this program will be discussed later, but at this point we might note that the technical achievements have not been substantial. The fundamental theoretical problems underlying all of these applications are very difficult and lie at the heart of current research in AI. It is therefore not surprising that they have yielded only minimally to this massive military effort. DARPA is well aware of the difficulties and seems to be committed to long-term support. In addition to its AI-based projects, DARPA is also involved in other important computer systems: VHSIC (very high speed integrated circuits), supercomputers, parallel processing, neurocomputing, and high-speed networks in the gigabit range (10^9 bits per second).

One important example that high technology is not infallible and that the consequences can be dreadful is the incident that occurred in July of 1988 in the Persian Gulf. At that time, the prime enemy was Iran, and the cruiser U.S.S. Vincennes, in the mistaken belief that it was under attack, shot down an Iranian airliner, killing 290 civilians. The Vincennes was equipped with the most advanced technology available, the $1 billion Aegis system, under which the captain issues commands from the Combat Information Center (CIS), a windowless room deep within the ship, connected to the outside world by radar and communications systems and relying on computers to process and display information rapidly. The information available to the captain was instantaneous and accurate and yet 290 people died. Why? The simple lesson is that too much data may overwhelm sound judgment, especially under battle conditions, exactly when such an advanced system is designed to make its major contribution.

Navy investigators, after studying the computer tapes, judged the data to be accurate but that two "key misperceptions led to the skipper's decision to shoot."[21] A radar operator reported that an F-14 fighter was headed directly towards the Vincennes, even though radar showed it climbing on a typical flight path. This report must be understood in the context of well-known previous events in the Gulf, specifically the attack on the frigate Stark by the Iraqis in 1987, which resulted in the loss of 37 sailors. The Stark captain's hesitant response in the face of a possible attack created a subsequent urgency not to let it happen again. Thus, a preconceived scenario was in place, and even when someone in the CIS announced that the radar blip might be a commercial airliner, it was noted but not really factored into the decision process. One recommendation was to improve computer displays to show an aircraft's altitude beside its radar track. The larger lesson is that human memories and emotions, heightened by stressful battle conditions, may compromise even the most sophisticated information technology system with dire consequences for all.

Many of these concerns were forgotten in the aftermath of the Gulf War, fought during January and February of 1991. Considerable publicity was directed towards "smart weapons," such as the Tomahawk cruise missile and the Patriot antiballistic missile. In fact, computers were seen as a major factor in the surprisingly quick and overwhelmingly massive victory over Iraq. High technology received an enormous boost, and increased funding for a new generation of weapons seems assured. At the same time, two points should be noted: the actual technology was developed in the 1970s and early 1980s, and a postwar analysis raised serious doubts about the actual effectiveness of computer-based weapons.

War by Accident

> On June 3, 1980, at approximately 2:26 a.m. Eastern Daylight Time, the SAC Strategic Air Command command-post display system indicated that two SLBMs (Submarine Launched Ballistic Missiles) had been launched toward the United States. Eighteen seconds later, the display system showed an increased number of SLBM launches. . . . After a brief period, the warning displays at SAC indicated that Soviet ICBMs had been launched toward the United States. After another interval, the NMCC (National Military Command Center) command-post received indication that SLBMs were launched toward the United States.[22]

At NORAD headquarters a warning was announced that within 20 minutes as many as 20 million Americans would be killed by the Soviet attack. A decision to launch a U.S. attack would have to be made quickly. All across the country, airplanes took off, missiles were readied, and everyone was put on alert. Within six minutes of the beginning of the crisis, humans at NORAD realized that it had been a false alarm. A faulty chip had been discovered; the back-up system had worked, this time.

It is to be hoped that this event was an isolated one. Even with very low probability, the consequences of a mistake are so dreadful, one would be too many. The increasing dependence on computers not only to analyze data but also either to suggest actions or to take actions independently is seen by many as a real danger. The warnings have come from within the military establishment itself. The concern is that the need to respond quickly requires putting more reliance on the information processing capability of computers. Fred C. Ikle, a former Undersecretary of Defense for Policy in the Carter administration, has stated, "The more we rely on launch on warnings (or for that matter, the Soviets do) the greater the risk of accidental nuclear war."[23]

An organization of computer scientists called Computer Professionals for Social Responsibility (CPSR) represents those professionals concerned about the social implications of their work. They are particularly concerned about the role of computers in the defense of the nation. DARPA's plan to employ AI in a more central role has stimulated CPSR to express more forcefully its apprehension about an increased reliance on automated systems.

> Like all computer systems artificial intelligence systems may act inappropriately in unanticipated situations. Because of this fundamental limit on their reliability, we argue against using them for decision-making in situations of potentially devastating consequence.[24]

The authors of DARPA's "Strategic Computing Plan" are certainly aware that current computer programs cannot begin to deal with the complexities of modern warfare. They have turned to AI and automatic decision-making as a means of coping with uncertainty. Furthermore, the scope of the new systems is expected to extend to strategic weapons.

> Commanders remain particularly concerned about the role that autonomous systems would play during the transition from peace to hostilities when rules of engagement may be be altered quickly. An extremely stressing example of such a case is the projected defense against strategic nuclear missiles, where systems must react so rapidly that *it is likely that almost complete reliance will have to be placed on automated systems.* At the same time,

> the complexity and unpredictibility of factors affecting decisions will be very great. (Emphasis added.)[25]

Although there are risks and problems, DARPA sees no alternatives.

In the summer of 1983 a very popular movie, *War Games,* explored the possibility of how a computer system penetrated by a bright teenager might accidentally start a nuclear holocaust. The film showed the use of computers in decision-making as a way of bypassing the inability of many soldiers to fire missiles when ordered to do so in a realistic war situation. Interestingly enough, the military itself resisted this option, arguing that better training of its soldiers would suffice. In response to the popularity of *War Games,* Thomas C. Brandt (Assistant Deputy Chief of Staff for Combat Operations) of NORAD took great pains to assure the public, "No, that could not happen as it's portrayed in the film because of the nature of the system, because at NORAD people make decisions, not computers."[26] Despite such reassurances, the public is concerned because this is one area in which computer errors cannot easily be corrected afterwards.

The Strategic Defense Initiative

The possibility of nuclear war has been a fact of existence for most of us. It represents the terrifying vision of a technology that, once created and implemented, is inevitably loosed upon the world (recall the discussion in Chapter 2).

On March 23, 1983, President Reagan delivered his now famous "Star Wars" speech, launching the Strategic Defense Initiative. Its goal is the development of a comprehensive defense system to identify, intercept, and destroy all or most of an enemy's ballistic missiles. The debate over the feasibility of such a system and its impact on the current strategy of mutual deterrence has been raging ever since.

It is clear that enormous computational resources will necessarily be involved in the Star Wars project. Thus, it is not surprising that the computer science community has been split by a debate over the practicality of such a project and the morality of participation in its development. The decision whether or not to work on defense related activities is of course not unique to computer scientists. The most obvious example is that of the many physicists who, after the dropping of nuclear bombs over Japan, were reluctant to contribute to the development of hydrogen weapons. The role of scientists in service to the military is an old story rife with tales of ambition and regret.

In discussing the various issues associated with the Strategic Defense Initiative (SDI), the emphasis will be mainly on computer software; the very real and difficult physics problems will not be mentioned. It has been recognized by many critics of SDI that the most serious area of concern is software—the programs that are intended to direct the many computers in the wide variety of tasks necessary to make the system work. SDI will place unprecedented demands on software, to such a degree that many computer scientists have publicly expressed serious doubts about it ever working. And it must operate correctly the very first time it is used. Anyone familiar with writing even short programs knows that such an event is almost nonexistent.

> Because of the extreme demands on the system and our inability to test it, we will never be able to believe, with confidence, that we have succeeded. Most of the money spent will be wasted.[27]

In 1988, the Office of Technology Assessment (OTA) of the U.S. Congress issued a comprehensive classified study together with an unclassified version, "to determine the technological feasibility and implications, and the ability to survive and function despite a preemptive attack by an aggressor possessing comparable technology, of the Strategic Defense Initiative Program. . . . This study shall include an analysis of the feasibility of meeting SDI software requirements."[28] Consider the following items from the principal findings of this important study:

> *Finding 1.* After 30 years of BMD (Ballistic Missile Defense) research, including the first few years of the Strategic Defense Initiative (SDI), defense scientists and engineers have produced impressive technical achievements, but questions remain about the feasibility of meeting the goals of the SDI.
>
> *Finding 2.* Given optimistic assumptions (e.g., extraordinarily fast rates of research, development, and production), the kind of first-phase system that SDIO [*Strategic Defense Initiative Organization*] is considering might be technically deployable in the 1995–2000 period. . . . such a system might destroy anywhere from a few up to a modest fraction of attacking Soviet intercontinental ballistic missile (ICBM) warheads.
>
> *Finding 4.* The precise degree of BMD system survivability is hard to anticipate.
>
> *Finding 7.* The nature of software and experience with large, complex software systems indicate that there may always be irresolvable questions about how dependable BMD software would be and about the confidence the United States could place in dependability estimates. Existing large software systems, such as the long-distance telephone system, have become highly dependable only after extensive operational use and modification. In OTA's judgment, there would be a significant probability (i.e., one large enough to take seriously) that the first (and presumably only) time the BMD system were used in a real war, it would suffer a catastrophic failure. . . . The relatively slow rate of improvement in software engineering techniques makes it appear unlikely to OTA that the situation will be substantially alleviated in the foreseeable future.
>
> *Finding 8.* No adequate models for the development, production, test, and maintenance of software for full-scale BMD systems exist. . . . Experts agree that new methods for producing and safely testing the system would be needed. Evolution would be the key to system development, requiring new methods of controlling and disseminating software changes and assuring that each change would not increase the potential for catastrophic failure. OTA has found little evidence of significant progress in these areas.

The inclusion of these extensive quotations is necessary and important in order to indicate the scope of the software engineering task facing the designers of SDI. SDIO seems to have recognized the enormous difficulty of its task: "If deployed, SDS (Strategic Defense System) will be more complex than any other system the world has seen."[29] The software manager, Colonel Charles W. Lillie agreed that "the software development and testing practice lags up to 10 years behind the state of the art. But he asserted that the SDI office has recently taken several steps to shorten the lag."[30] In addition, it has been argued by SDI officials that previous military systems have been used without complete testing and they point to the Aegis ship defense system mentioned earlier. OTA has also noted that computer simulations will be difficult to mount because of the lack of real-world data on nuclear explosions in outer space, multiple enemy missile launches, and unpredictable countermeasures by the enemy as well. In a bizarre example of military strategic thinking, indulged in by OTA, the following backhanded support of SDI is proposed: "But unless the Soviets had secretly deployed countermeasures, such as a software virus planted by a saboteur programmer, the Soviets could not be certain that a SDI software would *not* work, and therefore *might* be deterred from attack,"[31] (emphasis added). Thus, expenditures of billions of dollars have already been made, and much more will follow, to produce a system whose reliability is highly suspect, which cannot be adequately tested, and whose major impact has probably been economic by inducing the Soviet Union, with its weak economy, to struggle to spend similar amounts of money to keep up.

The day following President Reagan's "Star Wars" speech, Paul Thayer, the Deputy Secretary of Defense, convened a meeting of leading civilian advisors and military officials, which he opened with the following question: "What are we going to do with this mess?"[32] Between 1983 and 1989, more than $17 billion had been spent on SDI. Although Congress has never agreed to the annual amounts requested by the executive branch, it has continued to allot substantial funding. Nevertheless, it does appear that support for SDI is waning and in the words of Lawrence Korb, "The mess has been cleaned up and SDI has come back to where it belongs, and where it was before Mr. Reagan's speech—that is, to being a robust research program."[33] Whatever else it has done, the SDI program has forced computer scientists to think very hard about their professional responsibility, their duty to the nation, and their own ethical standards.

ISSUES AND PROBLEMS

Many issues could be discussed but the emphasis will be on two: the responsibility of the federal government for the dissemination of public information and the impact of military funding on higher education. Other issues such as the growing number of government databases and their impact on privacy will be examined in Chapter 9. Also to be discussed later in this book (Chapter 14) will be the very difficult questions associated with ethical and professional conduct. As noted previously, many scientists have long struggled with whether or not to engage in research that directly or indirectly has military applications. Computer scientists have had to face similar questions in recent years.

The Dissemination of Federal Information

The Federal government collects, processes, and distributes vast amounts of information used by all segments of the public. Up to fairly recently, most of this material was hard copy, or ink on paper, frequently published by the General Printing Office or the National Technical Information System. Many types of information, however such as technical, statistical, scientific, and reference may best be stored and disseminated by electronic means. For example, reference information such as Bureau of the Census statistics reports could be made available on optical disks. The crucial issues under discussion are how to maintain ready access to electronic media and to define the respective roles of the government and private information handlers in the electronic dissemination of information. Many of these questions are defined and discussed in a comprehensive report issued by the Office of Technology Assessment (OTA) of the U.S. Congress.

Some of the problems and challenges identified by the OTA are given as follows:[34]

- At a fundamental level, electronic technology is changing or even eliminating many distinctions between reports, publications, databases, records, and the like, in ways not anticipated by existing statutes and policies.
- Electronic technology permits information dissemination on a decentralized basis that is cost-effective at low levels of demand.
- Technology has outpaced the major government-wide statutes that apply to Federal information dissemination.
- The advent of electronic dissemination raises new equity concerns since, to the extent that electronic formats have distinct advantages (e.g., in terms of timeliness, searchability), those without electronic access are disadvantaged.
- *Technological advances complicate the Federal Government's relationships with the commercial information industry . . . the privatization of major Federal information dissemination activities has not yet been demonstrated to be either cost-effective or beneficial for important government functions.* [Emphasis added.]

There is disagreement within the government over how much and how fast information dissemination should be privatized, not whether or not it should be. Within the Office of Management of the Budget (OMB), officials argue that government agencies should only release information in bulk form, similar to the activity of wholesalers in consumer goods, while the private sector should act as retailers, packaging the information to meet market demands, the argument being that information companies are much more flexible and responsive than government bureaucracies. In opposition to this view, such groups as the American Civil Liberties Union and Computer Professionals for Social Responsibility claim "that information technology could greatly improve the public's ability to draw on government data. They call for new policies that would encourage the federal government to provide user-friendly access to its statistics and public records."[35] The battle is joined, largely on ideological and profit-motivated grounds. It appears that no comprehensive solution is in the offing, but rather a case-by-case approach in which the government is expected to provide services in those areas that are not economically viable for the private sector.

The Military and Computer Science

This discussion was initiated near the end of the previous chapter where the impact of military funding on university computer science research and curriculum development was briefly explored. We wish to extend that analysis in the light of this chapter's discussion of

SCI, SDI, and other military activities related to computer science. The issue in question is to what degree does the source of funding affect the kind, quality, and direction of scientific and technological research? With respect to scientific research, some would answer that there is no effect and that with respect to applied research it is difficult to determine the effects, but perhaps other answers can be proposed.

Some basic trends are becoming clear. Funding for both total and academic computer science has grown substantially from less than $80 million in 1976 to more than $460 million (in current dollars) in 1990 for the total.[36] DOD has increased its support much more rapidly than other sources such as National Science Foundation, Department of Energy, and NASA, and now accounts for about 63% of total funding. There has been a shift away from funding for basic research towards applied research with DOD leading the way, especially with the DARPA programs discussed earlier in this chapter. The consequences of these trends may be serious in the following ways: certain important but speculative research areas may be stifled because they do not fit DOD's current mission; some researchers may not obtain funding because of their objection to military support and the reduced availability of non-military funding; a certain cynical atmosphere may pervade the computer science community as results are appropriately colored to meet the requirements of military granting agencies;[37] the spin-offs of military research have been quite limited as the U.S. consumer electronics industries have discovered in their competition with Japan; the dependence on military funding tends to disrupt the structure of academic departments and thereby distort both the curriculum and the kinds of students attracted to it.

One final factor is that as DOD funds an increasing proportion of computer science research, it may tend to restrict the free flow of information among researchers on grounds of national security. Such restrictions have already occurred in the field of cryptography, crucial to the security of electronic communication. There is no necessary imperative about all these concerns, but past experience offers few examples of a kindly and understanding paymaster.

SUMMARY

Government is probably the largest single user of computers. These uses are incredibly varied and their impact is felt throughout society. The Federal Government has purchased and continues to purchase an enormous number of computers. It exerts considerable pressure on the market to conform to its requirements. One example is the ADA programming language designed by the Department of Defense for its software needs. Governments gather, store, and process vast amounts of information. The public may be concerned about how this information is safeguarded and how it is used. As the bureaucracy depends more heavily on computer systems, it may become less responsive to the needs of the public it is supposed to serve. It may hide behind the computer instead of providing human answers. The Congress has also benefitted from the use of computers and communication networks in a variety of ways.

More recently, the electoral process has witnessed the introduction of computers for purposes of identifying targeted special-interest groups and funding. The television networks use computers to monitor the voting process and, more controversially, to predict the outcomes, as early as possible. Voting and counting by computer is becoming more common with all the attendant risks of program error and even fraud.

The Department of Defense (DOD) is the largest user of computers within the Federal Government. The DOD has launched major programs to modernize its control and command structure and its weaponry, including advanced programs in artificial intelligence to equip airplanes and tanks with sophisticated computer systems. Major funding for AI has come from DOD, in pursuit of improvements in battlefield capabilities. Important and expensive research and development efforts such as the Strategic Defense Initiative and the Strategic Computer Initiative have been launched, with a significant impact on computer science research and education. Given the important role of computers in the detection and recognition of large-scale military threats, some people have expressed a deep concern that accidental war may occur because computer systems will respond before humans can intervene. In spite of assurances by the government that humans will always retain ultimate responsibility, the ability to respond quickly is a high priority for military decision-makers.

Finally, there is a considerable controversy over the role of the Federal Government in disseminating electronically stored information. The debate turns on the balance between the respective responsibilities of the private and public sectors in providing information, gathered by the government, to the public. The influence of DOD in the growth of computer science has been well-documented. What is of concern is whether or not this influence has been, and will continue to be, of benefit to the field, its practitioners, and the country.

NOTES

1. *Automated Data Processing Equipment in the U.S. Government: First and Second Quarter, Fiscal Year 1988 Summary* (U.S. General Services Administration, Federal Equipment Data Center).
2. *Ibid.*
3. Willie Schatz, "Government IS Projects: Getting the Presidential Nod," *Datamation,* April 15, 1988, p. 79.
4. *Paperwork Reduction: Mixed Efforts on Agency Decision Processes and Data Availability* (Washington, D.C.: U.S. General Accounting Office, GAO/PEMD—89.20, September 1989), p. 11.
5. *Ibid.*
6. *Managing Federal Information Resources, Seventh Annual Report Under the Paperwork Act of 1980* (Washington, D.C.: Office of Management of the Budget, December 1989).
7. David Burnham, "The I.R.S.'s Bumbling Efforts to Update Its Computers," *The New York Times,* April 8, 1990, p. F 12.
8. *Ibid.*
9. *Ibid.,* as quoted.
10. Willie Schatz, "The Pentagon's Botched Mission," *Datamation,* September 1, 1989, p. 22.
11. *Ibid.,* p. 22.
12. Robert Lee Chartrand, "Information Technology in the Legislative Process: 1976–1985," in Martha E. Williams (ed.), *Annual Review of Information Science and Technology (ARIST), Volume 21* (White

Plains, New York: Knowledge Industry Publications, Inc. (for the American Society for Information Science), 1986), pp. 203–239.

13. Stephen E. Frantzich, "The Use and Implications of Information Technology in Congress," in Karen B. Levitan (ed.), *Government Infostructures* (Westport, Connecticut: Greenwood Press, 1987), pp. 27–48.
14. Rodney N. Smith, "The New Political Machine," *Datamation,* June 1, 1984, pp. 22–24, 26, 27.
15. Ronnie Dugger, "Annals of Democracy: Counting Votes," *The New Yorker,* November 7, 1988, p. 40. Reprinted by permission; © 1988 Ronnie Dugger. Originally in *The New Yorker.*
16. Roy G. Saltman, "Accuracy, Integrity and Security in Computerized Vote-Tallying," *Communications of the ACM,* **31**(10), October 1988, p. 1191, 1218.
17. Tekla S. Perry, "TV Networks Vie for Viewer's Votes," *IEEE Spectrum,* October 1984, p. 68.
18. "New-Generation Computing Technology: A Strategic Plan for its Development and Application to Critical Problems of Defense," in *Strategic Computing* (Washington, D.C.: Defense Advanced Research Projects Agency, Department of Defense, October 28, 1983).
19. As quoted in Jonathan Jacky, "The Strategic Computing Program," in David Bellin and Gary Chapman (eds.), *Computers in Battle—Will They Work?* (New York: Harcourt Brace Jovanovich, 1987), pp. 171–208.
20. *Ibid.*, p. 181.
21. David Griffiths, "When Man Can't Keep Up with the Machines of War," *Business Week,* September 12, 1988, p. 36. Russell Watson, John Barry, and Richard Sandza, "A Case of Human Error," *Newsweek,* August 15, 1988, pp. 18–20.
22. Report of the U.S. Senate Committee on the Armed Services, as quoted in Christopher Simpson, "Computers in Combat," *Science Digest,* October 1982, p. 34.
23. As quoted in Arthur Macy Cox, "When Computers Launch the Missiles," *International Herald Tribune,* June 9, 1982, p. 4.
24. Severo M. Ornstein, Brian C. Smith, Lucy A. Suchman, "Strategic Computing," *Bulletin of the Atomic Scientists,* December 1984, p. 12.
25. "New-Generation Computing Technology."
26. As quoted in Lee Grant, "War Games: Separating Fact from Fiction," *Vancouver Sun,* July 6, 1983, p. D 17. Originally appeared in the *Los Angeles Times.*
27. Professor David Parnas, a distinguished software engineer, in his statement of resignation from a nine-member Star Wars advisory panel on computing, as quoted in Philip Elmer-Dewitt, "Star Wars and Software," *Time,* July 22, 1985, p. 39. See Chapter 14 for more of Professor Parnas's views, especially with respect to professional responsibility.
28. *SDI: Technology Survivability and Software, Summary* (Washington, D.C.: U.S. Congress, Office of Technology Assessment, OTA-ISC-354, May 1988).
29. From a SDI report on the National Test Facility as quoted in John A. Adam, "Star Wars in Transition," *IEEE Spectrum,* March 1989, p. 37.
30. *Ibid.*
31. *Ibid.*, p. 38.
32. As quoted in Lawrence J. Korb's review, "A Shield in Space?" *The New York Times Book Review,* Sunday, February 4, 1990, p. 9, of Sanford Lakoff and Herbert F. York, *A Shield in Space?* (Berkeley, California: University of California, 1990). Mr. Korb is a former Assistant Secretary of Defense in the Reagan Administration.
33. *Ibid.*
34. *Informing the Nation: Federal Information Dissemination in an Electronic Age* (Washington, D.C.: U.S. Congress, Office of Technology Assessment, OTA-CIT-396, October 1988), pp. 8–9.
35. Henry H. Perritt, Jr., "Government Information Goes On-Line," *Technology Review,* November–December 1989, pp. 60–67.
36. Joel S. Yudken and Barbara Simons, "Federal Funding in Computer Science: A Preliminary Report," *DIAC-87 (Directions and Implications of Advanced Computing),* Computer Professionals for Social Responsibility, Seattle, Washington, 1987, pp. 40–53. Much more detail on these issues will be found in a forthcoming book by Yudken and Simons. Terry M. Walker, "A Review of Federal Funding for Research

in Computer Science and Engineering," *Computing Research News,* April 1990, pp. 6–14.
37. Susan Faludi, "The Billion-Dollar Playbox," *San Jose Mercury News West Magazine,* November 23, 1986, pp. 12–17, 20–26.

ADDITIONAL READINGS

Information Processing: Issues and Problems

Anthes, Gary H. "IRS Tries Expert System for Fewer Errors." *Computerworld,* June 3, 1991, p. 33.

Little Real Paperwork Burden Change in Recent Years. Washington, D.C.: U.S. General Accounting Office, GAO/PEMD-89-19ES, June 1989.

Robertson, Jack. "Realism Invades Military Computing." *Datamation,* May 15, 1988, pp. 93–95, 98, 100.

Stoyles, Robert L. "The Unfulfilled Promise: Use of Computers by and for Legislatures." *Computer/Law Journal,* **IX**(1), Winter 1989, pp. 73–102.

Yang, Catherine and Gleckman, Howard. "Fred Goldberg and His Impossible Mission." *Business Week,* March 26, 1990, pp. 80–81.

The Political Process

Frenkel, Karen. "Computers and Elections." *Communications of the ACM,* **31**(10), October 1988, pp. 1176–1883.

McDonald, Evelyn C. "The Message Is the Medium." *Government Data Systems,* April 1988, pp. 6–8.

Saltman, Roy G. "Accuracy, Integrity, and Security in Computerized Vote-Tallying." Gaithersburg, Maryland: National Bureau of Standards, U.S. Department of Commerce, NBS/SP-500/158, August 1988.

Schmidt, William E. "New Age of Gerrymandering: Political Magic by Computer?" *The New York Times,* January 10, 1988, pp. A 1, A 7.

The Nation's Defense

Bellin, David and Chapman, Gary (eds.). *Computers in Battle—Will They Work?* New York: Harcourt Brace Jovanovich, 1987.

Bonasso, R. Peter. "What AI Can Do for Battle Management: A Report of the First AAAI Workshop on AI Applications to Battle Management." *AI Magazine,* Fall 1988, pp. 77–83.

Broad, William J. "What's Next for 'Star Wars'? "Brilliant Pebbles,'" *The New York Times,* April 25, 1989, pp. 19, 22.

Broad, William J. "Technical Failures Bedevil Star Wars." *The New York Times,* September 18, 1990, pp. C 1, C 5.

Clausen, Peter and Brower, Michael. "The Confused Course of SDI." *Technology Review,* October 1987, pp. 60–72.

Jackson, James O. "Thanks, but No Tanks: To Curb West German Complaints, the U.S. Army Plays War by Computer." *Time,* February 5, 1990, pp. 30–31.

Jacky, Jonathan. "Throwing Stones at 'Brilliant Pebbles.'" *Technology Review,* October 1989, pp. 20–21, 76.

Lewyn, Mark, Weber, J., Armstrong, L., Buell, B., and McWilliams, G., "The Army Marches on Silicon." *Business Week,* February 4, 1991, pp. 42–43.

Port, Otis, Magnusson, P., Payne, S., Smart, T., Levine, J. B., Schine, E., and Oster, P., "The High-Tech War Machine." *Business Week,* February 4, 1991, pp. 38–41.

Stefik, Mark. "Strategic Computing at DARPA: Overview and Assessment." *Communications of the ACM*, July 1985, pp. 690–703. (See also the February, March, and August 1985 issues.)

Van Creveld, Martin. *Technology and War: From 2000 B.C. to the Present.* (New York: The Free Press, A Division of Macmillan, Inc., 1989.

Issues and Problems

"Should the Government Subsidize Consumer Data Bases?" *At Home With Consumers.* Washington, D.C.: Direct Selling Education Foundation, November 1986.

"Technology & U.S. Government Information Policies: Catalysts for New Partnerships." *Report of the Task Force on Government Information in Electronic Format.* Washington, D.C.: Association of Research Libraries, October 1987.

Thomborson, Clark. "Role of Military Funding in Academic Computer Science." in Bellin and Chapman (eds.). *Computers in Battle—Will They Work?*, pp. 283–296.

8

COMPUTERS AND THE LAW

Bad laws are the worst sort of tyranny.

Edmund Burke (1729–1797)

The first thing we do, let's kill all the lawyers.

William Shakespeare, *King Henry VI Part II*

INTRODUCTION

A given technological innovation will inevitably secure its place in society as the existing system of laws is expanded to accommodate it. What is remarkable about computer technology is how fast this process has occurred and how many interesting and important legal issues have arisen. As many have noted, computer professionals and legal professionals share at least one thing: they both have an extensive and impenetrable jargon. In a very short time a new subdiscipline has come into being, usually called computer law. One lawyer (Thomas Christo) has argued that it is wrong to speak of computer law when in fact there is just the *Law*.[1] Nevertheless, a number of universities do offer courses in computer law and there are several journals in this area. What, then, are some of the issues that fall within the purview of computer law?

There are two major areas of concern. Computer crime involves the use of the computer, with or without computer networks, to steal or embezzle money in a manner that could not easily have been done otherwise. There are also such crimes as stealing computer time, unlawful access to files, the acquisition of privileged information, and the actual destruction of computer files. This last activity has probably become the most highly publicized, as such terms as "virus," "worm," and "hacker" have penetrated the public consciousness. While much computer crime has traditionally been perpetrated in banks, small and large companies, and government bureaucracies, viruses have had a direct impact on the ordinary citizen at home. Computer viruses seem to arrive as regularly as biological ones and with occasionally the same devastating effect.

The second major area is concerned with the relation between copyright and patent law and the legal protection of software. Much has been written about whether or not current law can be used in this area. There is the problem of distinguishing between the central idea captured in a program and the program itself. Other problems are occurring as the distinction between hardware and software becomes increasingly blurred. How does one protect programs implemented in ROM (read only memory)? There are questions about the copying of the masks used to manufacture microprocessor chips or, what is more subtle, the determination of the underlying logic by reverse engineering. More recently, the "look-and-feel" of application and system interfaces has become a frequent issue before the courts.

Developments in information processing have also affected the way law is practiced. Legal information retrieval systems help the lawyer in case preparation. Research is in progress to model legal reasoning in computer programs and to develop expert systems (ES) in various branches of case law, both examples of applied artificial intelligence. The computer has, of course, created new business for lawyers, such as liability litigation resulting from software errors in both application programs and ES. The legal status of evidence derived from computer records or simulations is still open to debate.

Other legal issues arrive in different contexts. The privacy issue with relation to computers has resulted in several pieces of legislation (see Chapter 9). Important legal problems arise around electronic funds transfer systems, transborder data flows, government regulation of the computer and telecommunication industries, and the control of technology transfer (see Chapter 11).

COMPUTER CRIME

One of the more glamorous products of the new technology is the crime story. Hardly a day passes without a report that yet another computer system has been broken into and money has been taken, or that a new virus from the East will begin destroying files in IBM PCs in two weeks; discussions of computer security and new anti-viral programs abound. The glamor factor used to arise because computers seemed to be so formidable that any breakdown in their security was clearly noteworthy. Now, with so many computers in homes and small businesses, a new virus has enormous economic and social impact. For stories dealing with violations of large computer networks, a "David and Goliath" image emerges of the lonely, clever computer programmer, or hacker, cracking the all-powerful system, thought to be invincible up to now. Many people are quite sympathetic to the human-versus-machine success story even if a crime has been committed. Given that crimes are indeed being perpetrated, however, measures must be taken to prevent them; security must be improved; and both professionals and the public at large must be educated about the dangers of such crimes.

The use of computers to commit crimes is not the only way they are associated with unlawful activities. Sabotage can be directed towards the computer installation itself in order to uncover information useful to crack various security codes. The computer can be the target of people who object—for political, social, and economic reasons—to the growing influence of computers in everyday life. The attack might be directed towards the communication network in which the computer is embedded—for example, phone lines might be tapped. These possibilities have stimulated an ongoing concern with computer security. Besides safeguarding the physical system, the data itself may need to be protected.

A Few Definitions

It will be helpful to clarify a number of terms used in the discussion of computer crime. The following definitions represent a compromise between technical details and general understandability. One cautionary note is to be careful about definitions that push biological analogies too far.

Virus. Simply put, a virus is a program that can insert executable copies of itself into other programs. In more detail, a computer virus must satisfy the following properties:

1. It must be capable of modifying software not belonging to the virus by attaching its program structure to the other program.
2. It must be capable of executing this modification on a number of programs.
3. It must have the capability of recognizing this modification in other programs.
4. It must have the ability to prevent further modification of the same program upon recognition of previous modification.
5. Modified software produced by the virus must have attributes 1–4.[2]

Bacterium. This is a program designed to cause a system to crash, that is, to cease operation without warning, thereby causing the loss of data. A bacterium does not attach itself to other programs but replicates itself to the limit of system capacity, preventing other legitimate programs from running.

Worm. A worm searches a computer system for idle resources and then disables them, not by replication of its own code, as do viruses and bacteria, but by systematically erasing various locations in memory. Thus, the system is unable to function as designed.

Trojan Horse. This appears to be a useful program but it contains within it hidden code that may have a destructive function. Viruses are typically spread by Trojan Horses. On the other hand, a programmer may include a "trap door" in the Trojan Horse to permit subsequent tampering, for example, a way to get into the system around the security envelope. (More detail is given later in this section.)

Time Bomb. Also called a logic bomb, this is one of the above infections modified to become operative on a given date or after its host program has run a certain number of times. Note the Burleson program described in the next section is a time bomb.

Hacker. This is a term with multiple meanings that have changed over time. Consider the following descriptions of a hacker:

1. a programmer who works long hours and seems to be strongly motivated by, and infatuated with, programming; or

2. a compulsive programmer who is driven to find solutions to problems, claimed to be extremely difficult or even impossible; or
3. a programmer who produces programs that are not particularly elegant and represent a collection of patches, or hacks, rather than a coherent whole; such programs are difficult to maintain, modify, or verify; or
4. a programmer who breaks into systems to prove that it is possible, and that no system can resist his, or her, efforts; such a hacker is sometimes called a cracker; or
5. a programmer who is a variant of 4 but in addition feels that society benefits by his, or her, actions in that hidden information is brought to light or proprietary software is made available to the entire community of programmers.

One attorney, who specializes in computer and communications law, prefers to use the term "rogue programs" to cover all these types of deviant programs and the term "computer rogues" to describe all individuals who devise, implement, and implant such programs as well as those who commit other crimes by using computers.[3]

Some Examples

Donn Parker, an expert on computer crime, prefers to use the term computer abuse. He defines it as follows:

> . . . any incident involving an intentional act where a victim suffered or could have suffered a loss, and a perpetrator made or could have made gain . . . associated with computers.[4]

Some figures have been made available from a report issued by the National Center for Computer Crime Data (NCCCD) in 1989. It estimates 1988 computer crime losses at $555 million, but notes that if salaries of personnel spent dealing with the associated problems are added in the total approaches $1 billion. Apparently, 485 serious incidents occurred, of which 31 resulted in prosecutions, about 6%, up from 2% in 1987.[5] As for the kinds of crimes committed, the NCCCD's Computer Crime Census of 1988 provides the following information: money theft (36%), theft of services (34%), information theft (12%), malicious alteration (6%), extortion (4%), deceptive alteration (2%), harassment (2%), damage to hardware (2%), and other (2%).[6] There has always been some uncertainty associated with computer crime statistics, however.[7] Here, then, are some examples of computer crimes,[8] presented for purely academic interest, of course.

The Burleson Revenge. In September 1985, Donald Gene Burleson, a programmer at a Fort Worth, Texas brokerage house inserted a special program into the company's computer that later caused 168,000 sales commission records to be suddenly deleted. Mr. Burleson had been dismissed three days before this event. He was charged and later "convicted of computer abuse under the Texas Penal Code which permits a felony charge to be filed if the damage exceeds $2,500 from altering, damaging, destroying data, causing a computer to malfunction or interrupting normal operations."[9] He was fined $11,800 and sentenced to seven years probation.

Kevin Mitnick: A True Compulsive. In early January 1989, Kevin Mitnick was arraigned in Los Angeles, held without bail, and charged with such crimes as illegally accessing computers at Digital Equipment Corp. and at the University of Leeds, in England, and stealing computer programs and long-distance telephone services. He was even able to change the credit rating of the judge in his case, which explains, in part, why he was denied bail and prohibited from making telephone calls. He was charged and convicted under the Federal Computer Fraud and Abuse Act of 1986, one of the first so treated, and sentenced to 12 months in jail, six months in a residential treatment program and three years of probation.[10] Given that he did not even own a computer, he was not fined.

The Pakistani Brain. During the period early 1986 to late 1987, shoppers, mostly American, purchased such brand-name software as Lotus 1-2-3 and WordStar at prices as low as $1.50 per disk at Brain Computer Services in Lahore, Pakistan. The brothers Alvi, owners of the store, also included, for free and of course unknown to the purchasers, a piece of hidden software, a virus, on each disk, which destroyed data and left behind the message, "WELCOME TO THE DUNGEON—Amjad and Basit Alvi." The copying of Pakistani disks was so extensive that before long, about 100,000 disks were so infected. Only disks bought by Americans were infected and Basit offered the reason, "Because you are pirating, you must be punished."[11] On a purely technical level, the virus designer, Amjad, is widely recognized as highly skilled and the virus as very elegant.

Breach of a Classified System. San Francisco, January 17, 1990—"Federal authorities today charged three men in California with engaging in a widespread pattern of breaking into Government and telephone company computers and obtaining classified information from a military computer. The prosecutor said the case might represent the first intrusion into a classified military computer by trespassers."[12]

Global Threat. "Three Australians have been arrested on charges of tampering with computers in the United States and Australia in a case that computer specialists say raises troubling questions about the vulnerability of technology to intruders operating beyond American borders and laws."[13]

Computergate. On September 7, 1990 John Kohler, executive director of the New Jersey Republican General Assembly staff resigned, admitting, contrary to previous denials, that he knew about "improper access to Democrat staff computer records."[14] Apparently the actual culprit was fired earlier in the year.

The INTERNET Worm

The most publicized and most discussed case of computer crime of recent years is known as the INTERNET worm, although all the early reports referred to it as a virus. Its importance goes beyond the event itself in November, 1988, to include possible legal repercussions, as lawmakers strive to formulate comprehensive legislation to deal with present and future threats to computers and networks. On September 26, 1988, *Time's* cover story was on computer viruses, and on August 1, 1988, *Business Week's* cover asked the question, "Is Your Computer Secure?" and mentioned hackers, viruses, and other threats.[15]

Curiously enough, within a rather short period, on November 4, 1988, a front page story in *The New York Times* announced "'Virus' in Military Computers Disrupts Systems Nationwide."[16] Over the next few weeks, stories appeared on a regular basis in many newspapers and magazines, and on television. Consider the following headlines on front-page pieces by John Markoff of *The New York Times:*

- November 5: Author of Computer 'Virus' is Son of U.S. Electronic Security Expert: Cornell Graduate Student Described as 'Brilliant'
- November 6: How a Need for a Challenge Seduced Computer Expert
- November 8: Loving Those Whiz Kids: Mischief Like the Computer 'Virus' Release Comes from Group That Is Indispensable
- November 9: The Computer Jam: How It Came About (p. 38)

The initiator of the INTERNET worm was Robert T. Morris, a graduate student in computer science at Cornell University in Ithaca, New York. On the evening of November 2, 1988, the first of about 6,200 computers allegedly affected, on a network of about 60,000, gradually slowed down or ground to a halt, as an unknown program began seizing computer resources. The activity began initially on ARPANET, a computer network created for academic users by the Defense Advanced Research Projects Agency (DARPA). It then spread to MILNET, an unclassified network of the Department of Defense, and finally to INTERNET, the major network for research facilities throughout the United States. All of these networks and others are connected by gateways across North America and indeed the world. Some local systems broke connections with the network as word of the unprecedented disaster spread and thereby avoided being infected. Within about 48 hours, life was back to normal everywhere.

The impact was so wide-ranging—NASA Ames Laboratory, Lawrence Livermore National Laboratory, The Massachusetts Institute of Technology, Stanford University, the Rand Corporation, among others, were affected—that the uproar in the research communities was deafening. The costs of containing the damage, clearing out the memories, and checking all programs for signs of the rogue program were estimated at $96 million, then $186 million, to $1 billion. Final estimates were considerably more sober, closer to $1 million and 2000 computers affected.[17]

In John Markoff's first report on November 4, he described a telephone call to *The New York Times* in which the unidentified caller, claiming to be an associate of the culprit, a university student, said that the program was an experiment that went awry. According to the caller, the worm, cleverly written except for the error that caused the explosion, exploited three flaws in the common operating system of computers on the networks. The next day the culprit was identified as Robert T. Morris, the son of one of the government's leading experts on computer security, chief scientist at the National Computer Center in Bethesda, Maryland, a branch of the National Security Agency. One of the flaws was in the basic electronic mail handling program, *sendmail,* which permits computers on the networks to communicate with one another. Another was a utility program, *fingerd,* which is called to identify users at a given location; this was its most successful means of migration. The last method was to guess passwords in order to gain access to trusted hosts where it might be able to migrate. What is disturbing to many of the users is that these flaws were generally known but were not exploited because that would have been a violation of collegiality, a breakdown in a system of trust shared by a large community.

Mr. Morris was indicted on July 26, 1989 by a federal grand jury in Syracuse, New York and accused under the Computer Fraud and Abuse Act of 1986 of gaining access to federal interest computers, preventing authorized access by others, and causing damage in excess of $1,000. The fact that there was a delay of more than six months between the date of the incident and the indictment suggests that government lawyers were in some disagreement over how to frame the charges. This uncertainty is probably the major legal legacy of the INTERNET worm, as the government struggles to amend current legislation to be more comprehensive and relevant. The trial began on January 16, 1990, and on January 23, a Federal jury found Mr. Morris guilty of intentionally disrupting a nationwide computer network, the first jury conviction under the 1986 act.[18] On May 5, 1990 a Federal judge fined Mr. Morris $10,000, placed him on three years' probation, and ordered him to perform 400 hours of community service. The judge stated that prison punishment did not fit the crime, although the act provided for up to five years in prison. An appeal was heard on December 4, 1990.[19]

The Computer Fraud and Abuse Act of 1986

The original act, the Counterfeit Access Device and Computer Fraud and Abuse Act of 1984 was signed into law by President Reagan in October 1984 as part of the Comprehensive Crime Control Act of 1984. In 1986, it was amended with the Computer Fraud and Abuse Act. The 1986 Act prohibits six types of computer abuse and provides for three types of felonies. The following computer abuses are defined as criminal conduct {§1030(a)(1)–(6)}:

> (1) Knowingly accessing a computer without authorization and obtaining restricted information with the intent to use that information to the detriment of the United States.
> (2) Intentionally accessing a computer without authorization and obtaining information in the financial record of a financial institution.
> (3) Intentionally, without authorization to access any computer of a department or agency of the United States, access[ing] such a computer of that department or agency that is exclusively for the use of the Government of the United States or, in the case of a computer not exclusively for such use, is used by or for the Government of the United States and such conduct affects the use of the Government's operation of such computer.
> (4) Knowingly, and with intent to defraud, accessing a Federal interest computer and obtaining something of value, unless the value so obtained is limited to the use of computer time.
> (5) Intentionally accessing a Federal interest computer without authorization, and by means of one or more instances of such conduct altering, damaging, or destroying information in any such Federal interest computer, or preventing authorized use of any such computer or information and thereby causing damage in excess of $1,000 or damaging records.
> (6) Knowingly, and with intent to defraud, trafficking in computer passwords.

Number (5) is the section under which Morris was charged and convicted. Although the number of computer-related crimes seems to have increased significantly, only a few convictions have taken place under this Act. There seems to be a number of limitations, both in the language of the Act and in the very nature of computer crime, which make such crimes difficult to prosecute. In the first instance, the Act focuses on computers used and owned by government departments without acknowledging the vast number of corporate computers equally likely to be abused. Access alone is not a crime, unless information is obtained, and neither is browsing, or the looking at files without causing damages.[20] Viruses or worms were not anticipated in the Act. Since many technical issues arise, prosecutors may have difficulty in dealing with such cases. Gathering evidence may also be difficult without violating the privacy of individuals whose files are on the system under investigation.

Other Related Issues: Education, Hackers, and Civil Liberties

Actions independent of new special-purpose legislation may be helpful and indeed necessary. Many have called for an education program, especially among computer scientists, to point out the underlying impact of violations of computers and networks. Stressing privacy issues may convince some potential violators that their actions could undermine the civil liberties of their colleagues. Furthermore, reaction to unauthorized access of individuals and programs may result in the introduction of constraints that severely limit the free flow of information, to the detriment of the considerate and law-abiding majority of users.

It must be acknowledged, however, that there does exist a small community, simplistically described as hackers, who maintain their *right* to enter any system for any purpose they deem appropriate. In an electronic forum held over a nationwide bulletin board in early 1990, a number of hackers expressed a variety of opinions on breaking into systems, perusing files, and the "virtues" of privacy.[21] Among the opinions expressed is a version of the "means justify the end" for hackers; that is, breaking into a system is warranted if the purpose is useful, a position countered by the analogy of entering an unoccupied house if there is something inside it of use to the perpetrator. Many hackers argue that the very concept of secret information is offensive and that if it were not collected, there would be no need to protect it. Thus, they claim that their role must be to "liberate" the data, to defeat the notion of secure systems, and thereby to inhibit the open-ended collection of information.

Despite the hackers' seemingly democratic principle of information for the people, their self-indulgence emerges, loud and clear: we define the issues, we say what is right and wrong, and by virtue of our skills, we reserve the right to act in whatever way we wish. How representative are these opinions? It is impossible to know, but even if they come from a very small minority, it is a highly skilled and a highly motivated one.

Kenneth Rosenblatt[22] makes the argument that good laws, even if available, would not guarantee more convictions or exert deterrence against potential perpetrators. The reason is that for the most part neither the police nor the district attorney in most jurisdictions are sufficiently well-informed about either computers or computer crimes. Mr. Rosenblatt proposes that the Federal government fund regional task forces composed of officers and prosecutors with expertise in these areas. In addition, he argues that certain convicted, compulsive hackers should be prevented from using computers as part of their probation requirements and should even have their own equipment confiscated, if the crime is severe. Indeed, the latter provision has been incorporated in California legislation co-authored by Mr. Rosenblatt.

As a final point in support of those concerned that in response to increased computer crime, or at least increased publicity, law enforcement officials will over-zealously pursue and persecute possible offenders, this case is offered. Early in 1990, the Justice Department indicted Craig Neidorf, 19, also known as "Knight Lightning," on charges of having downloaded the 911 emergency computer program from Bellsouth Telephone Company, obtained illegally, to his computer at the University of Missouri, and then editing it for inclusion in his bulletin-board newsletter for computer hackers, called *Phrack*.[23] The trial began in Chicago near the end of July. Sheldon Zenner, Neidorf's attorney argued that his client "was merely a journalist using an electronic bulletin board to disseminate a 'meaningless . . . bureaucratic' document. . . . Mr. Neidorf never broke into any computer system, never stole any file and never profited from this. . . . He is not a hacker—he's a journalist."[24] Four days into the trial, federal prosecutors dismissed charges against Mr. Neidorf because prosecution witnesses admitted that Mr. Neidorf had not been involved in the theft and further that the document itself was widely available; it could be purchased from Bellsouth for $13 although the indictment claimed that it was valued at $79,449.[25] The protection of free speech by the First Amendment must include electronic communication in its various forms, and reasonable approaches to dealing with computer crime must prevail.

The Morris case seems to have spurred only a few isolated efforts by industry and government to improve security, in spite of the enormous publicity the case received. As mentioned earlier, various initiatives were undertaken in the House and Senate to strengthen legislation related to computer viruses. In addition, law enforcement agencies have attempted to confront suspected computer crime by a number of raids across the U.S. in May, 1990, code-named Operation Sundevil. So far, only one indictment has taken place, and serious questions have been raised about the rights of computer users and bulletin board operators, whose computers were seized.

Also of recent concern is the invasion of voice-mail systems by hackers, who find it relatively easy to obtain access codes. They can then make long-distance calls, change passwords on company systems, and leave and receive messages.

Security Procedures

As in many other areas of life, prevention is far better than detection, indictment, and possible conviction. What steps can administrators of computing facilities take to ensure the physical security of the system itself, and the security of the communications network?

Physical security involves the computer itself, the peripheral equipment, and the rooms and buildings, including furniture, tape storage, and terminals. Obvious care must be taken with respect to fire, water, earthquakes, explosions, and other natural causes. Special care must be taken to control access by people in order to safeguard the equipment and physical surroundings. It may be necessary to require identification badges for those individuals who work in restricted areas. There must be alternative power supplies as well as back-up systems to be used in case of damage. An entire sub-industry has grown up to advise companies in physical security and to supply security equipment. As the dependency of society on computers increases, it becomes a basic necessity to take steps to guarantee physical security.

System security involves the basic operation of the computer itself. The issue is access—to the computer, the associated files, sensitive production programs, and even the operating system. The basic controls used to restrict access are computer identification numbers (IDs) and passwords. Within this system there may be privileged function levels, including user and program access control. An ID is typically issued by the computing center; it is the user's responsibility to choose a password as a second level of security. The operating system of the computer will permit access only to identifiable IDs and passwords. Once on a system, the ordinary user is restricted to his or her own files and system programs, including programming languages and library functions. Individual users may provide other users with access to their files, where access may mean reading the file, writing into it, or both. The operating system must ensure individual user security as well as protect itself from unauthorized access. There are a number of by-now-traditional means of cracking system security.

The following security procedures are generally advisable:

Concern with security must be built into the original design specification of the computer system, both in the physical surroundings and the hardware and software.

It is necessary to have a complete back-up system in case of damage from natural causes or sabotage.

A policy for prosecution of crimes should be drawn up, posted, and followed.

Have regular and unannounced audits of procedures to ensure compliance.

Rotate personnel regularly and be suspicious if there is any reluctance.

Screen personnel carefully, especially for sensitive jobs.

Be sympathetic to customer complaints; they may be the first sign that there is a problem.

THE LEGAL PROTECTION OF SOFTWARE

> Congress shall have Power . . . To promote the Progress of Science and useful Arts, by securing for limited Times to Authors and Inventors the exclusive Right to their respective Writings and Discoveries. (The Constitution of the United States, Article I, Section 8, 1788.)

The framers of the Constitution would have been surprised by the development of computers. The attempt to characterize software in order to design appropriate legal protection has been a long and torturous process that is by no means complete. Computers themselves are readily protected under patent law, as they are certainly inventions. But problems have arisen even here because of the difficulty in determining how to safeguard the masks used to produce integrated circuits. The major concern, however, lies with computer software, more specifically with applications programs. Congress has passed legislation that provides penalties for those who infringe upon the safeguards granted by patents or copyrights. There is the protection afforded by case law to protect trade secrets, and there is the law of contracts. Each has different background, advantages, and disadvantages.

One of the problems in protecting programs is a basic question of definition. As Gemignani has pointed out a program may be viewed as

> a particular form of expression of a flowchart or algorithm, a process for controlling or bringing about a desired result inside a computer, a machine part or completion of an incomplete machine, a circuit diagram of an incomplete machine, a circuit diagram or blueprint for a circuit board, a data compilation, a code writing. . . .[26]

The list does not end there. All the key terms in the constitutional mandate—limited time, author, inventor, and discovery—must be interpreted in the present context.

The growing debate over software protection is a part of the larger issue of protecting intellectual property rights. The big stakes in this area are of course related to technology, a clear indication of its importance. For example, some important cases of the 1980s are given below:[27]

- 1985: The Polaroid challenge against Kodak over violations of the patent for instant cameras is successful, and damages of $909.5 million were awarded on October 12, 1990, considerably less than the anticipated award of $10 billion.
- 1987: Corning Glass Works wins a patent suit against Sumitomo over the design of optical fibers.
- 1988: Fujitsu agrees to pay IBM over $1 billion over copyrights for mainframe operating systems but gains access to newer versions of this software.
- 1989: A five year suit between NEC and Intel ends when a judge rules that microprocessors can be copyrighted (and Intel lost its claim because it neglected to print the copyright symbol) but that the functions of a chip can be duplicated without a violation.

The 1990s will witness similar suits, and within the computer industry, the area of "look and feel" of computer interfaces in general and application program interfaces in particular will predominate. Current actions have been taken by Apple against Hewlett-Packard and Microsoft, by Xerox against Apple, by Lotus Development Corp. against Paperware Software International and Mosaic Software (Lotus won this case in June 1990), and Ashton-Tate (makers of dBase4) against Fox Software. These cases will be discussed in a following section. It is clear that the once relatively dormant area of patent and copyright law has become energized as developments in the computer industry continue to accelerate.

The economic stakes are very high: the worldwide software market in 1988 was about $50 billion, of which the U.S. controls about 70%, and of that total, export sales totalled $11 billion.[28] Thus the courts, in defining copyright and patent protection for software, will have to balance the rights of innovators to a fair return on their creative efforts and associated expenses against the rights of challengers to carve out niches in the marketplace, in order to maintain a vital and competitive environment.

Patents

Obtaining a patent is a long and involved process, but it does confer considerable advantages—a monopoly on use, as well as considerable tax benefits. Are computer programs patentable? The relevant portion of the U.S. Code, section 101, states:

> Whoever invents or discovers any new and useful process, machine, manufacture, or composition of matter, or any new and useful improvement thereof, may obtain a patent therefor, subject to the conditions and requirements of this title.[29]

Thus, a program would have to be considered a programmable process or a programmed machine. The history of attempts to patent programs is rife with controversy, confusion, and a basic inability to define the nature of a relatively new technology.

Companies and individuals wishing to patent their software are confronted by a tangled situation. The Patent Office has consistently rejected most patent applications. The Court of Customs and Patent Appeals has generally supported attempts to patent software. The Supreme Court has usually overturned decisions by the Court of Customs and Patent Appeals and has not clarified the question of the patentability of software. And, finally, Congress has so far not passed necessary and appropriate legislation. In 1968, the Patent Office made an official statement: "Computer programs per se . . . shall not be patentable."[30] In the following year, the Court of Customs and Patent Appeals, in hearing a patent appeal, set aside this opinion.[31] Since then a series of cases have proceeded to the Supreme Court, which consistently rejected patent claims until the case of Diamond v. Diehr in 1981. In this case, Diehr applied for a patent for a process for molding raw uncured synthetic rubber into cured products. This process involved measuring temperatures, using a computer to determine cure times, and opening a press accordingly. The Patent Board rejected the claim, and the Court of Customs and Patent Appeals reversed the rejection, arguing that the mathematical formula was embodied in a useful process. The Supreme Court upheld this opinion in a five-to-four decision. Three basic points of law emerged from the Court's opinion.[32] First, the mere inclusion of a mathematical formula, or programmed computer does not invalidate a claim. Second, in this claim, it was stated, "the respondents [did] not seek to patent a mathematical formula." Third, the claims sought "only to foreclose from others, the use of that equation in conjunction with the other steps in their claimed process." There will be more cases, more opinions, and eventually Congress will pass appropriate legislation. For now, there are a number of advantages and disadvantages to the patent process with respect to software protection.

Patent protection is broad and long-term (17 years). Independent development is no defense against an infringement charge. However, here are some serious disadvantages. Obtaining a patent is a long and costly process. Protecting a patent may also be quite costly. Only the "programmed machine,"—that is, application programs—is patentable, not data or documentation. Not all programmed machines are patentable, and more experience will have to be gained to determine the bounds. Before the Diehr decision, out of about 100,000 patent applications filed each year only about 450 were for program patents. However, patent applications for software have increased considerably in recent years.[33]

One important concern about patent applications is whether or not the entire program must be included to meet disclosure requirements. The simple answer is that flow charts or block diagrams, sufficiently detailed and complete, will suffice. To elaborate on a point made above, "[P]atents generally provide stronger protection than copyrights because a patent may be infringed even if there is no copying or even knowledge of the patent by the infringer."[34]

Copyright

A new Copyright act was enacted in 1976 and became effective in 1978. The new law was not meant to apply to computer software issues until a report was issued by the National Commission on New Technological Uses of Copyrighted Works (CONTU). On the basis of CONTU's recommendations, the Computer Software Copyright Act of 1980 was enacted. It contained the following definition:

> A "computer program" is a set of statements or instructions to be used directly or indirectly in order to bring about a certain result.[35]

(The noted author John Hersey, a member of CONTU, objected strenuously to the recommendation to provide copyright protection to programs. He argued that a program is not a "writing" in the Constitutional sense.) Permission was granted to an individual user to make copies or changes in a copyrighted program, for back-up purposes. In Section 102(a) of the Copyright Act the definition of what can be copyrighted is as follows:

> Copyright protection subsists . . . in original works of authorship fixed in any tangible medium of expression, now known or later developed, from which they can be perceived, reproduced, or otherwise communicated, either directly or with the aid of a machine or device.

A number of cases since 1978 have clarified some of the issues of copyright protection. Its advantages are (a) it is easy to obtain—inexpensive and quick; (b) it is appropriate for works which have wide circulation; (c) it endures during the author's lifetime plus 50 years; and (d) preliminary injunctions may possibly be much more easily obtainable than for possible patent violations. Nevertheless, there are some serious drawbacks. There are still some open questions about what is actually covered. For example, are object programs embodied in ROMs? What about the source program on tape? The scope of protection may be uncertain. For example, can one reproduce copyrighted subject matter in order to develop an object that cannot be copyrighted? Since software is widely proliferated, it will be difficult to enforce copyrights. Can the masks used to produce integrated circuits be copyrighted?

This last question can be answered: yes. In 1984, Congress passed the Semiconductor Chip Protection Act to protect the technology embodied in chips and the associated masks. Congress was concerned that chips and masks, representing one of the major achievements of American ingenuity, were vulnerable to copying and decided to explicitly create a new form of intellectual property protection to help stimulate continued investment in new chip design. While the copying of chips is prohibited, however, the reverse engineering of masks is permitted. Both chips and mask works are defined and the requirements for protection of masks delineated.[36]

Proving that infringement has occurred, under the Computer Software Copyright Act, may be extremely difficult. It is necessary to demonstrate that copying has taken place and that this constitutes an improper appropriation. The Act does permit a user to copy a program for private use. Improper use must be adjudged by a layperson, not a technical expert. The most critical issue arises from a statement issued by the Supreme Court in 1954: "Protection is given only to the expression of an idea—not the idea itself." Several important cases will be considered to illustrate the nature of the issues associated with software copyright cases.

Important Copyright Cases

Whelan Associates, Inc. v. Jaslow Dental Laboratories

This is the first of two cases relevant to the current impassioned debate on the "look and feel of computer user interfaces." Although not really a user interface case at all, Whelan is important because of the scope of its judicial decision. Jaslow hired Whelan to write a program to computerize Jaslow's office procedures, with a view to marketing it to other labs. Jaslow would pay development costs, Whelan would own the rights, and Jaslow would get a royalty on sales. Jaslow aided in the design, even to tailoring the interface to his own methods. The program, Dentalab, written in an obsolete language to run on an IBM mainframe, was delivered in 1979. A few years later Jaslow wrote his own version of the program called Dentacom, in BASIC, to run on PC's, without studying Whelan's code. When he began marketing his PC program, Whelan sued for copyright infringement.[37]

Although Whelan seemed to be concerned only that Jaslow had copied the underlying structure of her program, the similarity in interfaces became an important issue. In 1985, the court found for Whelan on all issues. With respect to copyright infringement, the court found "that the Dentacom system [Jaslow's program], although written in another computer language from the Dentalab, and although not a direct transliteration of Dentalab, was substantially similar to Dentalab because its structure and overall organization were substantially similar."[38] The decision was appealed and Whelan's victory upheld but the appellate court decision introduced a measure of confusion in that it ruled that screen displays that were similar were indications that the programs were also similar. The results of this case are evaluated by Pamela Samuelson, a professor of law, as follows:[39]

> The structure of the program was expression [of the idea] because it wasn't part of the general purpose or function of the program and because there were other ways for Jaslow [the defendant] to have structured such a program besides the way that Whelan had structured hers, so it was an infringement for Jaslow to have used a similar structure to Whelan's.

Broderbund Software v. Unison World

In another important case settled just a few months after Whelan, in 1986, Broderbund Software prevailed over Unison World in a decision that established that "'the overall structure, sequencing and arrangement of screens' in the user interface of a program are protected by copyright, or—broader yet—that a test of the 'look and feel' to an ordinary observer is applicable to software cases generally. . . ."[40] This raises the question, however, of what is required of a user interface that it be capable of existing independently of the working parts of a program. Answers are slowly being proposed in current cases, of which the most stunning decision is that in Lotus Development Corp. v. Paperback Software International and Mosaic Software.

Lotus Development Corp. v. Paperback Software International and Mosaic Software

This case was brought in February 1987 by Lotus, the very successful developer of the leading spreadsheet for IBM PC's and compatibles, Lotus 1-2-3. Paperback and Mosaic also produce spreadsheets but their software sells for $99 each compared to Lotus at $495. Lotus charged that the two companies had copied its screen format, a grid-like image, as well as its keystroke sequences, or macros. In his ruling in favor of Lotus, on June 28, 1990, federal judge Keeton stated, "I conclude that a menu command structure is capable of being expressed in many if not an unlimited number of ways, and that the command structure of 1-2-3 is an original and non-obvious way of expressing a command structure."[41] The immediate implication of this verdict is that once a program becomes a *de facto* industry standard, it will be extremely dificult for new products to challenge its dominance, if they are unable to employ a compatible interface. In the middle of October, Paperback Software announced that it would "stop marketing its VP Planner product line by December 1 and pay Lotus Development Corp. $500,000 for violating its 1-2-3 spreadsheet copyrights . . . [Paperback] also agreed not to appeal a June federal court ruling. . . ."[42] Following up on its courtroom success, Lotus launched a suit against Borland International, the maker of the spreadsheet Quattro Pro, also selling for $99. This time the issue is that Quattro has as an option the 1-2-3 menus and commands as an alternative to its own interface. Other suits dealing with these issues are in progress.

The Interface Debate

Considerable debate has erupted within the industry and elsewhere about the merits of copyright protection of interfaces, as currently guaranteed by the courts. Simply put, those supporting copyright protection argue that the original designers must have their work protected in order to earn a reasonable return on their investment, to encourage the design of new and innovative systems, and to attract and keep bright designers. Those in opposition might argue that copyright protection impedes innovation by freezing designs which may not be optimal, unfairly rewards those who happen to be first but not best, and discourages the free exchange of ideas for the benefit of all.

David Reed, the chief scientist, spreadsheets, at Lotus stated the following after the decision:[43]

> If the only way to better a product was to copy its interface, copyright might indeed halt innovation and restrict competition, because copyright prevents including all or part of a copyrighted work in another. As a designer, I'm challenged by trying to do something significantly better than the competition. . . . The notion that "programming freedom" precludes designers owning their original works seems like pure demagoguery.

A contrary position is held by G. Gervaise Davis, a founding partner of a law firm specializing in computer industry cases:[44]

> Lotus managed to convince a very bright but technologically unsophisticated judge [Keeton] that, because its one-word commands and macro functions were found somewhere in the underlying program, the use of those functional commands and similar command structure in a competing program was an infringement of 1-2-3. . . . This confuses protection of the underlying program with protection of the functions the program is intended to perform.

Pamela Samuelson's response to the Lotus decision is expressed in a characteristically blunt fashion:

> I am a lawyer. I interpret cases for a living. I have read Judge Keeton's opinion carefully and I have worked very hard to figure out what it means. I would tell you what it means if I could understand it, but I cannot. And neither can anyone else. So anyone who says he or she is sure the Lotus decision is a very narrow one and only makes copying the whole of someone else's interface illegal is giving his opinion and making a prediction. . . .

A considerably more radical position is taken by a founder of The League for Programming Freedom, Richard Stallman, a renowned MIT programmer and recipient of a MacArthur Foundation fellowship.[46] Stallman argues that software should not be copyrighted but should be freely available to everyone. This is based on the notion of a community of programmers, all of whose tools and products are shared resources. One fear of copyright can be seen by drawing an analogy with typewriters. If the typewriter interface, i.e., the specific keyboard layout, could be copyrighted, each manufacturer would be required to produce a different layout. For computers, interface copyright will inevitably lead to greater incompatibility. "Anything which impedes standardization impedes the social penetration of technology."

A preliminary decision in Apple Computer's suit against Microsoft and Hewlett-Packard for copyright infringement of its interface was won by Apple in March, 1991, much to the displeasure of Stallman. Although the issue of infringement has yet to be decided, the court ruling establishes that the Macintosh user interface programs are original works and therefore entitled to protection. At about the same time, AT&T informed a number of computer companies manufacturing workstations that they were violating patents obtained in 1985 by Bell Laboratories for the basic software necessary to display the simultaneous running of computer programs. This technology permits users to observe multiple windows on a display by means of a mouse. Although no claim for patent infringement has yet been made, this move by AT&T is similar to Apple's and would seem to carry with it a possible threat to small software developers.

Trade Secrets

The most favored method of protection, at least up to fairly recently before the surge in copyright cases, has been under trade secret laws. As there is no federal trade secrecy legislation, the relevant laws have been established, not in a uniform manner, in the individual states. One definition of a trade secret is "any formula, pattern, device or compilation of information which is used in one's business and which gives him an opportunity to obtain an advantage over competitors who do not know how to use it."[47] Three conditions are necessary to legally protect a trade secret: novelty, secrecy, and value in business. Trade secret law appears to cover programs as "processes comprising inventions, with documentation protectable as ancillary 'know-how'."[48] Databases and documentation could also receive protection as information of value. An attempt has been made to establish uniform laws on trade secrecy—the "Uniform Trade Secrets Acts" were drawn up in 1979, approved by the American Bar Association in 1980, and adopted by Minnesota and Arkansas in 1981.

The main advantages of trade secrecy laws are that preliminary injunctions are readily obtained, the applicability over a wide range of subjects is relatively clear, protection applies to both ideas and expressions, the waiting period is brief, and the application remains in force for a long period. Among the disadvantages are the lack of uniformity across the United States, the stress on secrecy as a bar to progress, the lack of protection against independent development, the difficulty in maintaining long-term secrecy—especially for widely proliferated software, and possible preemption by the Copyright Act. Despite these problems, trade secrecy is likely to continue to be the most favored method for protecting software.

Other Methods

To protect software, an employer may make a contract with the relevant employees as part of the terms of employment, which may include such stipulations as no unauthorized copies and no public discussion of programs under development. Whatever the specific terms of a contract, an employee is expected to respect confidentiality. Associated with the sales or licensing of software, there may also be contractual arrangements controlling disclosure. In such a rapidly evolving industry, employees tend to move readily among companies. Contractual arrangements are a reasonable way to maintain software protection, but the restrictions must not be too severe or they will not be upheld by the courts.

Finally, to protect secrecy it is certainly advisable to improve the effectiveness of security procedures. Also technology may be employed to increase the difficulty of making unauthorized use of programs. The copying of disks may be made quite difficult by special built-in protection. For example, the software may be restricted to run only on certain machines. Additional methods of foiling would-be violators have been and could be devised.

OTHER DEVELOPMENTS

Artificial Intelligence Applications

Traditional searches for information for case preparation have been aided by legal information retrieval systems. However, such systems depend heavily on appropriate indexing and keyword matching, procedures that occasionally fail to provide satisfactory results. What is needed to improve searches is to conduct them on conceptual grounds rather than by employing keywords. It will require natural language abilities far beyond what are now available. Even more difficult, but particularly relevant to legal matters, is retrieval based on analogy, a basic process in legal thought. This process clearly represents a stage beyond information retrieval on the road toward the modeling of legal reasoning. L. Thorne McCarty and N. S. Sridharan have been engaged for several years in the TAXMAN project. One of its major goals "is to develop a theory about the structure and dynamics of legal concepts, using corporate tax law as an experimental problem domain."[49] Their work is an application of AI techniques to the domain of legal knowledge representation and legal reasoning. Their current ideas are directed toward representing an abstract concept as a "prototype," a relatively concrete description, and as a sequence of "deformations" that can map the prototype into an alternative form. Since they began their research, many other projects in this area have been undertaken, both in North America and Europe.

One important area of current research is the attempt to formalize existing legislation in order to determine if it contains logical flaws. The very process of formalization, i.e., translating from legal English into a logical language, a difficult enough task, may itself reveal imprecise definitions and inconsistencies in reasoning. One important example is the representation of the British Nationality Act as a logic program.[50] Another interesting growth area is the application of expert systems to specific legal domains. Again, building an expert system requires the careful formalization of concepts and procedures, a valuable exercise in its own right. Expert systems have been developed in such areas as sentencing, tax law, naturalization, impaired driving, and remote damages. Donald H. Berman and Carole H. Hafner of the Center for Law and Computer Science at Northeastern University argue that AI may be a crucial element in dealing with the crisis in the U.S. legal system: "Expert systems can be used in the service of such algorithmic decision making, but they can also be used to organize and present the relevant facts and issues in the service of human decision makers."[51]

Liability and Malpractice

Suppose a navigator aboard an aircraft uses a computer, with appropriate application software, to plan a route that results in the aircraft's crashing into an unexpected mountain. Who is responsible? Among the candidates are the navigator, the pilot, the aircraft company, the computer manufacturer, and the software developer. The grounds for suit may include breach of warranty, breach of third-party beneficiary contract, negligence, and strict liability. In the last instance the programmer might be found liable, even though he was very careful in both the writing and debugging of the program. Under strict liability, a seller is liable for damages even if there is no contract between the seller and the person suffering the damages. As the dependence of society on computers grows, there will be a corresponding growth in litigation associated with computer malfunction, and it will be particularly interesting when the judgments of expert systems are challenged.

In a very important case, Diversified Graphics v. Groves, Diversified hired the consulting firm of Ernst & Whinney (now Ernst & Young) to recommend a turnkey computer system that could be operated without specially trained staff. It claimed that the system did not work as expected and many thousands of dollars were wasted in trying to make it satisfactory. Ernst & Whinney argued that in recommending a system it should be held only to an ordinary standard of care, not to a professional one. The jury, in finding for the plaintiff, Diversified Graphics, "held consultants from Ernst & Whinney liable for shirking the Management Advisory Services Practice Standards of the American Institute of Certified Public Accountants in their procurement of a turnkey system for Diversified Graphics."[52] In February 1989, the appeals court upheld the verdict. The strong message from this case is that even system programmers or application programmers as well as consultants will be held to professional standards.

Beyond programs or systems that fail to perform as advertised, there may be programs that actually cause physical harm. Computers in medical care can offer valuable services but there may be risks. For example, incorrect software may cause an X-ray overdose, as has actually happened, or a heart monitor may produce an incorrect reading that results in a doctor prescribing incorrect treatment.[53] Determining liability in computer-related cases is still a developing area of law. One possibility is the application of "strict liability to health care providers as a *seller* of computer products." Another is that the program may be viewed as incidental to the services provided and perhaps negligence, under the principle of torts, may apply. Or new legal principles may be required when computers or computer networks are involved.

A Final Comment

The Supreme Court ruled in Diamond v. Diehl that programs could be patented, although a number of issues remain to be clarified. One year earlier, in 1980, an equally important decision was handed down in which the Court ruled that a human-made organism could be patented. Thus, two dynamic technologies have been afforded patent protection. Finally, it is interesting that the major competitor to the United States in technology, Japan—despite having a quite different culture—has developed a patent practice similar to U.S. patent law.

SUMMARY

The introduction of computers in significant numbers into society has brought the legal system problems of new crimes and new ways to commit old ones. Computer crime has become one of the most publicized aspects of computer use. The various crimes associated with computers are difficult to evaluate in terms of either magnitude or frequency, but it seems safe to say that the number and variety are increasing and the stakes are growing. Victimized companies, including banks, have been reluctant to publicize such crimes for fear of endangering their reputations for security. Nevertheless, enough cases have been documented to indicate that computer crimes can be quite subtle and difficult to detect.

More recently, computer viruses and worms have taken the center stage, causing severe disruptions of systems and networks and loss of files for individual computer users. The most publicized case was the INTERNET worm initiated by Robert Morris, a Cornell graduate student, late in 1988. Although found guilty, Morris's actions prompted a flurry of congressional activity towards new legislation to deal with viruses and worms. The range of crimes made possible by computers is so wide that precise definition has proven elusive.

Legislation has been passed in various states to deal with computer crimes, but it was only in late 1986 that Congress passed the Computer Fraud and Abuse Act to provide penalties for illicit access to computers. The current generation of computer crimes seems to be less concerned with property-based activities and more focused on reckless behavior, which puts other users at risk. To deal with unauthorized entry, a variety of security methods have been proposed to protect against both physical and electronic trespassing. Only authorized staff should be able to gain direct entry to the computer. A system of passwords and priority levels should be used to restrict unauthorized sign-ons via remote terminals.

The development of software and computers must be protected against illegal copying to ensure that developers are properly rewarded for their work and to encourage others to enter the marketplace. Traditional means of protecting intellectual property are copyrights and patents. Patent protection for programs was first recognized in a 1981 Supreme Court decision but it has taken several years for the Patent Office to be receptive to software applications. First in 1980 and then in 1984, the Software Copyright Act extended copyright protection to computer programs. Also in 1984, Congress passed the Semiconductor Chip Protection Act to protect chips and the masks used to produce them. Of recent concern has been the attempt by some software and hardware companies to protect the "look-and-feel" of their user interfaces. In 1990, Lotus Development, the developer of the 1-2-3 spreadsheet program won an important suit to copyright its interface and command structure. Many in the industry believe this decision will have a detrimental effect on the free interchange of ideas as large companies seek to reinforce their control over commonly shared approaches.

AI approaches may make it possible to model legal reasoning and the attempt at the formalization of legal code may reveal hidden flaws. Finally, the increasing use of computers has created problems of failure and personal damage and questions of liability, which the law is currently ill-equipped to deal with properly.

NOTES

1. Thomas K. Christo, "The Law and DP: A Clash of Egos," *Datamation*, September 1982, pp. 264–265, 267–268.
2. R. Burger, *Computer Viruses: A High-Tech Disease* Second Edition (Grand Rapids, Michigan: Abacus, 1988), p. 15. As referenced in James Tramontana, "Computer Viruses: Is There a Legal 'Antibiotic'?" *Rutgers Computer & Technology Law Journal*, **16**(1), 1990, note 26, p. 255.
3. Anne W. Branscomb, "Rogue Computer Programs and Computer Rogues: Tailoring the Punishment to Fit the Crime," *Rutgers Computer & Technology Law Journal*, **16**(1), 1990, note 26, p. 4.
4. Donn Parker, *Crime by Computer* (New York: Scribner's, 1976), p. 169.
5. *Commitment to Security*, The Second Statistical Report of the National Center for Computer Crime Data (Santa Cruz, California: NCCCD, 1989).
6. *Ibid.*, p. 27.
7. An interesting bit of historical trivia is associated with computer crime statistics. In 1973, in a speech to the American Society for Industrial Security, Robert V. Jacobson, president of International Security Technology, Inc. reported that, "According to an unpublished study of white-collar crime in the United States, 86.2% of computer crime in 1972 was never detected!" This figure gained great currency in the computer crime lecture and publication circuit. As Mr. Jacobson admits, however, "At the time it never occurred to me that people would miss the irony. After all how could one generate an estimate with three figure accuracy about undiscovered events?" Letter from Robert V. Jacobson, SIGSAC, Spring 1987, pp. iii–v.
8. Deputy district attorney for the County of Santa Clara, California, and the lead attorney for the district attorney's High Technology Unit, Kenneth Rosenblatt, defines computer crime as "illicit activity directed at copying, altering, deleting and/or gaining access to information processes stored or transmitted by computers." In Michael Alexander, "Computer Crime: Ugly Secret for Business," *Computerworld*, March 12, 1990, p. 104.
9. Branscomb, "Rogue Computer Programs and Computer Rogues," p. 18.
10. Branscomb, "Rogue Computer Programs and Computer Rogues" pp. 18–21, and "Drop the Phone," *Time*, January 9, 1989, p. 15.
11. Philip Elmer-DeWitt, "You Must Be Punished," *Time*, September 26, 1988, p. 54.
12. Andrew Pollock, "3 Men Accused of Violating Computer and Phone Systems," *The New York Times*, January 18, 1990, pp. A 1, A 17.
13. John Markoff, "3 Arrests Show Global Threats to Computers," *The New York Times*, April 4, 1990, pp. A 1, A 16.
14. "Computergate Hits New Jersey," *Computerworld*, September 17, 1990, p. 147.
15. Katherine M. Hafner, Geoff Lewis, Kevin Kelly, Maria Shao, Chuck Hawkins, and Paul Angiolillo, "Is Your Computer Secure?" *Business Week*, August 1, 1988, pp. 64–67, 70–72, and Philip Elmer-DeWitt, "Invasion of the Data Snatchers," *Time*, September 26, 1988, pp. 50–55.
16. John Markoff, "'Virus' in Military Systems," *The New York Times*, November 4, 1988, pp. 1, 13.
17. Branscomb, "Rogue Programs and Computer Rogues," p. 7.
18. John Markoff, "Jury Convicts Student Whose Program Jammed Computers," *The New York Times*, January 23, 1990, p. A 13.

19. John Markoff, "Computer Intruder Gets Probation and Fine But Avoids Prison Term," *The New York Times,* May 5, 1990, pp. 1, 8. "Morris Appeal Due," *Computerworld,* November 12, 1990, p. 8.
20. Christopher D. Chen, "Computer Crime and the Computer Fraud and Abuse Act of 1986," *Computer/Law Journal* **X**(1), Winter 1990, pp. 71–86.
21. "Is Computer Hacking a Crime?" *Harper's Magazine,* March 1990, pp. 45–57. A transcript of selections of a nationwide forum held on a computer bulletin board over an eleven-day period, including a variety of perspectives.
22. Kenneth Rosenblatt, "Deterring Computer Crime," *Technology Review,* February–March 1990, pp. 34–40. (See 8.)
23. Michael Alexander, "Babes in High-Tech Toyland Nabbed," *Computerworld,* July 20, 1990, p. 8.
25. Peter H. Lewis, "Can Invaders Be Stopped But Civil Liberties Upheld?" *The New York Times,* September 9, 1990, p. F 12, and Michael Alexander, "Dial 1-800 . . . for Bellsouth 'Streets'," *Computerworld,* August 6, 1990, p. 8. The three individuals who actually broke into Bellsouth Corp.'s computers to obtain the proprietary information were not so fortunate. They were sentenced, on November 16, 1990 to terms varying from 14 months to 21 months in prison plus fines of $233,000 each. Reported in Michael Alexander, "Hackers Draw Stiff Sentences," *Computerworld,* November 26, 1990, pp. 1, 99.
26. Michael C. Gemignani, *Law and the Computer* (Boston: CBI, 1981), p. 84.
27. Paula Dwyer, Laura Jereski, Zachary Schiller, and Dinah Lee, "The Battle Raging Over 'Intellectual Property'," *Business Week,* May 22, 1989, p. 89, and Keith H. Hammond, "What Will Polaroid Do with All that Moola?" *Business Week,* October 29, 1990, p. 38.
28. Gregory C. Damman, "Copyright of Computer Display Screens: Summary and Suggestions," *Computer/Law Journal,* **IX**(4), Fall 1989, p. 444.
29. David Bender, *Computer Law: Evidence and Procedure* (New York: M. Bender, 1982), p. 4A-2.
30. As quoted in Gemignani, *Law and the Computer,* p. 102.
31. *Ibid.*
32. As quoted in Bender, *Computer Law,* pp. 4A-7–4A-8.
33. J. Michael Jukes and E. Robert Yoches, "Basic Principles of Patent Protection for Computer Software," *Communications of the ACM,* **32**(8), August 1989, pp. 922–924.
34. *Ibid.,* p. 923.
35. Bender, *Computer Law,* p. 4A-31.
36. Frederick L. Cooper III, *Law and the Software Marketer* (Englewood Cliffs, New Jersey: Prentice-Hall, 1988), pp. 91–96.
37. Pamela Samuelson, "Why the Look and Feel of Software Interfaces Should Not Be Protected by Copyright Law," *Communications of the ACM,* **32**(5), May 1989, pp. 563–572.
38. Paul R. Lamoree, "Expanding Copyright in Software: The Struggle to Define 'Expression' Begins," *Computer & High Technology Law Journal,* **4**(1), January 1988, p. 62.
39. Samuelson, "Why the Look and Feel of Software Interfaces Should Not Be Protected by Copyright Law," p. 567.
40. Lamoree, "Expanding Copyright in Software," p. 78.
41. As quoted in John Markoff, "Lotus Wins Copyright Decision," *The New York Times,* June 29, 1990, p. C 3.
42. Patricia Keefe, "Paperback Pulls Spreadsheet, Won't Appeal Lotus Victory," *Computerworld,* October 22, 1990, p. 7.
43. David Reed, "Airing both Sides of the 'Look-and-Feel' Debate," *Computerworld* August 13, 1989, p. 21. Copyright 1989 by CW Publishing Inc., Framingham, Massachusetts. Reprinted from Computerworld.
44. G. Gervaise Davis, "Airing both Sides of the 'Look-and-Feel' Debate," *Computerworld,* August 13, 1989, p. 21. Copyright 1989 by CW Publishing Inc., Framingham, Massachusetts. Reprinted from Computerworld.
45. Pamela Samuelson, "How to Interpret the Lotus Decision (And How Not to)," *Communications of the ACM,* **33**(11), November 1990, p. 32.
46. Prepared by Richard Stallman and Simson Garfinkel for the League for Programming Freedom, "Against User Interface Copyright," *Communications of the ACM,* **33**(11), November 1990, pp. 15–18.

47. Bender, *Computer Law,* p. 4A–78.
48. *Ibid.,* p. 4A-79.
49. L. Thorne McCarty and N. S. Sridharan, "The Representation of an Evolving System of Legal Concepts: II. Prototypes and Deformations," *Proceedings of the Seventh International Conference on Artificial Intelligence,* Vancouver, Canada, 1981, p. 246.
50. M. Sergot, F. Sadri, R. A. Kowalski, F. Kriwaczek, P. Hammand, and H. T. Cory, "The British Nationality Act as a Logic Program," *Communications of the ACM,* **29**(5), May 1986, pp. 370–386.
51. Donald H. Berman and Carole D. Hafner, "The Potential of Artificial Intelligence to Help Solve the Crisis in Our Legal System," *Communications of the ACM,* **32**(8) August 1989, p. 937.
52. J. J. Bloombecker, "Malpractice in IS?" *Datamation,* October 15, 1989, p. 85.
53. James M. Godes, "Developing a New Set of Liability Rules for a New Generation of Technology: Assessing Liability for Computer-Related Injuries in the Health Care Field," *Computer/Law Journal,* **VII**(4), Fall 1987, p. 521.

ADDITIONAL READINGS

Computer Crime

Alexander, Michael. "Hacker Probe Bogged Down." *Computerworld,* February 11, 1991, p. 1.
Alexander, Michael. "Suit Seeks to Define User Rights." *Computerworld,* May 6, 1991, p. 1.
Bloombecker, Buck. *Spectacular Computer Crimes: What They Are and How They Cost American Business Half a Billion Dollars a Year!* Homewood, Illinois: Dow Jones-Irwin, 1990.
"Computer Security: Virus Highlights Need for Improved Internet Management."Washington, D.C.: United States General Accounting Office, GAO/IMTEC-89-57, June 1989.
Cornwall, Hugo. *Datatheft.* London: Mandarin Paperbacks, 1990.
Denning, Dorothy. "The United States vs. Craig Neidorf." *Communications of the ACM,* **34**(3), March 1991, pp. 24–43. (Includes comments by colleagues and rebuttal by Dr. Denning.)
Denning, Peter J. "Computer Viruses." *American Scientist,* May–June 1988, pp. 236–238.
Denning, Peter J. "Stopping Computer Crimes." *American Scientist,* January–February 1989, pp. 10–12.
Fitzgerald, Karen. "The Quest for Intruder-Proof Computer Systems." *IEEE Spectrum,* August 1989, pp. 22–26.
Highland, Harold Joseph. *Computer Virus Handbook.* Oxford, United Kingdom: Elsevier Advanced Technology, 1990.
Lewyn, Mark. "Does Someone Have Your Company's Number." *Business Week,* February 4, 1991, p. 90.
McAfee, John. "The Virus Cure." *Datamation,* February 15, 1989, pp. 29–40.
Olenick, Lou. "Systems Managers Crucial in Computer Crime Protection." *Computerworld,* November 19, 1990, p. 134.
Parker, Donn B. *Fighting Computer Crime.* New York: Scribner's, 1983.

The Legal Protection of Software

Branscomb, Anne W. "Who Owns Creativity?" *Technology Review,* May–June 1988, pp. 38–45.
Chesterman, John and Lipman, Andy. *The Electronic Pirates.* London: Routledge, A Comedia Book, 1988.
Garfinkel, Simson. "Get Ready for GNU Software." *Computerworld,* August 6, 1990, p. 102.
Kahin, Brian. "The Software Patent Crisis." *Technology Review,* April 1990, pp. 52–58.
Markoff, John. "Patent Action on Software by A.T. & T." *The New York Times,* February 26, 1991, p. C 1.
Mueller, Janice M. "Determining the Scope of Copyright Protection for Computer/User Interfaces." *Computer/Law Journal,* **IX**(1), Winter 1989, pp. 37–59.

Samuelson, Pamela. "Interface Specifications, Compatibility, and Intellectual Property Law." *Communications of the ACM*, **33**(2), February 1990, pp. 111–114.

Samuelson, Pamela. "Survey on the Look and Feel Lawsuits," *Communications of the ACM*, **33**(5), May 1990, 483–487.

Samuelson, Pamela. "Should Program Algorithms be Patented?" *Communications of the ACM*, **33**(8), August 1990, pp. 23–27.

Tapper, Colin. *Computer Law, Fourth Edition*. London: Longman, 1989.

Von Hippel, Eric. "Trading Trade Secrets." *Technology Review*, February–March 1988, pp. 58–62, 63.

Legal Applications

Frank, Michael, Krassa, M. A., Pacek, A. C., and Radcliff, B. "Computers and the Law," *Social Sciences Computer Review* (6:3) Fall 1988, pp. 341–352.

Kerr, Susan. "Is the Computer Fostering a More Just System?" *Datamation*, January 15, 1988, pp. 45–48, 52, 55.

The Second International Conference on Artificial Intelligence and the Law, Faculty of Law, University of British Columbia and Association for Computing Machinery, Vancouver, Canada, 1989.

Warner, Edward. "Expert Systems and the Law," *High Technology Business*, October 1988, pp. 32–35.

Other Developments

Birnbaum, L. Nancy. "Strict Products Liability and Computer Software." *Computer/Law Journal*, **VIII**(2), Spring 1988, pp. 135–156.

Denis, Sabine and Poullet, Yves. "Questions of Liability in the Provision of Information Services." *Online Review*, **14**(1), 1990, pp. 21–32.

Turley, Tod M. "Expert Software Systems: The Legal Implications." *Computer/Law Journal*, **VIII**(4), Fall 1988, pp. 455–477.

9

PRIVACY AND FREEDOM OF INFORMATION

The makers of our Constitution undertook to secure conditions favorable to the pursuit of happiness. . . . They sought to protect Americans in their beliefs, their thoughts, their emotions and their sensations. They conferred, as against the Government the right to be let alone — the most comprehensive of rights and the right most valued by civilized men. To protect that right every unjustifiable intrusion by the Government upon the privacy of the individual, whatever the means employed, must be deemed a violation of the Fourth Amendment.

Justice Louis D. Brandeis, Dissenting, Olmstead v. United States, 277 U.S. 438, 1928

INTRODUCTION

The following are excerpts from newspaper articles in the United States and Canada:

- Organizations of librarians, authors and civil libertarians say they have been deeply troubled to discover that agents of the Federal Bureau of Investigation are looking into what books people are reading, who these readers are, and even whom they are associating with. At issue is the FBI's so-called Library Awareness Program, in which the bureau seeks information on possible Soviet-bloc intelligence-gathering by asking librarians to report seemingly suspicious requests by readers or to reveal the names of people who may be helping Soviet agents to obtain information. [At public libraries!] (Herbert Mitgang, *The New York Times,* June 26, 1988, p. E 6. Copyright © 1988 by The New York Times Company. Reprinted by permission.)
- Local telephone companies nationwide are beginning to offer customers a caller identification system that would display the number from which an incoming call was originating before the call was answered. [More detail later in this chapter.] (Calvin Sims, *The New York Times,* March 11, 1989, p. 1. Copyright © 1988 by The New York Times Company. Reprinted by permission.)
- . . . Alana Shears, 32, claims a manager at Epson America Inc. routinely read electronic messages and memos that employees exchanged with outsiders—correspondence everyone assumed was confidential. Fired for insubordination earlier this year, Shears now

is pursuing her unusual invasion-of-privacy case in the courts. (*The Vancouver Sun,* September 24, 1990, B 4, from the *Washington Post.* © 1990, The Washington Post. Reprinted with permission.)

• An Ontario police intelligence agency's request for routine access to confidential information on Bell Canada subscribers would circumvent court procedures requiring police to obtain warrants, privacy lawyers say. (Lawrence Surtees, *The Globe and Mail,* June 28, 1990, p. B 5.)

• A random computer-assisted investigation of wealthy New York State taxpayers claiming to live outside the state has found that the first 12 people audited all were falsely filing as out-of-state residents, officials said today. That has resulted in the collection of $28 million in back taxes. (Philip S. Gutis, *The New York Times,* February 8, 1989, p. 13. Copyright © 1988 by The New York Times Company. Reprinted by permission.)

• Is Nothing Private? Computers know more about you than you realize—and now anyone can tap in. . . . (Cover Story, *Business Week,* September 4, 1989)

• Dorcas R. Hardy, Commissioner of the Social Security Administration, told a Congressional committee today that the agency had verified millions of Social Security numbers for private credit companies. . . . In the disputed procedure, the credit companies send computer tapes with the Social Security numbers to the Federal agency, which then singles out incorrect numbers. The credit companies use the numbers in checking a person's credit ratings. (Martin Tolchin, *The New York Times,* April 1989, p. 8. Copyright © 1988 by The New York Times Company. Reprinted by permission.)

Probably the single most frequent charge levelled against computers is that they rob us of our privacy. Banks of computer disk drives and tapes are envisioned in some back room, on which the intimate details of the lives of many people are stored. Government agencies, law enforcement officials, insurance companies, banks, schools, credit agencies, and many others have access to private information about most people in society. This situation was true before the arrival of computers, but somehow the computer has added a significant new element—whether it is due to the computer's ability to store and search rapidly through vast amounts of data, the image of the computer as a malevolent force, the economic benefits available to companies that are able to precisely target large segments of the population, or the general trend in society towards the accumulation of information that is made possible by computers.

The national research firm, Louis Harris & Associates, has been conducting surveys on American attitudes toward privacy since 1970. He has been assisted on some of these by Dr. Alan Westin of Columbia University. These surveys represent the most comprehensive attempt to gauge U. S. public opinion on the issue of personal privacy and technological impact, over an extended period of time.[1] Figure 9-1 shows a rising concern by the public about threats to their personal privacy over the period 1970 to 1990. The rise between 1970 and 1978 probably reflects the post-Watergate and post-Vietnam disillusion with government. The rise to near 80% during the conservative Republican administrations of Presidents Reagan and Bush is somewhat more difficult to explain. The 1990 survey suggests a continuing distrust of institutions and a concern that control over personal information has been lost to credit bureaus, government, and other institutions. The distrust of large institutions of all kinds may be rooted in a realization that very little personal information remains private, that government seems to have an insatiable need to collect more

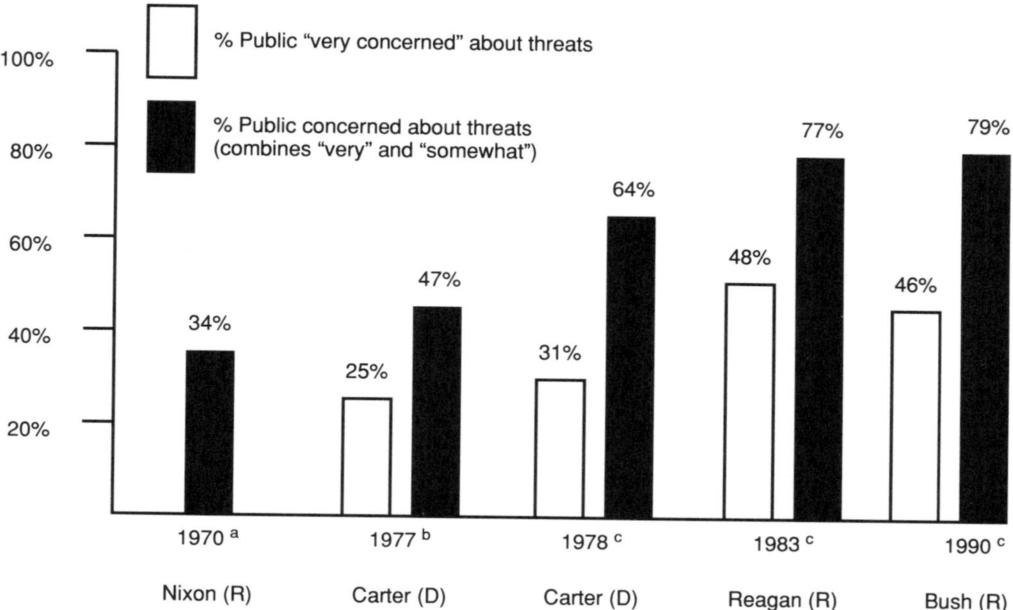

FIGURE 9-1 Concern by the Public about Threats to Their Personal Privacy.
a. For 1970, the Harris question asked, "Do you ever tend to feel that sometimes your sense of privacy is being invaded or not—that people are trying to find out things about you that are not any of their business?" (Yes, no.)
b. For 1977, the Harris question asked, "Now some people tell us they are concerned about what's happening to their personal privacy—the right to live their own life without others knowing more about it, or intruding into it, more than is absolutely necessary. I'd like to know if you've ever thought about that. Would you say you are very concerned about the loss of personal privacy, somewhat concerned, only a little concerned, or not concerned at all?"
c. For 1978, 1983, and 1990, the Harris question asked, "How concerned are you about threats to your personal privacy in America today?" (Very concerned, somewhat concerned, not very concerned, not concerned at all.)
Source: A national opinion survey conducted for Equifax Inc. by Louis Harris & Associates and Dr. Alan F. Westin, Columbia University. Equifax Inc., 1600 Peachtree Street, Atlanta, Georgia 30302.

and more information, that in the private sector banks, credit bureaus, and direct marketing companies also seem driven to reap economic benefits from large, detailed databases on consumers, and that the technology permits, and indeed encourages the collection and rapid processing of vast amounts of data.

In order to explore some of these issues more carefully, it will be helpful to look at the results of the three most recent surveys, to monitor the changes in opinion between 1978 and 1990. One problem is that the targeted groups varied somewhat over the years so that strict comparisons are not possible. Also as the general public has become more aware of computers, primarily through direct exposure to personal computers, the level of sophistication has increased, especially among professionals. With these caveats consider Table 9-1, which reveals some of the fears and concerns of the general public and of selected

TABLE 9-1

RESPONSES FROM VARIOUS GROUPS TO QUESTIONS ON COMPUTERS AND PRIVACY FROM THE YEARS 1978, 1983, AND 1990.

Questions	Responses	General 1978 (1511)	Credit Grantors 1978 (72)	Banks and Thrifts 1978 (36)	General 1983 (1256)	Credit Grantors 1990 (150)	Banks and Thrifts 1990 (157)	Direct Marketers 1990 (150)
1. Do you feel that the present uses of computers are an actual threat to personal privacy in the country or not?	Yes	54%	29%	22%	51%	35%	45%	37%
	No	31%	70%	78%	42%	64%	54%	62%
2. Computers have made it much easier for someone to obtain confidential personal information about individuals improperly.	Agree	80%	59%	36%	—	71%	75%	71%
	Disagree	10%	40%	58%	—	27%	24%	27%
	Not sure	10%	1%	6%	—	2%	1%	2%
3. In general, the privacy of personal information in computers is adequately safeguarded.	Agree	27%	71%	78%	34%	57%	46%	48%
	Disagree	52%	23%	17%	60%	40%	52%	48%
	Not Sure	21%	5%	6%	6%	3%	3%	4%
4. Computers have improved the quality of life in society.	Agree	60%	96%	89%	—	89%	90%	92%
	Disagree	28%	5%	11%	—	9%	9%	8%
	Not Sure	13%	—	—	—	3%	1%	—
5. How close are we to a "Big Brother" society as depicted in George Orwell's *1984?*	There already	8%	—	—	6%	—	—	—
	Very close	26%	—	—	23%	—	—	—
	Somewhat close	39%	—	—	40%	—	—	—
	Not close	19%	—	—	28%	—	—	—
	Not sure	8%	—	—	3%	—	—	—

Source: A national opinion survey conducted for Equifax Inc. by Louis Harris & Associates and Dr. Alan F. Westin, Columbia University. Equifax Inc., 1600 Peachtree Street, Atlanta, Georgia.

industries; this table represents only a very small and carefully selected part of three quite extensive surveys. A few points are clear, as follows:

- The general public is clearly concerned about computers and their effect on privacy. (See questions 1, 2, and 5). Even in responding to computers and the quality of life, the general public is much less enthusiastic than special interest segments of society, not surprisingly.
- It is surprising how many people accept the idea that we are reasonably close to a "Big Brother" society as envisioned by George Orwell (see question 5). Also of interest is that in the 1983 survey, only 27% of the general public had read Orwell's *1984*.
- The general public is more trusting in the belief that personal information is safeguarded than are the professional groups. Even among the professional groups, however, the support for this belief has substantially decreased between 1978 and 1990 (see question 3).

In the 1990 Equifax survey, when asked whether they believe that lists of consumer information should be sold, 69% of the public (out of a base of 2254) say that it is a bad thing and only 28% are favorable. More specifically, when asked if direct marketing companies should be permitted "to ask credit reporting bureaus to screen their computerized files for those who meet the requirements and then supply just the customer's name and address . . . [without obtaining] the customer's advance permission," 76% of the public find this an unacceptable practice, while 23% find it acceptable. Not surprisingly, among the direct marketing people sampled the reverse is found—it is acceptable to 75% and unacceptable to 21%.[2]

The public's level of sophistication about various privacy issues is revealed by their responses to the statements and questions (abbreviated for space limitations) in Table 9-2. Also included, for comparison, are responses from one of the "privacy-intensive industries," credit granting.[3] The public is obviously concerned about possible loss of privacy and values privacy as a fundamental right far more than do the credit granters and other representatives of such industries.

Clearly, there is a deep concern among most segments of society about the growing number of records being held in both private and government databases. The U.S. government maintains databases containing many billions of individual records, probably over 20 for each American. Credit bureaus, including TRW and Equifax, hold records on most Americans, and Canadians as well; they are used mainly to verify applications for credit, such as for life insurance, mortgages, and consumer loans. These records are now being used, as mentioned above, for other purposes by direct marketing companies, whose very existence depends on treating information as a commodity, to be bought and sold, independent of the wishes of the people themselves. The government records are needed for the various agencies to carry out their responsibilities. In the not too distant past, however, various departments did establish databases to collect information on individuals who were perceived as a possible threat to the stability of government. Such activities inhibited the free exercise of constitutional rights.

Privacy is a cultural, philosophical, and political concept. The formulation of legislation

TABLE 9-2

RESPONSES OF THE PUBLIC (2254) AND CREDIT GRANTORS (150) TO SELECTED QUESTIONS IN THE 1990 EQUIFAX SURVEY.

Questions		Public	Credit Grantors
Consumers have lost all control over how personal information about them is circulated and used by companies.	Agree	71%	40%
	Disagree	27%	57%
Since the Nixon Watergate episode in the early 1970s, there haven't been any really serious attempts by the federal government at invading people's privacy.	Agree	32%	27%
	Disagree	64%	61%
Would you favor the government requiring a national work identification card for all working Americans, both citizens and noncitizens? (Supporters: help identify illegal aliens; Opponents: dangerous threat to privacy.)	Favor	43%	—
	Oppose	56%	—
	Not sure	2%	—
Federal freedom of information laws have gone too far in letting individuals and businesses get government documents.	Agree	58%	—
	Disagree	37%	—
	Neither	1%	—
	Not sure	4%	—
If we rewrote the Declaration of Independence today, we would probably add "privacy" to the list of "life, liberty, and the pursuit of happiness" as a fundamental right.	Agree	79%	56%
	Disagree	19%	43%
	Neither	1%	1%
	Not sure	1%	—

Source: A national opinion survey conducted for Equifax Inc. by Louis Harris & Associates and Dr. Alan F. Westin, Columbia University. Equifax Inc., 1600 Peachtree Street, Atlanta, Georgia.

in this area clearly depends on how privacy is viewed and valued. Concern with privacy did not begin with computers. As Edward Coke (1552–1634), an English writer on the law, put it, "A man's house is his castle." The common person and the king should be equal with respect to the security of their home. The computer seems to have added several important new wrinkles to this principle. The collection, storage, and retrieval of large amounts of private information, by credit bureaus, for example, has become a major industry.

In response to a variety of problems associated with violations of privacy, legislation has been enacted in the United States to guarantee certain rights. This legislation addresses some issues, but others remain open. Privacy is a cultural issue, and different types of legislation exist in other countries.

The term *freedom of information* is generally applied to the concept that governments must make the information they collect accessible to the public at large unless they can demonstrate a pressing need for secrecy. The explication of this idea requires a distinction between privacy and secrecy. In general, governments are reluctant to reveal their operations. Eventually legislation was passed in the United States to provide public access to government under a set of regulations, the Freedom of Information Act.

Finally, future privacy issues will arise in connection with new technological developments. Given varying national privacy laws, international agreements will have to be developed to deal with the flow of data across borders. It seems that everywhere one turns, someone or some group is asking questions and gathering information. How was it used, who has access and for what purposes, and what rights do the people about whom the information was gathered have?

THE NATURE OF PRIVACY

> A man has a right to pass through this world, if he wills, without having his picture published, his business enterprises discussed, his successful experiments written up for the benefit of others, or his eccentricities commented upon, whether in handbills, circulars, catalogues, newspapers or periodicals. (Jurist Alton B. Parker, Decision, Robertson v. Rochester Folding Box Company, 1901.)

Privacy as a social issue has long been a concern of social scientists, philosophers, and lawyers. The arrival of the computer has sharpened this concern and made concrete a number of threats to personal privacy. But what does the word privacy mean? Is privacy a right?

> Privacy is the claim of individuals, groups or institutions to determine for themselves when, how, and to what extent information about them is communicated to others.[4]

Alan Westin, the author of the above statement, has probably made the most important recent contributions to both the definition and scope of the meaning of privacy in the age of computers. In fact, the definition given above is arguably the most common one in current use. Westin's definition has been criticized because it formulates the definition in terms of a claim. The counter-argument is that privacy "is a situation or freedom about which claims may be made."[5] This dissension may appear to be the usual legal hair-splitting, but it seems to suggest that the Westin definition represents an activist view that privacy should be a right. Two other criticisms of the Westin definition are that it limits the concept of privacy to information control, and only information about the individual who makes the claim at that.

It is not surprising that information and its control feature so prominently. After all, the forthcoming "information age" will certainly catapult individual privacy to the forefront of civil liberty issues (if it has not done so already). Information is not the only thing that comes to mind when one thinks of privacy, however. Also important are being alone or alone with one's family, not being exposed to displays one considers offensive, and the right not to have one's behavior regulated (for example, the right to use contraceptives, or to have an abortion). These issues arise in connection with such privacy problems as surveillance by the use of wiretapping, electronic bugs, and long-range microphones; possible censorship of the public media; and the tension between individual behavior and the demands of society.

The concept of privacy can be given three aspects: territorial privacy, privacy of the person, and privacy in the information context.[6] Territorial privacy refers to the very basic notion that there is a physical area surrounding a person that may not be violated without the acquiescence of the person. Laws referring to Peeping Toms, trespassers, and search warrants have been enacted to safeguard territorial privacy. The second category, in some sense, is concerned with protecting a person against undue interferences such as physical searches and information that violates his or her moral sense. The third category is the one most relevant here, as it deals with the gathering, compilation, and selective dissemination of information:

Privacy and Information

To live in contemporary society is to leave, stored in records held by institutions, a trail of the following kinds of information:

Vital statistics (birth, marriage, death).
Educational (school records).
Financial (bank records, loans).
Medical (health records both physical and mental).
Credit (credit cards, credit record, purchases).
City government (house taxes, improvements).
Employment (earnings, work record).
Internal revenue (taxation, deductions, earnings).
Customs and immigration (passports, visas, customs payments).
Police (arrests, convictions, warrants, bail, paroles, sentences).
Welfare (payments, history, dependents).
Stores (credit record, purchases).
Organizations (membership, activities).
Military (service record, discharge status).
Motor vehicles (ownership, registration, accident record).

This list represents only a sample of the kinds and sources of information being held about the average citizen. The computer has made it possible to store an enormous amount of information and to retrieve it in an efficient manner. Most of the above-listed records are held by government institutions at all levels. This fact is seen by some critics as evidence of the insatiable appetite of government to know more and more about its citizens. In the private domain there has been a corresponding increase in the amounts and uses of information.

In recognition of this explosion in information, the concept of privacy has undergone some changes. Inevitably there will be disclosures of information—if not, why has it all been collected? How can the rights of the affected person be protected? Perhaps the prior question is what should these rights be? A basic statement appeared in 1973, in an important U.S. government report, as follows:

> An individual's personal privacy is directly affected by the kind of disclosure and use made of identifiable information about him in a record. A record containing information about an individual in identifiable form must, therefore, be governed by procedures that afford the individual a right to participate in deciding what the content of the record will be, and what disclosure and use will be made of the identifiable information in it. Any recording, disclosure, and use of identifiable personal information not governed by such procedures must be proscribed as an unfair information practice unless such recording, disclosure or use is specifically authorized by law.[7]

This statement does not describe what information should be stored, or what the controls for its use should be, but it does argue for the legal establishment of privacy rights for the individual. Subsequent legislation did delineate and incorporate some of these rights by regulating the behavior of record-keepers.

The general public in the United States is concerned about threats to personal privacy, and this worry is growing, as Figure 9-1 illustrates. Many people would claim that there is a basic human need for privacy. Not all basic human needs are defended in law, however. It has been recognized that individual privacy, in its many manifestations, is a basic prerequisite for the functioning of a democratic society. In this light, the recommendations made in the 1973 government report have served as a basis for subsequent legislation.

- There must be no personal-data record-keeping systems whose very existence is secret.
- There must be a way for an individual to find out what information about him is in a record and how it is used.
- There must be a way for an individual to prevent information about him that was obtained for one purpose from being used or made available for other purposes without his consent.
- There must be a way for an individual to correct or amend a record of identifiable information about him.
- Any organization creating, maintaining, using or disseminating records or identifiable personal data must assure the reliability of data for their intended use and must take precautions to prevent misuse of the data.[8]

Records have been kept on individuals from time immemorial, but the use of computers has introduced a change in kind as well as in degree. Records can now be easily transmitted over long distances, searched efficiently, and merged if desired. Since the cost of storage is cheap, more data can be stored and so more is collected. As more information is collected, more uses are made of it, as if the availability drives the need. There seems to be an insatiable appetite for information in both the private and public domains. Since these trends are likely to accelerate in the future, much is to be gained by trying to understand the various implications of contemporary threats to privacy.

DATABASES

> The issue of privacy raised by computerization is whether the increased collection and processing of information for diverse public and private purposes, if not carefully controlled could lead to a sweeping power of surveillance by government over individual lives and organizational activity.[9]

Individual privacy is threatened by the possible use of government databases for surveillance. Such use may inhibit the free exercise of constitutionally guaranteed rights, such as freedom of speech and petitioning the government for the redress of grievances. With private databases, such as those maintained by the large credit bureaus, the impact could be quite serious. Without credit, a car, house and life insurance, and a mortgage are not available. A suspect credit rating may limit one's type of employment, housing, and one's children's educational possibilities. Quite clearly, the misuse of information by others could have a devastating effect on a person's life. With the increasing use of information systems to store personal records, the imbalance between the individual and the "system" has grown. It is therefore incumbent upon the record-keeper to establish guidelines to insure the protection of individual rights.

The Privacy Commission, set up after the passage of the Privacy Act of 1974, enunciated the three necessary objectives of a privacy protection policy as follows.[10]

Minimize Intrusiveness. This involves creating a balance between what is demanded of an individual and what is provided in return.

Maximize Fairness. This will make sure that information stored about an individual is not used unfairly.

Create Legitimate, Enforceable Expectations of Confidentiality. It is most important to guarantee that recorded information is subject to the most stringent security procedures.

Constitutional Guarantees

Some very complex privacy issues are highlighted by the First, Fourth, and Fifth Amendments to the Constitution. These amendments are concerned with the following rights and guarantees:

First Amendment. Freedom of religion, speech, the press, peaceable assembly, and the right to petition for redress of grievances.

Fourth Amendment. No unreasonable search and seizure by the federal government.

Fifth Amendment. A person may not be compelled to testify against himself or be deprived of life, liberty, or property without due process.

By the collection of large amounts of data and surveillance of individuals and groups (as discussed earlier), the government could inhibit the freedoms of speech and assembly guaranteed in the First Amendment. Threats to these rights have occurred in the past, against both active and passive participants in political meetings and demonstrations. A basic challenge arises whenever threats to First Amendment rights surface: "What have you got to worry about if you haven't done anything wrong?" Unfortunately, the collection of data by the government, as well as surveillance, can be repressive in itself, in that it creates the impression that an activity is not proper and that participants ought to reconsider their actions. In some cases, information has been used directly to affect the employment of individuals. First Amendment rights are crucial to maintaining a democratic society, and any attempts to limit them must be forestalled.

The interrelation between information systems and the Fourth Amendment turns on such issues as the use of personal or statistical data as a reason for search and seizure, the information itself as the object of the search, and the use of the system to facilitate the search and seizure. With the use of criminal record information systems, police may carry out searches on the basis of instantaneous access to the database. Courts may be concerned about whether such information provides reasonable cause. Computer systems could be employed to monitor the shopping activity of individuals by accessing appropriate electronic funds transfer systems. This activity would be much more intrusive than personal observation could be.

Possible Fifth Amendment violations may arise when data collected for one purpose is used by the government as evidence in an unrelated case. Another problem may arise in the use of criminal records in computer models to predict criminal behavior. Individuals' rights could be denied on the basis of predictions, not actual unlawful action. Since these records may include statements by the persons being modeled, self-incrimination is a definite possibility. More constitutional issues associated with databases and privacy will surface in the future.

Computer Matching

A final example of the possible misuse of the data that is collected and stored in government databases is particularly worrisome. It points out that the arrival of the computer has literally created new avenues for the exercise of bureaucratic power. The term *computer matching* probably reached public consciousness in late 1977, when Joseph A. Califano, Jr., the Secretary of Health, Education, and Welfare, announced a new program, "Project Match," to reduce welfare violations. The idea was to match computerized lists of federal employees against computerized lists of state welfare rolls. Any person whose name appeared on both lists, a so-called hit, would be a likely candidate for welfare fraud investigation.

The Privacy Act of 1974 (to be discussed later in this chapter) embodied the principle that information collected about individuals for certain purposes cannot be used without their consent for unrelated purposes. An individual's consent is not required if the information is to be used either in a manner consistent with the original purpose—the "routine use" provision—or for a criminal investigation. Computer matching has been justified by appeal to the routine use exception. In response to criticisms about the extensive use of computer matching, the Office of Management and Budget (OMB) drew up a set of guidelines in 1979. These have not satisfactorily addressed the critical issues, in the opinion of many critics.

In 1984, Richard P. Kusserow, Inspector General of the Department of Health and Human Services, argued that computer matching is just another necessary weapon in the government's arsenal against waste and fraud. Because the cost of such fraud is so enormous, the government is entitled to take whatever measures it deems necessary to protect the rights of innocent taxpayers. The Reagan Administration revised the OMB guidelines in 1982, in order, it was claimed, to "streamline paper-work requirements and reiterate requirements for privacy and security of records."[11] The government maintains that privacy safeguards are in place and that computer matching is not a threat to civil liberties. The critics argue that the safeguards are inadequate and that computer matching represents one more serious step in the erosion of personal privacy.

In 1986, the United States General Accounting Office (GAO) issued a report reviewing the activities of federal agencies in implementing the provisions of the Privacy Act of 1974 (to be discussed later in this chapter). Although computer matching is not explicitly mentioned in the Act, the OMB revised guidelines were an attempt to address some of the concerns raised by increasing government use of this technique. In the conclusions to the report, GAO notes that[12]

> Although computer matching is one of the most controversial activities generating privacy concerns, agencies (1) did not have current, complete data on the extent of matching programs, (2) did not always follow OMB's matching guidelines, and (3) differed in interpretation of the matching guidelines as to whether programs needed to be reported to OMB. In addition, two component agencies exempted their matching programs from OMB's guidelines. We found no evidence that OMB was previously aware of these discrepancies.

Without addressing the privacy concerns associated with computer matching, GAO makes the following bureaucratic recommendations to ensure that the OMB guidelines are effectively enforced:[13]

> • Computer matching guidelines should specifically state that agencies are to annually report to OMB all participation in matching programs initiated in prior years but conducted on a recurring basis. This would contribute to more complete data in OMB's Annual Report to the Congress.
>
> • Computer matching guidelines should provide for public notice of computer matching programs conducted by organizations not covered by the act when Privacy Act systems of records are disclosed by federal agencies.
>
> • Computer matching guidelines should instruct agencies to notify OMB when like IRS [Internal Revenue Service] and OCSE [Office of Child Support Enforcement], they believe they are exempt from OMB guidelines. This would provide OMB with the opportunity to review and concur. [What about the possibility of refusal on occasion?]

Hearings were held on computer matching in the Senate in 1986 and in the House the following year. On October 18, 1986 the Computer Matching and Privacy Protection Act was enacted. It will be discussed later in this chapter, in the section on Privacy Legislation.

Private Databases

> Let us not overlook a significant fact . . . people tend to state their case most favorably when they know that the information they supply will be the basis of their having their application granted. . . . It is essential that we be permitted to verify the information presented to us by the applicant through the credit bureaus and others. . . .[14]

A great deal of information is gathered by the private sector. Educational, employment, medical, financial, and insurance records all require protection to ensure privacy. Probably of greatest importance in the average citizen's life is the use of credit information. When an individual opens a charge account, applies for a credit card or life insurance, or takes out a loan, personal and financial records are created. Apparently, credit bureaus first opened their doors in the early 1890s to provide services for specific businesses. They produced reports in various forms on individuals applying for credit. As of the end of 1989, credit bureaus contained some 500 million consumer credit files, more than one, on the average, per adult, and in 1988, they issued about 450 million credit reports.[15]

PRIVACY LEGISLATION

> More important, however, is the fact that it [The Assault on Privacy] should bestir all Americans to claim their constitutional legacy of personal privacy and individual rights and to demand an end to abuses of computer technology before the light of liberty is extinguished in our land.[16]

Transactional Data Protection

Lawmakers frequently respond to public pressure by formulating legislation to deal with agreed-upon abuses. Since 1968, a series of laws have been passed that deal in the broad sense with credit protection where this includes a variety of financial matters. Coupled to these financial activities is a concern with the privacy of the associated information, or the transactional data, and recent laws have been passed to protect this data from improper use. Among these laws are the ones shown in Table 9-3.

Space precludes the discussion of all these laws, so we will focus on one of the earliest, the Fair Credit Reporting Act of 1970, and briefly describe the most recent ones, the Cable Act and the Video Protection Act.

Fair Credit Reporting Act

> . . . to insure that consumer reporting agencies exercise their grave responsibilities with fairness, impartiality, and a respect for the consumer's right to privacy. (Fair Credit Reporting Act, 1970.)

In 1967, the first Congressional hearings were held to address threats to personal privacy by some credit bureaus: false records, biased records, outdated material, and errors in data

TABLE 9-3

A SELECTION OF TRANSACTIONAL DATA PROTECTION LAWS.

Law (date enacted)	Purpose
1. *Consumer Credit Protection Act* (1968)	To state clearly the cost of borrowing.
2. *Fair Credit Reporting Act* (1970)	To permit the correction of mistakes on credit records.
3. *Currency and Foreign Transactions Reporting Act (Bank Secrecy Act)* (1970)	To keep certain records on individuals and to report certain types of financial transactions to the government.
4. *The Right to Financial Privacy Act* (1978)	To limit some of the broad interpretations of the Bank Secrecy Act.
5. *Tax Reform Act* (1976)	To restrict governmental use of tax information for other purposes.
6. *Debt Collection Act* (1982)	To regulate the federal government's release of personal information on bad debts to credit companies.
7. *Cable Communications Policy Act* (1984)	To protect the privacy of subscribers to cable television.
8. *Video Protection Privacy Act* (1988)	To protect records of individual borrowers held by video rental stores.

entry. The Fair Credit Reporting Act (FCRA) was passed in 1970 and came into law in April 1971. Below is a brief overview of the main points of the Act:[17]

Accuracy of Information. Credit agencies must take all reasonable steps to guarantee the accuracy of reports in collection, storing, and processing.

Obsolete Information. Certain information must not be included after a number of years have elapsed: bankruptcies, 14 years; suits and judgments, 7 years; criminal arrest, 7 years.

Limited Uses of Information. This point specifies the conditions under which an agency may supply a report. Examples are credit, employment, licensing, legitimate business needs, court order, and with written instructions from the concerned individual.

Notices to Individuals. If the results of the report adversely affect the individual, he or she must be notified and supplied with the name and address of the relevant agency. If an investigation is to be undertaken, the affected individual must be notified.

Individual's Right of Access to Information. The individual has a right to be fully informed about all information held about him (except for medical records), and the sources and recipients of the information—for the previous 2 years for reasons of employment, and 6 months for others.

Individual's Right to Contest Information. An individual can dispute the information held on him, which may require a reinvestigation. If the disagreement is not resolved, the agency must permit the individual to include a brief statement in the file.

In 1976, FCRA was criticized by the federal district court judge in Minnesota in the case Henry v. Forbes:[18]

> The Act does not provide a remedy for all illicit or abusive use of information about consumers . . . individuals are not protected against the abuse of the credit reporting appa-

> ratus unless their circumstances are within the narrow bounds of coverage under the Act. . . . [The individual has] no remedy unless the information were used in violation of common law privacy rights (requiring highly public, outrageous conduct to make a cause of action).

Another set of criticisms can be summarized as follows:[19] considerable vagueness exists with respect to who has access to the credit data. It permits disclosure to "anyone with a legitimate business need for the information in connection with a business transaction involving the consumer." The FCRA only requires the credit agency to provide an inquiring consumer with "the nature and substance of all information," and does not permit him or her to inspect the file in person. The importance of the accuracy of the information collected, stored, and disseminated is not recognized in the Act. And finally, the Act is directed only at credit reporting agencies and not at other institutions that may request the information.

In September 1989, *Business Week's* cover story, "Is Nothing Private?" revealed what to many Americans was a confirmation of their worst fears that nothing is private. An editor signed up with two super credit bureaus, using the small lie that he needed to run credit checks on one or two prospective employees. For $20 apiece, one of the superbureaus produced credit reports based on just the names and addresses of two of his colleagues. It gets more interesting. For an initial fee of $500, the editor was able to access the superbureau's database from his home computer. He ran two names through the system—Representative Richard J. Durbin (D–Illinois) and Dan Quayle, the Vice-President of the United States. These requests did not set off alarms and reports were produced. Various innocuous tidbits about J. Danforth Quayle, with a Washington address, turned up including that he has a big mortgage and that he charges more at Sears, Roebuck & Co. than at Brooks Brothers, and what his credit card number is. A spokesman for the Vice-President said, "We find the invasion-of-privacy aspect of the credit situation disturbing. Further controls should be considered."[20]

Cable Communications Policy Act of 1984

This important Act extended privacy protection to subscribers of cable television and would apply as well to videotex systems carried over cable. Subscribers to cable television may create a record of programs paid for, purchases made for home shopping, and other services as well. Videotex systems, still in their early stages (see Chapter 13), permit subscribers to take advantage of a number of services, including banking, reservations to musical, theatrical, film, and sporting events, bulletin boards, electronic mail, and news and information sources. Every action by a subscriber leaves a trail, gradually accumulating a record of preferences and interests, which direct mailing companies, advertisers, and even criminal investigators may find useful. The consumer needs protection and hence the passage of this Act. Some of the provisions of the Act are given below:[21]

- Cable operators have to provide subscribers to cable television services with a separate annual written statement, which clearly and conspicuously states the nature, uses, disclosures, retention periods and rights of access concerning the identifiable personal information to be collected with respect to the subscriber.

• A subscriber has to furnish prior written or electronic consent before a cable operator can use the cable system for the collection and disclosure of identifiable personal information, except that the cable company may collect, use, and disclose personal information in order to provide legitimate business services to the subscriber or to respond to a court order, and may disclose names and addresses, if the subscriber has had an opportunity to prohibit or limit such disclosure.

• A "governmental entity" may obtain such access pursuant to a court order, only if in a court proceeding it has offered "clear and convincing evidence" that the subject of the information is reasonably suspected of engaging in criminal activity, that the information sought would be material evidence in the case, and that the subject of the information is afforded the opportunity to appear and contest such entity's claim.

Video Privacy Protection Act of 1988: The Bork Bill

In 1987, when Robert Bork had been nominated by President Reagan to the Supreme Court and was being considered by the U.S. Senate, a reporter obtained unauthorized access to the video rental list of his family. Presumably, the purpose was to uncover evidence that Mr. Bork, or his family, rented questionable, read pornographic, movies as a way of further discrediting his nomination. Congress acted quickly to protect the privacy of video renters. Individual laws of this kind, however well-motivated, are indications of the lack of a well-thought, comprehensive approach to consumer privacy protection in the United States.

Government Personal Privacy Protection

Privacy Act of 1974

The passage of the Privacy Act of 1974 was the culmination of many studies and hearings, but the Watergate scandal was the major factor in its approval.

> The purpose of this Act is to provide certain safeguards for an individual against an invasion of personal privacy by requiring federal agencies, except as otherwise provided by law, to . . .
>
> (1) permit an individual to determine what records pertaining to him are collected, maintained, used or disseminated by such agencies;
> (2) permit an individual to prevent records pertaining to him obtained by such agencies for a particular purpose from being used or made available for another purpose without his consent;
> (3) permit an individual to gain access to information pertaining to him in federal agency records, to have a copy made of all or any portion thereof, and to correct or amend such records;
> (4) collect, maintain, use, or disseminate any record of identifiable personal information in a manner that assures that such information is current and accurate for its intended use, and that adequate safeguards are provided to prevent misuse of such information;
> (5) permit exemptions from the requirements with respect to records provided in this Act

only in those cases where there is an important public policy need for such exemptions as has been determined by specific statutory authority; and
(6) be subject to civil suit for any damages which occur as a result of wilful or intentional action which violates any individual's rights under this Act.[22]

With respect to subsection (5), records maintained by the CIA, any law enforcement agencies, prosecutors, courts, correctional institutions, or probation or parole authorities are exemptions as defined in the act. Because police work depends so heavily on informers, these records must be excluded from general access. Also exempt are records involving national defense or foreign policy, specific statute exclusions, trade secrets, and the protection of the President. Many other categories are given in the act. It also required the establishment of the Privacy Protection Study Commission, to conduct a study of the databanks, automated data processing programs, and information systems of governmental, regional, and private organizations in order to determine the standards and procedures in force for the protection of personal information.[23]

Implicit in all the legislation discussed so far is an after-the-fact philosophy. The assumption is that computerized personal record systems are here to stay, and it is only necessary to regulate their use in order to limit the worst abuses. The law is employed to establish procedures and provide recourse for injured parties. The prior question of whether there is justification and need for a particular database has not been legally addressed. Any government agancy can decide to set up a record-keeping system whenever it wishes. Most of the critical energy in the privacy issue has been directed toward the adequacy of procedures rather than the prior question of need.

Family Educational Rights and Privacy Act

In contrast to the omnibus approach of the Privacy Act, the Family Educational Rights and Privacy Act (FERPA), passed in 1974, was directed at educational records. This law gives the parents of minors and students over 18 the "right to inspect and review, and request correction or amendment of, an education record."[24] Educational institutions must inform parents and students of their rights and must draw up appropriate procedures to conform with the regulations of the Act. Since there are over 60 million students, this act covers a great number of people. A privacy law in this area was necessary, because in addition to grades, conduct, and attendance information, some schools keep track of the family life—its stability and economic and social level—and social life of the student, including relationships and membership in churches. The file may also contain psychological test data and teacher evaluations. The unauthorized use of this data could seriously affect the student's life both in and after school.

Schools tend to divulge personal information readily to other schools, law enforcement officials, and for research purposes to the government. Frequently, the interests of the student are secondary. The desire to collect more and more information seems to be increasing, because records are heavily used in decision making. This trend is especially strong in those institutions with large numbers of students. In many postsecondary institutions there is a history of cooperation with law enforcement officials, especially with respect to information about student radicals. It was this rather slipshod treatment of student records, with little access for students or their families, that motivated the passage of FERPA.

Privacy Protection Act of 1980

This Act defines regulations to be followed by law enforcement agencies in acquiring print media records, but it also provides "special protection against search and seizures of materials in the possession of the media and their representatives by federal, state, and local law enforcement agencies. Such materials are subject to seizure by law enforcement agencies *only* if the custodian of the materials is suspected of criminal activity or to prevent the death, serious bodily injury, or destruction of evidence."[25] Reporters may sue for damages if they feel that their right to privacy has been compromised.

Computer Security Act of 1987

This Act creates a means for establishing minimum acceptable security practices for federal computer systems. Responsibility was originally assigned to the National Bureau of Standards (now the National Institute of Standards and Technology, NIST) to develop standards and guidelines to guarantee the security and privacy of the federal computer system, with technical advice provided by the National Security Agency (NSA). The Office of Management of the Budget (OMB) has been working with NIST and NSA to assure the effective implementation of the Act. For example, in 1988, OMB issued guidance to agencies on computer security planning; it co-sponsored a workshop for federal employees on implementing the training and planning portions of the Act; in March of 1989, the inaugural meeting of the Computer System Security and Privacy Advisory Board established by the Act was held; and NIST and NSA reached an agreement that formalized their working relationship in computer security.[26]

Computer Matching and Privacy Protection Act of 1988

This Act amended the Privacy Act to require a biannial report by the President concerning the administration of the law. It was motivated by a concern with the increasing number of computer matches being carried out by various government agencies. In the opinion of Professor David Flaherty, a renowned privacy expert, the Act has a limited scope, "applying only to the 'computerized comparison of records for the purpose of (i) establishing or verifying eligibility for a Federal benefit program, or (ii) recouping payments or delinquent debts under such programs.' It does not apply to matches performed for statistical, research, law enforcement, foreign counterintelligence, security screening, and tax purposes."[27] The Act contains some measures to protect privacy, however: agencies wishing to carry out matching programs must design written agreements describing how the resulting records will be used; citizens to be affected must be given prior notice in the *Federal Register;* "agencies cannot take steps to deny or cut off a benefit to a person on the basis of adverse data uncovered, unless they have validated their accuracy and offered the individual an opportunity to contest the findings [; and] agencies that conduct or participate in matches are required to create Data Integrity Boards, made up of an agency's own senior officials, to oversee and approve matches."[28]

Communication Privacy Protection

Electronic Communications Privacy Act of 1986

Title III of the Omnibus Crime Control and Safe Streets Act of 1968, usually called the Wiretap Act, amended the 1934 Communications Act so that government officials at all levels could legally use wiretaps and other forms of electronic surveillance. This was in the spirit of the times to provide law enforcement agents with wider powers to combat crime. Such technological developments as cellular telephones, citizen band radios, and electronically transmitted information in computer-readable form have created new forms of communication not anticipated in the 1968 Act. Thus, the 1986 Act was enacted to deal with these deficiencies and includes digital communications, data communications, video communications, and a separate chapter on E-mail (electronic mail). Of primary concern with respect to privacy is an amendment that permits the government to contract out the task of monitoring communications pursuant to a court order. The ramifications of this amendment are quite complicated and beyond the scope of the present discussion, but what is clear is that "the infringement of privacy rights will be multiplied by an incalculable factor because of the use of contracting parties. Rather than delegating the responsibility for conducting these privacy-sensitive interceptions, Congress should have added additional staff to the law enforcement agencies charged with conducting interceptions."[29]

Also of considerable interest, given its increasing use, are the provisions with respect to E-mail. It is a criminal offense, in the words of the legislation, to either "intentionally [access] without authorization a facility through which an electronic communication service is provided; or intentionally [exceed] an authorization to access that facility." A fine line must be drawn to permit bulletin boards to function while protecting E-mail. Thus, criminal liability applies only if the person who gains access to a system actually obtains, alters, or prevents another's access to electronic communication. One final provision is that the Act "prohibits an electronic communications service provider from knowingly divulging the contents of any stored electronic communication."[30]

An Overseas Example

There seems to be a general consensus that privacy legislation should be concerned with three broad areas: (1) the setting up of databases and collection of data, (2) procedures for regulating the management of the information, that is, the right of access and data correction, and (3) monitoring and enforcement schemes. Different countries have chosen to emphasize these aspects to varying degrees. A major criticism of the U.S. system of privacy protection is the lack of regulation of private databases. There is nothing comparable to the data protection boards that exist in most European countries.

One country that has launched an approach to record-keeping at odds with the privacy concerns of the Western countries is Thailand. The Thailand Ministry of the Interior has created the Central Population Database (CPD), which "closely *tracks* the 55 million Thais living in 10 million households nationwide. The database, which is the only fully integrated demographics database system in the world, *can* be used to improve the country's standard of living."[31] (Emphasis added.) This comprehensive national database contains extensive demographic information, presumably permitting improved public health planning, educational planning, benefits administration, tax collection and law enforcement. Obviously necessary is a system of national identity cards with personal identification numbers (PIN), containing a thumbprint and photograph. Soon every Thai will have a card, which will also be used for passport, immigration, and refugee control. The director of the CPD center in Bangkok, sensitive to charges of a Big Brother society claims, "It's a system that people need. They accept it. CPD complies with government privacy laws." The Central Population Database was the recipient of a *Computerworld Smithsonian Award* in 1990.

FREEDOM OF INFORMATION

The freedom of information issue exists in uneasy tension with the question of personal privacy. The freedom of information concept is concerned with the rights of citizens to obtain access to information held by the government. The desire to obtain information from the government may endanger the privacy of individuals about whom records are kept. Thus, the situation is such that the individual demands the right to know but at the same time wishes to guard his or her privacy.

It is recognized that the vast amounts of information collected by the government are used to serve the public—for administrative purposes and for planning and research. Research uses—frequently by external agencies, research groups, and universities—involve statistical data in which information about individuals cannot be identified. Although there are some problems, it is generally agreed that information used for such statistical purposes usually protects privacy, and it is readily made available.

The following problem areas arise:

There must be a reconciliation between the freedom to obtain information from the government when that information contains personal information about other people.

Should there be absolute guarantees on the privacy of personal data or should the release of such information be discretionary?

There are currently restrictions on individuals obtaining access to information about themselves. How does this relate to a freedom of information scheme?

Various individual access procedures should be consistent with some overall freedom-of-information concept.

The Freedom of Information Act

The Freedom of Information Act (FOIA) was passed in 1966, went into effect on July 4, 1967, and was subsequently amended in 1974 and 1976. Its basic principle is that any person may request access to government records and may make copies of the same. Certain records are exempt from disclosure. "Record" is taken to mean all the documents either in the possession of an agency or subject to its control. Some of the features of the FOIA are as follows:

Requests must be made to the agency that holds the record—that is, any "executive department, military department, Government corporation, Government-controlled corporation, or other establishments in the Executive Office of the President or any independent regulatory agency."[32]

If an agency refuses to provide the records within a ten-day period, appeal is possible, first to a higher level and then to a district court.

A fee may be charged for searching, reviewing, and copying.

Each agency is required to publish, in the *Federal Register,* information about its organization, access methods, rules of procedure, and so forth.

Not all agencies are required to respond to requests; in fact, there are nine exemptions. The first refers to national defense and foreign policy, and includes executive privilege as it relates to state secrets. A 1974 amendment directed the heads of agencies claiming this exemption to turn documents over to the courts for a final decision. Other exemptions include trade secrets and commercial information, internal personnel rules and practice, information limited by appropriate statutes, inter- and intra-agency memoranda, reports prepared in the course of regulating or supervising financial institutions, and geological and geophysical information. Two exemptions are particularly significant. Exemption (6) excludes "personnel and medical files and similar files the disclosure of which would constitute a *clearly unwarranted invasion of personal privacy.*"[33]

> . . . under normal circumstancs, intimate family relations, personal health, religious and philosophic beliefs and matters that would prove personally embarrassing to an individual of normal sensibilities should not be disclosed.[34]

Exemption (7) deals with law enforcement records. The original wording in the act was criticized because it permitted the withholding of just about any file labelled "investigatory." Amendments introduced in 1974 defined this exemption more precisely. In part, they exclude access to investigatory files if such access "constitutes an unwarranted invasion of personal privacy."[35] This differs from Exemption (6) only in that it omits the word "clearly." The courts have not held this difference to be significant. The FOIA does protect privacy, but the distinction must be made between an individual requesting information about a third party or about himself or herself. The latter case has been dealt with under the terms of the various privacy acts. With regard to the former, the absolutist position would be to restrict all access to personal information about another individual. However, there seems to be general agreement that on occasion the cause of open government must have higher claim than that of personal privacy. For example, it may be necessary to examine information about public officials to determine if they are exercising their responsibilities as required by law. There is a "balancing" test in Exemption (6): For each request for access, privacy and confidentiality must be balanced. Appeal to judicial review is possible, and case law will determine appropriate guidelines over time. Another approach might be to specify, in advance, records for which privacy must be maintained and to exempt them absolutely from disclosure. This approach may not be satisfactory in all cases, as it makes no provision for public's right to know in special circumstances.

Technological innovations have also had an impact on the operation of the FOIA. With the increasing computerization of Federal record-keeping, the question arises as to what constitutes a record under the FOIA. Vast amounts of information can be assembled from various distributed databases, organized under a variety of categories, and selectively printed. As Alan Westin has said, "It's as if you've created a great no man's land of information. Traditionally, thinking has been in terms of paper environments and without any sophistication about electronic information."[36] John Markoff, a writer on technology issues for *The New York Times* notes, "There are no explicit legal guidelines that agencies must follow when programming their computers to extract information asked for under the act. Nor are there guidelines on the form in which agencies must release the data. Some experts argue that unless issues involving computerized records can be resolved by the courts or by new laws, the lack of guidelines will become a common way for agencies to deny requests."[37] The interesting question is how much computing, if any, the government is required to do in order to respond to a request for information. On the other hand, the government could release enormous quantities of paper instead of using computers to produce a succinct, directed response. Thus, there is considerable interest in amending the FOIA to accommodate electronic information.

ISSUES AND PROBLEMS: PRESENT AND FUTURE

Privacy as an issue will not disappear. In fact, it will become more pronounced as the computer makes even greater inroads in the functioning of society. Future problems are inextricably linked to the ability of the computer to process large amounts of information efficiently and rapidly. Although the computer has brought certain problems to the fore, the importance of privacy is a societal issue and its protection depends on a host of social concerns.

Caller ID

Telephone companies around the country have started to make available to consumers a service commonly called caller ID. Simply put, when a call is made, the receiver will be able to see the telephone number of the caller on a small liquid crystal display. Thus, by having access to the telephone number in advance, the receiver can decide whether or not to answer and in the case of obscene, threatening, or unwanted calls, to gain knowledge of the incoming number. On the other side, callers will be forced to reveal unlisted numbers thereby losing a certain measure of privacy. More advanced systems can automatically match the incoming call against a stored list of numbers and them display the name of the caller permitting the receiver to prepare a ready response. Of course the caller could use a public telephone to conceal his or her identity or take advantage of a newly available third-party service for rerouting calls at a cost. Caller ID seems to have obvious value but many concerned about privacy have voiced objections. Consider the following arguments against Caller ID:[38]

- Unblockable Caller ID clearly violates the "trap and trace" provision of the state wire-tap act.
- Bell's other new "IQ services," like Call Trace, Call Return, and Call Back, provide virtually all the opportunity for reducing harassing and obscene phone calls. . . .
- Caller ID will be used by commercial operations to compile phone lists for phone solicitation.
- I believe that unblockable Caller ID will sooner or later cause the death or injury of a police officer doing undercover work or a person hiding from an abusive partner. [A reverse directory will make this possible.]

One commentator in favor of Caller ID suggests remedies to allay the fears of those concerned about loss of privacy. He suggests that telephone companies offer blocking free to anyone who wants it, with the knowledge that some abusive callers will be the first to take advantage of this option. By using call tracing, the numbers of unwanted callers can be trapped at the phone company.[39]

Unregulated Databases

Companies have fired workers from jobs without cause, doctors have refused to take new patients who are able to afford medical care, and apartment managers have refused to rent to prospective tenants with regular jobs and sufficient income. Many similar cases have been documented with the common denominator that the companies, doctors, and managers have all taken advantage of special purpose commercial databases directed towards their concerns. Companies can turn to databases to determine if any of their workers have filed a worker compensation claim elsewhere, as well as the disposition of the case. Other blacklists will provide information to physicians if a prospective patient has ever sued a doctor for malpractice, or will provide information to an apartment manager if a prospective tenant has ever brought a claim for a violation of tenant's rights. The data for these lists is openly available in tenants' courts, small claims courts, worker compensation hearings, and civil court proceedings. All that is required is sufficient staff to extract relevant information from these records and then enter it into the database. By focusing on large population centers, companies with comprehensive databases find a ready market for their services. And it is all legal; the only possible danger may result from inaccurate data. Credit bureaus, banks, cable companies, and video rental stores are all subject to a certain degree of regulation with respect to the privacy of their clients but there do not exist uniform laws to protect the privacy of citizens in all their commercial activities.

The National Practitioner Databank

For years it has been difficult, if not impossible, to monitor the movements of health care professionals who, having been disciplined by one board, move to a new jurisdiction, leaving behind their flawed record and presenting themselves as competent professionals. In 1986, Congress passed a law to set up a national database, the National Practitioner Databank, of disciplinary actions taken against physicians, dentists, nurses, therapists, and other licensed health professionals. The databank, accessible to hospitals, licensing agencies, and other medical groups, but not the general public, will supply such information as professional misconduct (including making sexual overtures to patients), misdiagnosis, and mistreatment, but not personal matters such as arrests, non-payment of taxes, or drug or alcohol abuse (except when professional performance is affected). In more detail, the data bank will store the following information:[40]

- Disciplinary measures taken by state licensing boards regarding all licensed health practitioners.
- Malpractice payments made by all entities, including hospitals, medical groups and insurance companies.
- Restrictions of privileges invoked against doctors and dentists by hospitals and clinics; hospitals and clinics have the option of including restrictions imposed on other health professionals.
- Disciplinary actions made by medical and dental societies regarding doctors and dentists.
- State actions against hospitals, health maintenance organizations and other health care groups.

The data bank, popularly known as "docs in a box" opened for business on September 1, 1990, as names of offending health care professionals were entered. Doctors are permitted to inspect their own files and to enter explanatory statements, if they wish. The American Medical Association, which initially opposed the databank, now supports it but would like "nuisance suits" to be left off. Hospitals will have to improve their verification of doctors' records and to rationalize their disciplinary procedures, because of the serious consequences of including such actions in the National Databank. Presumably the public will benefit in that incompetent health practitioners will no longer be able to find new places to work where their past record is unknown. Here is an important case in which the need of hospitals to know about their staff's background, in order to provide competent medical care and to reduce costly malpractice suits, outweighs any claim to privacy by members of that staff.

Electronic Mail

An important component of office automation, electronic mail, or E-mail, was discussed in Chapter 4. Although it has proven to be an extremely useful communication tool and facilitates cooperation throughout the company, an important privacy issue has emerged, one strongly related to the growing concern with workers' rights. (See Chapter 10.) The basic question is to what degree management can monitor its employees' E-mail, either on an occasional or regular basis. A class action suit launched in August 1990 against Epson America Inc. for "allegedly violating its employees' privacy by intercepting their E-mail," was dismissed in January 1991 in a Los Angeles County Superior Court because "the company did not violate a state penal code prohibiting electronic eavesdropping on private communications."[41] Another suit was filed against Nissan Motor Corp. in January 1991 by two employees, again in California, accusing the company of intercepting their electronic messages and violating their privacy. Some companies argue that they reserve the right to intercept messages, without prior warning, as a means of ensuring that employees do not abuse the system with personal communications. What does seem necessary is that companies issue clear guidelines, based on discussions with their employees about the use and misuse of E-mail, and that both employees and employers adhere to them.

MarketPlace

On January 23, 1991, Lotus Development Corp. and Equifax Inc. announced that they were cancelling a product called Lotus MarketPlace: Households, a CD-ROM read-only database package for Macintosh computers, containing the names, addresses, estimated income, and buying habits of 120 million American consumers. Some 30,000 Americans complained to Lotus and demanded that their names be removed because prior permission had not been obtained by Lotus to sell their personal information. One of the leaders against the sale of MarketPlace was Marc Rotenberg, director of the Washington, D.C. office of Computer Professionals for Social Responsibility: "There is no product that would have made more detailed personal information available on more people than MarketPlace."[42] Robert Ellis Smith, the publisher of the newsletter *Privacy Journal*, wrote to Equifax demanding that the product be withdrawn: "It violates a century-old principle of American privacy law: that a person's name or likeness may not be used commercially without consent and without compensating the individual."[43]

In withdrawing the project, Jim Manzi, Lotus's president and chief executive officer said, "While we believe that the actual data content and controls built into the product preserved consumer privacy, we couldn't ignore the high level of consumer concern. . . . After examining all of the issues we have decided that the cost and complexity of educating consumers about the issues is beyond the scope of Lotus as an information provider."[44] The removal of MarketPlace from the marketplace represents an important success of the privacy advocacy movement and augurs well for the future protection of privacy.

Electronic Monitoring Systems

Across the country, the prisons are overcrowded and solutions are being sought for ways to alleviate these conditions. In some jurisdictions, judges have forbidden the imprisonment of convicted felons until the prison population is reduced. One answer is the home imprisonment of non-violent offenders and their control by means of electronic monitors in the form of bracelets or anklets. These devices, attached by tamperproof straps, contain a transmitter that broadcasts continuously to a receiver located in the offender's home telephone and then relays the signal to a computer in the probation office. The electronic monitor has a limited range, typically 100 feet, and if the wearer strays beyond this distance, the computer will warn the probation officer. Attempts to remove the device also produce warning signals. More recent technology depends on cellular telephones and portable automobile receivers as well as the possibility of administering a low level shock if the wearer moves beyond the restricted range.

Certainly, for the offenders, living at home away from all the dangers of prison is important, and in addition, by maintaining a semblance of normality, it is possible to repay society in a positive way. One serious drawback is the apparent loss of privacy, but if the offender has given informed consent, has voluntarily waived his rights, and has been assured of strict adherence to a set of rules by administrators, it may be a reasonable alternative. The usual bureaucratic concerns of cost-benefit analysis are still in question, and for many, the psychological problems associated with constant surveillance are unsettling, but for a society facing continued growth in crime and prison overcrowding, it is not surprising that such a technological fix has been chosen.

Transborder Data Flows

Individual countries have formulated privacy protection laws that may not be compatible. The European Economic Community has agreed to a convention for privacy protection that will cover the flow of information among member states. Problems arise when countries whose privacy laws are not compatible wish to exchange information. As there are international agreements in many areas, one might eventually expect treaties in this area as well. In the absence of such agreements, countries may refuse to permit personal data to be sent to other countries where the laws are weaker or do not apply to nonresidents. The urgent need for international treaties may not be apparent in the United States. Because it is so prominent in the data transmission field, the United States may be said to be a data-exporting country.

Concluding Remarks

The right to privacy is not viewed as an absolute right, especially with respect to information. In fact, the word "privacy" does not appear in the Bill of Rights. The major thrust of legislation has been to control, not to forbid, the collection and use of private information. Information about any individual is not always in that individual's control. Rather it can be gathered, stored, and disseminated by both private and public agencies. The law has provided protection, and one must continue to turn to the law for future protection. The distinguished jurist, William O. Douglas, referred to the police in the following quotation, but he might just as well have been concerned with other institutions and groups in society:[45]

> The free state offers what a police state denies—the privacy of the home, the dignity and peace of mind of the individual. That precious right to be let alone is violated once the police enter our conversations.

What do the 1990s hold for computer technology and privacy? The long-time contributor to the computer and privacy debate, Rein Turn, points out the following issues:[46]

- Creation of integrated personal information record-keeping systems as byproducts of services provided, or as the principal services or products themselves.
- Automated, autonomously operating data collection and transmission units (e.g., digital transponders) which directly involve, or permit, inferring personal information.
- Automated decision making about individuals based on computerized personal information profiles.
- Systems that permit linking of personal databases, or that increase the potential of illicit access to, use of, or dissemination of personal information. Systems that aid and abet in evading or circumventing privacy protection requirements and enforcements.

In the legislative arena, the major efforts may be towards the creation of data protection boards, in the European model, to apply both to the public and private sectors. Advocates admit that success in the near future is not likely, given strong opposition from companies in the information industries. Nevertheless, the Association for Computing Machinery issued a press release on May 7, 1991 urging "stronger governmental action to protect privacy." Among its resolutions was the following:[47]

> The ACM supports the establishment of a proactive governmental privacy protection mechanism in those countries that do not currently have such mechanisms, including the United States, that would ensure individual privacy safeguards.

SUMMARY

The impact of computers on privacy is one of the major concerns voiced by the public at large. Although most people agree that computers have improved the quality of life, there is a definite apprehension that some form of an Orwellian *1984* society is not far off. Privacy is an important but difficult right to maintain when so much information about individuals is gathered and stored by both public and private agencies. Personal data must be safeguarded and only used for the purpose for which it was originally collected.

One of the fears of legitimate groups is that databases built up by government surveillance will be used to harass lawful activities. The increasing use of computer matching is of concern to civil libertarians, because the searching of computer records in order to turn up possible violations seems to be an action contrary to the presumption of innocence. Credit bureaus play a major role in the marketing of information. Because credit ratings are so important in almost every aspect of life, it is necessary to guarantee that such data is as accurate as possible and that individuals be informed as to its use.

In response to public concern, a number of acts have been passed by the federal government to deal with the most serious violations. The European approach in the private sector is to establish government agencies to license and regulate companies which operate databases. Freedom of information occasionally conflicts with privacy rights, but balances must be struck to ensure that the public is able to obtain information about the actions of government.

NOTES

1. Louis Harris & Associates and Dr. Alan F. Westin, *The Dimensions of Privacy: A National Opinion Research Survey of Attitudes Toward Privacy* (Conducted for Sentry Insurance, New York: Garland Publishing, 1981). The poll was conducted between November 30 and December 10, 1978 and between November 27, 1978 and January 4, 1979.
   Louis Harris & Associates, *The Road after 1984: The Impact of Technology on Society* (for Southern New England Telephone, December 1983). The poll was conducted between September 1 and September 11 and between September 7 and September 23, 1983.
   Louis Harris & Associates and Dr. Alan F. Westin, *The Equifax Report on Consumers in the Information Age* (for Equifax Inc., 1990). This poll was conducted between January 11 and February 11 and between April 20 and April 30, 1990.
2. *The Equifax Report on Consumers in the Information Age,* pp. 69–70.
3. *The Equifax Report on Consumers in the Information Age,* pp. 7, 11, 23.
4. From Alan F. Westin, *Privacy and Freedom* (Atheneum Publishers, an imprint of Macmillan Publishing Company, copyright © 1967 by the Association of the Bar of the City of New York), p. 7.
5. Kent Greenwalt, "Privacy and Its Legal Protections," *Hastings Center Studies,* September 1974, p. 45.
6. *Privacy and Computers,* Department of Communications/Department of Justice, Canada (Ottawa: Information Canada, 1972), p. 13.
7. *Records, Computers, and the Rights of Citizens,* U.S. Department of Health, Report to the Secretary's Advisory Committee on Automated Personal Data Systems (Washington, D.C., 1973), pp. 40–41.
8. *Ibid.,* p. 41.
9. Westin, *Privacy and Freedom,* p. 158.
10. *Personal Privacy in an Information Society,* Report of the Privacy Protection Study Commission (Washington, D.C., 1977), pp. 14–15.
11. Richard D. Kusserow, "The Government Needs Computer Matching to Root Out Waste and Fraud," *Communications of the ACM,* **27**(6), June 1984, p. 543.
12. *Privacy Act: Federal Agencies' Implementation Can Be Improved.* (Washington, D.C.: United States General Accounting Office, GAO/GGD-86-107, August 1986), p. 47.
13. *Ibid.,* p. 49.
14. Written statement of J. C. Penney Company, Inc. to the Privacy Protection Study Commission, February 12, 1976, as quoted in *Personal Privacy in an Information Society,* p. 43.
15. "Resolved: Credit/Privacy Laws Need to Be Revised," *At Home With Consumers,* **10**(3), December 1989, pp. 2, 4. Published by the Direct Selling Education Foundation.
16. Senator Sam J. Ervin, Jr., Foreword to Arthur R. Miller, *The Assault on Privacy: Computers, Data Banks, and Dossiers* (Ann Arbor, Michigan: University of Michigan Press, 1971).
17. *Records, Computers, and the Rights of Citizens,* pp. 66–69.
18. As quoted in Warren Freedman, *The Right of Privacy in the Computer Age* (New York: Quorum Books, 1987), p. 14.
19. Richard F. Hixson, *Privacy in a Public Society: Human Rights in Conflict* (New York: Oxford University Press, 1987), p. 220.
20. Jeffrey Rothfeder, Stephen Phillips, Dean Foust, Wanda Cantrell, Paula Dwyer, and Michael Galen, "Is Nothing Private?" *Business Week,* September 4, 1989, p. 74.
21. David H. Flaherty, *Protecting Privacy in Two-Way Electronic Services* (White Plains, New York: Knowledge Industry Publications, Inc., 1985), p. 102.
22. Section s.2(b) of the Privacy Act of 1974, 5 United States Code, section s.552a, passed as part of Public Law 93-579.
23. *Personal Privacy in an Information Society,* p. xv.
24. *Ibid.,* p. 413.
25. Freedman, *The Right of Privacy in the Computer Age,* p. 15.
26. *Managing Federal Information Resources,* Seventh Annual Report Under the Paperwork Reduction Act of 1980, Office of the Management of the Budget (Washington, D.C., 1989), pp. 35–36.

27. David H. Flaherty, *Protecting Privacy in Surveillance Societies: The Federal Republic of Germany, Sweden, France, Canada, and the United States* (Chapel Hill, North Carolina: The University of North Carolina Press, 1989), pp. 357–358.
28. *Ibid.*
29. Russell S. Burnside, "The Electronic Communications Privacy Act of 1986: The Challenge of Applying Ambiguous Statutory Languages to Intricate Telecommunication Technologies," *Rutgers Computer & Technology Law Journal,* **13**(2), 1987, p. 508.
30. *Ibid.,* p. 512.
31. Carol Hildebrand, "Thailand's Database Aimed at Social Needs," *Computerworld,* July 30, 1990, p. 14.
32. *Public Government for Private People, Volume 2,* The Report of the Commission on Freedom and Individual Privacy, Province of Ontario, Canada (Toronto, 1980), pp. 455–457.
33. *Ibid.,* p. 114.
34. *Ibid.*
35. *Ibid.,* p. 115.
36. As quoted in John Markoff, "Freedom of Information Act Facing a Stiff Challenge in Computer Age," *The New York Times,* June 18, 1989, p. Y 13.
37. *Ibid.*
38. Joseph Rhodes, Jr. is a Commissioner on the Pennsylvania Public Utilities Commission. His arguments (reprinted from *Privacy Journal,* Providence, Rhode Island, March 1990, pp. 4–5) are taken from a dissenting statement to the Commission, which approved the proposal by Bell Telephone of Pennsylvania to offer Caller ID services. This approval was challenged in the courts and in May 1990, the courts rejected Caller ID as a form of illegal wiretapping.
39. Peter Coy, "Why All the Heavy Breathing Over Caller ID," *Business Week,* June 18, 1990, p. 34.
40. Martin Tolchin, "Agency Will Track Those Disciplined Over Medical Care," *The New York Times,* September 25, 1988, pp. 1, 18. Copyright © 1988 by The New York Times Company. Reprinted by permission.
41. Jim Nash and Maureen J. Harrington, "Who Can Open E-mail?" *Computerworld,* January 14, 1991, pp. 1, 88.
42. Richard Pastore, "Lotus Decision Impact Weighed," *Computerworld,* February 4, 1991, p. 36.
43. Robert Ellis Smith, "Lotus, Equifax Cave into Privacy Demands," *Privacy Journal,* January 1991, p. 1.
44. Press Release, "Lotus, Equifax Cancel Shipment of Lotus MarketPlace: Households," distributed over electronic mail, January 23, 1991.
45. William O. Douglas, Address to the American Law Institute, 1953.
46. Rein Turn, "Information Privacy Issues for the 1990s," *Proceedings of the 1990 IEEE Computer Society Symposium on Research in Security and Privacy,* May 7–9, 1990, Oakland, California, p. 398.
47. Press Release, "ACM Urges Stronger Governmental Action to Protect Privacy," Association for Computing Machinery, New York, May 7, 1991.

ADDITIONAL READINGS

The Nature of Privacy

Burnham, David. *The Rise of the Computer State.* New York: Random House, 1983.
Smith, Robert Ellis. *Privacy: How to Protect What's Left of It.* Garden City, NJ: Anchor/Doubleday, 1979.

Databases

Computer Matching: Assessing Its Costs and Benefits. Washington, D.C.: United States General Accounting Office, GAO/PEMD-87-2, November 1986.

Computer-Based National Information Systems: Technology and Public Policy Issues. Washington, D.C.: U.S. Congress, Office of Technology Assessment, OTA-CIT-146, September, 1981.
Federal Government Information Technology: Electronic Record Systems and Individual Privacy. Washington, D.C.: U.S. Congress, Office of Technology Assessment, OTA-CIT-296, June 1986.
Flaherty, David H. *Privacy and Government Data Banks.* London: Mansell, 1979.
Miller, Arthur. *The Assault on Privacy.* Ann Arbor, Michigan: University of Michigan Press, 1971.

Privacy Legislation

Campbell, Duncan and Conner, Steve. *On the Record: Surveillance, Computers and Privacy—The Inside Story.* London: Michael Joseph, 1986.
Federal Government Information Technology: Electronic Surveillance and Civil Liberties. Washington, D.C.: U.S. Congress, Office of Technology Assessment, OTA-CIT-293, October 1985.
Gulleford, Kenneth. *Data Protection in Practice.* London: Butterworths, 1986.
Linowes, David F. *Privacy in America: Is Your Private Life in the Public Eye?* Urbana and Chicago: University of Chicago Press, 1989.
Rothfeder, Jeffrey. "Congress Should Put a Lid on What Credit Bureaus Let Out." *Business Week,* July 2, 1990, p. 57.
Rubin, Michael Rogers. *Private Rights, Public Wrongs: The Computer and Personal Privacy.* Norwood, New Jersey: Ablex Publishing, 1988.
Rule, James, McAdam, Douglas, Stearns, Linda, and Uglow, David. *The Politics of Privacy.* New York: Elsevier, 1980.
Weingarten, Fred W. "Communications Technologies: New Challenges to Privacy." *The John Marshall Law Review,* **21**(4), Summer 1988, pp. 735–753.

Freedom of Information

Autin, Diana M. T. K. "The Reagan Administration and the Freedom of Information Act." In Richard O. Curry (ed.). *Freedom at Risk.* Philadelphia: Temple University Press, 1988, pp. 69–85.
"Keeping Secrets: Congress, The Courts, and National Security Information." *Harvard Law Review,* **103**(4), February, 1990, pp. 906–925.
Susman, Thomas M. "The Privacy Act and the Freedom of Information Act: Conflict and Resolution." *The John Marshall Law Review,* **21**(4), Summer 1988, pp. 703–733.

Issues and Problems

McCarthy, Belinda R. (ed.). *Intermediate Punishments: Intensive Supervision, Home Confinement, and Electronic Surveillance.* Monsey, New York: Criminal Justice Press (a division of Willow Tree Press), 1987.
Hilts, Philip J. "Oversight Phase I: Keeping Records of Doctors with Records." *The New York Times,* September 9, 1990, p. E 26.
Berman, Jerry and Goldman, Janlori. *A Federal Right of Privacy: The Need for Reform.* Washington, D.C.: Benton Foundation Project on Communications and Information Policy Options, 1989.
Rotenberg, Marc, Culnan, Mary J., and Rosenberg, Ronni. "Prepared Testimony and Statement for the Record on Computer Privacy and H.R. 3669, The Data Protection Act of 1990." The Subcommittee on Government Information, Justice and Agriculture, Committee on Government Operations, May 16, 1990.
Smith, Robert Ellis. "A First in New York City." *Privacy Journal,* April 1991, pp. 1–2. New York State has established eight privacy principles as guidelines that telephone companies must meet if they wish to gain approval for the introduction of new technologies.

10

EMPLOYMENT AND UNEMPLOYMENT

Any kind of machinery used for shortening labour — except used in a cooperative society like ours — must tend to less wages, and to deprive working men of employment, and finally, either to starve them, force them into some other employment (and then reduce wages in that also), or compel them to emigrate. Now, if the working classes would socially and peacefully unite to adopt our system, no power or party could prevent their success.

***Manifesto, Cooperative Community,* Ralahine, County Clare, Ireland, 1883 (on introduction of the reaping machine.)**

INTRODUCTION

The most serious and complex problem associated with the impact of computers on society has to do with work. The basic and simplistic expression of this concern is the question, does technological change create, or destroy, jobs? In the present context, technological change refers to innovations in computer and communications technology. Definitive answers are scarce; by way of exploration, the arguments may be briefly stated as follows. Yes, the introduction of new technology may reduce the number of jobs in the directly affected industry. On the other hand, it may actually increase the number, because increased productivity resulting from the new technology will increase demand, and more workers will be necessary to satisfy it. Even if there is a net loss of jobs in a specific industry, it is argued, new jobs will be created in support areas for the new technology, in whole new industries resulting from unpredictable technology, and in the service and white collar areas. For example, the introduction of robots will create a robot support industry to install, service, and monitor performance, to say nothing of design and manufacture. Jobs are eliminated in those industries that benefit from robots but are created in the robot support companies. The common term for this effect is *job displacement.* The question about technology and jobs can be restated in terms of the economy as a whole, to take job displacement into account.

Assuming that new jobs will be created, will there be a sufficient number to take up the slack? It is likely that in factories that manufacture robots, robots themselves will be a major factor in production. The technology associated with computers is qualitatively different from previous technologies. It brings not only ways to do things more efficiently, but also the possibility of doing many things with very few workers. The possibility that many of society's needs could be satisfied with a significantly reduced work force is of concern to many people.

What about the theory that an unending chain of inventions and discoveries will always be part of our future, creating new products and new jobs? In our time such inventions and processes as Xeroxing, Polaroid cameras, video cassette recorders, and personal computers have certainly created new industries and jobs in design, manufacturing, marketing, sales, and service. In the past 200 years, since the beginning of the Industrial Revolution in England, enough jobs have been created, it has been claimed, to accommodate growth in population, increasing urbanization and reduction of farm labor, and a rapidly accelerating chain of inventions. These observations apply only to the Western world, and not necessarily in the last few years.

Prior to the Industrial Revolution, most of the population was engaged in agriculture. With advances in farming machinery, fertilizers, and disease-resistant and weather-conditioned crops, productivity on the farm has soared. Currently, in the United States about 3% of the work force produces enough food for the entire country, as well as enormous quantities for export. Where did all the farm workers go? Most of them became blue collar workers in the rapidly growing industrial plants. Recently, the percentage of the work force in blue collar jobs has been decreasing. Most American workers are now employed in service and white collar jobs—that is, they do not produce things but work with people, paper, and information.

The expectation now is that as society moves from an industrial to an information base, the major source of new jobs will be in the office, in service areas such as restaurants, hotels, and entertainment, in the financial domain, and in government. The model of the future has a much-reduced labor force in production and an expanded number of people in the service and information areas. There is a serious problem with this view—the increasing rate of automation in the office. The introduction of computers, office networks, telecommunication systems, and fax machines has as its goal a major improvement in office productivity, but as a byproduct there will be fewer jobs. Of these, fewer will be the kind of low-skill jobs that have traditionally served as an entry point for many hundreds of thousands of workers.

Another major concern is with the changing nature of work. The Industrial Revolution spawned a number of responses from workers whose livelihood was threatened by the use of machines. Probably the most well-known were the Luddites, who flourished in the beginning of the eighteenth century. They are best known for having smashed newly introduced machines—in blind opposition to progress, according to the conventional view. The well-known British historian E. P. Thompson has argued as follows:

> At issue was the "freedom" of the capitalist to destroy the customs of the trade, whether by new machinery, by the factory-system, or by unrestricted competition, beating down wages, undercutting his rivals, and undermining the standards of craftsmanship.[1]

Since that time there has been an uneasy relationship between the worker and new technology. While welcoming the relief from drudgery and dangerous work that machines have provided, the worker has been concerned first with becoming merely an adjunct to the machine and then being replaced by it. In many cases the machines themselves were dangerous.

This fear has grown, especially in the factory, as work has become organized under such principles as scientific management (Frederick Taylor) and the assembly line (Henry Ford). The reduction of production to a series of small, repeatable actions encouraged a belief that the worker was easily replaceable, that his or her skill could be extracted, and that he or she would perform a boring, routine task efficiently for many years of working life. The computer can be seen merely as the most recent phase of technology or as a new force that gives management a powerful tool for extending its control, whether in factory or office. Computers and communications systems may reproduce the factory model in the office—at least this is the fear of many workers. The relatively open social system in the office may be replaced by a rigid, highly structured environment in which the performance of the worker at the terminal may be closely monitored.

EXPERIENCES OF WORKERS

> Workers are not all alike: they have different needs, interests and motivations. Moreover, these characteristics constantly change over the career of each worker, much as the modal work values of the society as a whole shift over time.[2]

Computers will make their presence felt in several ways in both factory and office. Computers have been used to automate various decision-making processes so that workers who formerly monitored ongoing production now must watch video terminals to see what is happening. The most dramatic innovation in the factory is the introduction of robots into the assembly line. (See Chapter 12). In both factory and office, there may be problems in integrating people and machines in an efficient, safe, and productive manner.

Workers Voice their Concerns

> The men and women who do the hard work of the world have learned from him [Ruskin] and Morris that they have a right to pleasure in their toil, and that when justice is done them they will have it. (William Dean Howells, *Criticism and Fiction,* 1981).

It is useful and important to characterize the nature of the workplace as seen through the eyes of the workers themselves. The opinions of satisfied or indifferent workers, probably a majority, are sometimes neglected in favor of the angry or frustrated one. Our interest is in real and potential problems, difficulties, and alienation, but how representative these angry voices are is a real question. It is also true that in times when unemployment rates are high, workers are less likely to complain openly.

What aspects of work are likely to be most affected by computers? In the words of a spot welder in an automobile assembly plant,

> I don't understand how come more guys don't flip. Because you're nothing more than a machine when you hit this type of thing. They give better care to that machine than they will to you. They'll have more respect, give more attention to that machine. And you know this. Somehow you get the feeling that the machine is better than you are. (Laughs.)[3]

The theme of the machine receiving preferred treatment is likely to become more common. The machine referred to above is in fact part of traditional assembly line equipment, which differs significantly from a new generation of equipment. Robots are a form of flexible automation that can be programmed to perform a variety of tasks. The relationship of the worker to such new machines will be different. Will workers perceive themselves as mere caretakers, or as surviving only until the next generation of even more sophisticated machines? Their concern derives from a real awareness of their place in the production process.

> You really begin to wonder. What price do they put on me? Look at the price they put on the machine. If that machine breaks down, there's somebody out there to fix it right away. If I break down, I'm just pushed over to the other side till another man takes my place. The only thing they have on their mind is to keep that line running.[4]

There is nothing unique about the American experience in this regard, of course. Witness the following account describing work in a Japanese automobile factory:[5]

> I have really been fooled by the seeming slowness of the conveyor belt. No one can understand how it works without experiencing it. Almost as soon as I begin, I am dripping with sweat. Somehow, I learn the order of the work motions, but I'm totally unable to keep up with the speed of the line. My work gloves make it difficult to grab as many tiny bolts as I need, and how many precious seconds do I waste doing just that? . . . If a different model transmission comes along, it's simply beyond my capacity. Some skill is needed, and a new hand like me can't do it alone, I'm thirsty as hell, but workers can neither smoke nor drink water. Going to the toilet is out of the question. Who could have invented a system like this? It's designed to make workers do nothing but work and to prevent any kind of rest.

Some Historical Issues

The history of technological innovation and its effect on the workplace is complex. To begin with, it is almost impossible to discuss the history of work without assuming a particular political viewpoint. In its starkest form, the capitalist or free enterprise position argues that the constant pressure to increase productivity, in order to meet competition, results in increased investment in capital equipment. The worker is gradually relieved of a dangerous environment, complex decision making, and the power to disrupt the productive process. From a Marxist point of view, the basic goals of capitalist management are simply to extract skills from workers and to achieve sufficient return on investment by reducing the cost of labor. Management also wants complete control over its workers—to use them as it wishes, independently of their needs and desires as human beings.

Free enterprise spokesmen point out that industrialization has permitted workers to improve substantially their standard of living. Marxists argue that the price has been high—loss of autonomy, loss of skills, and loss of respect. Technological optimists predict that the age of computers will accelerate benefits, with more and cheaper goods available, less work necessary to maintain income levels, and improved living conditions for the Third World. A closer examination of the industrialization process reveals a rather disturbing long-term trend: Workers have been losing control, initiative, and skills.

An important examination of this process was carried out by Harry Braverman. Written from a Marxist point of view, his book has been recognized even by non-Marxist economists and sociologists as a valuable contribution to the history of labor studies.[6] In his view, the most important implication of the Industrial Revolution for the worker was loss of control. In the evolution of the craftsman working on his or her own to the worker on the factory floor, the distinguishing feature is loss of control—over pace of work, the individual steps, and the quality of the product. From this loss—this sale of one's labor—many consequences follow. The worker and the work process have been endlessly studied in order to improve efficiency, reduce costs, and (in Marxist terms) squeeze out the last drop of surplus labor.

Scientific Management

As enterprises grew larger the problems of organization became paramount. Near the end of the nineteenth century serious attempts were made to apply new techniques to the management of large and complex companies. Initiated by Frederick Winslow Taylor, this principled effort was called scientific management. He bluntly stated that it was management's sole responsibility and duty to control every facet of labor's activity. Although previous thought and practice had recognized this domination, Taylor set out to demonstrate in painstaking detail how management could translate its power into the closely controlled supervision of the labor process. He based all his subsequent research on the notion of "a fair day's work"—apparently, the maximum amount of work a worker could do on a regular basis throughout his lifetime without damaging his health. In the eyes of management, when workers slow their pace, loaf or talk, they fail to fulfill their potential, and here scientific management comes into play. The worker attempts to conceal from management how fast the work can actually be done; so management is paying a salary that does not correlate with the realities of the situation. Supervision and discipline that are vague and general will not be adequate as long as the workers themselves control the labor process. From first-hand experience, and a series of experiments that took 26 years, Taylor derived a precise formulation by which workers could be carefully instructed in each movement of their prescribed tasks.

Taylor's contributions can be summed up in terms of three principles, as follows:[7]

1. Dissociation of the labor process from the skills of the workers. Management should organize the labor process independently of the workers' knowledge and craft.

2. Separation of conception from execution. Basically, the task of the worker is to perform a series of prescribed actions that do not involve planning or decision making. The worker must not introduce his or her ideas into the labor process because this compromises management's control.
3. The use of the monopoly over knowledge to control each step of the labor process and its mode of execution.

The implementation of these principles involves the systematic planning of each production step and the careful instruction of workers in its proper execution. Scientific management and its successor theories became a dominant force in the growth of large industrial enterprises.

The Modern Assembly Line

At the turn of the century, the production of automobiles was essentially a craft. Individual mechanics would move around a stationary work site until the assembly of the automobile was complete. After Henry Ford introduced the Model T in 1908, the demand was so enormous that new production techniques were needed. In 1914, the first continuous assembly line was introduced at his Highland Park plant near Detroit. The improvements in productivity were astounding. Within three months an automobile could be assembled in about one-tenth the time, and "by 1925 an organization had been created which produced almost as many cars in a single day as had been produced, early in the history of the Model T, in an entire year."[8] The pay structure was flattened, and bonuses and incentives were done away with. They were no longer necessary to stimulate productivity, because the combination of the division of labor and the moving assembly line meant that management could precisely control the rate of production. The assembly line principle quickly spread to other industries and served as a foundation for industrial growth.

Worker reaction was decisive and negative: they left in large numbers as other work was available. In 1913, the turnover rate was 380% and a major unionization drive began. In response Ford increased pay to $5.00 per day, considerably above the going rate. This measure stemmed the flow of workers and introduced another feature to the industrial scene—the use of higher wages to limit possible disruptions. This strategy has also been one of the responses appropriated by labor unions to accommodate to the potential and actual loss of jobs resulting from the introduction of computers.

COMPUTERS AND EMPLOYMENT

> They talk of the dignity of work. Bosh. The dignity is in leisure. (Herman Melville, *Redburn*.)

Before examining computers and employment, it will be useful to consider the broader perspective of technology in general.

Technology and Employment

> "I don't like making men redundant," he said, "but we're caught in a double bind. If we don't modernize we lose competitive edge and have to make men redundant, and if we do modernize we have to make men redundant because we don't need 'em any more."[9]

In a recent study by the National Academies of Sciences and Engineering and the Institute of Medicine on technology and employment in the United States, the following principal finding was given:[10]

> Technological change is an essential component of a dynamic, expanding economy. The modern U.S. economic system, in which international trade plays an increasingly important role, must generate and adopt advanced technologies rapidly, in both the manufacturing and nonmanufacturing sectors, if growth in employment and wages is to be maintained. Recent and prospective levels of technological change will not produce significant increases in total unemployment, although individuals will face painful and costly adjustments. Rather than producing mass unemployment, technological change will make its maximum contribution to higher living standards, wages, and employment levels if appropriate public and private policies are adopted to support the adjustment to new technologies.

In this carefully worded statement, the obvious is juxtaposed with the speculative. Yes, technology is important, no significant levels of unemployment will result, but "individuals" beware, and all will be fine if government and business cooperate.

As part of a comprehensive analysis on the relationship between technology and structural unemployment, the Office of Technology Assessment (OTA) of the U.S. Congress was concerned with the problems of reemploying workers displaced by technology.[11] It is clear that changes in technology can be disruptive, making some jobs obsolete and reducing opportunities for others. But perhaps a definition of technology itself would be helpful. It certainly includes tools, devices, machines, and all manner of equipment, but it also includes a body of knowledge incorporated in processes, skills, routines, and organization of work and social groupings. This latter component is frequently overlooked when the impact of new hardware is evaluated. It is also important to understand the dependent concept of productivity. There are several definitions but labor productivity is typically defined as the goods or services produced per employee-hour. This measure depends crucially on capital investment in technology to reduce the labor component and thereby increase labor productivity. That is, with more equipment or improved processes, fewer people may be needed to produce the same or greater amounts of products or services. One striking example may suffice: in 1950, some 244,000 operators were required to handle over 175 million long-distance calls; in 1980, about 128,000 operators handled over 2.64 billion calls, an increase in productivity of almost 60-fold. Of course, such a dramatic increase was only possible with improved switching equipment, which resulted in a steep increase in the number of direct long-distance dialings. So in fact, operators are probably not handling many more calls themselves, an observation that points out the weakness of the definition of labor productivity.

In any case, as OTA points out, labor productivity is only one factor in overall productivity and efficiency. Others include "good labor management relations, well-trained employees, improved design so that products can be made more easily and perform better, and higher quality in the sense of meeting design specifications more closely."[12] If the relationship between technology and productivity is complicated then the relationship between productivity and employment is equally complicated. In addition to technology, employment depends on international trade, domestic competition, changes in consumer preference, international relations, inflation, fiscal policy, and a host of other factors. Nevertheless, technology is a major factor and a country cannot hope to be competitive without employing advanced technology in its manufacturing and service industries. It is possible to see the impact of technology on the long-term shifts in the distribution of jobs by major occupational groups. For example, farm labor, which constituted over 70% of the labor force in 1820, was reduced to less than 50% by 1880, less than 40% by 1900, and is currently running at less than 3%, because of mechanization, fertilizers, and new crop varieties. Table 10-1 shows these changes for the major occupational groups, from 1900–1980.

The number of production workers has also declined, though not as sharply since the Second World War. Operatives, most of whom are semiskilled manufacturing workers, reached a peak of 20.4% in 1950 (not shown in Table 10-1) and then decreased to 14.2% in 1980. Furthermore, the proportion of production workers within manufacturing has decreased substantially, and in absolute terms, between 1979 and 1985, 1.7 million manufacturing jobs were lost. This decline will continue as fewer and fewer workers together with increasingly sophisticated technology and organizational structures produce all the goods required. The continuing increase in clerical workers and professional and technical workers should also be noted.

TABLE 10-1

PERCENTAGES OF TOTAL U.S. EMPLOYMENT ACCOUNTED FOR BY MAJOR OCCUPATIONAL GROUPS, FROM 1900–1980.

Occupational Group	1900	1920	1940	1960	1980
Professional and technical services	4.3	5.4	7.5	10.8	16.1
Managers and administrators	5.8	6.6	7.3	8.1	11.2
Sales workers	4.5	4.9	6.7	7.1	6.3
Clerical workers	3.0	8.0	9.6	14.1	18.6
Craft and kindred workers	10.5	13.0	12.0	13.6	12.9
Operatives	12.8	15.6	18.4	18.9	14.2
Nonfarm laborers	12.5	11.6	9.4	5.2	4.6
Service workers	9.0	7.8	11.7	11.2	13.3
Farm workers	37.5	27.0	17.4	6.0	2.8

Source: Technology and Structural Unemployment: Reemploying Displaced Adults (Washington, D.C. U.S. Congress, Office of Technology Assessment, OTA-ITE-250, 1986), p. 331.

TABLE 10-2

FASTEST GROWING OCCUPATIONS, 1988–2000, MODERATE ALTERNATIVE PROJECTION (NUMBERS IN THOUSANDS).

Occupation	Employment 1988	Employment 2000	Numerical Change	Percent Change
Paralegals	83	145	62	75.3
Medical assistants	149	253	104	70.0
Home health aides	236	397	160	67.9
Radiologic technologists and technicians	132	218	87	66.0
Data processing equipment repairers	71	115	44	61.2
Medical records technicians	47	75	28	59.9
Medical secretaries	207	327	120	58.0
Physical therapists	68	107	39	57.0
Surgical technologists	35	55	20	56.4
Operations research analysts	55	85	30	55.4
Securities and financial services sales workers	200	309	109	54.8
Travel agents	142	219	77	54.1
Computer systems analysts	403	617	214	53.3
Physical and corrective therapy assistants	39	60	21	52.5
Social welfare service aides	91	138	47	51.5
Occupational therapists	33	48	16	48.8
Computer programmers	519	769	250	48.1

Source: Monthly Labor Review, U.S. Department of Labor, Bureau of Labor Statistics, November 1989, p. 60.

Future Jobs

Given the previous discussion, can anything be said about what the jobs of the future will be? One important question is whether or not high technology will be a major contributing factor to job growth. The Bureau of Labor Statistics of the Department of Labor regularly issues job projections, based on a sophisticated model. Table 10-2 shows the fastest growing occupations, between 1988 and 2000, and Table 10-3 shows those with the largest job growth. Both present the moderate alternative projection. Some observations from these projections follow:

Fastest growing occupations:

- Fully one half of the 20 fastest growing jobs are health service occupations, reflecting an aging population with in-home and technical needs.
- There is rapid growth for occupations related to computer technology.
- Most of the growth areas are in service jobs: paralegals, securities and financial services, travel agents, and so on.

TABLE 10-3

OCCUPATIONS WITH THE LARGEST JOB GROWTH, 1988–2000, MODERATE ALTERNATIVE PROJECTION (NUMBERS IN THOUSANDS).

	Employment		Numerical	Percent
Occupation	1988	2000	Change	Change
Salesperson, retail	3,834	4,564	730	19.0
Registered nurses	1,577	2,190	613	38.8
Janitors and cleaners, including maids and housekeeping cleaners	2,895	3,450	556	19.2
Waiters and waitresses	1,786	2,337	551	30.9
General managers and top executives	3,030	3,509	479	15.8
General office clerks	2,519	2,974	455	18.1
Secretaries, except legal and medical	2,903	3,288	385	13.2
Nursing aides, orderlies, and attendants	1,184	1,562	378	31.9
Truck drivers, light and heavy	2,399	2,768	369	15.4
Receptionists and information clerks	833	1,164	331	39.8
Cashiers	2,310	2,614	304	13.2
Guards	795	1,050	256	32.2
Computer programmers	519	769	250	48.1
Food counter, fountain, and related	1,626	1,866	240	14.7
Food preparation workers	1,027	1,260	234	22.8
Licensed practical nurses	626	855	229	36.6

Source: Monthly Labor Review, U.S. Department of Labor, Bureau of Labor Statistics, November 1989, p. 60.

Largest job growth:

- Retail—salespersons, for example—will have the largest growth.
- Food-related jobs are among the fastest growing—waiters and waitresses, food counter and fountain related, and food preparation.
- Health services are also growing very fast—registered nurses, nursing aides, orderlies, and attendants.

From the point of view of high technology's contribution to employment, it can be seen in Table 10-3 that most of the new jobs in the next 12 years will be traditional, low-skilled, service jobs: salespersons, janitors and cleaners, waiters and waitresses, general office clerks, secretaries, nurses aides and orderlies, truck drivers, receptionists, cashiers, guards, and food counter and food preparation persons. Computer programmers and computer systems analysts are also included in both tables, but both make rather small contributions compared to the other occupation groups. Among the fastest growing occupations are paralegals, medical assistants, home health aides, medical records technicians, medical secretaries, and travel agents, again not exactly technology-rich jobs. As part of these projections, the Bureau of Labor Statistics estimates that manufacturing is expected to continue decreasing in its percentage of the work force, from 26.4% in 1988 to 24% in 2000. Note these figures are somewhat inflated because they include laborers as well.

Clearly, the manufacturing sector will not provide the majority of new jobs in the economy and has not done so for some time. As shown, although high technology industries are growing very fast, they will not provide many new jobs, in comparison to the more mundane areas. There are three reasons: the high technology sector is relatively small, its productivity is growing faster than many other manufacturing sectors, and many jobs created by U.S. companies are actually off-shore, typically in the Far East. The products of high technology, computers, microprocessors, communication equipment, robots and advanced manufacturing equipment, software, and computer peripherals will improve productivity in application areas, and so will have a deleterious effect on other manufacturing employment. The recession of the early 1980s resulted in the loss of some three million manufacturing jobs. Most of these will never be replaced.

As mentioned in the previous paragraph, in the early 1980s, recessions led to large-scale job losses, especially in manufacturing. Displaced workers were defined as those who, through no fault of their own, lost their jobs as well as their investment in training. In the last few years, however, the focus has shifted from manufacturing workers to "the firing of middle managers, financial industry employees, and, with increasing automation in office equipment, clerical workers."[13] A survey carried out in 1988 revealed that between 1983 and 1988, 4.6 million workers over age 20 were displaced. This is a considerable number given that during this period total employment rose substantially. The most significant fact about this recent group of displaced workers is that the jobs they lost were less likely to have been in manufacturing industries. Thus, we may be witnessing the first indication that information processing technology is having an impact on office employment. If this is indeed the case, then it may now be a segment of white-collar workers' turn to enter a long period of decline.

In summary, part of the cause of the unemployment, or displacement discussed above is the increasing tendency towards industrial automation as a means to improve manufacturing productivity and towards office automation as a means to improve white-collar productivity. For example, Japan, the world's leading country in the introduction of robots, has presented a serious challenge to other industrialized nations. The message is quite clear: increase productivity or cease to compete on the world scene, with an accompanying loss of jobs and a lowering of the standard of living. In some sense, while Japan may be seen to be exporting unemployment as well as VCRs, cameras, and television sets, the dilemma of industrialized countries may be seen as follows:

> Automate rapidly (thereby increasing unemployment, only temporarily it is hoped) in order to compete internationally and perhaps restore the immediate loss in jobs with an increase in total production or in a lowering of service costs.
>
> Don't automate aggressively, in order to save jobs in the short run. Because cheaper goods may be produced elsewhere or cheaper services may be available elsewhere, however, domestic jobs will eventually be in jeopardy.

A serious question arises here about society's responsibility for unemployment due to technological innovation.

It seems likely that the bulk of future jobs will be produced not in manufacturing but in the service area, especially in the more menial sector. Are we heading towards a society in which a relatively small percentage of the labor force produces sufficient food and manufactured goods and performs professionally in such areas as education, medicine, engineering, science, finance, computers and government, while most workers are involved in health services, food preparation and serving, custodial work, salesclerking, leisure, clerical work, and other relatively low-skilled and low-paying jobs?

The Computer and the Office

> Office automation will enable American business to create 20 million new jobs before the end of the century.[14]
>
> There are 20 million office workers in this country whose jobs will be put at risk in one way or another by office automation.[15]

There are at least two possibilities for the office of the future. The promising model includes an increase in productivity, more jobs, improved skills for office workers, and increased opportunities for executives. The pessimistic version suggests that the industrial model will be reproduced in the office, with rows of women at desks and terminals, automatically monitored by the computer, with a major reduction of the traditional social intercourse of the office. The clerical work force is heavily dominated by women: 62% in 1970, but 80% in 1980. Although the office and the typewriter have been a major source of employment for women, the next stage of technological innovation may not be so kind. In 1978 Siemens, a West German company, estimated that office automation could result in a reduction of the labor force by 25 to 30%. Occupations such as file clerk, bookkeeper, typist, and bank teller, which are predominantly filled by women, are the leading candidates for automation.

Interestingly enough, the term *word processing* was first introduced by IBM in the early 1960s to sell dictation equipment. In 1967, IBM also used it as part of an advertising campaign for its magnetic tape Selective typewriters. The goal for the future office is clearly stated in an encyclopedia entry for word processing (WP): "WP represents a further stage in modern society's application of automation, reaching beyond manufacturing and production lines into the office."[16]

Those who look forward to increased office automation, especially (but not exclusively) equipment manufacturers and software developers, have an optimistic view. In the long run the routine and ordinary will be automated, and the number of employees with higher technical skills will increase. Office work will be more satisfying as the drudgery is relegated to machines. The level of human interaction will rise among those employees who need to communicate and who have sufficient time. Besides word processing, office automation includes communication networks, electronic mail, scheduling of meetings, information retrieval, and other applications. The complete package will arrive in stages because of high capital costs as well as associated technical problems. Productivity improvements will not be spectacular and in fact may not initially appear to justify the expense and effort. Over the next few years the office will undergo a transformation that will affect work in many ways. The shape of the future is difficult to predict. A concerned and informed public can help to humanize the new technology.

The Organization of Work

> His [Taylor's] "system" was simply a means for management to achieve control of the actual mode of performance of every labor activity, from the simplest to the most complicated.[17]

The contributions of Frederick Taylor to the organization of the productive process concerned scientific management, time studies, and the assembly line. His goal was to separate the planning process from the execution process. Management's prerogative is to decide how a product is to be manufactured and then assign workers specific tasks to perform. Because of this division of labor and the separation of thought and action, work on assembly lines has been characterized as boring, mind numbing, and alienating. The trade-off of job security and good wages for mediocre working conditions has been justified by many commentators of the labor scene. However, with the rise of Japan as a major world competitor, it became clear to many observers that the traditional means of production still dominant in the United States could not compete successfully.

Many reasons have been offered for the Japanese success story: American aid; a modern industrial plant; a special relationship among government, business, and labor; new management techniques; a premium on quality control; the use of advanced technology such as robots; and the encouragement of worker participation in industrial decision making. Much has been written about the involvement of Japanese workers in the decision-making process. Workers are organized into groups for specific tasks and are permitted to carry out these tasks as they wish as long as production goals are met. On a regular basis, workers meet with management to suggest improvements in production. This system reverses the Taylor maxim. It must be working, or management would not continue to operate under such a system. In addition, management makes a long-term commitment to its workers—to train them appropriately and find alternative work if market conditions change.

Many of the above methods actually originated in the United States and were imported to Japan, where they were enthusiastically accepted and widely used. In an interesting turn of events, the same methods are being returned to the United States. Unfortunately, the economic recession of the early 1980s has limited to a considerable degree the willingness of many companies to experiment. In fact, certain industries took advantage of high unemployment rates to renegotiate major changes in work rules with their unions. For example, in the steel, automobile, and airline industries, crews have been reduced in size and jobs enlarged with new duties. Management has gained more power to schedule work and required workers to give up relief periods in some cases.

Finally, what direct impact will computers have on the organization of work? In direct contrast to the problems associated with computers and workers, current approaches to the enhancement of work, especially in the Scandinavian countries and Germany, sometimes referred to as computer-facilitated cooperative work, offer a work place in which the computer, with appropriate software, provides the necessary resources to encourage workers to realize their full potential. The goal is to provide computer and communication facilities to enable people to perform their jobs better by cooperating with their fellow workers wherever they may be located. Management must be prepared to surrender part of its autonomy in the belief that a well-trained, well-motivated work force, operating with work-enhancing tools will produce better products and provide better services. Thus, computer technology, in the view of supporters of the cooperative approach, can indeed be a liberating force in the work place, freeing people from the drudgery of routine work, and permitting them to produce quality work.

Whether management will be sufficiently enlightened to recognize this potential is questionable, for it will require a break with long-held beliefs and the exercise of a measure of trust that computers, as a new technology, are indeed different and that their potential is unlimited. The major component of the trust is actually in the workers, in their desire to excel and their interest to explore the possibilities of the new technology—in other words, a return to workers of some degree of control over the work process. Experiments are in progress in many countries to develop both software and hardware to realize some of these aims. In the real world, however, computers for the most part are not at all liberating. They are management's current tools to reinforce control, to extract knowledge, and ultimately to reduce the labor component, in order to increase profits and minimize potential work disruption.

The Service Sector

> . . . A McDonald's outlet is a machine that produces, with the help of unskilled machine attendants, a highly polished product.[18]

The impact of computer technology in manufacturing and in the office has received most of the attention when a concern with employment and the changing nature of the work place is discussed. The service sector can benefit greatly from technology, however, and given its overwhelming importance in the economy, serious attention must be paid to understanding something about its operation. First, the definition of services is usually given as that sector of the economy "whose output is not a physical product or construction, is generally consumed at the time it is produced and provides added value in forms (such as convenience, amusement, timeliness, comfort or health) that are essentially intangible concerns of its purchaser."[19] Note that services go beyond fast food and football, and include finance, communications, education, health care, transportation, legal assistance, entertainment, and travel. In 1986, the service sector accounted for about $3 trillion of the over $4.25 trillion gross national product and about 80 million of the full and part-time work force of over 108 million.

Capital investment in services has been growing rapidly, and in an investigation of some 145 industries by the Bureau of Labor Statistics, nearly half of the 30 most capital-intensive were services. One of the concerns about technology investment in the service area is that the desired payoff in terms of increased productivity has not generally been achieved. Although it is difficult to define productivity for services in general, carefully constructed measures can be produced for individual segments. In some of these areas, productivity has clearly increased (recall long-distance calls as well as the caveat) and in others it has not, if complaints about the limited return of office automation are to be believed.

Recently, the service sector has been the job engine of the economy. Between 1976 and 1986, about 85% of the new jobs in the private sector have been in services. In Bureau of Labor Statistics projections, about 18 million new jobs will be created between 1988 and 2000, of which 16.6 million are wage and salary jobs in the service sector.[20] The real question, however, is not just job numbers but job quality. In terms of income, of the ten jobs expected to grow most quickly over the next decade, eight, all in the service area, will pay less than the median income, and five will pay less than the poverty level for a family of four.[21] Furthermore, none of these areas is likely to benefit from computer technology in any way that will improve job availability, wages, or quality of work. In addition, these are areas with an increasing frequency of part-time or contingency workers, which means that the jobs lack many benefits that provide a safety net in difficult times. Those parts of the service sector in such areas as communications, finance, insurance, and transportation will benefit from increased capitalization in technology. Salaries will be higher, work will probably be more interesting, and advancement more possible, but in terms of the service sector as a whole, these areas do not provide a large percentage of the jobs.

THE RESPONSE OF UNIONS

> With all their faults, trade unions have done more for humanity than any other organization of men that ever existed. They have done more for decency, for honesty, for education, for the betterment of the race, for the developing of character in man, than any other association of men.[22]

> Labor unions are the worst thing that ever struck the earth because they take away a man's independence.[23]

Unions have their supporters and their detractors, but they are concerned about the welfare of a large segment of the work force. This segment is currently diminishing, however. Their activities represent an attempt to protect the workers they represent from threats to job security and loss of benefits. How they perceive the challenge of technology is indicative of the feelings of the workers themselves as opposed to the intentions of management.

The unions have been caught in a difficult position. Faced with the loss of jobs during the recession of the early 1980s, unions have negotiated contracts in which hard-won concessions gained over the years have been given up. They have tried to protect current jobs for a reduced work force. In this context, technological change has not been in the forefront of most unions' bargaining positions. For some unions, however, the handwriting has been on the wall for quite a while. After a series of bitter strikes, the printers' union in New York settled for a contract that essentially means the end of the industry and the union. Typographers and printers have fallen victim to computerized composition and typesetting. At large newspapers reporters can enter their stories directly into the computer, where they can be edited and subsequently put together in the newspaper's layout. In a significant technological innovation, the computer-stored information can be sent across the country, and such papers as *The New York Times* and *USA Today* can be printed simultaneously in many parts of the United States.

As an example of the ability of management to take advantage of computer networks and the internationalization of labor, consider the operation of one "global office."[24] New York Life Insurance, finding it difficult to hire workers skilled enough to process insurance claims, has turned to rural Ireland. Insurance claims are sent daily to Ireland by air, leaving Kennedy International Airport in the evening and arriving at Shannon Airport early the next day. They are then driven to Castleisland, 60 miles away, processed within seven days, and sent to a service center in New Jersey via a trans-Atlantic communications network linking computers in Ireland and the United States. An explanation and perhaps a check is printed overnight and then mailed to the beneficiary. The system works because wages in Ireland, for comparable work, are about half those in the United States and the unemployment rate in Ireland is about three times the U.S. rate. This is only one example of the export of jobs made possible by international computer networks and global salary inequities and unemployment. It is one reason, among many, that labor unions in the United States are consistently losing relative membership, as the work force grows.

Bureau of Labor Statistics figures show that the percentage of union membership among non-agricultural workers grew from 11.6% in 1930 to a peak of 35.5% in 1945. This growth was not continuous and there was a dip in 1933, a sudden jump in 1937, and dips in 1940 and 1942. The decline was continuous from 1945 to the present except for a slight rise in 1952 and 1954. In 1978, membership was 23.6% but the total number at about 20 million had remained relatively constant over the previous five years. After 1978, the statistics include employee association membership as well and indicate that by 1982, the percentage had declined to 20.6% with about 19.8 million members.[25] The 1989 numbers show that the percentage excluding the government sector stands at about 12%, rising to only 16% if government employees are included. Thus, out of a work force of over 100 million, union membership is only about 16 million.

Not only have the numbers decreased substantially, but the composition of the membership has also altered dramatically, in a not surprising way, to mirror the new reality. Thus, there has been a movement away from manufacturing towards services. In 1955, the largest affiliates of the AFL-CIO (American Federation of Labor-Council of Industrial Organizations) were auto workers (1,260,000), steelworkers (980,000), carpenters (750,000), machinists (627,000), and electrical workers (460,000). By 1989, only the auto workers remained in the top five with their membership reduced by more than 25%. The five largest were teamsters (1,161,000), state, county, and municipal employees (1,090,000), food and commercial workers (999,000), auto workers (917,000), and service employees (762,000).[26] Thus, unions have had to move away from their industrial roots and attempt to organize the growing numbers of service and white collar workers. This effort has created tensions within the union movement between blue collar and white collar workers, between private and public sector workers, and between a traditionally white, male-dominated institution and the large numbers of women, blacks, and hispanics in the new labor force.

Union membership in Europe and elsewhere is considerably higher than in the United States: in fact, the average percentage of membership rose from 48% in 1970 to 55% in 1979 and has not changed much since then. Currently, both Denmark and Sweden are well over 90%, Belgium is near 80%, Germany and Britain are between 40 and 50%, Canada is near 40%, and France is about 20%. One interpretation of the decline in U.S. union membership is that the unions have been too successful, that the gap between union pay and non-union pay has become so large that unionized companies are no longer competitive and companies have substantially increased their efforts to combat unionism.[27] Thus, the advice to unions is to forego wages as their main focus in negotiations and move to other areas such as job security and benefits. In addition, unions must come to terms with the increased numbers of part-time workers and their different needs, as well as new compensation programs such as profit-sharing, employee stock option plans, and even joint ownership and management.

Given that the major impact of technology is in the information-intensive industries, the question that emerges is when, or perhaps if, unions will succeed in representing professionals whose work has been affected by computers. Up to now, no major professional organization has adopted collective bargaining, except for the American Nurses' Association. Engineering societies seem to be too diverse and fragmented to fall under a single umbrella organization and also a large percentage of members, about one-third, are management. Professionalism also remains an obstacle, given the common perceptions that unions are only suitable for factory workers.[28] Thus, unions may find much more fertile areas among the large numbers of low-paid, relatively low-skilled data-entry clerks, office workers, and others whose work place environment has deteriorated because of computers and insensitive management. Even more, concern about possible dangers of radiation from computer terminals, or muscular damage from keyboard use must be negotiation issues for unions. One final statement about work and life, from a union, is an appropriate way to end this section.[29]

> Work, and not just income, is an essential condition of well-being in society. Through the activity of human work in all its forms, people should be able to realize their human dignity and self-expression, participate in social and economic life, secure decent personal and familial incomes, and contribute to the building of a more just world.

WOMEN, COMPUTERS, AND WORK

> For this country to attend to the health of science, as well as provide for the common defense . . . and increase the national productivity, greater participation of women and minorities in science and technology [is necessary].[30]

The widespread use of computers has provided, and is expected to provide, many jobs for women. The impact of computers on employment is expected to affect women significantly, given their high representation in office work. Do computers represent new opportunities for women or merely a reinforcement of the old inequities? An increasing number of women have been choosing careers in computer science and engineering. Society has tended to discourage women in the sciences, and how the schools react to the challenge will be very important to girls and women.

Early indications of the situation in schools are not encouraging. Girls are being excluded, either overtly or subtly, from computer-related activities. Arguments are formulated that girls are just not suited for computers, that their minds are not logical, and that if computer time is in short supply, boys should be given priority. Whether girls think differently from boys—girls (supposedly) intuitively, boys (supposedly) logically—is neither proven nor relevant, but actions based on this assumption should be examined. In almost every area of computer use—video games, computer courses at school, computer games—boys are in the majority and in effect define the associated culture. One feature of this culture is the excitement of shared expertise. If the environment were made less competitive and less aggressive, girls could be encouraged to participate more fully.

Recent studies have shown that programming style can vary among children according to temperament. Sherry Turkle, a professor of sociology at Massachusetts Institute of Technology, has been observing young children, boys and girls, learning to program in LOGO.[31] She has identified two basic styles exemplified by the majority of these children. The attitudes of most boys toward programming is to achieve mastery over a formal system, to cause the objective world of the computer to behave in a desired manner, to control a piece of the external world. Girls—at least those who are attracted to the computer—develop a much more subjective relationship. They tend to project themselves into the objects and events on the screen, achieving a much more intimate connection with their programs. The boys are willing to use ideas developed by the girls to improve their programs. An important lesson is that in a supportive environment, girls can enjoy programming and begin to fulfill their potential.

Encouragement of girls in their formative years may increase the proportion of women in information systems but the trends are not promising. Recent statistics from the U.S. Department of Labor Women's Bureau show that, although the number of women employed in computer-related professions (a very broad category) increased by 245,000 between 1985 and 1990, most of the growth took place in lower paying, non-management jobs, and women were paid 30% less than their male counterparts for equivalent jobs.[32] In 1988, of the top layer of 53,000 computer managers, 25% were women, up by only 7% from the 1980 proportion of 18% women out of about 24,000. Given that the size of the profession more than doubled, this gain by women represents slow progress indeed. The situation is even worse if minorities and minority women are considered. In 1980 and 1985, managers were 92% white and 8% minority and exactly the same proportions held in 1988.[33] The proportion of women has remained about the same over the last five years of the 1980s, in the lower level jobs such as computer operations (64.7% out of 713,000 in 1984, and 64.2% out of 870,000 in 1989), data entry/keypunch (91.3% out of 351,000, 87.8% out of 414,000), and programmers (35.4% out of 507,000, 35.2% out of 561,000).

In academia, the story is discouraging as well. Although the percentages of women pursuing bachelors, masters and Ph.D.'s in Computer Science increased from 1980 to 1986, they declined in 1987 and 1988 (except for Ph.D.'s, which declined only in 1988).[34] 1989 figures for Ph.D.'s were up, but the long-term trends are bound to show a decrease as the effect of fewer women in undergraduate programs comes into play. It should not be surprising, therefore, that women are poorly represented as faculty members in computer science and computer engineering departments. In a 1988–1989 survey of 158 such departments, 6.5% of the faculty were women, 30% of the departments had no women faculty at all, 34% had only one, and 20% had only two.[35] If role models mean anything for women considering computer science as a profession, most will find little encouragement within computer science departments. Furthermore, women in graduate school face challenges beyond the academic curriculum, namely confronting hostile and frequently sexist male students and faculty.

Professional women now face an unfair struggle for career advancement and adequate recognition of advanced degrees. There seems to be an unstated reluctance to choose equally qualified women over men for management positions. The explanation frequently offered, that men simply feel more comfortable working with men, does not do justice to the depth of the problem. Men tend to patronize women at a professional level. Women have only recently increased their representation in professional ranks and lack the widespread "old-boys" network that has traditionally provided contacts, support, and information for successful men. This situation is changing, as several women's organizations are now in operation: the Association of Women in Computing, the Society of Women Engineers, and the Aerospace Women's Committee, among others. These societies work to keep women informed of educational and professional opportunities, provide support in stressful situations, and promote the visibility of their members.

Much of the discussion, so far, about women and computing has focussed on professional women, but most women who work with computers are in data entry and computer operator positions. For them the serious issues are working conditions and job termination, more than career opportunities. On-line monitoring by employers, the well-publicized dangers of video display terminals, and the possible deskilling of jobs are of concern. The increasing use of computers in the workplace has the potential to improve working conditions, but only if management takes appropriate steps.

One group of women connected to the computer industry has generally been overlooked in the discussions of success stories—Asian women who may work in sweatshop conditions to produce microprocessors and peripherals. For example, wafers containing chips manufactured in the United States are sent to Third World countries such as Thailand and Malaysia, where they are separated, have their leads soldered, and are then returned for incorporation into products. The work pays little by Western standards and produces considerable eye strain. Another very interesting example is the assembly of compact disk drives. One of the most successful companies in this area is Seagate Technology, Inc., with 1990 sales estimated at about $2.5 billion. Of its 40,000 employees, 27,000 are in Southeast Asia, about half in Singapore, and most of these are women. As Seagate chairman Alan Shugart says, "In Thailand, there is a lot of close work under microscopes. It is pretty tough to find people in the U.S. to do that kind of work."[36] The pay in Singapore is about $2 per hour, while in Thailand it starts at 50 cents. Here is the description of one of the factories: "At one location, the employees, nearly all women, piece together drives while facing each other across three-by-three-foot tables. They rarely speak, rarely look up. One American Seagate manager described them as 'mini-robots' and then was cautioned by an aide to display more sensitivity."[37] Advances in technology sometimes rest on a foundation of human blood, sweat, and tears.

Job Safety: VDTs and Other Problems

The video or visual display terminal (VDT) or unit (VDU) is the most common evidence of the increasingly widespread distribution of computers in the workplace and at home. Estimates vary but there are probably more than 30 million VDTs in use today and the number if growing rapidly. Large numbers of workers, mainly women, will be spending many hours in front of VDT screens. Over the years a number of fears have been expressed about possible threats to health from long-term interaction with VDTs and keyboards. These concerns can be grouped into four main categories: visual, physical, psychological, and most controversial, radiation-related. The greatest fears have been aroused because of potential genetic defects. A number of incidents have been reported of what appear to be unexpectedly high rates of miscarriages and birth defects among women working with VDTs. During a one year period between 1979 and 1980, at a Sears Computer center in Dallas, there were seven miscarriages and one premature infant death out of twelve pregnancies that year. In the same period, four of seven babies born to VDT operators at the *Toronto Star* had birth defects.

Subsequent investigations have revealed that screens do not emit sufficient ionizing radiation to cause any damage, but questions are being asked about the effects of pulsed low-level magnetic radiation. Similar radiation is produced by electric blankets, electric razors, hair dryers, and the human body itself. There is considerable debate in the scientific community about the dangers of low-level radiation and the experimental evidence is inconclusive at present. Consider the following reports:[38]

> • In an article in the American Journal of Epidemiology in 1988, Dr [David] Savitz [of the University of North Carolina] concluded that children living in homes which had continual exposure to a magnetic field of between two and three milligauss—roughly the amount received living 15 meters from a power line—had a one-and-a-half to two times greater risk of developing cancer.
>
> • A [1988] study by the Kaiser Permanente Medical Centre of Northern California [of 1,583 pregnant women who attended obstetrics and gynecological clinics] found a statistical link between computer work and miscarriages, although the bulk of epidemiological evidence contradicts this. [The authors of the study did not measure other factors that might have accounted for the higher miscarriage rate and so are unable to establish a direct cause.[39]]
>
> • Dr. Bernhard Tribukait and his colleagues at the Department of Radiobiology at the Karolinska Institute in Stockholm exposed pregnant mice to weak, low-frequency magnetic fields. Significantly, the fields were pulsed, like those radiated by VDUs. They noted a small number of malformations in some of the mice fetuses.
>
> • A more recent study, coordinated by Dr. Ezra Berman of the EPA [Environment Protection Agency] . . . exposed chicken embryos to the same weak, pulsed magnetic fields. Some

> laboratories saw abnormalities while others did not. . . . So did the pulsed magnetic fields produce the malformations? 'While our answer is not a full yes, it's definitely not no,' Dr. Berman concludes.

There are other studies that seem to provide some weak evidence that pulsed, low-radiation fields can cause biological damage, but how this relates to dangers from VDTs is not clear. Nevertheless, in late 1989, IBM began shipping VDTs with reduced electromagnetic emissions, while strenuously maintaining that existing VDTs posed no safety hazards. Careful statistical analysis of the clusters of birth defects, mentioned earlier, indicate that such clusters are bound to occur by chance alone and do not demonstrate that there is a connection between birth defects and VDT work. A seemingly definitive study released by the National Institute of Occupational Safety and Health in March 1991 states that "Women who use video display terminals do not run an increased risk of miscarriages . . . no increase in the risk of spontaneous abortion [is] associated with the occupational use of VDTs, or the electronic fields they produce."[40]

Although reproductive issues have received considerable attention, there are many other important health-related issues. Other problems are eye strain (even the formation of cataracts has been documented successfully), and back, neck, arm, hand, and finger trauma. In some cases a solution is achieved by better background lighting, reduction of glare, proper height of tables and chairs, regular breaks, and the elimination of stress attributable to excessive monitoring. A report by the International Labor Organization states that, "One out of every four workers in the industrialized nations is likely to suffer from mental illness at some point in his or her working life."[41] The vision problems that arise from extended work with VDTs include eye strain, fatigue, blurring, and double vision similar to those associated with other visually demanding work. There are other problems related to screen flicker and cursor blinking, which can cause headaches.

Another problem, recently discovered, is that women may be highly sensitive to a barely audible, high-pitched squeal, a 16 khz pure tone, emanating from some VDTs. Experimental results indicate "that women exposed to the noise made more errors and were more prone to headaches and other stress-related complaints than women who were not exposed to the sound."[42] There a group of physical problems associated with long-term use of the keyboard that are known under a variety of terms, namely, repetitive strain injuries, cumulative trauma disorder, VDT disease, and upper-limb disorders (ULD). One specific nerve disorder resulting from thousands of repetitive movements is carpal tunnel syndrome, a painful condition that may debilitate the hands and arms. In 1989, out of 284,000 occupational illnesses, 147,000 were repetitive motion disorders, up 28% over the previous year, making it the fastest growing occupational complaint.[43] In general, ULD may involve damage to muscles, nerves, and tendons, as well as swelling and inflammation. It is important to recognize the onset of these disorders as they may be difficult to alleviate at a later stage. Much more research needs to be undertaken but for the present, careful attention to furniture design, keyboard height and location, arm and wrist angles, and frequent breaks must be observed.

If companies do not take independent action to improve working conditions and if regulatory agencies are slow to recognize the special problems in the office, local government may step in. In 1988, Suffolk County, New York passed legislation regulating the use of VDTs in the workplace, that included rest breaks, special training, eye examinations, and glasses. Four companies filed suit against the law, claiming that existing federal and state laws provide sufficient protection and ensure uniform coverage. In late 1989, a New York Supreme Court Justice struck down the law, ruling that Suffolk County had overstepped its authority. More recently, the San Francisco County Board of Supervisors passed a measure to establish working conditions in offices with more than 15 employees. Among the requirements are a fifteen minute break every two hours, antiglare screens, nonglare lighting and light intensity, adjustable chairs and desks, a minimum of three feet between a worker and the back of a VDT, and regular reports by the director of public health on electromagnetic radiation.[44]

Telecommuting: Electronic Cottage Industry

The phrase "electronic cottage," aparently first used by Alvin Toffler,[45] conjures up visions of people working at home by means of computers and communications networks. The cottage part is a preindustrial vision of workers at home, performing piece work that they return upon completion to central locations and then pick up new supplies. There are remnants of this mode of labor in the Western world today. In northern Scotland, tweed fabrics are woven on home looms. In late 1984, the U.S. Labor Department permitted home knitters to sell their work for profit. (They are still required to observe minimum wage and child labor laws. Much of this work is done in New England and had been illegal since 1942.)[46] Two other terms are occasionally used:[47] *telework,* organizational work performed outside of the normal organizational confines of space and time, augmented by computer and communications technology; and *telecommuting,* the use of computer and communications technology to transport work to the worker as a substitute for physical transportation of the worker to the location of the work.

A number of companies have chosen to encourage part of their staff to remain at home while performing their information processing activities. Other companies, not particularly in favor, have nevertheless permitted telecommuting as a way of hiring information systems staff in a highly competitive market. The number of company employees working at home during normal business hours reached 3 million in 1989 and is estimated to have grown to 3.6 million in 1990.[48] Furthermore, it is believed that President Bush is strongly in favor of telecommuting as being "good for business and good for relieving the nation's traffic, energy and pollution problems. . . . Cars that don't leave the garage don't pollute the air or congest the freeway."[49]

Proponents of remote office work, or telecommuting claim that an increasing number of employees will be working at home because it makes economic sense. Commuting is eliminated, which means savings in fuel costs and time and a general reduction in the stress associated with driving. Employees have an increased flexibility for arranging their working hours around their family responsibilities. People will be able to choose where they live, independently of the need to be close to a job. There must also be advantages for the employer or new working arrangements will not be implemented. Productivity improvements are supposedly a major reason for physically decentralizing work. One difficulty in measuring productivity is that more work may be accomplished because more time is being spent rather than because the worker is more efficient.

From management's point of view, employees may be easier to attract if flexible work arrangements are possible. If the number of staff at a central location is reduced, the building rental costs can also be reduced, a saving somewhat offset by increased telephone charges. For many women with children who want a career, however, there are problems with staying at home. It may appear to be convenient to work at home, but women who work there may not be taken seriously, even if child care can be adequately arranged. The problem is a general one for remote workers—if they are out of sight, will they be out of mind at promotion time?

One critic of the electronic cottage, Tom Forester, the author and editor of several books on technology and society, proposes the following reasons that this idea will not inevitably be translated into social reality:[50]

> 1. Not many people are or will be in a position to work at home in future because of space constraints and the nature of their occupations.
> 2. Of those who could work at home, not many will choose to do so, because homeworking suits only some people and not others. Even fewer people can cope with the psychological problems on a long-term basis.
> 3. We are thus most unlikely to see a major increase in homeworking (or the 'mass return home after the industrial revolution' envisioned by the electronic cottage theorists).
> 4. We may, however, see a small but steady increase in the number of people doing some rather than all of their work at home, as flexible working patterns become more widespread and more people seek to 'get the best of both worlds.'

THE CHANGING NATURE OF WORK

> The man whose whole life is spent performing a few simple operations, of which the effects are perhaps always the same, or very nearly the same, has no occasion to exert his understanding or to exercise his invention in finding out expedients for removing difficulties which never occur. He naturally loses, therefore, the habit of such exertion, and generally becomes as stupid and ignorant as it is possible for a human creature to become.[51]

The importance of work in our lives can hardly be overestimated and therefore anything that affects the many hours we spend working has an impact well beyond the work place. The physical and psychological challenges to the well-being of workers both in the office and the factory raise many important social issues. For all the talk about the potential liberating power of the new technology, there may be a price to pay, especially for women and especially in the office. More specifically, there is a growing concern with threats to worker autonomy and self-respect posed by various kinds of technology including drug testing, television and telephone surveillance, and sophisticated body searches. Careful attention must be paid to computer-based technology such as computer monitoring, which is only the most recent version of the process of determining basic line work levels and adherence to pre-established work regimens. Such monitoring is physically unobtrusive, although the employee, typically a woman, must be constantly aware that every few milliseconds her activities are being measured. The result usually is an increase in stress level with detrimental psychological side effects.

Somewhat more abstract but still of concern is the growing uncomfortable relation between people and machines, especially when these machines may pose a challenge to human dignity. Thus, it is all the more important that the introduction of sophisticated computers into the work place be accompanied by proper training, which stresses the long term benefits of computer-aided work and assures employees of their on-going value. Part of their fear is that they will ultimately be replaced by the computer. Even though there is little likelihood of this occurring in the short run, sufficient evidence exists to warrant some apprehension. A more realistic concern is that an increasing number and variety of jobs will be deskilled, that is, they will consist of nothing more than "tending" machines.

Deskilling

Does the introduction of new technology—computer systems, to be specific—raise or lower the overall skills of employees? The pessimistic viewpoint is that the new technology, for example, office automation, will certainly raise the skills of some of the workers, but most of the office staff will have a reduced range of responsibilities. Their work will be narrowly constrained to data entry—that is, sitting at a terminal all day, rapidly typing rows and columns of numbers. Under this scenario, skills have been reduced for many of these employees, most of whom are likely to be women. As jobs are deskilled, they are also reclassified and downgraded in terms of wage scales. Thus, entry level jobs will pay less and be less secure, more routine and monotonous. Consistent with this view is the assumption that office managers are always interested in maximizing volume and speed in data processing. The only restraints are such side effects as absenteeism, high turnover, poor quality, or even sabotage. This view justifies the fears of many critics that management wishes to reproduce the factory model in the office.

Many women are concerned that the new automation will reinforce sex segregation in the office. With more women employed in routine jobs, their path for advancement will be much longer and more difficult. In fact, most women will have no opportunity for advancement because there will be no opportunity to improve their skills. On the factory floor, many workers see their future as adjuncts to powerful, computerized machines. Here also deskilling is an issue. Fewer workers will be able to exercise a broad range of skills, and most workers will be narrowly constrained. From a historical point of view, the process of separating the actions of the worker from their planning and organization will culminate in the computerized factory, where very few workers are required. An alternate scheme is to incorporate workers in the planning process in order to make use of their skills at the manufacturing level.

A number of government reports have appeared in the last few years that attempt to directly address this issue of the impact of technological change on the workplace and the worker. Consider the following presentation of the debate:[52]

Two opposing points of view are prominent:

- technological change leads to upgrading of skills, making for better jobs but also requiring more training or education, so that less skilled people may have trouble finding jobs;
- or, on the contrary, that advanced technology deskills jobs, making them narrower, more repetitious and perfunctory, and leaving workers as nothing but machine tenders at relatively low pay.

A third view has also emerged:

[T]echnological changes are increasing the quality and number of some higher level jobs while eliminating or downgrading middle-level positions, thus creating a skills gap between lower and higher level jobs.

It is also important and necessary to point out that it is not just technology that affects the nature of jobs. The technology is implemented in a matrix of economic, historic, and social forces that present a variety of decisions for management and labor. To succumb to a belief in technological determinism is to abrogate responsibility; certainly the range of decisions may be constrained, but there are decisions to be made and both management and workers must cooperate, if possible, to produce a humane work place. Just a few years ago, the following advice on how to use their equipment and deal with their workers was recommended to factory managers:[53]

> If skills can be progressively built into machines, then workers need not be especially skilled themselves. . . . [G]ear up for long production runs, buffer yourself with enough inventory to keep the lines moving, inspect for defects—if at all—at the end of those lines, treat workers primarily as a reservoir of costs that can be bled out under pressure as the need arises, and you will boost your market share, your profits, your stockholder's good disposition, your bond ratings, your own compensation, and the Nation's industrial health.

In 1985, the Panel on Technology and Employment was created by the Committee on Science, Engineering, and Public Policy of the Council of the National Academy of Engineering to study the impact of technological change on employment opportunities, productivity, and the quality of work life. It published its findings in 1987,[54] which included a comprehensive review of existing literature. When discussing worker skills, it is necessary to distinguish between *basic skills,* those which workers have typically acquired before entering the labor force, such as literacy, problem-solving, and written communication, and *job-related skills,* typically provided by employers and required by employees to perform the job. Although studies have been carried out for more than 50 years, the overall results are surprisingly inconclusive:[55]

1. Process innovations in skill-intensive manufacturing processes often eliminated high-skill jobs and generated low-skill jobs. The opposite was true, however, for the adoption of data- and word-processing-technologies in offices, which eliminated low-skill jobs and created high-skill jobs.
2. No evidence [has been found] to support claims of significant upgrading or downgrading in aggregate skill requirements as a result of technological change.

3. [Using] educational attainment as a proxy for skill requirements . . . the educational requirements of projected 1995 jobs were virtually identical to those needed for 1982 jobs.

4. [T]he automation of high-skill jobs shifted their content from the direct operation of a machine to monitoring the operations of a different machine that was more nearly self-controlling. . . . The changes resulting from new technology reduced skill requirements.

5. . . . [T]he shift toward increased responsibility required higher-order mental skills to ensure quick and appropriate responses to mechanical breakdowns.

6. . . . [T]he introduction of automated manufacturing technologies reduced the number of job classifications while broadening the scope of activities within each classification.

7. . . . [A]utomation fragmented and standardized clerical work, requiring lower-level and narrower skills.

8. . . . [T]he introduction of minicomputers, personal computers, and higher-level programming languages has restructured office work. . . . [T]his worker will be responsible for a wider range of tasks. . . .

Surveillance and Monitoring

The rights of workers in the workplace are not clearly defined. By providing jobs, management would seem to have power over its workers that threatens their basic civil liberties. For example, drug tests, polygraph tests, and psychological evaluation may be required to qualify for a job and to keep one. On the job, employees may be subject to television surveillance, telephone and computer monitoring, and even regular body searches. Professed reasons are to deter and detect criminal activities, to measure performance in order to establish basic rates of work, and to maintain such rates. Management maintains its right to control the labor process by whatever means it deems necessary. Workers argue that monitoring creates an atmosphere of suspicion and recrimination resulting in decreased productivity and unacceptable levels of stress.

Table 10-4 shows the kinds of monitoring and testing that have increased concern about the challenges to privacy and civil liberties in the workplace. It is taken from an Office of

TABLE 10-4

SOME CATEGORIES OF BEHAVIOR SUBJECT TO MONITORING, MEASUREMENT, OR TESTING.

Monitoring, Measurement, Testing	Performance	Behaviors	Personal Characteristics
Output: keystrokes, and so on.	x		
Use of Resources: computer time, phone.	x	x	
Communications contents: eavesdropping.	x	x	
Location: cards, beepers, TV cameras.		x	x
Concentration, mental activity: brainwave.		x	x
Predisposition to error: drug testing.		x	x
Predisposition to health risk: genetic screening.			x
Truthfulness: polygraph, brainwave.			x

Source: The Electronic Supervisor: New Technology, New Tensions (Washington, D.C.: U.S. Congress, Office of Technology Assessment, OTA-CIT-333, September 1987), Figure 1, p. 13.

Technology report called *The Electronic Supervisor*.[56] The first three categories seem to be directed towards measuring work performance and are sometimes called work monitoring or work measurement and are of primary concern in the present context. Others investigate more personal issues both in and outside the workplace and are beyond the scope of this discussion. A review of some of the following findings in the above report reveals the depth of concern that this issue has raised (the numbers are as given in the report):[57]

> 2. Computer-based systems offer opportunities for organizing work in new ways, as well as means of monitoring it more intensively. Electronic monitoring is most likely to raise opposition among workers when it is imposed without worker participation, when standards are perceived as unfair, or when performance records are used punitively. Worker involvement in design and implementation of monitoring programs can result in greater acceptance by workers, but despite activities of labor unions in some industries and recent progress in labor-management cooperation in others, most firms do not have mechanisms to do this.
>
> 3. There is reason to believe that electronically monitoring the quantity or speed of work contributes to stress and stress-related illness, although there is still little research separating the effects of monitoring from job design, equipment design, lighting, machine pacing, and other potentially stressful aspects of computer-based office work.
>
> 4. Monitoring the content of messages raises a different set of issues. Some employers say that service observation (listening to or recording the content of employees' telephone conversations with customers) helps assure quality and correctness of information and the protection of all parties in case of dispute. However, service observation also impacts the privacy of the customer, and workers and labor organizations have argued that it contributes to stress of the employee, and creates an atmosphere of distrust. Monitoring the content of electronic mail messages or personal computer (PC) diskettes also raises privacy issues.

It is obviously very difficult to obtain accurate statistics about how much monitoring goes on and who gets monitored. Typically, routinized work and low-level work such as simple data collection are likely candidates for monitoring. Thus, word processors, data-entry clerks, telephone operators, customer service workers, telemarketers, and insurance claim clerks are subject to monitoring, but certainly not all are. Alan Westin, who produced a report used in *The Electronic Supervisor,* estimated that the great majority of clerical workers are not monitored (65% to 80%) and that most professional, technical, and managerial workers are not (95% or more). But note that if 20% to 35% of clerical workers are monitored this amounts to 4 to 6 million workers.[58]

SUMMARY

Of all the issues associated with technology, especially computers, the most important is work—how much, and what kind. The subject of jobs and computers will be with us for a very long time, and all will be affected.

The relation between technology and work is a complex one. Historically, except for periods of worldwide economic dislocation, technological innovation has not decreased the number of jobs. The open question is whether or not computers are a fundamentally different kind of technology. The contributions of Frederick Taylor and Henry Ford were key to the development of the assembly line. The separation of actual work from planning has serious consequences for workers. The process continues, with the introduction of robots into the factory and computer networks into the office. The voices of the workers themselves should be listened to. What workers really want, whether or not they are dissatisfied, and the role of computers in their lives are issues of concern to society at large.

Which jobs will be most affected by computers and how? Granted that many jobs will be lost, where will the new jobs come from? Will there be enough? Blue collar jobs are decreasing. Service and information jobs are increasing. Agricultural jobs are now only about 3% of the total. Fewer people are producing the products and food for society.

How does office automation affect the social organization of the office? Since women represent by far the largest number of office workers, they will be most affected. Will their jobs be more interesting, or less? Will their skills be broadened and improved, or narrowed and decreased?

Unions are dedicated to the welfare of their members. Unfortunately, in recent difficult economic times job security has overridden considerations of working conditions, wages, and other benefits. However, some unions have attempted to include technological issues in their contracts.

Women are affected in many important ways by computers because of their large representation in the office. Problems of job advancement, equal pay for equal work, and discrimination in the workplace and in academia exist. Serious questions have been raised about the physical, psychological, and long-term genetic effects of video display terminals. Other ergonomic concerns, such as glare, background lighting, and seating are more amenable to correction. With the availability of high speed communication networks, it is now possible for an increasing number of workers to work at home. There are, however, some drawbacks and the process has not been accepted as quickly as its advocates had expected.

Some of the changes in the lives of the workers and in the nature of their jobs as a result of the introduction of computers into the workplace have not been for the better. Considerable debate exists over whether or not the skill level of both workers and jobs have increased or decreased, the so-called deskilling issue. Also very serious is the increasing use of computer systems to monitor performance and to threaten individual privacy.

NOTES

1. E. P. Thompson, *The Making of the English Working Class* (Middlesex, England: Penguin, 1980), p. 600.
2. From James O'Toole, *Making America Work: Productivity and Responsibility,* p. 5. Copyright © 1981 by the author. Reprinted by permission of The Continuum Publishing Company.
3. Phil Stallings, as quoted in Studs Terkel, *Working* (New York: Avon Paperback, 1975), p. 223. Copyright © 1972 by Random House, Inc. and Alfred A. Knopf, Inc.
4. *Ibid.*
5. Described in Satoshi Kamata, *Japan in the Passing Lane,* (New York: Pantheon Paperback, 1983), p. 22. Copyright © 1982 Random House, Inc. and Alfred A. Knopf, Inc.

6. Harry Braverman, *Labor and Monopoly Capital: The Degradation of Work in the Twentieth Century* (New York: Monthly Review Press, 1974).
7. *Ibid.*, pp. 112–121.
8. *Ibid.*, p. 147.
9. Quoted from David Lodge, *Nice Work* (New York: Viking Penguin, 1989), p. 126.
10. Richard M. Cyert and David C. Mowery (eds.), *Technology and Employment: Innovation and Growth in the U.S. Economy*, Panel on Technology and Employment; Committee on Science, Engineering, and Public Policy; National Academy of Sciences, National Academy of Engineering, and Institute of Medicine (Washington, D.C.: National Academy Press, 1987), p. 168. Reprinted with permission from *Technology and Employment*, © 1987 by the National Academy of Sciences. Published by National Academy Press, Washington, D.C.
11. *Technology and Structural Unemployment: Reemploying Displaced Adults* (Washington, D.C.: U.S. Congress, Office of Technology Assessment, OTA-ITE-250, February 1986), pp. 321–367.
12. *Ibid.*, p. 321.
13. Diane E. Herz, "Worker Displacement in a Period of Rapid Job Expansion: 1983–87," *Monthly Labor Review*, May 1990, p. 21.
14. Paul Strassman, vice-president, Information Product Division of Xerox, as quoted in Englebert Kirchner, "At the Mercy of Machines," *Datamation* (Cahners Publishing Co.), September 1982, p. 252.
15. Karen Nussbaum, president of 9 to 5, *Ibid.*
16. Edward W. Gore, Jr., in *McGraw-Hill Encyclopedia of Science and Technology*, Volume 14, Fifth Edition (New York: McGraw-Hill, 1982), p. 708.
17. Braverman, *Labor and Monopoly Capital*, p. 90. Copyright © 1974 by Harry Braverman. Reprinted by permission of Monthly Review Foundation.
18. George Cohon, CEO of McDonald's Restaurants of Canada Ltd., as quoted in *Report on Business Magazine, Globe and Mail*, Toronto, Canada, April 1988, p. 14.
19. James Brian Quinn, Jordan J. Baruch, and Penny Cushman Paquette, "Technology in Services," *Scientific American*, December 1987, p. 50.
20. George Silvestri and Jay Lukasiewicz, "Projections of Occupational Employment, 1988–2000," *Monthly Labor Review*, November 1989, p. 47.
21. John J. Sweeney and Karen Nussbaum, *Solutions for the New Work Force: Policies for a New Social Contract* (Cabin John, Maryland: Seven Locks Press, 1989), pp. 18–19.
22. Clarence Darrow, in *The Railroad Trainmen*, November 1909.
23. Henry Ford (booklet distributed to Ford employees during CIO drive), as quoted in *Time*, August 20, 1945.
24. Steve Lohr, "The Growth of the 'Global Office'," *The New York Times*, October 18, 1988, p. 29.
25. Michael Goldfield, *The Decline of Organized Labor in the United States* (Chicago: The University of Chicago Press, 1987), pp. 3–25.
26. Bureau of Labor Statistics as included in John Holusha, "Unions Are Expanding Their Role to Survive in the 90's," *The New York Times*, August 19, 1990, p. F12.
27. "Workers of the World Disunite," *The Economist*, August 18, 1990, p. 57.
28. Sar A. Levitan and Frank Gallo, "Collective Bargaining and Private Sector Professionals," *Monthly Labor Review*, September 1989, pp. 24–33.
29. From *The Facts*, published by the Canadian Union of Public Employees and reprinted in the *Globe and Mail* (Toronto, Canada), March 2, 1988, p. B 10.
30. Shirley Macom, Head of the Office of Opportunities in Science of the American Association for the Advancement of Science, as quoted in Carol Truxal, "The Woman Engineer," *IEEE Spectrum*, April 1983, p. 59. © 1990 IEEE. Reprinted, with permission, from The Institute of Electrical and Electronic Engineers.
31. Sherry Turkle, *The Second Self: Computers and the Human Spirit* (New York: Simon and Schuster, 1984).
32. Maryfran Johnson, "Women Under Glass," *Computerworld*, December 3, 1990, p. 93.
33. *Ibid.*

34. Karen A. Frenkel, "Women & Computing," *Communications of the ACM,* **33**(11), November 1990, p. 38.
35. *Ibid.*
36. As quoted in Evelyn Richards, "Asia's Taskmaster: How One U.S. Company Drives Employees," *The Vancouver Sun* (Canada), June 30, 1990, p. D 10. Originally published in *The Washington Post.*
37. *Ibid.*
38. "Very Debatable Units," *The Economist,* September 1, 1990, pp. 73–74, 76. © The Economist Newspaper Ltd. Used by permission.
39. Tamar Lewin, "Pregnant Women Increasingly Fearful of VDT's," *The New York Times,* July 10, 1988, p. Y 13.
40. *Visual Display Terminals and Workers' Health* (Geneva: World Health Organization, 1987), pp. 137–158. "Miscarriage link to VDTs not found in U.S. Study," *Vancouver Sun* (Canada), March 16, 1991, p. B 9. Taken from *Newsday.*
41. "ILO Study Finds Mental Illness in Workplace," *The Globe and Mail* (Toronto, Canada), February 20, 1987, p. B 15.
42. Ellis Booker, "VDT Tones May Cut Productivity, Study Says," *Computerworld,* August 27, 1990, p. 10.
43. Mitch Betts, "Repetitive Stress Claims Soar," *Computerworld,* November 19, 1990, p. 1.
44. J. A. Savage, "San Francisco Considers VDT Employee Safety Legislation," *Computerworld,* September 3, 1990, p. 12. J. A. Savage, "San Francisco Businesses Decry VDT Proposal," *Computerworld,* October 8, 1990, p. 18. The requirement for a one meter separation between VDTs and adjoining workers was dropped, "in a compromise with businesses that said it would cost too much." *Computerworld,* December 3, 1990, p. 120.
45. Alvin Toffler, *The Third Wave* (New York: Bantam, 1981).
46. "Home Work," *Fortune,* December 10, 1984, pp. 10–11.
47. Margrethe H. Olson, "Organizational Barriers to Professional Telework," in Eileen Boris and Cynthia R. Daniels (eds.), *Homework: Historical and Contemporary Perspectives on Paid Labor at Home* (Urbana and Chicago: University of Illinois Press, 1989), pp. 215–216.
48. Mitch Betts, "Bush to Push Work-At-Home," *Computerworld,* November 26, 1990, p. 1.
49. *Ibid.*
50. Tom Forester, "The Myth of the Electronic Cottage," *Futures,* **2**(3), June 1988, p. 232, published by Butterworth-Heinemann, Oxford, United Kingdom, © 1988 Tom Forester.
51. Adam Smith, *The Wealth of Nations Volume II,* (London: Everyman's Library, J.M. Dent & Sons Ltd., 1947), p. 278.
52. *Technology and Structural Unemployment,* p. 336.
53. W. Abernathy, K. Clark, and A. Kantrow, *Industrial Renaissance: Producing a Competitive Future for America* (New York: Basic Books, 1983).
54. Cyert and Mowery (eds.), *Technology and Employment.*
55. These studies are all referenced in Cyert and Mowery, *Technology and Employment,* as follows:
    1. P. M. Flynn, "The Impact of Technological Change on Jobs and Workers," Paper prepared for the U.S. Department of Labor, Employment Training Administration, 1985.
    2. K. I. Spenner, "The Upgrading and Downgrading of Occupations: Issues, Evidence, and Implications for Evidence," *Review of Education Research,* **55**, 1985, pp. 125–154.
    3. H. Levin and R. Rumberger, "Educational Requirements for New Technologies: Visions, Possibilities, and Current Realities," Working Paper 86-SEPI-2, Stanford Education Policy Institute, 1986.
    4. Flynn, "The Impact of Technological Change on Jobs and Workers."
    5. Larry Hirschhorn, *Beyond Mechanization: Work and Technology in a Postindustrial Age* (Cambridge, Massachusetts: MIT Press, 1984).
    6. National Research Council, Committee on the Effective Implementation of Advanced Manufacturing Technology, *Human Resources Practices for Implementing Advanced Manufacturing Technology* (Washington, D.C.: National Academy Press, 1986).
    7. B. Baran, "The Technological Transformation of White-Collar Work: A Case Study of the Insurance Industry," In H. Hartmann (ed.), *Computer Chips and Paper Clips: Technology and Women's Em-*

ployment, Volume 2, Case Studies and Policy Perspectives (Washington, D.C.: National Academy Press, 1987), pp. 25–62.

8. Ibid.

(Compiled from *Technology and Employment,* © 1987 by the National Academy of Sciences. Published by National Academy Press, Washington, D.C.).

56. *The Electronic Supervisor: New Technology, New Tensions* (Washington, D.C.: U.S. Congress, Office of Technology Assessment, OTA-CIT-333, September, 1987).
57. *Ibid.,* pp. 9–12.
58. *Ibid.* p. 32.

ADDITIONAL READINGS

Introduction

Zuboff, Shoshana. *In the Age of the Smart Machine: The Future of Work and Power.* New York: Basic Books, 1988.

Experiences of Workers

Aronowitz, Stanley. *False Promises.* New York: McGraw-Hill, 1974.

Garson, Barbara. *All the Livelong Day.* Middlesex, England: Penguin, 1977.

Littler, Craig R. (ed.). *The Experience of Work.* Aldershot, Hants, England: Gower, 1985.

O'Toole, James. *Work and the Quality of Life.* Cambridge, Massachusetts: MIT Press, 1974.

Rice, Berkeley. "The Hawthorne Effect: Persistence of a Flawed Theory." *Psychology Today,* February 1982, pp. 70, 72–74.

Computers and Employment

Bjerknes, Gro, Ehn, Pelle, and Kyng, Morten (eds.). *Computers and Democracy.* Aldershot, Hants, England: Gower, 1987.

Guile, Bruce R. and Quinn, James Brian (eds.). *Technology in Services: Policies for Growth, Trade, and Employment.* Washington, D.C.: National Academy Press, 1988.

Leontief, Wassily and Duchin, Faye. *The Future Impact of Automation on Workers.* New York: Oxford University Press, 1986.

Olson, Margrethe H. *Technological Support for Work Group Collaboration.* Hillsdale, New Jersey: Lawrence Erlbaum Associates, 1989.

Quinn, James Brian and Paquette, Penny C. "Technology in Services: Creating Organizational Revolutions." *Sloan Management Review,* Winter 1990. pp. 67–78.

"The Mechanization of Work." Special Issue, *Scientific American,* September 1982.

The Response of Unions

Davies, Annette. *Industrial Relations & New Technology.* Dover, New Hampshire: Croom Helm, 1986.

Heckscher, Charles C. *The New Unionism: Employee Involvement in the Changing Corporation.* New York: Basic Books, 1988.

Montgomery, David. *Workers' Control in America: Studies in the History of Work, Technology, and Labor Struggles.* New York: Cambridge University Press, 1979.

Computers, Women, and Work

Brodeur, Paul. "The Hazard of Electromagnetic Fields: III Video-Display Terminals." *The New Yorker,* June 6, 1989, pp. 39–68.

Brodeur, Paul. "The Magnetic-Field Menace." *Macworld,* July 1990, pp. 136–144,

Fierman, Jaclyn. "Why Women Still Don't Hit the Top." *Fortune,* July 30, 1990, pp. 40–42, 46, 50, 54, 58, 62.

Hartmann, Heidi I., Kraut, Robert E., and Tilly, Louise E. *Computer Chips and Paper Clips: Technology and Women's Employment, Volume I.* Washington, D.C.: National Academy Press, 1986.

Johnson, Maryfran. "Career Boosters for Women." "The Feminine Technique in IS." "Women Out on Their Own." *Computerworld,* December 10, 1990, pp. 95–96, 98.

Mallory, Maria and Bradford, Hazel. "An Invisible Workplace Hazard Gets Harder to Ignore." *Business Week,* January 13, 1989, pp. 92–93.

Pearl, Amy, Pollack, Marth E., Riskin, Eve, Thomas, Becky, Wolf, Elizabeth, and Wu, Alice. "Becoming a Computer Scientist: A Report by the ACM Committee on the Status of Women in Computer Science." *Communications of the ACM,* **33**(11), November 1990, pp. 47–57.

Schatz, Willie. "Suffolk Law, New Studies Reinvigorate VDT Debate." *Datamation,* August 15, 1988, pp. 39–41.

Working with Visual Display Units, Occupational Safety and Health Series (Geneva: International Labour Office, 1989).

Vitalari, Nicholas P., Venkatesh, Alladi, and Gronhaug, Kjell. "Computing in the Home: Shifts in the Time Allocation Patterns of Households." *Communications of the ACM,* 28(5), May 1985, pp. 512–522.

Wright, Barbara Drygulski, Feree, Myra Marx, Mellow, Gail O., Lewis, Linda, H., Samper, Maria-Luz Daza, Asher, Robert, and Claspell, Kathleen. *Women, Work, and Technology.* Ann Arbor: University of Michigan Press, 1987.

The Changing Nature of Work

Barba, Connie. "'That's No 'Beep', That's My Boss: Congress Seeks to Disconnect the Secrecy of Telephone Monitoring in the Workplace." *The John Marshall Law Review,* **21**(4), Summer 1988, pp. 881–902.

Berger, Joseph. "Companies Step in Where the Schools Fail." *The New York Times,* September 26, 1989, p. A 1, A 12.

Brod, Craig. *Technostress: The Human Cost of the Computer Revolution.* Reading, Massachusetts: Addison-Wesley, 1984.

Danann, Sharon. "Cracking the Electronic Whip." *Harper's Magazine,* August 1990, pp. 58–59.

Garson, Barbara. *The Electronic Sweatshop: How Computers Are Transforming the Office of the Future Into the Factory of the Past.* New York: Simon and Schuster, 1988.

Howard, Robert. *Brave New Workplace.* New York: Viking, 1985.

Moad, Jeff. "It's Time to Retrain!" *Datamation,* August 1, 1990, 20–22, 24.

Owen, John W. "Working at Home." *Datamation,* July 1, 1989, pp. 63–65.

Rothfeder, Jeffrey, Galen, Michele, and Driscoll, Lisa. "Is Your Boss Spying on You?" *Business Week,* January 15, 1990, pp. 74–75.

Smith, Robert Ellis. *Workrights.* New York: E. P. Dutton, 1983.

Tepperman, Jean. *Not Servants, Not Machines.* Boston: Beacon, 1976.

Westin, Alan F. and Salisbury, Stephan (eds.), *Individual Rights in the Corporation: A Reader on Employee Rights.* New York: Pantheon Books, 1980.

11

BUSINESS AND GOVERNMENT

The business of America is business.

Calvin Coolidge, Address to the Society of American Newspaper Editors, January 17, 1925.

INTRODUCTION

In Chapter 4, a variety of applications of computers in the business world were presented and discussed. In Chapter 7, a similar exercise was carried out for the role of computers in government. The primary purpose in each of these cases was to focus on specific innovative uses within a given domain. Of course, many information processing problems do not respect arbitrary boundaries. Several issues naturally reside in the murky area between government and business.

The relationship between business and government has been long and complex. Most companies wish to pursue their activities with minimal interference from government. Government has a variety of responsibilities, among them the creation of a climate in which companies may compete openly and the protection of its citizens' welfare. To these ends, governments have to pass antitrust and consumer protection legislation. In countries where the state owns and manages all the companies, the goals of these companies and the people are taken to be indistinguishable. And even in a free enterprise system, government has found it necessary, over the years, to intervene in the marketplace in order to ensure that all companies have a fair chance to compete. The following is a list of relevant issues:

Antitrust Cases. The U.S. government charged IBM with antitrust violations in a suit that lasted 13 years until it was finally dropped in January of 1982.

Regulation of the Telephone Industry. Up to fairly recently, long distance telephone lines were a monopoly run by AT&T (American Telephone and Telegraph). In January of 1982,

AT&T agreed to separate itself from a number of local telephone companies under an agreement arranged by the Federal courts. The agreement took effect on January 1, 1984.

Industry Standards. The government plays an important role in helping to set standards in the computer and communication industries (and other areas as well).

Legal Protection of Software and Hardware. The government protects programs by such means as copyright and patent laws (as discussed in Chapter 8).

Protection of Privacy. Issues arising from the growth in the use of computer-based information systems have led to problems and legislation.

Electronic Funds Transfer Systems (EFTS). Future regulation of the banking and financial industries must take into account the increasing use of computer and communication systems for banking services.

Transborder Data Flows. As information becomes a major resource, governments must develop policies to control the flow of information across national borders. This process is complicated by differing national policies on privacy and freedom of information.

Technology Transfer. Individual countries are concerned with protecting their technological developments. In the United States this concern covers both economic competitors such as Japan and political ones such as the Soviet Union. In the United States open discussion of technical issues is a way of life, and restrictions will be resisted.

National Industrial Policy. Many voices have been raised proposing solutions to economic difficulties in the United States. One important proposal is that the government should formulate a plan for future industrial development.

Thus, the federal government must intrude into the marketplace from time to time. In general, its policy is to set rules for the players, monitor the resulting performance, and take specific actions only if violations occur. This is the usual procedure for competitive industries such as computers, automobiles, and household appliances. In regulated monopolies such as the telephone system and radio and television stations, the government has traditionally exerted control by the issuance of licenses, their renewals, and the setting of rates. There has been much debate about the proper role of government, which acts from a variety of motives, ranging from the accommodation of public opinion to the exercising of a particular political philosophy.

The computer industry has grown very rapidly since 1945 and no company has been more successful than International Business Machines. In fact, as of March 1991, IBM was the top U.S. company in terms of stock market value, the fourth leading company in sales at $69 billion, and first in profits at $6.02 billion. As a further indication of its dynamism and flexibility, IBM became the world leader in income from sales of personal computers in 1983, having just entered the market two years earlier, and in 1990 it was still the major world player, although with a reduced market share. In one of the final acts of the Johnson administration, in early 1969 IBM was charged with a variety of antitrust violations. After much expense on both sides, the charges were finally dropped thirteen years later. How IBM's domination of the computer market was achieved and maintained was an important issue in the government's suit.

The other major government suit of the late 1970s and early 1980s was directed against AT&T. "Ma Bell," as it was sometimes called, had been a gigantic company composed of a number of local telephone companies, a long-distance service, a manufacturing division, Western Electric, and a world-famous research facility, Bell Labs. During the 1970s, AT&T's monopoly over long-distance service was challenged, and the result was a consent agreement between the company and the federal courts that required AT&T to divest itself of its local telephone companies.

Since money plays such an important role in our lives, the new developments in banking and bill paying will have an important impact. Already, automatic teller machines (ATMs) are everywhere and are changing long-established banking habits. Additional changes taking place now include: point-of-sale terminals (POS terminals), debit cards, and regional and national banking networks. Several social issues naturally arise with the growth in electronic banking (usually called electronic funds transfer systems, EFTS). Among these are privacy, new possibilities for large scale theft and sabotage, system reliability, reduced competition, and consumer protection.

Of major concern to governments is the competitiveness of their industries in response to worldwide challenges. The United States is currently locked in technological combat primarily with Japan but increasingly so with Europe. Japan has made enormous advances since World War II, in becoming a major economic force and technological leader. It has invested heavily in new technology and now challenges the United States across a broad range of products and services, especially computers and microelectronics. In response, the U.S. government, in the guise of meeting its defense requirements, has sponsored research and development in many areas of high technology. Many economists and politicians have urged the development of a national plan to maintain economic superiority. The centerpiece of most proposals is a national resolve to continue world leadership in computer hardware and software. Except in times of war, national mobilization has not been a hallmark of U.S. society. Nevertheless, even with a White House hostile to any suggestion of adopting a national industrial policy, some small steps have been taken.

Another important area of the economy in which some degree of government involvement has taken place are the nation's stock exchanges. Computers have made possible the trading of enormous quantities of securities very rapidly and have contributed to a certain degree of instability. The flow of information around the world via communication networks has become an important factor in the conduct of international business. This development coincides with the growth in multinational corporations and their increasing dependence on the rapid and efficient transmission of information. The host of factors associated with this worldwide flow is called transborder data flow (TBDF).

Because it is vitally interested in maintaining technological as well as military superiority, the government has initiated attempts to control technology transfer. More recently, as the Cold War has diminished because of the far-reaching changes in Eastern Europe, the West has reduced, and even removed, many of the restrictions on the export of computers.

INDUSTRY REGULATION

> What is good for the country is good for General Motors and what's good for General Motors is good for the country.[1]

The U.S. government has recognized two major forms of environments in which businesses can operate. One is the typical free marketplace situation in which companies compete against one another. The other is a monopoly situation, in which the government permits a single company to operate without competition, under an agreement that its rates will be regulated. Up to fairly recently the telephone industry was the prime example of a regulated monopoly. An intermediate form is represented by the radio and television industries. Individual stations must apply for licenses, which are renewed at regular intervals if no violations occur. Governments have seen fit to try to ensure that the competition in the open marketplace is as unrestricted as possible. For example, in 1890 Congress passed the Sherman Antitrust Act in reaction to the activities of large railway and industrial trusts. In later years various companies—such as Alcoa Aluminum, American Tobacco, and Hughes Tool—were charged with antitrust violations. The longest antitrust case to date involved IBM.

IBM and the Computer Industry

> Our industry is healthy and competitive, and IBM has not violated the antitrust laws.[2]

On January 17, 1969, the last possible day it could take action, the Justice Department of the Johnson administration launched an antitrust suit against IBM. Almost thirteen years later, on January 8, 1982, the Justice Department of the Reagan administration dropped the longest antitrust suit in history. In the interim, many millions of dollars were spent in legal fees, 66 million pages of documents were collected, and IBM was somewhat restrained in its activities. The government originally charged IBM with monopolizing the computer industry.

Since it is the undisputed leader in the industry, IBM's every move, announced or predicted, has been carefully watched and evaluated. This situation has given IBM extraordinary power in manipulating the market to suit its own needs. The government's antitrust case depended, in part, on proving that certain practices of IBM in controlling the computer industry were illegal. For example, when competitors began marketing new models that were faster and cheaper than the current IBM versions, IBM might announce a price cut or its own new models. Generally customers were forced to wait until the details of IBM's new machines were released. Making inroads into IBM's domination was not easy under the best of conditions. In order to convince an IBM customer to switch, a price reduction in equipment would not be sufficient. It was necessary to guarantee that existing programs would continue to run properly on the new computer. Nevertheless, IBM's share of the market did slowly diminish. In response to the government's charges, IBM argued that its practices were commonly accepted in other businesses, that it did not really control the market, and that in such a technically active field no single company could ever maintain control very long.

After almost 13 years, the government finally dropped the case. William F. Baxter, Assistant Attorney General in charge of the antitrust division of the Justice Department, stated: "The government is not likely to win this case. Even if it won, there is no relief I could recommend in good conscience."[3] During the trial some had suggested that IBM be broken up into a number of smaller independent companies. Others had argued that these new companies would still be larger than their competitors and even more aggressive than the monolithic IBM.

It had been felt that IBM had assumed a much less competitive stance during the years of the trial, to avoid the possibility of further charges. While IBM appeared to be dormant, though, there was considerable ferment below the surface. The best example of the "new" IBM was its stunning achievement in the personal computer market. From its introduction of the PC (Personal Computer) in 1981, IBM took the lead in dollar value of personal computers sold in 1983. IBM's worldwide domination of the computer market was described in Chapter 3. The IBM name once again demonstrated its worth in the personal computer area. First-time buyers found comfort in dealing with a company that had a proven track record and was not likely to go out of business. In order to survive in the personal computer market, it became necessary for IBM's competitors, save Apple, to market PC-compatible machines. This strategy has resulted in IBM's share of the total market, in 1989, being considerably reduced, while it still holds a substantial lead over its next leading competitor, Apple's Macintosh, IBM with a 22.3% market share, yielding \$8.34 billion, and Apple with a 9.6% market share, yielding \$3.57 billion.

A whole industry has come into being that produces equipment compatible with IBM. Companies in this market are referred to as PCMs, Plug Compatible Manufacturers. Only the existence of a relatively stable industry, guaranteed by such a major company as IBM, would encourage the growth of PCMs. In general, industries dominated by a few large companies are certainly more stable but perhaps less innovative, although in the personal computer market, including software, competition and innovation are the hallmark, so far. IBM has dominated nearly every segment of the computer industry except for minicomputers, where Digital Equipment leads, and the new growth area, workstations, led by Sun, Digital, and Hewlett-Packard. Those who favor minimal government involvement in business point to the computer industry as an example of a successful and innovative field, neglecting to consider the influential role of the Department of Defense, the National Aeronautics and Space Administration, and the National Science Foundation. Nevertheless, even with the IBM giant, there has been room for Silicon Valley and Route 128.

AT&T and the Telephone Industry

> Mr. Watson, come here; I want you.[4]

The American Telephone and Telegraph Company has been referred to as the biggest company on earth, and it is not an exaggeration. On January 1, 1984, AT&T underwent a dramatic change, which will have a significant impact on society. The combination of computers and communication systems is rapidly changing the way we live and work. The distinction between the processing of data by computers and the transmission of data by communication systems is becoming blurred. What is the role of AT&T and its competitors in this process?

Alexander Graham Bell invented the telephone in 1876. Bell Telephone Company, the predecessor of AT&T, was founded on July 8, 1877. Under the leadership of Theodore Vail, a shrewd and visionary businessman, AT&T was formed in 1885, after an early battle with Western Union. It had purchased Western Electric as its manufacturing division and forced Western Union to withdraw completely from the telephone business. The company began a period of rapid growth, stringing telephone lines across the country, fighting off competitors, and purchasing independent telephone companies. By 1910, it had even achieved control of Western Union. In 1913, under the threat of antitrust action, an understanding with the Justice Department was reached, the Kingsbury Commitment, by which AT&T promised to sell its Western Union stock, desist from purchasing any additional competitors, and permit interconnection with independent companies. After the passages in 1921 of the Willis-Graham Act, which excluded telephone mergers from antitrust charges (if they were approved by the regulatory agencies), AT&T launched a new wave of acquisitions until by 1932 its market share had reached 79%.

In order to protect its position, AT&T strongly advocated regulation, arguing that where there was no serious competition public control should be in force. It prospered under the regulatory system, which after 1934 included the Federal Communications Commission (FCC). In practice, regulation precluded the entrance of competitors and protected AT&T's monopoly. In 1956, after several years of dealing with a new antitrust suit filed in 1949, AT&T and the Justice Department agreed to a Consent Decree that generally accepted AT&T's position that the basic issues of the suit should be resolved by Congress. Existing arrangements were to continue, except that AT&T was not permitted to engage in any businesses other than the furnishing of common carrier communications services. Thus, AT&T and its subsidiary, Western Electric, could only be involved in regulated services. This seemed to confirm AT&T's mandate, but the new age of computer communications was fast approaching and AT&T was excluded.

Challenges to AT&T began to appear. Besides the telephone, there are other kinds of terminal equipment: modems for connecting computers or computer terminals, key telephone sets for small businesses with several lines, and Private Branch Exchanges (PBXs) for large businesses with internal switching centers. Telephone companies only permitted their own equipment to be connected to telephone lines. In 1966 the FCC ruled that though the telephone companies could set standards, they could not prohibit devices manufactured by other companies from being attached to their networks. Both PBXs and key telephone sets entered the competitive market. This was an important development, because PBXs were soon to become the basic infrastructure of the office and its interface to the existing telephone system.

Perhaps the most significant assault on the telephone companies was launched by Microwave Communications Incorporated (MCI), which applied in 1963 for the right to build a microwave system between St. Louis and Chicago. MCI planned to offer such services as voice, data, and facsimile transmission, in direct competition with AT&T. After initial approval by the FCC in 1966 and final approval in 1969, a court challenge by AT&T was instituted and withdrawn in 1971, more than seven years after the date of the original application. The telephone companies correctly anticipated that the MCI application would have immense repercussions far beyond its modest beginnings. Other companies entered the field and MCI itself soon expanded to a nationwide network, primarily providing private-line service. Next it offered direct competition to AT&T in public, or dial-up, long-distance service. A dial-up call would use the telephone companies' lines to reach the local MCI office, then go over the MCI network to the destination city's MCI office, and finally over local telephone lines to the destination telephone. The Execunet service offered by MCI in 1975 operated in this manner. AT&T appealed to the FCC and was upheld, but eventually the case went to the courts. In May 1978 the Supreme Court supported a lower court ruling that overturned the FCC decision. Thus, after almost 100 years of operating as a monopoly, AT&T faced serious competition in the long-distance market.

The development of satellite-based communications systems also challenged AT&T's monopoly of long-distance communication, and the boundary between computer and communications technologies has continued to blur. Computer manufacturers began to compete with communications companies in the production of a range of products. The FCC permitted a policy of free market competition in the satellite communication industry in 1972. AT&T could use domestic satellites for its public long-distance monopoly service but was not allowed to compete for three years in the private satellite market. In November 1974, convinced that new technology had made the Consent Decree of 1956 outdated, the Justice Department initiated the largest antitrust suit ever against AT&T. The suit argued that AT&T should be broken up into separate companies: Western Electric for telephone equipment, Long Lines for long-distance service, and the operating companies for local service. Finally, on January 8, 1982, an agreement was reached between AT&T and the Justice Department along the lines suggested in the original suit.

> An historic agreement has been reached: AT&T agreed to a consent order divesting the company of all facilities used to provide local telephone service, and the Department of Justice dropped its antitrust case against the company.[5]

After divesting itself of its local telephone companies, AT&T was organized in two main divisions, as follows:[6]

- AT&T Communications.

Long-distance. 1984 sales: $35 billion.

- AT&T Technologies. 1984 sales: $17 billion.

AT&T Bell Laboratories: Research and development.

AT&T Network Systems: Telephone equipment, manufacturing and sales.

AT&T Technology Systems: Manufacturing and sales of components, e.g. chips.

AT&T International: Overseas marketing of equipment and services; foreign partnerships.

AT&T Information Systems: Computers and business systems.

On January 1, 1985 AT&T Information Systems—set up as an arms-length, deregulated subsidiary by the government—was reorganized along three lines of business: computers, large business systems, and small business systems. The remaining parts of the AT&T empire—the twenty-two local operating companies, about two-thirds of its assets—were reorganized into seven independent regional Bell operating companies (BOCs), the *Baby Bells:* Pacific Telesis, U.S. West, Bellsouth, Nynex, Bell Atlantic, Southwestern Bell, and Ameritech, and the Central Services Organization, a research and development division jointly owned by these companies and now called Bell Communications Research (Bellcore). AT&T has begun to compete in the office automation market. Its Information Systems division is in direct competition with such companies as Wang, Xerox, and Digital Equipment. In the communication switching equipment area, it competes with such companies as Northern Telecom (Canada), Rolm (United States), and L. M. Ericson, Philips, and Plessey (Europe), and in the long-distance carrier market its major competitors are MCI, GTE-Sprint, and Allnet. It was expected, however, that the major confrontation would be with IBM.

IBM and AT&T: When Giants Collide?

> The stage is set for a bout of worldwide dimensions: never before have two private corporations brought such resources and so many years of preparation into a head-on competition.[7]

During the 1970s, when the government's antitrust suit had an inhibiting effect, IBM seemed to be biding its time, reluctant to appear too aggressive. Then, in anticipation of the suit's ultimate dismissal, it took steps to prepare for the future. Probably its most dramatic action was to launch the IBM PC. One year after the suit was dropped, IBM bought a share of Intel, the large semiconductor manufacturing company, and Rolm, a leading manufacturer of PBXs. IBM has shown remarkable flexibility for such a large, well-established company. With the restraints imposed by possible government action removed, IBM has served notice that it will enter any sphere of computer applications it views as profitable. By virtue of its partnership in Satellite Business Systems, IBM also has a stake in the international telecommunications market.

It was anticipated that IBM would also be confronting the newly deregulated AT&T Information Systems along a number of fronts, among which are the following:

Office Automation. Work stations, PBXs, local voice and data transmissions.

Data Processing Services.

Long-Distance Networks. Interfaces to local systems, industry standards, cable operators.

Telephone Equipment. Modems, telephone switching equipment, terminals.

Office Equipment. Printers, Fax.

Banking Equipment. Automatic teller machines (ATMs), Point of sale terminals (POSs).

The Communications Battleground

As we have noted, AT&T's monopoly of long-distance communication has been eroding since the early 1970s. Furthermore, the 1982 consent agreement opened up the market to increased, vigorous competition. A major player in the game is MCI Communications, which has challenged AT&T at every step. Consider Table 11-1, which shows revenues and market percentages for AT&T and its major competitors from 1981 to 1987. MCI and other companies have been able to undercut AT&T's rates, because AT&T's Communications division remains regulated in order to give new companies a chance to compete. However AT&T will become more competitive as access charges, which local telephone companies charge to interstate carriers, are equalized. In 1990, AT&T's share of long distance revenues had decreased to 67%. All these changes will have a serious impact on data communications, because there will be active competition to serve the computer and communications needs of both large and small businesses.

The competition is becoming particularly vigorous at the international level. In 1987, the worldwide telecommunication equipment market totalled some $95 billion: Western Europe, 32%, United States, 32%, Japan 12%, the rest of the world, 24%.[8] The projected market in 1992 is $140 billion. The major components are customer premises equipment, transmission, cable and outside plant, and switching. Many large companies are attempting to obtain a share of this growing market. AT&T has launched joint international ventures with Philips, a Dutch-based company. The integration of computers and communication systems is necessary to serve a variety of traditional and novel needs: data communications, teleconferencing, electronic mail, Fax, and delayed voice messaging. The rapidly evolving information age is dependent on the growing sophistication of the telecommunications industry. Although all of this is happening, it has taken several years for the convergence to become a reality; up until fairly recently, companies were either in computers or in communications but not both. For example, while the growth in telecommunications was almost entirely dependent on the private sector, the computer industry, especially in the United States owes a considerable debt to the government.

The communications industry has been heavily regulated, but over the last few years the tendency of the U.S. government seems to have been towards a hands-off approach. In a period of rapidly changing technology, it is argued that government should permit the companies to fight it out before reintroducing guidelines. In Europe, especially in France, governments are more protective of their state-run post, telephone, and telegraph agencies. In the early years of the 1980s, IBM undertook a number of initiatives to position itself in the telecommunications market. Its forays into telecommunications have run into a variety of problems, however, among them the following:

- In 1982, IBM "repatriated" its Information Network, which had been operating in Europe since the early 1970s. Set up as an Independent Business Unit (IBU) to offer network services, it failed to return a profit between 1982 and 1984.

TABLE 11-1

AT&T AND ITS MAJOR LONG-DISTANCE COMPETITORS. (DOLLAR AMOUNTS IN MILLIONS.)

Company	1981		1983		1985		1987	
	Dollars	Percent	Dollars	Percent	Dollars	Percent	Dollars	Percent
Other common carriers (OCC):								
MCI	413.1	1.9	1,326.3	4.9	2,330.8	7.7	3,938.4	12.5
GTE-Sprint	230.9	1.1	740.0	2.7	1,121.9	3.7	2,591.5	8.2
Allnet					309.2	1.0	394.6	1.3
OCC Total	726.6	3.3	2,229.6	8.2	4,663.0	15.4	7,541.6	24.0
AT&T Long-Lines	21,252.0	96.7	24,833.5	91.8				
AT&T Communications					25,598.3	84.6	23,906.7	76.0

Source: Taken from Table 2, pp. 68–69, in Leonard Waverman, "U.S. Interexchange Competition," in Robert W. Crandall and Kenneth Flamm (eds.), *Changing the Rules: Technological Change, International Competition, and Regulation in Communications* (Washington, D.C.: The Brookings Institution, 1989).

• Also in 1982, IBM signed an agreement with the Canadian company Mitel to develop an advanced digital PBX for local networking purposes. This venture ended a year later, and in 1984, IBM purchased Rolm, Inc., a leading U.S. manufacturer of communication switches, for $1.25 billion. After four years, and considerable losses, IBM partly sold off Rolm to the German company Siemens AG.

• IBM has been involved since 1974 in Satellite Business Systems, in which it holds a 60% share. This company, involved in the highly competitive long-distance market, is a consistent money loser.

Other actions taken by IBM in communications include a joint computer network project with Motorola to enable salespeople and repair personnel to communicate with computers using cellular telephone, a national videotex system, called Prodigy, in cooperation with Sears, Roebuck (See Chapter 13 for more detail), and most importantly, in 1985 it purchased 16% of MCI Communications, with an option to buy up to 30%. In this area, IBM has stressed joint ventures and acquisitions rather than the development of in-house products. Up until now success has proven elusive as computers and communications are not as obvious a match as had been anticipated by industry experts:[9]

> The recent attempts by AT&T and IBM to invade one another's markets have been remarkably unsuccessful. Despite the obvious similarities in the basic technologies of the two industries, large computer firms like Apple, Digital Equipment Corporation (DEC), or Unisys are not major players in either the communications equipment or telecommunications services market, nor are communications companies like Northern Telecom, GTE, CIT-Alcatel, or Plessey important competitors in the computer industry. . . . It appears that specialization and product differentiation are as important as technological convergence in explaining the structure of these two industries.

A Status Report

In 1985, IBM expected to quadruple its sales, from $48.6 billion, in 10 years, an incredible rate of growth for a company its size. Its 1990 computer sales were $69 billion, suggesting how unrealistic the earlier prediction had been. During the mid-1980s the entire computer industry suffered a slow down and the frequent cry was heard: "What's wrong with IBM?" IBM seemed unable to respond to shifting industry demands, resulting in decreasing market share in personal computers, failure in early introduction of a RISC workstation, major failure in the Rolm purchase, major failure in the worldwide Automatic Teller Machine market, growing threat from Japanese companies in mainframes, DEC's control of the minicomputer market, and complaints from large customers that IBM was not listening to their problems. In the late 1980s, IBM began to turn things around, under its CEO John Akers, by tightening its organizational structure: IBM USA was reorganized into seven autonomous business units and an eighth for marketing. This action represented a flattening of the management hierarchy and a decentralization of decision making. The foreign operations, extremely profitable, were left untouched. Maintaining its tradition of no layoffs, IBM convinced several thousand employees to take early retirement and transferred some 20,000 from staff and laboratory to sales.

New products were being introduced at a faster rate, including the successful AS/400 minicomputer in 1988; some 25,000 systems worth about $3 billion were sold in less than a year. In 1990 it introduced, to considerable acclaim, a range of competitive workstations. It re-entered the home computer market with a low-priced version of its PS/2. It has moved to strengthen its foreign operations, especially in Japan, where IBM is highly admired amongst U.S. companies. Between 1984 and 1988, two IBM researchers won Nobel prizes in physics for work on superconductivity and the scanning tunneling microscope, respectively. In 1990, IBM was the first to announce the fabrication of a 16-megabit memory chip, another indication of its continuing research and development expertise. IBM has continued to invest in a variety of companies to complement its own activities and to position itself to take advantage of new developments. Consider the following moves taken by IBM:[10]

- investing in Supercomputer Systems run by Steve Chen, former designer for Cray Research;
- licensing programming technology from Stephen Jobs's NEXT, Inc.;
- joining a consortium of investors in U.S. Memories, to compete more effectively against Japan in memory chips;
- forming an alliance with International Telemanagement Corp. to allow Netview, IBM's network management product, to support non-Systems Network Architecture (SNA) architectures; and
- most surprisingly of all, joining with its long-term rival, Apple Computer, in a pact to "transform computing in the 1990s." Signed on October 3, 1991, this technology accord between two fierce rivals will include the development of object-oriented software environments and multimedia computing, and an improvement in the interfacing of Apple Macintoshes to larger IBM computers.

IBM will expand its maintenance and service facilities to tap this very important growth area. IBM already leads in maintenance with 1989 revenues of $7 billion in a worldwide market of $29.3 billion, but only has a 5.3% share of the $22.5 billion worldwide market in services. 1990 witnessed a major improvement in overall sales, up 10% to $69 billion, and more significantly profits, up 60% to $6 billion, number one among U.S. companies. Uncertainties remain, however, especially because of the recession of 1991, which was reflected in a 85% drop in earnings for the third quarter of 1991. IBM stated that overall earnings for 1991 would be considerably lower than predictions made by stock market analysts, and in a surprising speech by IBM chairman, John Akers, managers were severely criticized for underachievement.[11]

IBM's challengers will not disappear but some have suffered severe setbacks, especially DEC, with a loss of $95 million in 1990 on flat sales, Unisys, with a loss of $437 million, and Wang, down $584 million. The growth in the workstation market is significant and it remains to be seen if IBM can establish a presence. Its mainframe dominance continues to be challenged by Japanese companies, but the enormous worldwide capital investment in

IBM mainframes provides a major long-term buffer. It is unlikely that IBM will be subject to further government challenges, since its international success endows it with considerable power as a bulwark against the technological and economic assaults of Europe and Japan. As noted in previous comments, IBM has made little inroads into the communications market, neither in equipment nor services, and does not seem likely to do so in the near future. The anticipated earthshaking confrontation between IBM and AT&T was a bust.

AT&T has not fared as well as IBM, at least in the five years following its breakup. As a regulated monopoly, it lacked sufficient experience in the highly competitive markets where IBM has thrived. In the future, AT&T's enormous research, manufacturing, marketing, and service resources will undoubtedly help make its presence felt in a wide range of markets. For the average telephone user, however, the immediate results of the breakup were increased local telephone rates, a confusion in the choice of long-distance services and telephone equipment, and an apparent lowering in overall service quality. For the business community, the benefits are lower long-distance rates and equipment and system costs, because of increased competition, and a more rapid introduction of technological innovations.

In its primary business activities as a long-distance carrier and a developer and manufacturer of communications equipment, AT&T's market share will gradually decrease in the face of increased competition, but its revenues will increase as the overall market grows. To position itself as a lean competitor, AT&T has reduced its workforce over the last six years by 92,000, to 281,000 employees. In the computer business, AT&T's performance has been undistinguished, to say the least. For example in 1986, it lost $1.2 billion in its computer operations.[12] In October 1988, AT&T achieved an important boost when it won a $929 million contract from the Department of Defense to supply some 20,000 minicomputers over the following five years. IBM was one of the losers. Of additional importance is that these computers use AT&T's Unix System V as their operating system and will certainly help to establish this system as a way to go for government computing.[13] On May 6, 1991 NCR, the nation's fifth largest computer company, accepted a stock bid from AT&T, in a major step by AT&T to achieve a significant presence in the computer industry.[14] Finally, in its attempts to control the long-distance market, AT&T has regularly challenged the Federal Communications Commission to remove restrictions on its operations, but as long as it maintains such a dominant position, the restrictions will be removed only gradually.

EFTS: ELECTRONIC FUNDS TRANSFER SYSTEMS

> EFTS constitute an array of automated payment systems, in which the merger of computer and telecommunications technology is employed to improve the efficiency of our present payments system.[15]

Financial transactions are such a common occurrence in everyday life, it is not surprising that computers have found eager acceptance in the banking community. The sheer mass of numerical computations required to record, update, and process banking records has made the industry a major purchaser of equipment and employer of data processing professionals. Early applications involved the use of keypunches to prepare financial information that was then read into the computer. Accounts were then updated and financial statements produced. As software and hardware became increasingly sophisticated, banks have modernized their method of operation. Tellers could enter transaction information into a local computer via terminals at the counter. For independent banks, this information would be useful directly; for branch banks, the local computer would send the information over a communication system to the central computer. The marriage of computers and communication systems is a marriage made in heaven, for financial institutions. The next step has been to permit the customer direct access to the electronic system.

Banking in America

> The key to cutting costs, and the central challenge in retail banking . . . is "to migrate customers from the brick and mortar system to electronic delivery systems."[16]

Banks can be chartered by both the federal government and the states. The history of banking reflects the tension between the desire of rural, frontier America for local control over banks and the seeming expansionist tendencies of the international banks. This confrontation has turned on the issue of branch banking—which banks can set up branches and what constitutes a branch bank. "By 1988, 45 states has passed some type of legislation permitting regional or nationwide branching. Many states allowed for the formation of regional compacts designed to give regional banks enough time to prevent themselves from being absorbed by the money center banks."[17] The past 25 years have witnessed considerable consolidation of banks, as the number of truly independent banks has decreased from 13,400 in the mid-1960s to 9,800 by the end of 1988. This trend will continue as deregulation of interstate banking continues, as banks close because of depressed regional economies, and as hostile takeovers become more frequent.[18]

The Dimensions of EFTS

The term EFTS covers a multitude of processes, services, and mechanisms that depend on computers and communication systems for their operation. Some components have been in existence for quite a while, others have been introduced recently, and still others are in the planning stage. The full array will certainly change the way we shop, bank, and generally carry out our financial transactions. The impact on society will be in such areas as employment, privacy, social relations and patterns of interaction, centralization of control, financial transactions, and possible major consolidations of financial institutions.

Preauthorizations and Automated Banking

The following were probably the first procedures that could legitimately be included in the term EFTS:

Direct deposits of regular payments: paychecks, royalties.
Direct payments of recurrent expenses: mortgages, loans.
Direct regular contributions: charity.
Payment of bills by telephone.

Once a person authorizes deposits or payments, these are made automatically without further interaction. Typically, large companies deliver tapes of employees salaries to banks for disbursement into appropriate accounts. Such tapes are of course generated by the companies' computers. Since these procedures do not require sophisticated computer techniques, they were instituted quite early in the course of electronic banking.

The use of ATMs for depositing and withdrawing money, transfers between accounts, and other services—and the authorization of credit and checks—have become a way of life for many people. As of 1988, there were 72,500 ATMs installed across the country (an impressive growth rate given that the first appeared in September 1969). They have proven to be convenient, easy to use, and extremely popular because of their availability at all hours of the day and night. For their part, the banks find that ATMs, which can operate 24 hours a day, save them a considerable amount of money because employees are not needed. The banks are encouraging the use of ATMs during regular banking hours as well, by reducing their staff size and reserving the remaining staff for special problems. Although ATMs permit a variety of banking functions, about 75% are cash withdrawals, 15% inquiries, and 9% deposits. In 1988, there were 3.5 billion cash withdrawals using machines and 2.5 billion checks cashed with tellers.[19] The direct economic benefits of ATMs are obvious: 40 to 60 cents per transactions compared with 90 cents to $1.20 for a teller transaction. Even though the range of available functions is continually growing, as of 1987 only 8.7% of all branch transactions employed ATMs.

Another part of EFTS is the use of terminals to perform credit checks. Before authorizing a purchase, a store is able to verify electronically that a customer has sufficient funds on hand or that the balance available on a credit card is sufficiently large. This kind of checking can also be carried out by telephone, with only slightly more difficulty, but the communications networks necessary for electronic banking discourage the use of the telephone in this context.

POS (Point-of-Sale) Operations

The common feature of POS operations is that the electronic financial transactions are made directly at the time of purchase. Thus, instead of using cash, a check, or a credit card, the customer will have a debit card that when placed in a POS terminal transfers money from the customer's bank account to the store's. The card used in ATMs is really a debit card, since its use may result in instantaneous transfers into and out of bank accounts. If the customer has insufficient funds or lacks a line of credit, the purchase will not be completed. The widespread use of the debit card will be a major step along the way to the cashless society. Another important implication is the loss of the "float period" between the time a purchase is made and the time it must be paid for. The float period is not desirable for the banks, because it gives the customer use of the bank's money interest-free. In periods of high interest rates, substantial amounts of money are involved. With the debit card the float period is effectively eliminated and at the same time payment to the vendor is guaranteed.

What benefits do debit cards have for consumers? Consider the following list proposed by Jane Bryant Quinn:[20]

> 1. For the prudent, debit cards are pure discipline. You don't spend more money than you have in the bank.
> 2. The cards can be easier to use than personal checks, especially in places where you're not known.
> 3. For couples with joint checking, debit cards eliminate the need to juggle two checkbooks or carry loose checks.
> 4. If you use a debit card for small purchases, you run no risk of paying interest on them. With a credit card, by contrast, interest might be due even if you pay off the bill at the end of the month. (That usually happens when you roll over debt or when your card has no grace period.)
> 5. If you're short of cash, a debit card can see you through a supermarket, a gas station, a fast food restaurant—places that generally don't take credit cards.

Debit cards are much more common in Europe and Japan than in the United States, and in Japan there is a variation, the prepaid card used to pay for a wide range of goods and services. The initial value of the card is coded on a magnetic strip and subsequent payments result in a corresponding reduction in its value. In 1989, some $2.1 billion were spent using prepaid cards.

Automated Clearinghouse

A major part of the cost of processing a check is the physical movement of the check itself from the merchant, to a local bank, to a central clearinghouse, to the customer's bank, and eventually back to the customer, with perhaps additional stages involved. The replacement of all this paper processing by an electronic system is well under way. Such networks have been in existence for some time to facilitate the movement of money among financial institutions. Thus, EFTS have a well-established infrastructure for servicing money flows among banks. Large networks of ATMs and POS services are being built. Banks are getting larger through mergers, acquisitions, and the formation of networks to permit customers access to banking services on a regional basis. Such growth is necessary if the costs of constructing both regional and national EFTS are to be financed.

Problem Areas

One of the byproducts of EFTS is an increase in financial information. For example, the use of a POS terminal results in a record indicating that an individual spent a particular amount of money at a particular time and place. Because these records are created electronically and stored in computer databases, they are relatively straightforward to retrieve. EFTS operate on-line and in real time (i.e., transactions take effect instantaneously) and could be used to locate individuals whenever they initiate a transaction. Furthermore, more institutions will have access to an individual's financial records. In 1978, Congress passed the Right to Financial Privacy Act, limiting the government's access to financial records. The act outlines the procedures necessary to obtain such financial records as follows:

Customer authorization.
Administrative subpoena or summons.
Search warrant.
Judicial subpoena.
Formal written request, a copy of which is filed in court.

The government must notify individuals that their financial records are being requested and advise them that they may under law have the right to attempt to keep those records from the requesting agency. Records obtained by one agency cannot be provided to any other government department or agency. Such legislation represents legitimate concerns about the increasing availability of private information, in this case financial, even though the act is primarily concerned with specifying the conditions under which the government *can* have access.

Future Developments

Smart Cards

The credit or bank card, with its magnetic stripe on the back, has taken its place among the indispensable objects of modern life. It is used to obtain credit from a merchant and the credit card company and cash from an ATM. A further significant change has already begun—the development and distribution of the "smart card," a credit card-sized device containing one or more integrated circuit chips, which perform the functions of a microprocessor, memory, and input/output interface. Such a card can contain an enormous amount of information about an individual and his or her commercial transactions.

Visa International, which developed the supercard with Toshiba, began tests in Japan in mid-1988. Various demonstration projects have been undertaken, but only very small specialized niches have been found, probably because of the relatively high costs of card production, about $5 per card compared to 50 cents per regular credit card. There seems to be a number of important benefits to be derived from their use, including the following, but so far none have proven to be profitable or cost-effective:[21]

1. Placement of the PIN [Personal Identification Number] securely enough on the card to eliminate today's inefficient signature verification system, preclude expensive on-line PIN verifications, and reduce fraud costs in a cost-effective way.
2. Reliance on dynamic, individually determinable transaction control parameters that would help reduce fraud, curb excessive cardholder activity, and control the burgeoning cost of on-line authorizations.

3. Capture and storage of transaction data, for both control and record-keeping purposes.
4. Integration of nonfinancial data such as medical history, insurance requirements, hotel and airline reservations, frequent flyer numbers, tickets, product warranties, and so on.
5. Reduction of some operating costs such as frequent card reissuance, paper-based card bulletins, and data entry of paper sales drafts.

Additional ATM Applications

ATMs currently perform straightforward banking operations: deposits, withdrawals, and transfers between accounts—the basic, high volume transactions that are easily automated. In the works are more specialized functions such as the following:

- buying or selling stocks (which would require that brokerage companies hook into the EFTS networks),
- investment in term deposits,
- dispensing foreign currencies at airports or border crossings,
- accessing line-of-credit facilities, and
- providing access to an increased number of accounts.

Whenever banks can reduce their overhead by encouraging the use of automatic facilities, they will be readily introduced.

Banking at Home

By connecting a personal computer via a telephone to the bank's computer, all the usual functions of an ATM should be available in the comfort of one's home. It would be possible to determine which checks have cleared, to reconcile checkbooks, to pay bills for goods and services, and to send queries to the bank for later response. At-home banking permits 24-hour access and increased control over one's financial activities. In spite of these benefits, home banking is a very minor part of overall banking: about 100,000 subscribers at the end of 1988, whose transactions numbered less than one-tenth of one percent of the number of checks written. Some of the difficulties associated with home banking are lack of consumer preparation, high costs, and ongoing technical problems. At the end of 1987, only about 4.6% of American homes owned modems, which are necessary to connect personal computers via telephone to central computers, and of these less than one-quarter were interested in home banking. This acceptance rate of only 1% is a formidable barrier.[22] Despite an investment of tens of millions of dollars, Chemical Bank closed down its home banking system after attracting about 20,000 subscribers.

COMPETITIVENESS

Is the United States still competitive? If we are to believe the many journalists, economists, and historians who have written over the past ten years, the answer is, perhaps yes, but the future holds a diminished economic role internationally for the United States. Large trade deficits have become endemic; whole segments of the consumer electronics industry, such as television receivers, video cassette recorders, television cameras, and still cameras have vanished; the automobile industry has suffered a continuing reduced market share; major segments of the computer industry, such as memory chips, printers, laptop and notebook computers, and even supercomputers are being dominated by Japan; in international banking, Japanese banks have taken eight of the top ten positions in terms of total assets, with only one American bank making the top ten. In all these areas, the trends do not favor the United States and some have even argued that the United States should forego international industrial competition and become the world's provider of services and handler of information. Opposing voices have argued that it is impossible for the United States to maintain world leadership without a strong and thriving industrial base, especially in the computer, communications, and information technology sectors.

The two major challengers to U.S. dominance are Japan and the newly unified Western Europe. Given that Japan is the single country that competes successfully against the United States across a broad range of products, it is important to characterize Japan's success before attempting to describe U.S. actions to reclaim its previously unchallenged supremacy. Although one important factor in the Japanese success story is the intimate cooperation among business, government, and labor to achieve advances in carefully chosen areas, the U.S. government has officially resisted the design of a national industrial policy as a way of focusing energy on well-defined goals. Nevertheless, certain steps have been taken to mount challenges, including cooperative efforts among leading computer companies, the control of the export of designated technologies, government support of certain advanced technologies, restrictions on the dissemination of research results in sensitive areas, and occasional refusal of foreign acquisitions of particular U.S. high technology companies.

Japan and High Technology

In recent years books, television shows, and special issues of magazines have appeared, with some regularity, that purport to explain Japan to Americans. The work ethic of the Japanese is continually extolled in comparison to the well-publicized but unverified negative attitudes of the American worker. Characterizations of Japan are varied and numerous, including the following:

The Japanese are copiers not innovators.

Their success is based on unfair cooperation among government, industry, and labor.

IQ tests show the Japanese to be smarter than Americans.

They prevent fair competition by restricting entry to their domestic marketplace.

They compete unfairly abroad by taking initial losses in order to penetrate a new market.

Although they lost World War II, the Japanese obtained an advantage in the complete rebuilding of their industrial plant.

A Record of Achievement

Since 1981, the extent of Japan's growing domination of technology and economic power has become more evident:[23]

- In the memory chip market, Japan produced about 70% of the worldwide production in units, in 1989, up from less than 40% in 1981. (In the same period, the United States share was down from about 55% to 15%.)
- Even more significantly, Japan's worldwide market share in semiconductor manufacturing equipment has increased from about 5% in 1979 to over 70% in 1988. (The United States share was down dramatically from over 90% to about 20%).
- The next generation of chip fabrication will require the expensive technology of X-ray lithography. In the United States only IBM has plans to construct the required $1 billion dollar plant and the entire output will be used by IBM. Japan has 19 X-ray lithography projects in progress.
- Japan's five largest laptop computer manufacturers hold a combined 43% of the U.S. market.
- Japan's worldwide computer sales reached $53 billion in 1988, growing at a compound annual rate of 45% between 1984 and 1988, compared to U.S. sales of $148 billion, growing at only 10% annually over the same period.
- Japan's overall trade surplus with the United States has averaged above $50 billion since 1986.
- Japan's direct investment in the United States has increased from about $6 billion in 1985 to almost $23 billion in 1989.
- Japan is the world leader in the following emerging technologies: flat panel displays (both monochrome and color) CD-ROM drives (used to read information stored on optical disks), erasable optical disk drives, and laser printer mechanisms.

In the consumer electronics market, Japan is by far the world leader in video cassette recorders, citizen band radios, stereo systems, color television sets, and compact disk players. In the application of new digital electronics to consumer products, Japan has shown the way and is the leader in 35 mm cameras, with self-focusing and automatic film advance, calculators, and watches. The quality of these products has totally reversed an earlier reputation for shoddy workmanship.

During the 1980s, Japanese researchers have become second only to the United States in the number of scientific publications published per year—about 25,000 compared to a U.S. total of over 100,000—and in addition have increased their percentage of articles in American journals from 2% to 10%.[24] In another important measure based on influential patents, Japan is second only to the United States and is rapidly narrowing the gap.[25] Japan's investment in research and development as a percentage of gross national product has now equalled that of the United States. There are two major features of this funding that are unique to Japan: almost no funds are directed towards defense research, and Japanese industry receives less than 20% of its research and development funds from the government, compared to about 50% in the United States and Europe.[26] This latter point is generally ignored in the West as the Japanese government is frequently accused of massive financial support for industry.

Other factors contributing to the success of "Japan, Inc." are a stable and hard-working labor force, progressive management (although there is some debate about how progressive), effective cooperation among business, government, and labor, a serious concern with productivity and quality, aggressive worldwide marketing coupled with a protectionist home policy, and a focus on consumer production under the U.S. military security umbrella.

In cooperation with some U.S. computer companies, Japanese computer manufacturers are attempting to establish a foothold in the lucrative U.S. market. For example, Japan's share of the personal computer market was 13% in 1989. Also in 1989, Hitachi bought 80% of National Advanced Systems. IBM's main competitor in the mainframe market, Amdahl Corp., is half-owned by Fujitsu Ltd. Fujitsu and NEC have become serious challengers to Cray in the supercomputer market, as Control Data has declined substantially. Software development is an important area in which the Japanese have yet to prove themselves. The United States controlled 70% of the $55 billion worldwide software market, in 1989, but the Japanese have launched a major effort to leap to the forefront: the Fifth Generation research project and its recent successors.

The Fifth Generation Project

In October 1981, Japan held an international conference on fifth generation computers, to which 86 foreigners were invited. From the Japanese point of view, the term fifth generation has two meanings, as follows:

Structural. The sequence of generations is based on the basic building blocks of computers: vacuum tubes, transistors, integrated circuits, very large-scale integrated (VLSI) circuits, and ultra large-scale integrated circuits.

Functional. Most of the publicity associated with the fifth generation project has to do with the concept of a computer able to perform a variety of tasks requiring intelligence, such as inference, natural language understanding, and image understanding.

Japan announced a 10-year project to develop the fifth generation computer and called for international cooperation. The development of such a computer will require faster hardware, new forms of computer organization, new programming languages, and breakthroughs in AI. Japan has demonstrated expertise in the hardware aspects, but its underlying purpose in pursuing this project is to challenge U.S. leadership in software. The stakes are high. Edward Feigenbaum and Pamela McCorduck issued the following call-to-arms in *The Fifth Generation:*

> We are writing this book because we are worried. But we are also basically optimistic. Americans invented this technology! If only we could focus our efforts we should have little trouble dominating the second computer age as we dominated the first.[27]

In November 1984, the Second International Conference on Fifth Generation Computer Systems was attended by about 700 researchers from Japan and 300 from 30 other countries. It was an opportunity to report on the three years of research of the Fifth Generation project. The formal presentation of papers and status reports revealed that some of the early projections had been scaled down and certain goals had become more focussed. Post-conference demonstrations clearly indicated that the project had achieved some significant advances in a rather short time. In terms of hardware, a high resolution computer similar to recently developed Lisp machines was shown. Called a personal sequential inference machine, it was a concrete implementation of a computer with an operating system written in an extended version of Prolog, a logic programming language. The Japanese commitment to logic programming has distinguished their approach from the North American effort and has also stimulated research in this area. Another interesting achievement is Delta, a relational database machine with large storage capabilities. Most striking is the degree to which the project has achieved, at this early stage, an integrated implementation of hardware, software, and application programs—all based on logic programming.

More recently, ICOT (The Institute for New Generation Computer Technology, founded in 1982 to manage the project) has produced a 64-processor computer with plans for a 1,000 processor version by 1992. ICOT is the largest project under the direction of MITI, Japan's somewhat infamous, at least in the United States, Ministry of International Trade & Industry. The followup to the Fifth Generation project is being planned, the development of a neurocomputer based on a highly parallel organization, similar to the structure of a simplified version of the human brain. Work in this area is also being carried out in the United States under the sponsorship of the Department of Defense. The general consensus is that the Fifth Generation project has not been successful in fulfilling its early goals. Nevertheless, it has contributed to the development of Japanese expertise in a number of areas, particularly AI, and it has created products which may lead to more powerful versions down the road. What it has certainly accomplished is to rouse the West to meet this technological challenge as well as others posed by Japan.

NATIONAL INDUSTRIAL POLICY

> Industrial policy remains an elusive concept. It encompasses ideas, some of them contradictory, ranging from the establishment of an industrial development bank to support winning industries, to an industrial conversion agency to rehabilitate losing industries and their workers. Many proposals prescribe some type of three-way bargaining process, in which business and labor make concessions in return for Government help.[28]

Governments regulate, monitor, allocate, draw up guidelines, enforce statutes, and generally attempt to create a favorable climate for business. Periodically, the U.S. government involves itself more directly in business activities. For example, it guaranteed massive loans to the Chrysler Corporation to enable it to survive. In the early 1980s a number of voices urged the government to become a partner in future industrial development. The following reasons were among those offered:

Japan's stunning industrial success has been attributed to the long-range planning and adequate financing provided by industry and government in cooperation with labor.

High technology is so volatile and important to the economic well-being and security of the nation that government involvement is mandatory.

Other more traditional industries such as steel and automobiles—the so-called smokestack industries—are seen as supplying fewer jobs in the future, and so the government is urged to stimulate other areas of the economy.

The serious recession of the early 1980s has convinced many economists that active government participation in a national plan for growth is necessary to stabilize the economy in the future.

The government has already been so involved in piecemeal economic activities—through its funding of research, its investment credits, its antitrust prosecutions, and its import/export regulations—that a coherent, long-range strategy is quite appropriate.

Critics maintain that the United States has arrived at its current dominant position precisely because the government has not become involved in a serious way in major business activities. Many prefer the government to act as a referee, not player. They suggest that the strength of the free enterprise system is that it is self-regulating and that any interference by the government will disturb this system. They ask what special skills the government has to enable it to predict winners independent of market forces. This confrontation is not new, but current economic, social, political, and military factors have given it a new urgency.

U.S. Actions

Given that our focus is not on a national industrial policy in general but rather on a national policy related to computer technology, the present discussion will be concerned with steps taken in this direction. Although no national policy has ever been enunciated by the U.S. government, steps have been taken, such as the following:

- The Department of Defense, through DARPA (see Chapter 7 for details), has supported research and development in a variety of military-related, high technology areas including artificial intelligence (smart land rovers, battle management systems, pilot's assistant, expert systems), integrated circuits, supercomputers, parallel processing, and neurocomputing.
- The Microelectronic & Computer Technology Corporation (MCC) was formed in 1983 by 21 electronics companies, including Motorola, Digital Equipment, General Electric, Control Data, National Semiconductor, and Sperry Univac (but not IBM), to share costs to develop the next generation of computers to exceed Japan's efforts. These companies have contributed both money and people and will share in whatever technology is developed. MCC has a rather small annual budget of $65 million and up to now has not achieved notable results probably because it has been unable to recruit leading researchers. It has current projects in the packaging of chips, office automation, neural networks and supercomputers.
- Sematech is a consortium of chip producers, founded in 1988, with 14 members in

1989, funded by its members and the Federal and Texas governments to attempt to restore the lost U.S. lead in DRAM (dynamic random access memory) chips. The board of the Semiconductor Industry Association, with 37 members, unanimously approved this effort in 1989. A major source of funding is $100 million from the Pentagon. Both IBM and AT&T donated chip technology to the fledgling consortium: IBM, the design and manufacturing specifications for its 4-megabit DRAM, and AT&T, the technology for a 1-megabit static RAM. Sematech suffered a major blow in June 1990 when its first chief executive, the legendary Robert N. Noyce died.

• Within the Department of Commerce, the Technology Administration was founded, perhaps as a civilian version of DARPA. The initial program, called the Advanced Technology Program (ATP), funded at a miniscule $10 million for 1990, has as its aim the funding of leading edge research. Its budget for 1991 was increased to $36 million and there are indications that Congress may increase it substantially in the future. The Technology Administration's director Robert M. White wants to transfer technology developed in the Federal government's laboratories to industry and also to help small manufacturers adopt new technology. The future role of this agency will be a harbinger of the administration's plans for government-industry cooperation.

All these efforts may be valuable but they represent piecemeal attempts to deal with a perceived problem, namely the gradual loss of technological domination by the United States. The debate over a national industrial policy has gone through several stages, and as the 1990s begin it has been renewed. The economist Robert Kuttner points out that in fact the United States has had an industrial policy since the end of World War II and it has been implemented by the Pentagon, which subsidizes technological development every time it buys a new weapons system, supports a research project in a national laboratory, or contracts with the private sector through projects supported by DARPA. The Pentagon can even claim considerable success in such major innovations as integrated circuits, advanced composite materials, supercomputers, optics, computerized machine tools, telecommunications, and AI.[29] Many of the Pentagon needs are also important to society in general and should properly be supported by agencies other than the Department of Defense. Among these technologies are integrated circuits, robotics, fiber optics, biotechnology, and superconductivity. Private companies are not investing enough in research in these areas to keep the United States competitive, but the White House, as of late 1990, was strongly resistant to any arguments that the government should take leadership in this area.

Surprisingly, President Bush's budget for fiscal 1992, released in February 1991, indicated support for high technology. More specifically, he asked for $683 million for high performance computing and communications, up 30%, to be divided as follows: $156.8 million for high performance computing systems, with about two-thirds to be allocated by DARPA; $265 million for advanced software technology and algorithms, with about 40% to the allocated by the National Science Foundation; $91.9 million for the National Research and Education Network, a program to develop a gigabits-per-second network; and $124.5 million for basic research and human resources. At the same time, Senator Albert Gore Jr. of Tennessee introduced a bill with similar aims, the High-Performance Computing Act of 1991.[30]

With all the discussion about revitalizing "our" (U.S.) competitiveness, the Harvard economist Robert Reich asked, "Who is us? Is it IBM, Motorola, and General Motors? Or is it Sony, Thomson, Philips, and Honda?"[31] He describes two corporations: corporation A with headquarters in New York, with top managers and directors American but with most of its employees non-American, and much of its research and most of its manufacturing plants located outside of the United States; and corporation B, which is headquartered abroad, with most of its management foreign but most of its employees American and much of its research and most of its manufacturing carried out in the United States. In improving U.S. competitiveness, which corporation is most crucial? As Reich notes, ". . . the competitiveness of American-owned corporations is no longer the same as American competitiveness. Indeed, American ownership of the corporation is profoundly less relevant to America's economic future than the skills, training, and knowledge commanded by American workers—workers who are increasingly employed within the United States by foreign-owned corporations."[32] Thus the answer to the question, "Who is us?" is the American work force, not necessarily the American corporation, and this answer of course changes the terms of reference of any discussion about what steps, if any, the government should take with respect to U.S. competitiveness. For example, by the early 1990s, Honda will be manufacturing more cars in the United States than in Japan and will even be exporting cars to Japan. In fact, 10% of the U.S. manufacturing work force is currently employed by foreign employers.

Another important move by Japan, beyond buying American companies and setting up partnerships with U.S. firms to gain access to emerging technology, and building manufacturing plants within the United States, is the opening of research laboratories to carry out basic research in the United States. The crucial aspect of this venture is that Japanese companies intend to hire top U.S. computer scientists to work in them by offering salaries considerably higher than the going rate. Academics may find these offers hard to refuse given current cutbacks in research funds and the promise of state-of-the-art equipment. Examples of such laboratories are a NEC Corp. lab in Princeton, and two new labs being considered, one in San Francisco by Matushita Electric Industrial Co. and the other in Cambridge, Massachusetts by Mitsubishi Electric Corp. Following the American model, the Japanese companies intend to establish their facilities near leading universities to attract U.S. scientists.[33] Japanese influence in the United States is already of some concern because of their supposed excessive lobbying efforts in Washington on behalf of their economic interests. A recent book[34] claims expenditures of $400 million per year are made to win support for policies favorable to Japan.

Japan will not go away; neither will Europe nor that fast rising group of Asian contenders including South Korea, Taiwan, Singapore, Hong Kong, and Malaysia. What is clear is that to a lesser or greater degree, the U.S. government will play an important role in America's economic future especially in the high technology arena, whether through the fiction of non-interference in the marketplace or overtly through direct support for emerging technologies. One final point should be noted, however, that international trade is not limited to goods. More than 20% of U.S. exports in 1988 are accounted for by services in such industries as banking, insurance, telecommunications, consultancy, and transport. In the United States nearly 70% of the gross domestic product and 75% of employment derives from the service sector.[35] Future economic strength will depend on recognizing the importance of and building up a viable and thriving service industry.

European Responses

In 1984, the European Community proposed the European Strategic Programme for Research and Development in Information Technology (ESPRIT). It has five components: microelectronics, software technology, advanced information processing, office systems, and computer integrated manufacturing. Its aims are to develop the technologies needed for the European information technology industry to be competitive in the 1990s, to promote European industrial cooperation, and to make sure that Europe has an important international role to play. About 3,000 researchers were working on more than 200 projects in 1987. In 1985, under the initiative of France to create a larger technological home market for European countries by improving cooperation, EUREKA was created, currently involving the twelve European Community countries, six other European countries, and Turkey. The Eureka program is much more applied than ESPRIT and for the most part is aimed at producing marketable products and processes. More recently, a communications-oriented project has been undertaken, called RACE (Research and Development in Advanced Communications for Europe). The goals are to introduce integrated broad-band communication in the context of the emerging ISDN (Integrated Systems Digital Network) protocols.[36]

OTHER ISSUES

Stock Market Regulation

> From the close of trading on Friday, October 16, to its lowest point on Tuesday, October 20, a period of just 10 trading hours, the S & P 500 Index fell 22%. During the same 10 hours, the S & P Futures Index fell 36%. This precipitous drop in prices on October 19 and 20, 1987, and the events that surrounded it, are now known as the Crash of 1987. The 1987 stock market plunge was the worst ever.[37]

Sometimes called Black Monday as well, this event set off a flurry of accusations and was seen as yet another crime committed by Wall Street insiders and traders against the small investor. In the wake of the crash, studies were initiated by several authorities, including the Presidential Task Force (the Brady Commission), the Commodity Futures Trading Commission (CFTC), the Securities Exchange Commission (SEC), the General Accounting Office (GAO), the New York Stock Exchange (NYSE), and the Chicago Mercantile Exchange (CME). All these reports addressed two major questions: What caused the crash? Are the financial institutions flawed? The answers are surprising, especially in the light of the instant analyses following the crash. The SEC report does not answer the "what" and indeed says that the precise combination of causes may never be known. It was, indirectly critical of computerized strategies involving the simultaneous buying and selling of stocks and stock index futures.[38] (This practice will be discussed later in this section). The Brady Commission report notes (p. x), "The precipitous market decline . . . was 'triggered' by specific events: an unexpectedly high merchandise trade deficit which pushed interest rates to new high levels, and proposed tax legislation which led to the collapse of the stocks of a number of takeover candidates."[39] Note that nothing is said about the internal workings of the stock exchanges themselves. After analyzing all of the above reports, the author of the opening quotation, Franklin Edwards of Columbia University, attempts to capture the common opinion, perhaps a generalization: ". . . a combination of speculative euphoria in world stock markets and serious underlying macroeconomic disequilibria set the stage for a crisis of confidence that inevitably would have, and finally did, precipitate a market break."[40]

In the early reactions to the crash, a likely major candidate was the computer in two respects, first as initiating and responding to trades in a manner that produced a frenzied, uncontrollable cycle of selling, and second as an inadequate record keeper and monitor of the overheated market. These charges were not supported by the subsequent studies. Nevertheless, immediately following the crash, the New York Stock Exchange suspended program trading ("Program trading exacerbated the decline"[41]), an act that falsely suggested a major contributing role for computers. Perhaps three definitions would be helpful at this point:[42]

Program Trading. Prior to the entry of computers, program trading involved the purchase or sale of a portfolio, or "basket" of stocks, as if the portfolio were a single stock. With the advent of computers, the term "computerized trading" is frequently used and the image is evoked of huge blocks of stock bought or sold with a single keystroke.

Stock-Index Arbitrage. Arbitrage is the simultaneous purchase and sale of similar securities on different markets in the hope of achieving a gain based on small differences in prices on the two markets. In the most popular form of arbitrage, called stock-index arbitrage, a portfolio of stocks is traded instead of a single stock. Traders prepare a basket of stocks that mirrors the Standard & Poor (S&P) stock index and monitor the value of that index on the Chicago Mercantile Exchange, which deals in futures, that is, in contracts to deliver a fixed quantity of stocks at a fixed price and a fixed time. Simultaneously, the value of the basket is monitored on the New York Stock Exchange, where the sum of the momentary values of each stock determines the overall value. Because of discrepancies which arise between these two markets and last only a few minutes, it is possible for a trader, by instantaneously issuing buy or sell orders, for large baskets at values, for example, between \$10 and \$100 million, to profit by moves of the two markets in opposite directions. It has been possible for vast amounts of money to be made by this process.

Portfolio Insurance. One way for an investor to hedge against losses is to program his or her own computer to monitor the instantaneous behavior of the portfolio. If it falls below a certain value, a warning can be triggered and the investor can issue a sell, with a few keystrokes, or if it rises, a buy order can be similarly issued. It is possible for the computer program to issue such orders automatically, if the conditions are well-defined. Portfolio insurance is commonly used by corporations, pension funds, endowments, and mutual funds.

Index arbitrage and portfolio insurance played some role in the crash, although they probably did not initiate it. The question for regulatory authorities, such as the internal ones run by the Exchanges, and especially SEC, the federal agency responsible for the operation of all the nation's exchanges, is to ensure that all investors, large and small, have equal opportunity. The destabilizing impact of computers, if any, must be eliminated or reduced.

Among the recommendations in the SEC study that are relevant to the use of computers are the following:[43]

- Program trading information should be publicly disseminated, and the NYSE's DOT (designated order turnaround) system should be enhanced.
- Better market-surveillance systems are needed.
- Various improvements should be made to increase the efficiency of the automated settlement systems used by clearing associations.

Several other recommendations relate to stock index futures and options, and to index frontrunning. This latter activity involves buying futures contracts on the S & P index and then attempting to influence the index by buying shares in stocks on the index. As the index rises so do futures on the index, which are then sold at a profit. The SEC banned frontrunning in July 1990.[44] The creative use of computers to manipulate stocks in ways not previously anticipated will require regulators to exercise constant vigilance. To this end, the New York Stock Exchange (NYSE), the National Association of Securities Dealers (NASD), and the American Stock Exchange (AMEX) have invested in sophisticated computer programs to identify suspicious abnormal trading. Given the enormous number of daily transactions, it requires considerable computing power to detect such suspicious activities. The NYSE has a system with more than one million records on individuals who might have access to private information and therefore could be involved in a stock purchase or leveraged buyout. It also has a system for monitoring every transaction, which is first alerted by some unusual activity, the exact nature of which is not publicly available for obvious reasons. The second level is then triggered by analysis and comparison with normal behavior. The company is alerted and newspapers are consulted to uncover any information to explain the unusual occurrence. If no satisfactory explanation is discovered, a full investigation is initiated by the NYSE's surveillance staff.[45]

Another trend, which may bypass all these security efforts and the exchanges as well, is the growing use of electronic networks to match buyers and sellers. Such "fourth market" systems as Reuters's Instinet can provide a "blackboard" for investors and buyers to post buying and selling prices. In some sense this represents a return to a precomputer period except that the walls have been removed and the players have been globally distributed. Such networks are not limited to the United States and truly global, 24 hour per day trading is now a reality. Regulation on a global scale offers interesting and difficult challenges.[46]

Transborder Data Flow (TBDF)

> Because of advances in computer communications, many experts are forecasting a global communications revolution that will see the processing of information as the principal activity of a post-industrial society.[47]

The increasing rate of growth of global communications has serious implications. The term transborder data flow (TBDF) refers to the communication by computer of information across national boundaries. Because the United States is the leading country of the world in large multinational corporations, computer production, and far-flung communications systems, much of the concern about controlling or regulating information flow seems to be directed toward the United States. There are two major issues involved: protection of the transmitted data and the economic implications of information processing control.

The term data protection is used in Europe to refer to privacy concerns. Since countries have different approaches to such concerns, there is apprehension that the transmission of information across borders could jeopardize desired security. Thus, most European countries have government agencies that must approve the setting up of a database and then monitor its performance. In the United States, the basic approach has been to pass laws that define the privacy rights of individuals, who must then seek redress from the courts. When records containing information about individuals are sent across a national border, there is concern on both sides. From the U.S. point of view, Europe's preoccupation with data protection is an attempt to reduce the U.S. role in international data processing.

Technology Transfer

> The purpose of export controls is to deny the Soviet bloc access to Western technology that contributes to the effectiveness of their defense establishment.[48]

Besides TBDF, governments are also concerned with preventing technology developed within their countries from illegally reaching their political and economic competitors. The technology includes the hardware itself (computers and peripherals), the microelectronics (microprocessors and memory chips), production processes (masks and strategies for manufacturing integrated circuits), software (operating systems and application programs), and algorithms (mathematical results in cryptography). In general, technology transfer involves much more than the computer field, for example, military electronics, specialized metallurgy, crop control, and so forth. Technology flows out of the United States by the following channels:

I. Legal transfers made possible by the open nature of Western society, e.g., transfers occurring through perusal of open scientific literature, academic exchanges, trade fairs, etc.
II. Legal transfers through purchase of technologies under general license.
III. Legal transfers through purchase of technologies under validated license.
IV. Illegal transfers through purchase, e.g., by agents, through third countries or foreign embassies, dummy corporations, etc.

V. Illegal transfers through industrial espionage or the theft of materials classified by the U.S. government.[49]

Attempts to control, or limit, technology transfer have focused on government relations with universities and academics and with business.

Technology Controls

At no previous time in history has one nation been able to prey so deeply and systematically on the fruits of its adversary's genius and labor.[50]

The two major problems of technology transfer have to do with economic competition and military or political competition. Economic competition involves the political allies of the United States, who are mounting a serious challenge to U.S. trade dominance in such high technology areas as computers and communications. Most of this competition is carried out in the open, but periodically cases of industrial espionage are revealed. One of the most famous of these cases involved the attempts by Hitachi to obtain IBM trade secrets in 1982. Such acts are appropriately dealt with by criminal law. Political espionage directed at industrial and military secrets is a more difficult problem.

The flow of technology is currently under the control of two bodies of regulations: The Export Administration Regulations (EAR) are administered by the Department of Commerce and cover products that can be used for civilian or military purposes. The countries of destination were in the communist bloc. The list of affected products appears on the Commodity Control List (CCL). International Traffic in Arms Regulations (ITAR) are administered by the State Department. They cover all military items and the export or publication of data on items on the CCL or the U.S. Munitions List. There is another list, called the Military Critical Technologies List (MCTL), which is mainly concerned with the technology of processes used to manufacture the items on the other lists. When attempting to make a ruling, the Departments of State and Commerce regularly consult with the Department of Defense. An international organization called CoCom (The Coordinating Committee on Export Controls), consisting of the North Atlantic Treaty Organization nations (plus Japan but minus Iceland) also has a prohibited list of exports. The current system in the United States has become overly cumbersome; businessmen have been subjected to long waits and conflicting rulings. The Commodity Control List has grown to over 100,000 items.

East Germany has unified with West Germany; Poland, Hungary, and Czechoslovakia all have elected pro-Western governments; the Soviet Union is in the throes of opening and liberalizing itself; the Cold War is certainly receding from world attention. As might be expected, this thaw has initiated a reevaluation of East–West trade relations, among many other major changes. At a June 1990 meeting in Paris, CoCom, comprising 17 countries, liberalized its trading rules, with the somewhat reluctant agreement of the United States. Thus, export licenses for 30 different types of equipment, such as vacuum pumps and electric furnaces, were dropped, and the Soviet Union and Eastern European countries would have been granted access to more advanced computers, telecommunications equipment, and machine tools. The U.S. computer industry had expected to expand its markets substantially as most personal computers and peripherals would now be permitted to be sold. This would have permitted the unrestricted sale of computers using Intel 80386 and Motorola 68040 chips as their microprocessors, including IBM PS/2 and all Apple Macintoshes. Approval of sales of large minicomputers and even mainframes used for scientific purposes would have been facilitated. Some remnants of Cold War attitudes remained as Eastern European countries would have been required to safeguard their equipment from uncontrolled access by the Soviet Union.[51] Although Congress subsequently passed a bill to ease the restrictions as discussed above, it was vetoed by President Bush because "provisions mandating sanctions against countries using chemical and biological weapons would 'severely constrain presidential authority in carrying out foreign policy.'" The President did order federal agencies to facilitate regulations with respect to the export of high technology equipment to U.S. allies.

SUMMARY

Relations between government and business in the United States have been involved, torturous, occasionally acrimonious, sometimes beneficial, usually controversial, and always unpredictable. In this chapter, we have focussed on certain industries—computers and communications—and certain problem areas—transborder data flows and technology transfer. The development and significance of electronic banking has been discussed, with special emphasis on the dimensions of EFTS and the potential problem areas. In somewhat more detail, the following points have been covered:

Although committed to the free enterprise system, the U.S. government has at times found it necessary to challenge the activities of certain large companies. On January 8, 1982, the Justice Department dropped a 13-year antitrust suit against IBM. On the same day it also dropped an antitrust suit against AT&T, after AT&T agreed to divest itself of the local telephone companies.

IBM, freed of the antitrust suit, launched an aggressive challenge on all fronts to extend its domination of computer-related business. For example, within three years after the personal computer, the PC, was introduced in 1981 it held the lead in sales. AT&T's first steps after divestiture were somewhat more tentative. It was challenged in the profitable long-distance market by a number of companies and has yet to make its presence felt in the computer market.

In a major change fostered by technological innovation, the banking system is being transformed by the introduction of electronic funds transfer systems. Examples of this process are the appearance of automatic teller machines, point-of-sales terminals, and electronic banking via home computers. Concerns about EFTS include security of financial records, potential increased frequency of electronic crime, impact on competition, and impact on consumers.

Governments are extremely concerned about the competitiveness of their industries and prepared to provide support in a variety of ways. With the rise of Japan and Western Europe as the major economic competitors of the United States, many have called for the government to design a national policy to deal with the technological challenge. Some small steps have been taken but there is no support in the White House for a government led approach.

Other areas in which the government must play a role with respect to business activities are the regulation of stock exchanges, especially problems arising from the use of computers, transborder dataflow, and technology transfer.

NOTES

1. Charles E. Wilson, former president of General Motors, in testimony before the Senate Armed Forces Committee, 1952.
2. John Opel, president of IBM, as quoted in Bro Uttal, "Life After Litigation at IBM and AT&T," *Fortune,* February 8, 1982, p. 59.
3. As quoted in Robert Pear, "Antitrust Policies Affect Not Just Corporate Futures," *The New York Times,* January 10, 1982, p. E 2.
4. Alexander Graham Bell, first complete sentence transmitted by telephone, March 10, 1876.
5. Charles L. Brown, chairman of AT&T, as quoted in a full-page advertisement in *The New York Times,* January 10, 1982, p. 9.
6. Jeremy Main, "Waking up AT&T: There's Life after Culture Shock," *Fortune,* December 24, 1984, pp. 66–68, 70, 72, 74.
7. Frederic G. Withington, "Sizing Each Other Up," *Datamation* (Cahners Publishing Co.), July 20, 1982, p. 8.
8. "A Survey of Telecommunications: Netting the Future," Special Section, *The Economist,* March 10, 1990, p. 14.
9. Robert W. Crandall and Kenneth Flamm, "Overview," in Robert W. Crandall and Kenneth Flamm (eds.), *Changing the Rules: Technological Change, International Competition, and Regulation in Communications* (Washington, D.C.: The Brookings Institution, 1989), pp. 3–4.
10. This material is taken from four sources: Joel Dreyfuss, "Reinventing IBM," *Fortune,* August 14, 1989, p. 38; Joe Queenan, "Big Blue is Back," *Barron's,* May 28, 1990, p. 26; Jeff Moad and Susan Kerr, "How Allies Fit With the New IBM," *Datamation,* January 1, 1990, pp. 34–35; and John Markoff, "Executives of Apple and IBM Discuss Aims of New Tie," *The New York Times,* September 24, 1991, p. C2.
11. "IBM Chairman Reads Riot Act," *The Globe and Mail* (Toronto, Canada), May 30, 1991, p. B 1. (Taken from reports in the *Wall Street Journal* and *The New York Times.*)
12. Trudy E. Bell, "Bell Breakup Plus Five: Mixed Reviews," *IEEE Spectrum,* December 1988, p. 27.
13. *Ibid.,* p. 28.
14. Andrew Pollock, "Big Deal That Poses Little Threat," *The New York Times,* May 7, 1991, p. C 5.
15. August Bequai, *The Cashless Society: EFTS at the Crossroads* (New York: Wiley, 1981), p. 27. Copyright © 1981 by August Bequai. Reprinted by permission of John Wiley & Sons, Inc.
16. Stephen T. McLin, strategic planning chief, Bank of America, as quoted in Orin Kramer, "Winning Strategies for Interstate Banking," *Fortune,* September 19, 1983, p. 118. Copyright © 1983 Time Inc. All rights reserved.
17. Thomas D. Steiner and Diogo B. Teixeira. *Technology in Banking: Creating Value and Destroying Profits* (Homewood, Illinois: Dow Jones-Irwin, 1990), p. 10.
18. "A Survey of International Banking: A Question of Definition," Special Section, *The Economist,* April 7, 1990, p. 16.
19. Steiner and Teixeira, *Technology in Banking,* p. 92.
20. Jane Bryant Quinn, "The Era of Debit Cards," *Newsweek,* January 2, 1989, p. 51.

21. Thomas D. Steiner and Diogo B. Teixeira, *Technology of Banking: Creating Value and Destroying Profits,* Business One Irwin, Homewood, Illinois, © 1990, pp. 141–142.
22. *Ibid.,* p. 108.
23. Geoff Lewis, Neil Gross, Jonathan Levine, John W. Verity, Lois Therrien, and Patrick E. Cole, "Computers: Japan Comes on Strong," *Business Week,* October 23, 1989, pp. 104–105.
24. "Can Japan Make Einsteins Too?" *The Economist,* August 11, 1990, p. 83.
25. William J. Broad, "In the Realm of Technology, Japan Looms Ever Larger," *The New York Times,* May 28, 1991, pp. B 5, B 8.
26. "A Survey of Japanese Technology: Thinking Ahead," Special Section, *The Economist,* December 2, 1989, p. 4.
27. Edward A. Feigenbaum and Pamela McCorduck, *The Fifth Generation* (Reading, Massachusetts: Addison-Wesley, 1983), p. 3.
28. Karen W. Arenson, "Debate Grows Over Adoption of National Industrial Policy," *The New York Times,* June 19, 1983, p. 1. Copyright © 1983 by The New York Times Company. Reprinted by permission.
29. Robert Kuttner, "Industry Needs a Better Incubator Than the Pentagon," *Business Week,* April 30, 1990, p. 16.
30. Gary Anthes, "U.S. Budget Shines on High-Tech," *Computerworld,* February 11, 1991, p. 90. "President Proposes $638 Million for HPCC," *Computing Research News,* March 1991, pp. 1, 4.
31. Robert B. Reich, "Who Is Us?" *Harvard Business Review,* **68**(1), January–February 1990, p. 53.
32. *Ibid.,* p. 54.
33. Gina Kolata, "Japanese Woo High-Tech Wizards," *The Globe and Mail* (Toronto, Canada), November 12, 1990, p. B 5. (Taken from *The New York Times* wire service.)
34. Pat Choate, *Agents of Influence: How Japan's Lobbyists in the United States Manipulate America's Political and Economic System* (New York: Albert A. Knopf, 1990).
35. "A Survey of World Trade: Nothing to Lose But its Chains," Special Report, *The Economist,* September 22, 1990, pp. 36–37.
36. International Organizations Services, J. C. Bus, Wedgewood & Co. in collaboration with The Commission of the European Communities (eds.), *Information Technology Atlas—Europe* (New York: Elsevier Science Publishing, 1987).
37. Franklin R. Edwards, "The Crash: A Report on the Reports," from Henry C. Lucas, Jr. and Robert A. Schwartz (eds.), *The Challenge of Information Technology for the Securities Markets: Liquidity, Volatility, and Global Trading* (Homewood, Il: Business One Irwin, © 1989), p. 86.
38. *Ibid.,* p. 87.
39. As quoted in *ibid.,* pp. 87–88.
40. *Ibid.,* p. 88.
41. New York Stock Exchange Chairman John J. Phelan as quoted in Gary Weiss, "Two Key Questions: Was Program Trading to Blame . . ." *Business Week,* November 2, 1987, p. 51.
42. M. Mitchell Waldorp, "Computers Amplify Black Monday," *Science,* October 30, 1987, pp. 602–604.
43. Edwards, "The Crash," pp. 98–99.
44. Gary Weiss and David Greising, "Program Trading's Ugliest Wrinkle," *Business Week,* August 1989, pp. 72–73.
45. David Stamps, "The IS Eye on Insider Trading," *Datamation,* April 15, 1990, pp. 35–36, 38, 43.
46. David Zigas, Gary Weiss, Ted Holden, and Richard A. Melcher, "A Trading Floor on Every Screen," *Business Week,* November 5, 1990, pp. 128–30.
47. Michael J. Kirby, president, Institute for Research on Public Policy, in preface to W. E. Cundiff and Mado Reid (eds.), *Issues in Canadian/U.S. Transborder Computer Data Flows* (Montreal, Canada: Institute for Research on Public Policy, 1979), p. iii.
48. William Schneider, Jr., Undersecretary of State for Security Assistance, Science and Technology, as quoted in Walter Guzzardi, Jr., "Cutting Russia's Harvest of U.S. Technology," *Fortune,* May 30, 1983, p. 108.
49. *Technology and East-West Trade: An Update* (Washington, D.C.: U.S. Congress, Office of Technology Assessment, OTA-ISC-209, May 1983), p. 10.

50. Richard N. Perle, Assistant Secretary of Defense for International Security Policy, as quoted in Guzzardi, Jr., "Cutting Russia's Harvest of U.S. Technology," p. 112.
51. Paul Magnusson, Igor Reichlin, and Gary McWilliams, "The Dismantling of a Cold-War Icon," *Business Week,* June 25, 1990, pp. 41–42.
52. Gary H. Anthes, "Bush Vetoes Export Bill But Seeks Loosened Restrictions," *Computerworld,* November 26, 1990, p. 8.

ADDITIONAL READINGS

Industry Regulation

"Breaking up the Phone Company." Special Report, *Fortune,* June 27, 1983, pp. 60–97.
Brock, Gerald W. *The Telecommunications Industry.* Cambridge, Massachusetts: Harvard University Press, 1981.
Carlyle, Ralph Emmett and Moad, Jeff. "The Rise of an Information Utility." *Datamation,* January 1, 1989, pp. 26–31, 34.
Coll, Steve. *The Deal of the Century: The Breakup of AT&T.* New York: Simon and Schuster (Touchstone), 1986.
Coy, Peter and Lewis, Geoff. "How AT&T Learned to Act Like a Computer Company." *Business Week,* January 22, 1990, pp. 68–69.
Critical Connections: Communications for the Future. Washington, D.C.: U.S. Congress, Office of Technology Assessment, OTA-CIT-407, 1990.
DeLamarter, Richard Thomas. *Big Blue: IBM's Use and Abuse of Power.* New York: Dodd, Mead & Company, 1986.
"Did it Make Sense to Break up AT&T?" Special Report, *Business Week,* December 3, 1984, pp. 86 ff.
Irwin, Manley R. "The Telecommunications Industry." In Adams, Walter (ed.). *The Structure of American Industry.* New York: Macmillan, 1986, pp. 261–289.
Keller, John J., Lewis, Geoff, Mason, Tod, Mitchell, Russell, and Peterson, Thane. "AT&T: The Making of a Comeback." *Business Week,* January 18, 1988, pp. 56–62.
Lewis, Geoff, Field, Anne R., Keller, John J., and Verity, John W. "Big Changes at Big Blue," *Business Week,* February 15, 1988, pp. 92–98.
"Refashioning IBM," *The Economist,* November 17, 1990, pp. 21–22, 24.

EFTS: Electronic Funds Transfer Systems

Andrews, Edmund L. "The Internationalization of the Cash Machine." *The New York Times,* September 9, 1990, p. F 9.
Bartel, Henry and Arbuckle, Gavin. *Electronic Banking in Canada and the United States.* Montreal, Canada: Gamma Institute, 1987.
Business International and Financial Executives Research Foundation. *Automatic Global Financial Management.* New York: John Wiley, 1988.
Mitchell, Jeremy. *Electronic Banking and the Consumer.* London: Policy Studies Institute, 1988.
Perry, Tekla. "Electronic Banking Goes to Market." *IEEE Spectrum,* February 1988, pp. 46–49.
Selected Electronic Funds Transfer Issues. Washington, D.C.: U.S. Congress, Office of Technology Assessment Background Paper, OTA-BP-CIT-12, 1982.
Shogase, Hiro. "The Very Smart Card: A Plastic Pocket Bank." *IEEE Spectrum,* October 1988, pp. 35–39.

Competitiveness

Boyer, Edward. "Japan is No Threat to U.S. Freedom." *Fortune,* November 5, 1990, pp. 167–68.
Chen, Katherine T. "Contrasting Strategies Are Pursued by Big Three Economic Powerhouses." *IEEE Spectrum,* October 1990, pp. 76–78.
De Bony, Elizabeth. "Japan May Find Closed Doors in Europe." *Computerworld,* March 4, 1991, p. 66.
Dickson, David. "Eureka!" *Technology Review,* August–September 1988, pp. 26–33.
Fallows, James. *More Like Us: Making America Great Again.* Boston: Houghton Mifflin, 1989.
"The Global Economy: Can You Compete?" Special Report, *Business Week,* December 17, 1990, pp. 60 ff.
Guile, Bruce R. and Brooks, Harvey (eds.). *Technology and Global Industry: Companies and Nations in the World Economy.* Washington, D.C.: National Academy Press, 1987.
"Japan/United States, The Challenge of the 90s: Achieving the Trade Balance." Special Advertising Section, *Business Week,* July 16, 1990. Note that the dollar amounts in the graphs on pp. 77 and 78 should be billions of dollars, not millions of dollars.
Matley, Ben. "National Computer Policies in High-Tech Times." *Abacus,* Summer 1988, pp. 44–49.
Porter, Michael. *The Competitive Advantage of Nations.* New York: MacMillan, The Free Press, 1990.
Reich, Robert. *The Next American Frontier.* New York: Times Books, 1983.
Rifkin, Glenn. "R & D Group Finds Shoes It Can Fill." *Computerworld,* September 24, 1990, pp. 1, 87–88, 90–91.
Prestowitz, Clyde. *Trading Places: How We Allowed Japan to Take the Lead.* New York: Basic Books, 1988.
Rosenblatt, Alfred. "Who Leads? A Poll's Surprising Answers." *IEEE Spectrum,* April 1991, pp. 22–27.
Rosenblatt, Alfred and Perry, Tekla. "Formula for Competitiveness." *IEEE Spectrum,* June 1991, pp. 49–62.
Sanger, David. "Mighty MITI Loses Its Grip." *The New York Times,* July 9, 1989, pp. F 1–F 9.
Tatsuno, Sheridan. *The Technopolis Strategy: Japan, High Technology, and the Control of the 21st Century.* New York: Prentice Hall, A Brady book, 1986.
Warshofsky, Fred. *The Chip Wars: The Battle for the World of Tomorrow.* New York: Charles Scribner's Sons, 1989.
Wood, Robert Chapman. "The Real Challenge of Japan's Fifth Generation Project." *Technology Review,* January 1988, pp. 66–73.

Other Issues

"Automating Financial Markets: The Human Cost." *The Economist,* March 10, 1990, pp. 19–20, 24.
Lucas, Jr., Henry C. and Schwartz, Robert A. (eds.). *The Challenge of Information Technology for the Securities Markets: Liquidity, Volatility, and Global Trading.* Homewood, Illinois: Dow Jones-Irwin, 1988.
Magnusson, Paul, Coy, Peter, Boyle, Rosemarie, and Schiller, Zachary. "High-Tech Exports: Is the Dam Breaking?" *Business Week,* June 4, 1990, pp. 128, 130.
Markoff, John. "Export Restrictions Fail to Halt Spread of Supercomputers." *The New York Times,* August 21, 1990, p. A 1, C 9.
"The Future of Wall Street." Special Report, *Business Week,* November 5, 1990, pp. 118–122, 124–126, 128–130, 132.

12

ROBOTICS AND INDUSTRIAL AUTOMATION

To labor unions, robots presented the specter of automation in the extreme — motorized androids that would drive real people out of their jobs. To industry, they were expected to be an uncomplaining solution to round-the-clock production.

It turns out that people still work better than robots in many jobs, and where they do not, more mundane forms of automation work better.

Robots have found a place in industry, but mostly in arduous, dangerous or monotonous jobs that workers shun anyway, like wielding a 200-pound welder on an automobile assembly line or handling radioactive materials in nuclear reactors.

Peter T. Kilburn, *The New York Times,* July 1, 1990, p. 14.

INTRODUCTION

Hardly a day goes by without the media reporting that robots are coming—to the factory, office, mines, oceans, and even farms. Joseph Engelberger, a robotics pioneer, has told of being approached by an Australian sheep rancher who wanted to develop a robot for shearing. The expectations are high that robots will increase productivity, do the dirty and dangerous jobs for which humans are ill-equipped, be cheaper and more efficient than human labor, and make no demands on their employers for health plans, time off, or better working conditions.

Although the first robot patents were issued in the United States, Japan has become the leading manufacturer and exporter of robots in the world. The Japanese have made an early and serious commitment to robotics as a way of reducing the costs of the labor component of production. The average age of their work force has been increasing, and robots are seen as a necessary substitute for human workers. Somewhat slow to respond, the United States has recognized that in order to compete worldwide its industrial plant must be modernized and made more efficient, and the United States has begun to make a concerted effort in industrial robotics.

A variety of acronyms have been used to describe the various aspects of the merger between the computer and factory automation. Computer-aided design and computer-aided manufacturing (CAD/CAM) were probably the first terms to enter common usage with respect to computers in the plant. Subsequently, they were followed by computer integrated manufacturing (CIM) and flexible manufacturing systems (FMS), among others. The use of computers in every stage of the design and production process is accelerating. Companies of the future may be able to integrate planning, design, sales, marketing, and inventory control functions with automated manufacturing systems.

What are the actual details of factory automation? What are the structures and functions of contemporary robots? Industrial robots, with several current applications, are now distributed worldwide. This chapter considers the various factors associated with their use, aside from the major goal of improved efficiency, as well as a number of social issues that arise from the increased use of industrial robotics.

INDUSTRIAL ROBOTICS

What Is a Robot?

The major application of robots in the foreseeable future will be in the industrial environment. Automobile manufacturers are taking the lead in integrating robots into the assembly line. Automation is not a new feature on the assembly line, and it is sometimes difficult to determine what distinguishes a robot from a more traditional piece of machinery. As robots have made their appearance several definitions have been proposed. The following "semi-official" definition was adopted by the Robot Institute of America in 1979 and the International Society for Robots in 1981.

> A Robot is a reprogrammable multi-functional manipulator designed to move materials, parts, tools, or other specialized devices, through variable programmed motions for the performance of a variety of tasks.[1]

This doesn't sound very much like C3PO or R2D2, but it should be remembered that industrial robots are designed for specific tasks in the factory. Before science fact meets science fiction, considerable research and development will be required.

Brief History

It is generally agreed that George Devol is the father of the industrial robot. He has 30 patents for it, beginning with one in 1946 for a magnetic recording system that stores spatial positions for manipulators such as gripping devices. In 1954 he applied for a patent for "Universal automation," or "Unimation," which was granted in 1961. Eventually, Devol—together with Joseph Engelberger, a young engineer—formed a company called Unimation. It was financed by and became a division of Consolidated Diesel Electric (Condec). It manufactured its first robot in 1961, but did not turn a profit until 1975. In late 1982, Unimation was sold to Westinghouse as part of its major commitment to robotics.

Although developed in the United States, the robot has achieved widespread use in Japan. The Japanese have become the world leaders in the application and installation of robots. Japan entered the robot race in 1967, when Tokyo Machinery Trading Company began to import and market the Versatran robot made by AMF in the United States. In 1969, Kawasaki Heavy Industries began to manufacture robots under a licensing agreement with Unimation.

One view of the evolution of the robot industry in the United States up to about 1987 divides the period from 1961 into four stages as follows:[2]

Stage 1 (1961–mid-1970s). This is the very slow growth period as robots made their first appearance. The entire market was barely $15 million by the mid-1970s with Unimation the leader and Versatron its main competitor. Subsequently both Unimation and Versatron were sold.

Stage 2 (mid-1970s–1979). Sales rose to $45 million, with automobile companies the major buyers. The industry was now dominated by Unimation and Versatron plus four other companies: Cincinnati-Milicron (CM), ASEA, DeVilbiss, and Autoplace. CM capitalized on its expertise in numerical control equipment. In 1987, it ranked second among U.S. robot producers, having surpassed Unimation in 1984; CM even sells robots in Japan, one of the few U.S. manufacturers in the Japanese market. ASEA, a Swedish-based company, sells and services robots worldwide. DeVilbiss has a major presence in spray painting robots, and Autoplace, a major producer of small robots and an early developer of vision systems, acquired by Copperweld in 1979, went out of business in 1984.

Stage 3 (1979–1983). Many new firms entered the market, vision systems appeared, and special-purpose software for controlling and integrating robots into the entire production system was developed. Despite the recession of the early 1980s that certainly reduced robot growth, sales increased to $240 million in 1983. There was considerable diversification in the market as some companies specialized in controls, software, and vision, others in specific applications such as arc welding, and still others in flexible automation. Collaborations with foreign firms increased substantially in both robot parts, such as arms, and in entire robots. Some of the new entries to the U.S. market included Adept, Automatix, and American Cimflex in small parts handling and assembly, and GMF, Kuka, Graco Robotics, IBM, and Cybotech in applications. GMF, a joint venture of General Motors and Fanuc, of Japan, is by far the largest robotics company in the United States. Most of its sales are to General Motors, with such applications as painting, finishing, coating, and assembly. IBM uses its own robots almost exclusively in the assembly of small parts in its computer factories. A group of companies, including General Electric, Westinghouse, and

Bendix see robots as part of the factory of the future and have acquired robots through arrangements with established robot companies.

Stage 4 (1983–1987).[3] This was a period of consolidation and several more companies, including Copperweld and Bendix left the robot business. Further diversification has taken place into such areas as end effectors, stand-alone vision systems, vision guidance systems, programmable controllers, and computer-aided engineering (CAE) hardware and software. Most American robot companies have imported robots from Japan and Europe and a small number sell them abroad as well. Profits have been scarce for many companies.

Sales rose substantially in 1984 and 1985 to about $500 million, and predictions that $2 billion would be reached by the end of the decade were frequently heard. The next three years sales fell below $400 million, however, and in 1988, the American companies sold less than $300 million, with about $60 to $80 million in sales from Japan. Predictions now talk about no real growth through 1992.[4] One interesting historical note is that in 1988, Westinghouse sold its automation business to the Swiss company, Staubli International, thus ending U.S. ownership of the first robot company, Unimation. The bloom is clearly off the U.S. robot industry and possible reasons will be presented later in this chapter.

CURRENT USE AND DEVELOPMENT

Worldwide Distribution

To determine the number of robots at work in different countries is not an easy task. There is a problem of definition and of counting. The definitions given earlier stress the notion of programmability, and this is the crucial distinction between robots and other types of machinery associated with automation. Japan holds a substantial lead over the rest of the world in the manufacture and installation of robots, but the size of this lead depends on what is counted as a robot. Even if a uniform and consistent definition is accepted, the count varies, and it is difficult to determine reasons for the discrepancies. The highly competitive nature of the industry means that only estimates, not accurate counts, are generally available. The results presented here, in Table 12-1, are derived from statistics gathered and compiled by the International Federation of Robotics (IFR), in cooperation with the Working Party on Engineering Industries and Automation of the United Nations Economic Commission for Europe (ECE), based in Geneva.

Japan was clearly the world leader in installed robot base with 219,700, an increase of 25% over 1988, and will remain so into the foreseeable future. A comparable increase for Western Europe was about 20%, but the United States only increased by 13.5%. In 1986, worldwide sales totalled $1.7 billion but decreased to $1.4 billion in 1987. Another indication of the state of world markets is that the number of true producers, that is, those that manufacture robots for external sales, decreased from about 300 in 1985 to fewer than 100 in 1988.

TABLE 12-1

INSTALLED INDUSTRIAL ROBOTS IN SELECTED COUNTRIES.*

Country	1982	1983	1984	1985	1986	1987	1988	1989
Australia	—	—	528	—	800	925	1,200	1,350
Belgium	361	514	775	975	1,035	1,117	1,231	1,403
France	—	—	—	—	—	4,376	5,658	7,063
Italy	1,000	1,510	2,600	4,000	5,000	6,600	8,300	10,000
West Germany	3,500	4,800	6,600	8,800	12,400	14,900	17,700	22,395
Japan	32,000	47,000	67,000	93,000	116,000	141,000	176,000	219,700
Spain	—	433	525	688	859	1,149	1,420	1,751
Sweden	1,273	1,452	1,745	2,046	2,383	2,750	3,042	3,463
United Kingdom	1,152	1,753	2,623	3,208	3,683	4,303	5,034	5,908
United States	7,000	8,000	13,000	20,000	25,000	29,000	32,600	37,000

Source: International Federation of Robotics and National Robot Societies, "Industrial Robot Statistics," an extract from *Annual Review of Engineering Industries and Automation* (Geneva: United Nations Economic Commission for Europe, 1990) and *IFR Newsletter,* November 1990.

* *Note:* It is clear that the figures for Italy, West Germany, Japan, and United States are rounded but the exact amount is not known. Some examples of discrepancies can be seen by comparing the 1982 figures in this table with similar figures for 1982 reported in a survey, published in 1983: West Germany, 4300; Italy, 1,100; Japan, 31,900; Sweden, 1450; United Kindgom, 977; United States, 6301.

TABLE 12-2

Comparison of Applications of the 1988 Supply of Industrial Robots in Japan and in the United States.

	Japan		United States	
Applications	Units	Percent	Units	Percent
Material handling, loading and unloading	3,381	9.7	865	24.3
Spot welding	3,094	8.6	719	20.2
Arc welding	5,144	14.4	556	15.6
Assembly	16,025	44.7	702	19.7
Painting	603	1.7	424	11.9
Casting	1,020	2.8	—	—
Plastic moulding	3,129	8.7	—	—
Unspecified and other	3,433	9.6	264	7.4
Total	35,829	100	3,561	100

Source: International Federation of Robotics, *IFR Newsletter,* November 1990, pp. 17, 29.

Applications

Industrial robots are used in a wide variety of applications, as shown in Table 12-2. Welding is a major application of robots in the automobile industry, especially in the United States, in terms of the proportion of robots targeted for this task, namely 35.8%. The surprising and significant percentages in Table 12-2 are those concerned with assembly. The ability of robots to assemble parts, by insertion, mounting, screwing, bonding, sealing, gluing, soldering, and other means, has serious implications for long-term, blue-collar employment. Note that of the 35,829 robots purchased in Japan in 1988, 16,025 were used in a variety of assembly operations. Of these, 10,000 were computer numerical control robots and 2,291 were classified as intelligent. In this context, the designation intelligent is not well-defined, but usually means that they employ special sensors for vision and tactility and also sophisticated programming for responding to the information associated with these sensors.

In 1972, Ford used Unimation robots to weld Maverick car bodies—the first major use of robots in the automobile industry. The company had 300 to 400 robots in 1981 and planned to have 4000 worldwide by 1990. General Motors announced its intentions to install 14,000 robots by 1990. To this end it formed a joint venture with Fanuc Ltd. of Japan, GMF Robotics Corp., as mentioned earlier, to manufacture robots for a variety of applications.

The range of robot industrial applications is continually growing and diversifying. While most robots have been used in dirty and noisy factory situations—indeed, this use is put forth as one of the reasons that they should be welcomed by factory workers—opportunities have also emerged in the ultra-clean environments of semiconductor production. GMF Robotics and IBM, not surprisingly, have been producing special versions of their robots to operate in this setting. Also available are smart carts that can carry parts and finished products and can navigate around the factory floor by following reflective tapes. By equipping robots with television cameras and their controlling computers with complex image processing programs, robot manufacturers have begun to develop systems to detect defects in both components and finished products. Although the first attempts to market "personal" robots were notoriously unsuccessful, the next generation of home robots may find a more hospitable reception, especially if they serve genuine needs, such as security, vacuuming, and maintenance. Obviously safety is of prime concern.

The Impact of Artificial Intelligence

Beginning in the mid-1960s and continuing through the early 1970s there was a major concern within the AI community with robotics, or what was then termed integrated AI (see Chapter 2). It was felt that many aspects of intelligent behavior such as vision, natural language, and problem solving should be treated simultaneously in a uniform manner.

One of the most important "microworlds" for research was the hand-eye system. It consisted of a mechanical arm that was able to manipulate simple objects such as children's blocks and work in concert with a television camera, which was also under computer control. Such systems were in use in the 1970s at MIT, Stanford, and the University of Edinburgh in Scotland. It is possible to interact with such a system by typing in commands on a terminal in something close to English. In the early systems the experimenter might enter "Put the red block on top of the yellow block." A natural language program translated this request into an internal form, which provided the appropriate information for the vision and planning programs. The camera looking down at this scene provided input to the image analysis program, which identified the position of the two blocks. Finally a planning program, using this information, constructed a plan—a sequence of movements, grasps, and ungrasps. After some delay, the arm would begin moving to carry out the command. In terms of elapsed time, the image processing and plan construction took much longer than the actual movements.

It was soon realized that each of the component systems represented a major research area best pursued independently. Image processing did benefit significantly from its development in the hand-eye context. Researchers started with systems that could manage simple, brightly colored blocks sitting on black velvet in a shadowless environment. Construction has now begun on systems to enable industrial robots to deal with considerably less predictable environments.

One research project stands apart from the others—a mobile robot called "Shakey" by its designers at SRI International (formerly the Stanford Research Institute). Shakey was the first mobile intelligent robot. At some places such as shopping centers, movie theaters, and fairs, robots roll around and greet people with a "Hi, how are you doing?" or "Glad to see you here." These are all packaged devices, something like a tape recorder put inside a mannequin—a little more sophisticated, but not much more. Off to the side there is a person using a remote control device to determine the movements of the robot. In considerable contrast to this particular kind of robot, Shakey exhibited a degree of autonomous behavior. It moved about on wheels that were driven by a stepping motor under battery power. It had a television camera with a range-finder, and was connected to its computer, first by a cable and later by a radio receiver/transmitter. In operation it was similar to the hand-eye systems already discussed, except for a few important differences.

A task was given to Shakey in a simple command language from a terminal. At the same time, Shakey's television camera takes a picture of the world, a very simple room with the baseboard clearly distinguishing the walls from the floor. Scattered about were a large cube, block, and pyramid. The lighting was quite diffuse in order to avoid shadows. A task might be to push the block and the cube into a specified corner. On the basis of its initial "view" of the world, Shakey formulated a plan and began to execute it. It might roll over to the block first and push it into the corner, then move to the cube and push it into the corner as well. If by some chance an unexpected obstacle were in its path (perhaps placed there by a mischievous experimenter), a collision might take place. Shakey had a wire sensor (like a cat's whisker) that stopped its motor instantly if it brushed against an object that it was not expecting to push. If this happened, a new picture of the room was taken and analysed, and a revised plan was formulated. Such image processing is very time-consuming, but it is probably the most important legacy of robotics research in AI, besides the development of mechanical arms.

The key issues in research on robotics from an AI point of view are the following:[5]

Mechanisms. New flexible, light, fast, and compliant mechanisms open up possibilities for innovative robot applications. Distributed applications such as "snake" robots for nuclear power stations are under development. Micromanipulators, increased dexterity of hands and wrists, and legged robots are also being studied.

Sensing and Control. Sensors such as force, touch, sonar, infrared, vision, range, and various combinations are being explored. Appropriate control architectures are under investigation. These include hierarchical and distributed architectures.

Reasoning. Real intelligence will involve the ability to reason under conditions of uncertainty. Such issues as collision detection and avoidance, planning, and recovery from error are important.

Computing Systems. The underlying computer systems to support robots in work environments must be real-time. In addition, other architectures, such as distributed and parallel, with graceful degradation and reliability built-in are necessary.

Service Applications

Up to now and into the foreseeable future, the major applications area for robotics will be industrial, but as the advanced economies continue to reduce manufacturing's role in labor requirements and contribution to gross domestic product, the service sector will increasingly become a market for robots. In certain service areas such as hospitals, fast food, and commercial cleaning, the work is characterized as labor-intensive, repetitive, and

TABLE 12-3

SERVICE SECTOR APPLICATIONS AS ENVISIONED BY JOSEPH ENGELBERGER.

Chapter	Title	Description
7	Parasurgeon	The robot assists the neurosurgeon by precisely drilling a hole in the human skull for exploratory purposes.
8	Paranurse	To perform lower-level tasks such as delivering and picking-up trays.
9	Parapharmacist	Selecting from bulk containers to fill prescriptions.
10	Commercial Cleaning	Mopping, vacuuming, sweeping, dusting, and cleaning washrooms.
11.	Fast Food Service	"Constructing" hamburgers, pizzas, and tacos.
12.	Farming	Fruit picking, grain harvesting, sheep shearing.
13.	Gasoline Station Attendant	Pumping gasoline.
16.	Aiding the Handicapped and the Elderly	"Seeing-eye" robot, aid to paraplegics, aid to walking.

Source: Joseph F. Engelberger, *Robots in Service* (London: Originally published by Kogan Page, now © Chapman & Hall, 1989).

heavy, so these areas seem to be good candidates for robots to assist humans. Mobility seems to be an important requirement for many applications in the service sector. Joseph Engelberger, sometimes referred to as the Father of the Robot, has recently written a book, almost a book-length commercial in fact, arguing that robots in the service sector will be the largest class of robots. The chapter titles of Engleberger's book are indicative of his vision, and a selection with descriptions appears in Table 12-3.[6] Most of these examples are still in the imagination stage, but preliminary versions of a few with restricted abilities are being field tested or are in early production. For example, HelpMate, developed by Transitions Research Corporation, is being tested at a Danbury hospital as a courier. A robot is being developed at Carnegie-Mellon University to assist in pizza making. A robot french fry maker is in operation at a Macdonald's restaurant in Colorado. Security robots are in operation and one called Sentry, manufactured by Denning Mobile Robots, sells for $55,000.[7] The Veterans Administration Medical Center in Palo Alto has been working on a robot system to respond to voice commands from a paralyzed patient, to perform such functions as feeding, providing a drink, brushing teeth, and shaving.[8]

WHY USE ROBOTS? WORK AND PRODUCTIVITY

> Without robots, and the savings they bring, American manufacturers will continue to lose ground internationally.[9]

The Case for Robots

Robots have not been introduced into the workplace as rapidly as proponents had hoped or expected. Factors were reliability deficiencies in the current technology, high costs, and high interest rates. In reaction to the massive onslaught of "Japan Inc.," however, North

America and Europe have come to view the robot as the key to restoring their lost economic superiority, at least with respect to manufacturing. Especially in the industry that has suffered the most—the U.S. automobile industry—hopes for increased productivity have focussed more and more on a large investment in improved industrial automation, including robots.

Robots can effect the industrial process in the following ways:

Improvement of Productivity. Increased plant operating time because of fewer shutdowns, ease of retooling, automation of small batch production.

Stability and Improvement in Product Quality. Reduced quality variation, 24-hour working days with elimination of changeover problems.

Improvement in Production Management. Reduction of manpower allocation problems, benefits of durability and accuracy of robots, overcoming of skilled manpower shortages.

Humanization of Working Life. Release of humans from dangerous, unhealthy, and monotonous work.

Resource Conservation. Saving of materials by efficient robots, saving of energy by robots working in environments with reduced lighting, air conditioning, and so forth.

Will robots be used to humanize the workplace? To convince management to use robots for this purpose, it will be necessary to demonstrate that they will reduce the costs of illness and injury resulting from a dangerous environment. It is claimed that the savings to employers in terms of reduced incidence of occupational diseases (for example, exposure to noxious chemicals) and work-related injuries can be the crucial factor in the decision to install robots.

Productivity

The very large, sustained budget deficits and trade imbalances in the United States, and the low rates of increases in productivity over the past 20 years have given rise to a serious concern about America's future, especially in manufacturing. Many studies and books have appeared debating the weaknesses and strengths of the U.S. economy, challenging the very idea of a post-industrial society, and arguing that manufacturing is fundamental to threatened U.S. leadership. The argument frequently turns on the issue of productivity, that it must be increased, and how that goal is to be achieved. For many industries, a major infusion of capital investment is required, and robots, computers, and factory automation have become the symbols of the new manufacturing. Not unexpectedly, considerable debate exists with respect to the definition of productivity itself, especially in the service sector (and therefore not considered here) and also about what it will take to improve it.

Two kinds of productivity are usually considered: labor productivity and multifactor productivity. Labor productivity is expressed in terms of dollars of output (necessarily adjusted for inflation) per hours worked. Thus, one can compare productivity within different industries in one country, or the same industry across different countries, or one can even compare productivity among countries by taking the total output of the economy, the gross national, or gross domestic, product and dividing it by the total number of hours worked by all contributing workers. Multifactor productivity "is a composite measure of how efficiently an economy makes use of both labor and capital inputs. Growth in multifactor productivity reflects such factors as the introduction of new technology, improvements in skill and motivation of the work force, and better techniques of management and organization."[10] Other factors may be interest rates, the quality of the educational system, and the financial support for research and development by both government and industry. Labor productivity depends on all these factors as well, even as it is determined solely on the basis of output per hours worked. This formula occasionally produces anomalous results:[11]

> The inadequacy of this conventional measure is perhaps better illustrated if it is applied to assess the effects of the progressive replacement of horses by tractors in agriculture. Dividing the successive annual harvest figures first by the gradually increasing number of tractors and then by the reciprocally falling number of horses yields the paradoxical conclusion that throughout this time of transition the relative productivity of tractors tended to fall while the productivity of the horses they were replacing was rising. In fact, of course, the cost-effectiveness of horses diminished steadily compared with that of the increasingly efficient tractors.

In attempting to evaluate the U.S. position with respect to productivity, we must expect to encounter data presented in a variety of ways, but one fact should be kept in mind: the U.S. worker is still the most productive in the world but other nations, especially Japan are catching up fast. Consider the following statistics:

- One way of comparing manufacturing productivity between the United States and Japan is by computing the labor index, the ratio of the number of hours of U.S. labor to the number of hours of Japanese labor to produce a given product. As the number of manufacturing steps increases, that is, the product becomes more complex, Japan's efficiency also increases and so does the labor index. Some examples of products and associated labor indexes, with the number of manufacturing steps in parentheses, are as follows: color TV (80), 1.15; automatic transmission (200), 1.41; automobile engine (250), 1.62; automobile (1,200), 1.98.[12]
- From the Bureau of Labor Statistics, in May 1988, the following shows the average annual overall productivity growth in the United States, in percent per year for three periods, and for both labor productivity and multifactor productivity, in terms of output per unit of combined labor and capital input:[13]

Period	Labor productivity	Multifactor productivity
1948–1973	2.9	2.0
1974–1979	0.6	0.1
1980–1986	1.4	0.5

The same statistics for manufacturing productivity alone are given next.

Period	Labor productivity	Multifactor productivity
1948–1973	2.8	2.1
1974–1979	1.4	0.5
1980–1984	3.1	2.2
1985–1988	3.6	3.3*

* Multifactor productivity is for 1985–1987.

For the periods 1948–1973 and 1974–1979, Japan's manufacturing labor productivity was 7.2, 4.6, respectively, and 5.0 for 1980–1988.

• In 1988, the gross national product (GNP) per worker, as measured by purchasing power in dollars, was $39,400 for the United States, $33,800 for West Germany, and $30,100 for Japan. The growth of the GNP per work hour in the United States gradually decreased from just above 2% in the interval 1950–1960 to about 1.5% in 1981–1988. For Japan, it rose from about 5% in 1950–1960 to 10% in 1960–1970 and then down to about 3% in 1981–1988.[14]

The average U.S. worker currently produces about a third more than the average Japanese worker, but part of the difference can be attributed to inefficient performances in agriculture and services in Japan. When small farms and "mom-and-pop" stores inevitably disappear, the overall productivity gap will narrow considerably. The recent productivity gains in U.S. manufacturing are based to a significant degree on negative factors, such as the closing of inefficient plants and the permanent laying-off of workers at others, rather than direct improvements in manufacturing. Furthermore, given that the productivity gains occurred following a recession, they may represent a one-time expansion of productivity to fill a slow time in the economy. Finally, the U.S. Department of Commerce admitted in 1988 that its methods of calculating manufacturing output were flawed and that therefore the growth in manufacturing productivity in the 1980s was probably overestimated.[15]

Why Is Japan Ahead?

What has been the experience of that country most heavily involved in robot use? Robert H. Hayes, of the Harvard Business School, asserts that the Japanese have achieved their success through the use of solid management techniques along with a premium on quality control.[16] The details are as follows:

Creating a clean, orderly workplace.
Minimizing inventory.
Stability and continuity in the manufacturing process.
Preventing machine overload.
Comprehensive equipment monitoring and early warning systems.

No-crisis atmosphere.

Concepts of "zero defects" and "thinking quality in," in planning, training, feedback, and materials.

Emphasis on long-term commitments: partnership ("codestiny") and lifetime employment (actually less than one-third of workers).

Equipment independence—much of the production equipment is in-house.

The Japanese companies provide greater engineering support for their workers, in on-site consultation. These electronics companies attempt to hire the best workers available and depend on their intelligence and motivation. The wage structure in the Japanese companies rewards experienced employees with high wages, and new employees must start with substantially lower pay. Whereas the Japanese invest a considerable amount in equipment per employee, "this equipment is not more technologically advanced than machinery in American factories—there is simply more of it." [17]

A recent book written by the founders of the International Motor Vehicle Program at the Massachusetts Institute of Technology describes some very interesting features of Japanese automobile production. More specifically, they note how efficient Toyota has become by revealing that it can "achieve identical levels of productivity and quality in luxury cars with *one-sixth* the European manpower." [18] The genius of Toyota's production strategy, Taiichi Ohno, enunciated the following principles that have made Toyota such a world leader in automobile production: [19]

- teamwork,
- communication,
- efficient use of resources,
- elimination of waste, and
- continual improvement.

Furthermore, these principles flow up from the factory floor to the research and design divisions and down to the automobile dealer and showroom. This comprehensive attention to the entire design, manufacturing, and sales processes is unique to the Japanese automobile companies. Thus, while they have not hesitated to invest heavily in advanced technology, including large numbers of robots, their success has been based on the careful integration of technology and people under the working guidance of the many principles described in this section. Clearly, the answer to an improvement in the rate of growth of American productivity is not just more robots, or more advanced machines.

Labor and Technology

In the United States, the introduction of robots, up to very recently, has taken place much more slowly than in Japan. As the pace has quickened, concerns of labor and management about the introduction of new technology have come to the fore. The economic difficulties in the United States that began in the mid-1970s have convinced many manufacturers that only by reducing the labor component of production can they compete internationally. This viewpoint has been especially well articulated by the automobile industry. In 1983, General Motors announced a new subsidiary, called Saturn, that would produce automobiles as efficiently and cheaply as possible in order to challenge Japan's world leadership.

The Saturn concept was to integrate computers into the entire production process from the office to the factory floor. One of the goals was to reduce the labor component per car from the current level of 55 to about 20 hours. Robots would play a major role. Saturn "is going to advance significantly the state of the art in automated assembly. It will be the most robotized of any GM plant—and probably any plant in the world."[20] The plans were impressive: robots would position sheet metal for other robots to weld as car roofs. They would install windshields and rear windows and doors, and they would attach wheels and install seats. Such applications would require the development of robots with advanced vision systems.

The vision of 1983 was not translated into reality until late 1990, when the first Saturns rolled into dealer showrooms. It was already clear in 1988 that massive expenditures on advanced production technologies, centered on robots, were not going to work. Instead of trying to produce a workerless "lights out" factory, Saturn will be focussing on building a car that can compete with the best Japan can offer. "We're still exploring, but Saturn is no longer an experiment. We're not a laboratory. We're not a social program. We're a business."[21] The Saturn plant in Spring Hill, Tennessee, intended to be the most technologically advanced of all the GM plants may now be known as the most advanced in terms of management-worker relations:[22]

> The ranks of robots and armies of car-carrying automatic guided vehicles that populate GM's newest plants will be thinned. Instead Saturn is pouring its money [some $3.5 billion] into people management. It plans to hire exceptionally motivated workers, put them through intensive training, give them more say in how their jobs get done, and pay them a salary plus a performance bonus—just like Saturn executives.

In late 1990 as Saturn made its appearance, a great deal was riding on its success. Lester Thurow, dean of the Massachusetts Institute of Technology's Sloan School of Management argued that the importance of Saturn could not be overestimated. Its success, if it came, would show that the large, old bureaucracy could be pushed aside and a giant company could still adapt and learn, that management and labor could forge a new relationship, and that market share could be recovered.[23] Failure would be devastating. As noted, the enormous changes that have accompanied the Saturn project are not technological. Some crucial points in the *new* relationship between management and labor at GM, which thoroughly involves the United Auto Workers in every aspect of plant management, are given as follows, and it is not an exaggeration to state that they are indeed revolutionary, especially in the context of a history of lengthy and bitter confrontation:[24]

- The labor agreement establishes some 165 work teams, which have been given more power than assembly-line workers anywhere else in GM or at any Japanese plant. They are allowed to interview and approve new hires for their teams.

- They are given wide responsibility to decide how to run their own areas; when workers see a problem on the assembly line, they can pull a blue handle and shut down the entire line. They are even given budget responsibility.
- All teams must be committed to decisions affecting them before those changes are put into place, from choosing an ad agency to selecting an outside supplier.
- Instead of hourly pay, they work for a salary (shop-floor average: $34,000), 20% of which is at risk. Whether they get that 20% depends on a complex formula that measures car quality, worker productivity and company profits. In the company's first year, employee salaries will depend largely on car quality.
- At Saturn, team members rejected the traditional U.S. form of assembly line, where workers do two things at once—toil and shuffle—as they struggle to keep up with car bodies creeping down the line. On the Saturn "skillet" line, workers ride along on a moving wooden conveyor belt as they do their jobs, which enables them to concentrate on their work.

The Saturn plant is a unique GM experiment and an interesting gamble for an American institution not particularly known for its spirit of adventure. Given that it will take several years for Saturn to make a profit, the question arises as to whether or not management and labor relations can last the course. In an attempt to establish its independence, Saturn's advertisements make no mention of GM. Furthermore, it will try to tap the large reservoir of animosity towards Japan that many believe lies just below the surface. If Saturn proves to be a quality car with the right price and styling it could achieve enormous success; if not, Japan will inexorably continue its move towards domination of the world automobile market. What is also significant, and particularly humbling for GM, is that after years of spending billions of dollars to become more competitive, the answer is not just better machines but better people—more knowledgeable, committed, involved, and motivated.

GM has learned a great deal from its joint venture with Toyota, the New United Motor Manufacturing, Inc., usually called Nummi, in Fremont, California, which began late in 1984 in a re-opened GM plant. This is only one of a host of plants set up in the United States and Canada by Toyota, Honda, Mazda, and Nissan, primarily to deal with quotas and tariffs on imported cars. Noteworthy among these is the joint venture between Mitsubishi Motor and Chrysler Motors, Diamond-Star Motors, the most technologically advanced assembly plant in the world. Japanese cars made in the United States have increased their share of the market from less than 2% in 1984 to almost 15% in 1989. This rate of growth has certainly been a stimulus to U.S. manufacturers and also a threat that serious steps must be taken, and soon.

Finally, we turn briefly to explore the question, what is the impact of robots on the quality of work and on the work environment? The answers are neither new nor surprising, especially given the Japanese experience. Almost every commentator on these issues has stressed one point: advanced planning and consultation with labor is necessary. It has been maintained that success often depends on paying special attention to the problems of displaced workers, gaining line management support for the change, and educating employees in the use of the equipment before installation. Unions would like to be informed early in the planning process, to be able to help their displaced members assimilate into new jobs. It also seems to be ordinary common sense that the workers who are actually going to be involved with the new machines should be consulted about the selection of these machines. Many companies, including Ford, Westinghouse, IBM, and even GM, have taken pains to consult with those workers who will be most affected by robots. This responsibility must be extended, however, to include retraining and compensation.

INDUSTRIAL AUTOMATION

> . . . today's industrial pioneers are hooking new technologies into electronic networks, creating "spinal cords" and "central nervous systems" for factories that can streamline operations in everything from control rooms to assembly lines to shipping docks.[25]

A number of key terms are used to describe the various important areas of computerized manufacturing technology.[26]

Computer-Aided Design (CAD). CAD serves as an electronic drawing board for design engineers and draftsmen, with applications in aircraft design, automobiles, and integrated circuits. Included in this heading are *computer-aided drafting* and *computer-aided engineering* (CAE). CAE is concerned with interactive design and analysis.

Computer-Aided Manufacturing (CAM). CAM includes those types of manufacturing automation used primarily on the factory floor to help produce products. Some of the important subfields are *robots, numerically controlled* (NC) machine tools, and (of increasing importance) *flexible manufacturing systems* (FMS). An FMS is a production unit capable of producing a range of discrete products with a minimum of manual intervention. It consists of production equipment work stations (machine tools or other equipment for fabrication, assembly, or treatment) linked by a materials handling system to move parts from one work station to another. It operates as an integrated system under full programmable control. Two other areas included in CAM are *automated materials handling* (AMH) and *automated storage and retrieval systems* (AS/RS).

Management Tools and Strategies. These include, most importantly, *computer-integrated manufacturing* (CIM) and *management information systems* (MIS) (see Chapter 4). CIM involves the integration and coordination of design, manufacturing, and management using computer-based systems. It is currently an approach to factory organization and management. Other areas are *computer-aided planning* (CAP) and *computer-aided process planning* (CAPP), which are concerned with scheduling the flow of work in an efficient manner as well as establishing the optimal sequence of production operations for a product.

CAD/CAM

Robots are only part of the manufacturing process. The factory of the future is expected to be organized around (a) computers and sophisticated graphics systems at the design stage (CAD) and (b) computers, numerically controlled machines, routing systems, and robots at the manufacturing stage (CAM). Timothy O. Gauhan, vice-president of the CAD/CAM industry service of Dataquest, a California research company, has described the boundaries of CAD/CAM as follows:

> It extends to the entire process of conceptualizing, designing, and manufacturing a product—any place the computer is involved. It can be said to go right down the line from MIS . . . to design and simulation, redesign, material handling and maintenance, process control, quality control and inventory.[27]

CAD/CAM is not a well-defined production strategy, but rather a developing set of systems and strategies that are being applied to various aspects of the design and manufacturing process.

For Gene Bylinsky (a frequent contributor to *Fortune*) computer graphics are the major component of computer-aided design. The real payoff will come when CAD and CAM are linked.

> When the linkage works smoothly, the on-screen designing and testing of a product generates a bank of computer instructions for manufacturing it—or making the tools, dies, and molds used in manufacturing it. Even the tool paths, visible on the screen, can be specified. This CAD/CAM linkage greatly shortens the time between design and production. It is less costly to move to new models, make midstream design changes, customize products, set up short production runs.[28]

CAD/CAM has taken off in recent years as both substantial improvements in hardware technology and research developments in graphics, computational geometry, and AI have provided enormous power at reasonable costs. In terms of CAD/CAM's contribution to the design and production cycle, these improvements will have their effects in the following ways:[29]

- Computer systems will allow engineers to design parts and assemblies by specifying readily understandable physical features.
- Product definition databases will provide complete descriptions of components and assemblies, in a form that can be transferred not only within a company but throughout an interlinked network of organizations such as parts suppliers, service providers, and distributors.
- Mechanical engineers will begin to use tools for product design that are roughly comparable to the engineering workstations now commonly used by electrical engineers to design circuits and circuit boards.

CIM: Computer Integrated Manufacturing

Currently superseding CAD/CAM as the most talked-about computer-related manufacturing strategy is CIM. Its virtues have been hailed by IBM, General Electric, and many other companies. Large expenditures have already taken place—in 1988, worldwide sales of manufacturing systems and software totalled $52 billion—and predictions for 1992 are

$91 billion[30], of which perhaps one-half will be spent directly on CIM, including computerized manufacturing, process controllers, automatic testing, robots, programmable controls, material transport, numerical control machine tools, and manufacturing information systems.

An exact definition of CIM is not possible, as most commentators characterize it as a concept or approach rather than a well-established manufacturing system. Still, it can be characterized in a variety of ways. CIM has been discussed in regard to two different organizational schemes: vertical and horizontal. Vertical integrated manufacturing, the most commonly understood reference to CIM, involves the use of CAD to design a product and a CAM system to produce it directly from the CAD instructions. The entire process, including inventory control, shipping strategies, and production schedules, and other procedures that depend on MISs and CAP systems, is controlled and regulated by CIM. The horizontal approach, on the other hand, is concerned only with systematizing the manufacturing process itself—the computer control and coordination of equipment on the factory floor. This latter approach is also subsumed under the term flexible manufacturing systems (FMS).

New Japanese Approaches

Although they are the world leaders in the use of industrial, as well as service, robots (and even call their country, Japan, the robot kingdom), the Japanese have trailed in factory automation, but not in productivity as has been made clear earlier in this chapter. To rectify this situation and to ward off the challenges of the newly industrializing countries such as South Korea, Taiwan, and Singapore, Japan's Ministry of Trade & Industry (MITI) proposed a $1 billion cooperative program, Intelligent Manufacturing Systems (IMS), with the United States and Europe to develop "the computerized, 'intelligent' manufacturing systems of tomorrow—with Japan picking up most of the . . . tab."[31] Considerable interest was aroused among university scientists and a few large companies, but responding to complaints by U.S. government officials and a number of companies that it was all a plot to steal American technical knowledge, the Department of Commerce temporarily halted the initiative until international negotiations among Japan, the United States, and Europe produced "an agreement in principle to form an ambitious partnership in advanced manufacturing technologies,"[32] late in November 1990.

One important development in Japan, which may have significant repercussions elsewhere and which represents in the fullest sense the power of industrial automation, is the concept of customized manufacturing. One connotation arising from computer-related production is uniformity, the idea that to be efficient the manufacturing line must minimize diversity. This is exactly the wrong way of looking at computers. If used appropriately, they permit a wide range of possible outcomes without the requirement that each such outcome be explicitly specified. Thus a small Japanese company, with 20 employees, produces custom-made bicycles in three hours, versus 90 minutes for mass-produced ones, using robots and a CAD system. Customers have a choice of 11,231,862 variations on 18 models of racing, road, and mountain bikes. After having been fitted in a store, the customer's specifications are faxed to the factory, entered into a program that produces a blueprint and a bar code attached to a collection of tubes and gears. Then a computer reading the code directs a robot to weld at precise points and a painter to use a particular color and pattern. Wiring the gears and setting up the chain and brakes are done by craftspeople. The bikes are considerably more expensive than mass produced ones but are comparable to traditionally handmade ones.[33] This plant has aroused considerable interest, and the obvious extrapolation is to automobiles, where a customer can have his or her choices entered into a computer terminal by the salesperson, electronically sent to the appropriate factory, produced and even personalized in an automated plant, with people performing tasks that are appropriate for them.

Social Concerns

In Chapter 10, the work of Frederick Taylor was introduced and discussed; its influence has persisted to the present day. Indeed, the terms Taylorism and Fordism have come to stand for a style of management, predominantly American, that seeks to reduce substantially the worker's role in manufacturing. More recently, two new terms have come into use, mainly in Europe, which have been employed to differentiate two approaches to the application of automated systems in the factory, namely, human-centered and technocentric. Although these approaches rarely appear in a pure form, of all countries in the world, the United States is the most technocentric, the Saturn example notwithstanding. In somewhat more detail, the following characterizes the technocentric style:[34]

> It denotes an attempt to gradually reduce human intervention in the production process to a minimum and to design systems flexible enough to react rapidly to changing market demand for high quality products. Workers and technicians on the shop-floor are sometimes seen as unpredictable, troublesome and unreliable elements capable of disturbing the production and information flow which is best controlled centrally through computers. The "unmanned factory" is the ultimate goal. It represents the division of labor carried to its extreme whereby subdivided and simplified tasks executed by a mass of low-skilled labour are progressively taken over by increasingly flexible intelligent and versatile industrial robots and machines communicating among each other via networks and computers.

There are some serious questions about whether this goal is at all viable. Experience seems to show that to make flexible manufacturing systems work, highly skilled and motivated workers must be involved and able to deal quickly and effectively with breakdowns and other problems. Advocates of the technocentric approach might argue that it is only a matter of time until the technology is sufficiently well-refined to achieve the goals set for it.

The human-centered approach depends on the purposeful integration of people into the entire manufacturing process, from planning and design to execution, problem-solving, and redesign. Machines are valued for their role in replacing workers in dangerous and uncomfortable situations and in those involving endless repetitive actions, as well as for enhancing human abilities. People are valued for their creativity, adaptability, and special abilities to respond quickly to unforeseen events as well as their motivation, pride, and intelligence. Given that humans do make mistakes, that they do forget aspects of their jobs, that they do become irritated, and that they do lose concentration, is the answer to replace them with machines, when this becomes possible? The question is badly formed, not just because people are invaluable, but because even with advanced technology, it is a well-trained and well-motivated work force that provides the essential ingredient to make technology work.

SUMMARY

Although robots were first invented in the United States, Japan has taken the initiative and become the unchallenged world leader in their production and use. Major U.S. corporations such as IBM, General Electric, and General Motors have entered the market, in some cases in partnerships with Japanese and European manufacturers. There is some confusion about the numbers and kinds of robots being used around the world. Japan is dominant, and has about five times as many robots as its nearest challenger, the United States.

Some of the major applications of robots in the factory are welding, painting, machining, assembly, materials handling, and machine loading and unloading. Robots of the current generation are severely limited in their ability to react to unplanned events. Very active research areas, deriving in part from work in AI, are vision, tactile abilities, and planning. The major arguments for introducing robots are improvements in productivity, quality control, and production management. Human workers might be replaced in hazardous and unpleasant environments. It is important to note that Japan's success in manufacturing is not based solely on robotics. It would be a mistake for U.S. companies to introduce robots unaccompanied by good management and improved labor relations. With respect to the latter, the successful introduction of robots will depend on careful planning, consultation, monitoring, and retraining of displaced workers.

Robots are only part of the automation picture. Such important developments as CAD/CAM and CIM are gradually changing the nature of production. CIM is still probably more philosophy now than working system, but the promise is great and the stakes are high. Two contrasting approaches to industrial automation are technocentric and human-centered.

NOTES

1. *Robot Institute of America Worldwide Robotics Survey and Directory* (Dearborn, Michigan: Robot Institute of America, 1982), p. 1.
2. Steven Klepper, "Collaborations in Robotics," in David C. Mowery (ed.), *International Collaborative Ventures in U.S. Manufacturing* (Cambridge, Massachusetts: American Enterprise Institute/Balinger, 1988), pp. 228–235.
3. *Ibid.*, p. 233. The author of these stages had Stage 4 from 1983 to the present, that is 1987, the year of his paper.

4. John Holusha, "Ailing Robot Industry is Turning to Services," *The New York Times,* February 14, 1989, p. 27.
5. This is based on notes taken during a lecture early in 1990 at the University of British Columbia by Mike Brady, director of the robotics laboratory at Oxford University. He of course is not responsible for my interpretation.
6. Joseph F. Engelberger, *Robotics in Service* (London: Kogan Page, 1989).
7. George Harrar, "The Service Robot Lumbers off the Drawing Board," *The New York Times,* August 12, 1990, p. F 9.
8. Gene Bylinsky, "Invasion of the Service Robots," *Fortune,* September 14, 1987, pp. 84–85.
9. Richard M. Cyert (President of Carnegie-Mellon University), "Making a Case for Unmanned Factories," *The New York Times,* July 15, 1984, p. F 3. Copyright © 1984 by The New York Times Company. Reprinted by permission.
10. Michael L. Dertouzos, Richard K. Lester, Robert M. Solow, and the MIT Commission on Industrial Productivity, *Made in America: Regaining the Productive Edge* (Cambridge, Massachusetts: MIT Press, 1989), pp. 26–27.
11. Wassily W. Leontief, "The Distribution of Work and Income," *Scientific American,* September 1982, p. 189. Leontief received the Nobel prize in economics in 1973.
12. Otis Port, "The Push for Quality," Special Report, *Business Week,* June 8, 1987, p. 134.
13. U.S. Department of Labor, Bureau of Labor Statistics, *Monthly Labor Review,* May 1988 and May 1989.
14. Peter Passell, "America's Position in the Economic Race: What the Numbers Show and Conceal," *The New York Times,* March 4, 1990, p. E 4.
15. Dertouzos, Lester, Solow, and the MIT Commission on Industrial Productivity, *Made in America,* p. 31. Louis Uchitelle, "Strength in Manufacturing Overstated by Faulty Data," *The New York Times,* November 28, 1988, pp. 21, 31.
16. Robert H. Hayes, "Why Japanese Factories Work," *Harvard Business Review,* July–August 1981, pp. 57–66.
17. Andrew Weiss, "Simple Truths of Japanese Manufacturing," *Harvard Business Review,* July–August 1984, p. 124.
18. Alex Taylor III, "New Lessons from Japan's Carmakers," *Fortune,* October 22, 1990, p. 165.
19. *Ibid.,* pp. 165–166.
20. Jimmy L. Haugen, vice-president for automotive assembly systems, GMF Robotics Corp., as quoted in David Whiteside, Richard Brandt, Zachary Schiller, and Andrea Gabor, "How GM's Saturn Could Run Rings Around Old-Style Carmakers," *Business Week,* January 28, 1985, p. 128.
21. Saturn president, R. G. "Skip" LeFauve, as quoted in Alex Taylor III, "Back to the Future at Saturn," *Fortune,* August 1, 1988, p. 64.
22. Alex Taylor III, "Back to the Future at Saturn."
23. S. C. Gwynne, "Does U.S. Industry Have the Right Stuff? GM's Saturn Division Aims to Show that America Can Still Compete," *Time,* October 29, 1990, p. 42.
24. *Ibid.,* pp. 44, 46, 48. Copyright © 1990 The Time Inc. Magazine Company. Reprinted by permission.
25. William J. Broad, "U.S. Factories Reach into the Future," *The New York Times,* March 13, 1984, p. Y 19. Copyright © 1984 by The New York Times Company. Reprinted by permission.
26. *Computerized Manufacturing Automation: Employment, Education, and the Workplace* (Washington, D.C.: U.S. Congress, Office of Technology Assessment, OTA-CIT-235, April 1984), pp. 32–98. This report is an invaluable reference on industrial automation.
27. As quoted in Kenneth Klee, "CAD/CAM: Who's in Charge?" *Datamation,* February 1982, p. 110.
28. Gene Bylinsky, "A New Industrial Revolution is on the Way," *Fortune,* October 5, 1981, p. 107. Copyright © Time Inc. All rights reserved.
29. Herb Brody, "CAD Meets CAM," *High Technology,* May 1987, p. 12.
30. Willie Schatz, "Making CIM Work," *Datamation,* December 1, 1988, p. 19.
31. John Carey and Neil Gross, "Is Uncle Sam Going to Bust Up Japan's R&D Party?" *Business Week,* November 26, 1990, p. 55.

32. Gary Anthes, "Manufacturing Alliance Takes Shape," *Computerworld,* December 3, 1990, p. 97.
33. Susan Moffat, "Japan's New Personnalized Production," *Fortune,* October 22, 1990, p. 132.
34. Karl H. Abel, *Computer-Integrated Manufacturing: The Social Approach* (Geneva: International Labour Office, 1990), p. 6. Copyright © 1990, International Labour Organization, Geneva.

ADDITIONAL READINGS

Industrial Robotics

Schodt, Frederick L. *Inside the Robot Kingdom: Japan, Mechatronics, and the Coming Robotopia.* New York: Kodansha International (distributed through Harper & Row), 1988.

Sharon, D., Harstein, J., and Yantian, G. *Robotics and Automated Manufacturing.* London: Pitman Publishing, 1987.

Current Use and Development

Broad, William J. "Proliferation of Sophisticated Robots Opens a New Age of Ocean Exploration." *The New York Times,* November 13, 1990, pp. B 5, B 9.

Davis, Bob. "Weird-Looking, Costly Robot Not Every U.S. Marine's Pal." *The Globe and Mail* (Toronto, Canada) November 29, 1990, p. A 9. (Originally in the Wall Street Journal).

Edson, Daniel V. "Giving Robot Hands a Human Touch." *High Technology,* September 1985, pp. 31–35.

Grimson, W. Eric and Patil, Ramesh S. (eds.). *AI in the 1980s and Beyond.* Cambridge, Massachusetts: MIT Press, 1987.

Horn, Berthold K. P. and Ikeuchi, Katsushi. "The Mechanical Manipulation of Randomly Oriented Parts." *Scientific American,* August 1989, pp. 100–106, 08; 110–112.

Why Use Robots? Work and Productivity

Bellon, Bertrand and Niosi, Jorge. *The Decline of the American Economy.* Montreal, Canada: Black Rose Books, 1988.

Cohen, Stephen S. and Zysman, John. *Manufacturing Matters: The Myth of the Post-Industrial Economy.* New York: Basic Books, 1987.

Hoerr, John. "Go Team! The Payoff from Worker Participation." *Business Week,* July 10, 1989, pp. 56–62.

Holusha, John. "No Utopia, but to Workers It's a Job." *The New York Times,* January 29, 1989, pp. F 1, F 10.

Making Things Better: Competing in Manufacturing. Washington, D.C.: United States Congress, Office of Technology Assessment, OTA-ITE-444, February 1990.

Safety in the Use of Industrial Robots. Geneva: International Labour Office, 1989.

Taylor III, Alex. "Why Toyota Keeps Getting Better and Better and Better." *Fortune,* November 19, 1990, pp. 66–72, 74, 76, 79.

Technology and the American Economic Transition: Choices for the Future, Washington, D.C.: United States Congress, Office of Technology Assessment, OTA-TET-283, May 1988.

Treece, James B. and Ingersoll, Robert. "GM Faces Reality." *Business Week,* May 9, 1988, pp. 114–18, 122.

Treece, James B. and Hoerr, John. "Shaking Up Detroit: How Japanese Auto Plants in the U.S. Are Changing the Big Three." *Business Week,* August 14, 1989, pp. 74–80.

Yonemoto, Kanji. "Robotization in Japan: Socio-Economic Impacts by Industrial Robots." Japan Industrial Robot Association, June 1986.

Industrial Automation

"Costing the Factory of the Future." *The Economist,* March 3, 1990, pp. 61–62.
"Factory of the Future: A Survey." *The Economist,* May 30, 1987.
Hodges, Parker. "Manufacturing Automation's Problem." *Datamation,* November 15, 1989, pp. 32–35, 38.
Jaikumar, Ramchandran. "Postindustrial Manufacturing." *Harvard Business Review,* November–December 1986, pp. 69–76.
Kaplan, Robert S. "Must CIM be Justified by Faith Alone?" *Harvard Business Review,* March–April 1986, pp. 87–95.
Noble, David F. *Forces of Production: A Social History of Industrial Automation.* New York: Alfred A. Knopf, 1984.
Poe, Robert. "American Automobile Makers Bet On CIM to Defend Against Japanese Inroads." *Datamation,* March 1, 1988, pp. 43–45, 48–49, 51.
Rosenbrock, H. H. (ed.). *Designing Human-Centred Technology: A Cross-Disciplinary Project in Computer-Aided Manufacturing.* New York: Springer-Verlag, 1989.

13

THE INFORMATION SOCIETY

In 1982, a cascade of computers beeped and blipped their way into the American office, the American school, the American home. The "information revolution" that futurists have long predicted has arrived, bringing with it the promise of dramatic changes in the way people live and work, perhaps even in the way they think. America will never be the same.

Time, January 3, 1983

INTRODUCTION

Time declared the computer "Machine of the Year" for 1982. In the form of the personal computer, it had truly arrived as a major factor in the national consciousness. On television and in magazines a Charlie Chaplin look-alike shows how a personal computer, the IBM PC, will save your small business. The once almost mystical mainframe has emerged from the cloistered computing center, transformed into a terminal and television set. Other companies are heavily engaged in trying to convince American families to purchase a computers. Such names as Apple, Commodore, Radio Shack, Digital Equipment, and Texas Instruments have become quite familiar. The competition is fierce, and there have been and will continue to be many casualties.

Families will continue to buy computers in great numbers to give their children a head start, to manage the family accounts, to file recipes, and to play games. Personal computers have another important role to play—as terminals to connect to two-way television systems, usually called videotex. The "information age" is a vision of comprehensive communication networks that link homes, businesses, and government offices. Banking, shopping, education, entertainment, and more will all be accessible from the comfort of one's home. How will such possibilities affect society? Part of the answer must be speculative, but a number of issues have already emerged.

Another aspect of the information society is the replacement of letters by electronic mail and of face-to-face meetings by teleconferencing. In the first case, information in physical form is converted to electronic form, for long-distance transmission. The transmission will be initiated and ultimately received in a variety of ways. Perhaps videotex systems play a role here as well. Teleconferencing is not a new idea, but one that has evolved somewhat more slowly than anticipated. In order to interact meaningfully, humans require a host of visual and verbal signs. The new technology must find a way to provide these efficiently and economically.

THE HOME/PERSONAL COMPUTER

> Though the personal computer was born less than a decade ago, it already ranks up there with soap and soft drinks in ad expenditures.[1]

Throughout the 1980s, computers have been advertised in newspapers, magazines, and of course, on television. When the home computer first appeared, it was possible to distinguish it from the personal computer in the office, mainly by price, internal memory, and manufacturer. Although there was no clear dividing line, the home computer was generally considered to be under $1,000, usually under $500. In the early 1980s, the most popular of these computers were the enormously successful Commodore 20 and 64. The basic model was a keyboard with internal memory varying from 4K to 64K bytes and requiring a hookup to a television set, resulting in a picture less sharp than on a dedicated monitor. For all but the simplest tasks, peripheral devices are necessary, such as cassette recorders, floppy disk drives, and modems. Printers varying in price from $200 to $2000 are usually necessary as well. Thus, what begins as a rather modest investment can quickly accelerate to a substantial amount, to say nothing of open-ended expenditures for software.

Another early computer, the Texas Instruments 99/4A, was popular until the 1983 price wars drove the company out of the market after having suffered losses of $624 million. At the low end of the price spectrum was the Timex (or Sinclair) ZX81, which could be bought for less than $50, including an expansion 16K memory module and built-in BASIC interpreter. It also has been discontinued. This market has largely disappeared as more powerful computers have come on the scene and as more serious applications have arisen. In some sense the home computer has become the low end of the personal computer market. In fact, near the end of 1983, IBM introduced the PCjr, a stripped-down version of its very successful PC, which had given legitimacy to the personal computer market. The PCjr was one of IBM's few major failures and was pulled from the market in April 1985, despite the famous "Charlie Chaplin" ads. This action by the world's major computer company signalled a clear abandonment of the home market, leaving it to such companies as Radio Shack (with its Tandy line), Commodore (with its new line, Amiga), Atari (put out of the game market), and Apple (with its venerable Apple II, and then its successful Macintoshes), as well as a variety of IBM clones and compatibles. By the end of 1989, the U.S. home computer market leaders were Apple (24%), Commodore (19%), IBM (13%), Tandy (11%), and all others (33%).[2] The U.S. market, in terms of millions of units shipped, was

4.1 in 1990 and estimated to grow to 7.5 in 1994. The world market is about twice as large in 1990, as well as in the 1994 projection.

It has been well-documented that the personal computer has transformed the office and become one of the pillars of the information age, was well as a major and fast growing industry in its own right. In 1989, worldwide sales of PCs exceeded $37 billion and associated sales of peripherals, including printers, terminals, and storage devices was $56 billion. Not unexpectedly, IBM led both markets but was being challenged by Apple, NEC, Compaq, Groupe Bull, Olivetti, and many others in PCs, and Digital Equipment, Hitachi, HP, Fujitsu, and NCR among others in peripherals. There seemed to be a slump in the PC market in 1990, but the long range prospects are definitely excellent. Much of this material has been presented earlier, but it is included again to emphasize the importance and penetration of computers in every facet of society, worldwide. If indeed the information society is to be fully realized, in a yet undetermined form, computers and communication systems at work and at home will obviously play the fundamental role.

The Home

For most of the 1980s, the selling of the home computer represented a triumph of American marketing ingenuity more than a fulfillment of a genuine need. The home computer was a machine in search of a purpose. Consumers were assaulted by advertisements that used the following strategies:

Induce Guilt. Parents will be denying their children "a piece of the future" if they do not immediately buy a computer.

Promise Immediate Solutions. You can save your bakery or hat factory by organizing production with a personal computer.

Urge Additional Purchases. The computer itself is only a small part of the story. It is also necessary to buy more software, a disk drive, a printer, and a modem.

Argue for the Complete Package. For very little, you can buy the whole thing.

Remind the Customer of Video Games. Although computers are useful, a wide range of exciting video games will be sure to please the whole family.

But in 1990, for a number of reasons, IBM decided that the time was right to return to the home market and a short time later Apple repackaged its Macintosh into a competitive product, the Macintosh Classic. IBM executives learned that 20% of its PS/2 computers were being used at home and that the home PC market had grown substantially, to 3.7 million units in 1989. At the end of June, IBM announced the PS/1, a specially tailored computer for the home market, designed to avoid the earlier mistakes.

As computer technology has advanced, including much more sophisticated software, the home computer has become much more useful. In a survey of recent purchasers, the following reasons were given, with percentages of respondents in parentheses: bringing work home from the office or running a home business (57), doing school work (47), and writing letters, budgeting, and other personal chores (19). (Some respondents bought a computer for more than one reason.) The first reason was obviously a major factor in IBM's decision to market the PS/1, especially since almost 35 million Americans operate a full- or part-time business at home. Very few intend to use their PCs to play games—actually less than 3%, compared with more than 30% in 1985—given the overwhelming popularity of Nintendo and other new generation video games. The current generation of improved software has greatly simplified computer use and has made it much easier for first-time users to feel comfortable with computers. The leader in this direction has been Apple with its graphical user interface (GUI) for the Macintosh. In 1990, Microsoft introduced its Windows software, with much success, to provide a GUI for IBM PCs and compatibles. The new computers from IBM, Apple, and Tandy will be priced between $1000 and $2000 depending on extras.

A comparison between the computer and the automobile in their early stages of development offers an interesting lesson: the car would never have become so popular had the consumer been required to acquire the skills of a mechanic to use it. The computer is being sold as a powerful device, immediately useful without much knowledge of its inner workings. However, the parallel between cars and computers breaks down in a fundamental way. A car has a straightforward, but narrowly defined purpose, and knowledge of how to operate it enables the driver to use it. A computer can do so many things that a knowledge of programming gives great power to the user. In its current state, however, programming is not particularly easy, and so most users depend on others to program for them.

At Large

The computer has become a media star, in its ubiquitous personal form. The newsstands are becoming saturated with computer magazines—general interest ones such as *Byte, Personal Computing,* and *Popular Computing,* and others that appeal to owners of computers made by IBM, Apple, Commodore, Atari, and others. Everyone seems to be talking about home computers, either trying to decide which one to buy or justifying purchases already made. Much of this activity has the feel of a typical fad, but a substantial and important residue should remain after the initial novelty has worn off, for reasons given above. Many people have become disillusioned because of the unexpected limitations of their home computers; for many others, though, a new world has been revealed. With a computer connected via a modem to the telephone, the user has access to a growing number of services and databases. The variety of databases is expanding rapidly in response to the increasing number of people with computers, modems, and specialized interests.

Networks have been developed for professional and research reasons. INTERNET links research facilities at universities, private institutions, and others, which carry out research funded by the Defense Advanced Research Project Agency of the Department of Defense. This network, and others like it, encourages researchers to exchange information prior to publication in journals. A network called CSNET provides a communication system for computer science researchers across the country. It actually spans several existing networks and allows geographically remote researchers to work together. Ideas can readily be exchanged and joint papers written without face-to-face interaction. One researcher prepares a draft and sends a message to a colleague, who then makes corrections or additions over the network.

A larger community of interested researchers can also share in the articulation of new ideas. One researcher writes a proposal and then sends out a message over the network to his fellow researchers encouraging them to criticize his work. In some sense, an electronic forum has been created for the free and open exchange of information. Distributed computing power, communication networks, and sophisticated software have made possible an extended, underground college. The early exchange of ideas should help advance research and accelerate the diffusion of new results in the community at large.

ELECTRONIC MAIL, TELECONFERENCING, AND BULLETIN BOARDS

> . . . computer networks often become electronic communities that give people thousands of miles apart the feeling of being connected in a small village, with all the intimacy and ease of communication that implies. Known as "electronic bulletin boards," "computer conferences," or "electronic mail" exchanges, these networks are made up of computers linked by telephone lines and equipped with software that allows them to send and receive messages.[4]

One of the most important aspects of the "office of the future," described in Chapter 4, was electronic mail, the computer facility by which messages could be distributed simultaneously within an organization and to geographically remote points. In-house networks have been interconnected via telephone lines and satellite communication systems spanning countries and continents. The telephone conference call is a familiar event, but by using computers, conferences can be established over networks that operate independently of time and space. Another important use of networks is the electronic bulletin board, a system by which individuals can post messages, announcements, and opinions to make them available simultaneously to many other participants. Bulletin boards can be operated from homes and serve a small community of local users, or they can be nationwide and serve thousands. Over the past decade networks have spread across most countries, instantaneously linking interested people eager to share information. During the terrible events in 1989, in Tiananmen Square, in Beijing, electronic mail was used to keep people in the West informed.

Electronic Mail

For computer-generated documents, electronic mail has become an efficient means for distributing information. Within organizations, meetings can be announced by "broadcasting" time, place, and agenda to the relevant parties. Individuals can use electronic mail to avoid "telephone tag"; that is, a message is sent over a hard-wired line, or by use of a modem over a telephone to a network and will be available whenever the receiving party signs on and checks the incoming mail. The number of networks linking the United States and indeed the world is large and growing. There are gateways between many of these networks so that users can send messages to almost anyone on some network. Almost every company, large and small, has an in-house electronic mail system so that employees can easily exchange information and so that management can reach employees quickly and efficiently. Large, worldwide companies employ intercontinental networks to facilitate interaction among employees who are separated by long distances. The earliest users of electronic mail were universities and research institutions, who had developed the necessary software. It is now inconceivable to imagine a research environment without electronic mail. Preliminary versions of papers, early research results, and tentative proposals are circulated among researchers for immediate comment and analysis.

Beyond the specialists and hobbyists, it is estimated that some 40 million Americans now use electronic mail. The large networks, INTERNET and USENET provide services for millions of users and thousands of small networks link special interest groups. In addition, nationwide information service and conference providers such as Compuserve, Prodigy (a joint venture of IBM and Sears Roebuck, to be discussed in the next section), Dow Jones/News Retrieval, and The Source have a growing number of subscribers. The first two had 550,000 and 380,000 respectively, as of May 1990.[5] Users of these services must own a computer and modem, and pay subscriber fees of several dollars a month to several dollars an hour, as well as telephone charges.

An interesting coding system has arisen among users of electronic mail to replace the missing vocal, facial, and body signals that usually accompany face-to-face conversations. These symbols are scattered throughout the message to "flesh-out" the bare words appearing on the monitor. The following are a few of the more commonly used ones, which are more easily appreciated if the head is tilted to the left:[6]

:-) smile ;-) wink :-0 bored
:-D laughter :-(frown :-x angry
:-/ skeptical :-e disappointed :-7 wry

and some weird and obtuse ones:

:-F buck-toothed vampire with one tooth missing *:o) clown
+-:-) holds religious office @:-) wears a turban
@= pro-nuclear

Another method of sending printed material rapidly and efficiently and one which has grown extraordinarily fast is, of course, Fax. Fax is not really a new technology, but it is an example of how the microprocessor has transformed and indeed created a vital new industry. Every office has a Fax machine, and an enormous amount of information is now Faxed worldwide. Fax boards can be inserted into personal computers so that computer-generated documents are immediately available for transmission and reception. The volume of information transmitted over the new electronic media continues to expand and technological innovations contribute to more ways to transmit information, a direct reflection of the ever-increasing importance of information to advanced societies.

Teleconferencing

> Computer-mediated communication systems [*CMCSs*] use a computer to create, store, process, and distribute communications among groups of humans. The users can exchange ideas and information on a regular basis without having to be in the same place or to communicate at the same time.[7]

Teleconferencing may be viewed as an evolution of electronic mail systems to include the simultaneous exchange of information among several conversants. Telephone teleconferencing has been used for quite a while, not altogether successfully. There are problems in conversation when participants are not able to see one another. Visual cues are very important in turn-taking, and visual feedback indicates to speakers what effect their contribution has on the other participants. It seems necessary to expand the teleconferencing mode of operation to include visual interaction via a television system. As a preliminary or even alternate step, an electronic mail system can be expanded to manage multi-user interaction. The lack of face-to-face contact will still be a problem, but other features may help.

One form of computer teleconferencing uses the computer to send messages instantaneously to all the other participants. As with electronic mail, these messages can be read as soon as they are received or stored for later access. A typical system, operating over an efficient, low-cost, packet-switched network, might operate in the following way: Once on the network, the user would be told which other members of his group were currently active, whether any messages were waiting for him, and whether there were any comments on matters currently under consideration—the conference issues. The user has a variety of options: (a) scan the messages, (b) read some or all of them, (c) scan the conference comments, (d) reply to some or all of them either directly to on-line members or others, or (e) review previous comments in the conference prior to making a new contribution. The system permits, in fact encourages, user interaction over long distances and at all times, either in real-time or by stored messages. The size of the group can grow quite large without affecting the degree of participation of the individual members. One advantage over face-to-face communication is that in some real sense, all participants can "speak" simultaneously and the messages are broadcast to everyone. This situation represents a real democracy in that no member of the group has precedence. Because the interaction takes place over computers, a host of services not otherwise available are immediately accessible. Among these are editing facilities, immediate access to computer-stored data, the scheduling of face-to-face meetings, person-to-person messages, and administration of votes. One obvious drawback is the necessity to type all information. Although typing rates are slower than speaking, typed information can usually be understood (or perhaps skimmed) more quickly than spoken language. For the input phase, a variety of text-editing aids assist in the preparation of messages and reduce the usual difficulties of typographical error corrections. A computerized conferencing system has been developed at the New Jersey

Institute of Technology by Murray Turoff. Called the Electronic Information Exchange System (EIES), it has been used to determine which features are most conducive to teleconferencing.[8] Standard electronic mail systems were found to be too limited for long-term users. They must be able to tailor the system to their own needs by defining their own computer commands. Sophisticated word processing is mandatory for a system of communication that relies heavily on typing.

Bulletin Boards

Near laundromats, supermarkets, and community centers, people post notices on public bulletin boards advertising coming attractions, wanting to buy and sell furniture, rent apartments, sell airline tickets, and meet new friends. Bulletin boards are a common feature of most communities, serving to reinforce community ties and indicative of community vitality. In 1977, the first electronic bulletin board in the United States, the Community Memory Project was founded in Berkeley, California. Terminals were placed in retail stores and community centers in 1984 and people were encouraged "to speak [their] mind, check the city council's agenda, find toxic hot spots in the neighborhood and locate used cars and housing."[9] Other bulletin boards appeared all over the country, organized by community groups, clubs, and individuals. From the comfort of one's home a person could connect with like-minded individuals to sell, buy, inform, advertise, commiserate, rejoice, and complain. Furthermore, distance is no obstacle as electronic bulletin boards are nationwide, and even worldwide.

Legal issues quickly arose as to the responsibility of the bulletin board operator, the "sysop," with respect to the behavior of subscribers. If somebody posted an identification code and password for a proprietary computer system, is the sysop at fault? The law is not entirely clear but "people have been prosecuted for using the bulletin boards to post stolen credit card numbers, pirated software or, in one recent case, information traded among members of a pedophile ring."[10] Are the users protected by free speech rights? Marc Rotenberg, director of the Washington Office of Computer Professionals for Social Responsibility, is concerned about suggestions that the government might assume responsibility for regulating bulletin boards: "People should be providing an open forum. Open and unstructured communication is important . . . electronic communication systems should be treated in the same context as the public library with few if any restrictions on ideas and how they are communicated."[11]

VIDEOTEX

> . . . an interactive service which, through appropriate access by standardized procedures allows users of Videotex terminals to communicate with databases via telecommunication networks.[12]

What if a two-way communications network linked the homes of the nation via regional computer centers to a large number of businesses and services? From the comfort of one's home a vast array of transactions could be carried out, using a personal computer or a specially equipped television monitor with keyboard. Among the possibilities are the following:

Information Retrieval. Probably the most basic service, it includes electronic newspapers and specialized databases and directories including stock market, entertainment, and sports, community and health services information.

Transactions. Making reservations for entertainment, sporting events, and travel, paying bills, electronic funds transfer (EFTS), teleshopping.

Messaging. A "switchboard" to store and forward messages from one user to another, electronic mail, electronic bulletin board (one-to-many communication), computer conferencing.

Computing. The keyboard can act as a computer terminal providing access to games and financial analysis programs, as well as more sophisticated activities such as the transmission of software from the central computer facility to the home computer.

Telemonitoring. Provision of home security by the remote sensing of fire or intruders with alarms triggered at security agencies; the control of systems within the home for energy management.

Working at Home. Accelerating current trends, stockbrokers, data processing professionals, designers, draftsmen, architects, real estate agents, travel agents, secretaries, editors, and so forth can do some or all of their work at home.

Services for the Disabled. Disabled people can be monitored at home and communication with them facilitated by the use of Bliss symbols, Braille printers, and voice synthesizers.

Education at Home. Extension of current television education courses can be carried out as part of regular curricula and continuing education.

Although the prospects are mind-boggling, this potentially massive transformation of the marketplace, entertainment, education, and work will not take place overnight and probably much more slowly than had been predicted. On the technological front, although significant investments in computers, telecommunications, videotex decoders or special purpose software are necessary, the real obstacles seem to be sufficiently large numbers of interested information providers and most importantly a public convinced that videotex is something worth paying for. In fact there seems to be something of a chicken-and-egg dilemma: many people are not interested in the few videotex services available, because they do not provide a sufficiently broad range of useful or interesting services; potential information providers are not interested because the number of current users is too small. A few systems are currently in operation in the United States, although many experiments have failed. Of all countries in the world, France has had the most success and the reasons will be carefully examined. Major investments have taken place in England, Germany, and Japan.

Three forms of information services may be distinguished, as follows:

Information Retrieval Via On-line Databases. Large databases storing many different kinds of information can be accessed on personal computers via telephone lines by paying a fee for services. Examples are newspaper indexes, financial information, and computer hardware and software specifications. The user must access a database, formulate a query, and interrogate the database.

Teletext. This system provides a continuous stream of information that is available over television channels. The information could be repeatedly broadcast in the "blanking interval" between frames on a television channel or the normal channel itself could be used. Using a special keypad, the viewer types in a number to designate a teletext frame, that is, a screen image, and the decoder freezes it for viewing. The amount of information available and the time needed to cycle through it determine how long the user must wait until the frames of interest appear.

Videotex. (The "t" is usually dropped at the end of this word, probably to lend it a high-tech gloss). This term is used for a two-way information system. Typically, telephone lines are used to connect the central computer of the system to each individual user. The home user, by means of a special keypad or a home computer with appropriate software, requests information after viewing a "menu" of possibilities. The computer retrieves information from its own databases (or from others to which it has access) and transmits it. This information consists of text as well as graphics and can appear in color.

Information retrieval has generally been used by professionals—for example, stock brokers, lawyers, reporters, and financial analysts. Computer hobbyists have been using such systems as Compuserve and the Source, more often for the electronic mail and bulletin board facilities rather than as information utilities. Teletext is more widely used than videotex because it is considerably less expensive. Videotex is far more flexible but much more costly to implement, and thus, much-acclaimed developments are proceeding considerably more slowly than advocates had expected or desired.

Canada: Telidon

Canada's version of videotex was announced in 1978, after almost 10 years of development. Although it is no longer viable, it does have historical importance and provide some interesting lessons. Telidon operated with menus and direct page numbers in the usual manner, but was more advanced than European systems in the quality of its graphics. The European systems—Oracle, Prestel, and Antiope, sometimes called first generation videotex—use a method of pictorial representation called *alphamosaic.* Pictures are built up from a pattern of blocks in which both color and intensity can be controlled. The resolution leaves much to be desired, as straight diagonal lines look like staircases.

Telidon is a more advanced, second generation system, employing a graphics method called *alphageometric.* A system of points, line, arcs, and polygons are used to produce a much more sophisticated image. Underlying the picture transmission is a communication protocol, the Picture Description Instructions (PDIs). For example, using PDIs, a line is described by its endpoints. A microprocessor in the Telidon terminal decodes the description of a picture, which has been transmitted in terms of PDIs, and then displays it on the screen. The description is independent of the display characteristics so that on a high resolution monitor, finer increments can be used and greater fidelity achieved. Telidon is well-suited to the representation of detailed graphics such as architectural plans, circuit diagrams, and weather maps, and such cursive alphabets as Arabic and Chinese.

Telidon was developed under the leadership of the Department of Communication, and unlike the situation in the United States, considerable government financial support was made available. As in Britain, forecasts of market growth were wildly over-optimistic, with 3 to 4.3 million units predicted for 1990. By the end of 1981 there were 2,000 Telidon terminals in use in several experimental projects, such as an information system for modern farmers containing farm management information, market reports, weather reports, financial news, and crop data. U.S. trials were undertaken, as well as one in Venezuela. The North American Presentation-level Protocol Standards (NALPS) incorporated a substantial portion of the Telidon specifications, which seemed to indicate an important role for Telidon. By 1985, when its direct financial support ended, the Canadian government had spent $50 million (and the private sector $200 million) for research, development, and marketing. Since then Telidon has essentially disappeared in homes and exists, to a limited degree, as an interface to on-line databases in public places—shopping centers, convention centers, and hotels. It may be that personal computers connected via modems over telephone lines to information providers, banks, bulletin boards, and other services will negate the need for central systems.

France: Télétel

This system is more commonly known by the name Minitel, which is actually the name of the videotex terminal. In the late 1970s, a number of French laboratories were involved in the design of the representation of visual images for videotex (the Antiope standards), of the decentralized architecture of the computer system and databases, and of the videotex terminal. The French Telecommunications administration made a very important decision at this time to adopt a program to convert the telephone directory to an electronic form (the Electronic Directory) by distributing to all phone subscribers a free-of-charge terminal. Thus, a potential market of up to 30 million terminals was possible in the 1990s and by the end of 1988, there were 3.6 million in use, after only 12,000 had been installed by the end of 1982.[13] This captive market of users encouraged information providers to participate. The growth in the number of services was also quite rapid, from 146 at the end of 1981 to some 9,000 in 1987. The major uses, in terms of the number of hours connected to Minitel in 1987 was as follows, with percentage of total use in parentheses:[14] professional applications, for example, stock market reports (23%); messaging, chatting (22%); electronic telephone directory (18%); games (14%); practical services, such as train reservations, home shopping (10%); banking, finance (9%); general information, such as weather reports (4%).

One of the more popular services is known as Kiosque, a bulletin board, which provides "the user with anonymity as they [sic] can enter into date relationships with strangers."[15] Apparently such interactions have frequently been sexual in nature, bringing considerable notoriety to Minitel as well as the government's attention, in the form of an increased sales tax. What does not seem to be happening is the use of the system as an electronic newspaper, that is, as a source of general and broad-based information. It is clear that users want customized services, appealing to special interests. France's Telecom expects to give away about 8 million terminals reaching about 25 million subscribers and hopes to pay off its investment by 1993. Surely the key step in this enormous venture has been the decision to give away the terminals in order to create a mass market for services. No other country has taken this step, or is likely to do so. Other reasons for the success of France's Minitel are as follows: a specially-designed portable video monitor without the inconveniences of ordinary television sets; the immediate availability of a service, the Electronic Book, lacking in other videotex programs; preliminary social experiments were undertaken to test the service, including the communication hardware and the information sources; and, the charging mechanism was designed to encourage use.[16]

The United States

During much of the early development of videotex, the United States was content to wait and watch as developments unfolded in Britain, Germany, Japan, France, and Canada. Meanwhile, commercial on-line information retrieval systems were being developed by such companies as Mead Data Central, Dow-Jones News/Retrieval, and Lockheed's Dialog Information Service, the world's largest electronic information retrieval company (sold to Knight-Ridder for some $353 million in 1988). With the appearance of the foreign videotex systems, a number of U.S. companies began their own field trials. The earliest interactive system, QUBE, was implemented over cable by Warner Amex in 1977 in Columbus, Ohio. It offered a variety of services including instant political polls. After presidential speeches, a question would appear on viewers' television screens asking them to rate the effectiveness of the speech by pressing an appropriate button on a small keyboard connected to the set. Results would be tabulated very quickly and displayed on screen. Some 32,000 potential QUBE subscribers could have participated in a meeting of the town planning commission in 1978. No more than 2,500 actually tuned in and cast non-binding votes. Although our concern here is not interactive participatory democracy, this application of two-way systems obviously has significant impact in the future. In January 1984, Warner Amex ended the interactive QUBE experiment because of its inability to attract larger audiences.

One of the most important videotex ventures was the Viewtron system launched in October 1983 by Knight-Ridder Newspapers. Their long-term aim was to sign up 150,000 subscribers in the Miami-Fort Lauderdale area. Prelaunch expenditures were $26 million. Customers were required to purchase a special terminal, manufactured by AT&T, for $600 (later to rise to $900), and pay a monthly fee of $12 along with an estimated telephone bill of $14 per month. The requirement to purchase a terminal was criticized because it ignored the many people who already owned a home computer and would have been able to use it as a terminal with appropriate software. Knight-Ridder in response did design some software for the Radio Shack TRS-80 computer. The service sold no more than 1000 terminals, and even the introduction of a leasing arrangement did not help much, nor did the opening up of the system to personal computers. The resolution of the monitor was quite poor compared to ordinary television, the color choices were limited, figures appeared to be constructed out of Lego blocks, and transmission rates were slow. Viewtron was terminated in 1986 after total expenditures of about $50 million. Keycom, another videotex attempt in Chicago by Field Enterprises, owner of the *Chicago Sun-Times,* and Times Mirror, publisher of the *Los Angeles Times* also failed.

Thus, a *Business Week* article, in January 1985, seemed to say it all: "For Videotex, The Big Time Is Still a Long Way Off,"[17] and in somewhat more detail:[18]

> Potential customers have not been willing to buy expensive terminals—or pay hefty monthly fees to lease them—because they did not see any services they particularly needed that they could not find elsewhere for less. And service providers with no ready audience have been slow to develop new offerings.

Despite all the failures, much was expected, but many concerns were voiced when IBM and Sears Roebuck teamed up in 1984 in a joint venture called Trintex. For example, in September 1987, *Fortune* asked, "Are IBM and Sears Crazy? Or Canny?"[19] By that time they had invested about $250 million in what came to be called Prodigy, a major videotex system. Initial service began in the summer of 1988 in San Francisco, Atlanta, and Hartford and has since spread across the country. Prodigy began with news from USA Today and the Associated Press, business news and stock market quotes from Dow Jones, the ability to order merchandise from Neiman Marcus, J. C. Penney, and Levi Strauss, and to check airline schedules and make reservations. Near the end of 1990, Prodigy had 690,000 subscribers, making it the most successful videotex system in the world, except for France's Minitel. Users pay a fixed monthly fee of $12.95, with no additional time charges, and they also require a program to run on IBM compatible computers. To encourage use, IBM is including a 90-day subscription with every PS/1, its computer designed for the home market. The number of services has expanded substantially:[20]

Travel. Airlines and hotel reservations via EASY SABRE.

Financial Services. Stock quotes, discount brokerage, and banking.

Shopping. Items from Sears, J.C. Penney, Spiegel, and others.[21]

Information. Road & Traffic, Consumer Reports, PetCare Guide.

Education. Weekly Reader, Academic American Encyclopedia.

Classified Ads. Listings from small businesses and individuals.

Prodigy has banked on a number of innovations to succeed where others have failed. It has planned on millions of subscribers, which means that instead of central mainframe computers to handle requests over long distance lines, the computing power will be distributed among minicomputers located in the cities being served as well as the personal computers of the subscribers themselves. Prodigy has already signed agreements with local telephone companies to manage the local minicomputer. Most information is handled by the local minicomputer, which communicates with the mainframe in White Plains, New York, only when it needs information it does not already have. The program running on the user's home computer is able to interpret the messages from the minicomputer and display them appropriately. For example, the request to display a weather map results in an overlay being sent to the user's computer and superimposed on a map supplied with the software.[22]

Because of the large numbers of home computers currently in use, a videotex system based on their availability has a much better chance of succeeding than the earlier systems, which required a special-purpose terminal. Furthermore, its basic flat monthly fee (except for recent charges described in the next paragraph) encourages exploration by removing the per-minute charges of competing systems, such as Compuserve. Finally, both IBM and Sears Roebuck have deep pockets (with current expenditures exceeding $600 million) and believe that Prodigy is the wave of the future for marketing and many other services.

One interesting development surfaced in October 1990. Prodigy management claimed that a small number of users had made excessive use of the E-mail facilities and that therefore it was placing a limit on this free service. When some users attempted to coordinate opposition by using E-mail to reach other like-minded users, their E-mail privileges were suspended. Considerable criticism was raised regarding violation of free speech and privacy rights. Prodigy issued new messaging guidelines and "reaffirmed that personal messages sent to other users were private communications. But the service restricted communications between users and advertisers. Under the new guidelines, advertisers can be contacted only to purchase goods and services and to communicate about specific orders."[23] Chain letters are also prohibited. The new pricing strategy permits 30 free messages per month and charges a fee of 25 cents for each additional message. The restrictions on bulletin boards and electronic mail may result in a considerable loss of business, however, as subscribers turn to other services, such as H&R Block's CompuServe, McGraw-Hill's BIX, and General Electric's GENIE.

Another privacy-related issue has arisen because of the ability of the system to write information into the user's home computer. Could Prodigy download programs which would continually monitor the activities of the subscriber's computer? Such information could be used, perhaps, by direct marketing firms. Prodigy has denied that it has any such intentions and no evidence exists that Prodigy has ever uploaded information from users' hard drives.[24]

Social Issues

Customers are ultimately the most important group in the videotex story, but there are other players whose cooperation is necessary, including the information and service providers such as the media, finance, and retailing; information packagers; videotex carriers, such as common and cable; and equipment manufacturers. Very large and powerful corporations will play a major role in the development and management of videotex systems. Some critics, however, see videotex as a continuation of long term trends towards the consolidation of media worldwide, resulting in a diminished variety of news sources. For example, the number of cities served by a single newspaper is steadily increasing as fewer and more powerful information conglomerates emerge. This condition is in striking contrast to the claims made for videotex of the future, that it will usher in a new age of convenience, information accessibility, and improved communication. Aside from the concern about the large companies behind videotex, there is a feeling that the benefits will not be equally distributed. Poorer, less educated people will be unable to afford the service or perhaps unprepared to use it. The supposed universality of two-way information systems may be seen by a large segment of the population as yet another important institution from which they are excluded.

Other social concerns that accompany the growth of videotex include standards and industry regulation, possible job dislocations as a result of home shopping and electronic mail facilities, the control of content, legal liability for misuse of the system, and the protection of consumer rights. One of the most important concerns is privacy and security. Videotex systems store enormous amounts of information for the use of their subscribers and maintain a record of each subscriber's interactions with the system. Of particular significance for privacy and security are banking records, home shopping records, types of information accessed, educational programs, entertainment choices, opinions solicited, and charitable donations. This kind of information, collected on a regular basis, can form a profile of a selected household and is obviously of interest to direct marketing firms, charitable organizations, political fund raisers, and police investigators. The Federal government's Cable Communications Policy Act of 1984 (see Chapter 9) provides protection for users of cable systems and thereby for videotex systems carried over cable, but it seems to offer little or no protection for videotex systems for which the information is transmitted by common carriers, that is, telephone companies. The Electronic Communications Privacy Act of 1986 controls the misuse of electronic mail and remote computing services, but it says little about the legitimate collection of information acquired in the process of operating videotex systems over common carriers.

How responsible are systems operators for the content of the information they carry? Are they like newspapers that must stand behind their stories and perhaps face charges of libel, or like bookstores that usually can not be held liable for the books that they sell, given that it would be impossible for them to read all their books. Even so, book stores have on occasion been charged with selling obscene books. For videotex systems the law is not yet available, and the danger exists that in order to forestall possible government regulation, operators may institute their own regulations that may inhibit legitimate expression of opinion. Recent actions by Prodigy suggest that self-regulation may indeed be too timorous. While videotex systems are again beginning to grow, debate should be encouraged among the government, the operators, and the public in order to lay the groundwork for workable legislation to protect the public interest and encourage responsible behavior by the operators.

PERSPECTIVES ON THE INFORMATION SOCIETY

> From the time of Gutenberg, and even before, information production has been controlled and has led to social stratification based on unequal access. What is of special significance about the current situation is the centrality of information in all spheres of material production, as well as its increasing prominence throughout the economy. Today, information increasingly serves as a primary factor in production, distribution, administration, work, and leisure. For these reasons, how information itself is produced and made available become crucial determinants affecting the organization of the social system.[25]

That the United States, Canada, Western Europe, and Japan are moving towards an information society seems to be accepted dogma, even if the shape of that society is not well-defined. Throughout this book, the various building blocks of the emerging information society have been discussed and associated societal implications described. It may be useful, at this point, to step back and attempt to assess some of the major overall features and large-scale impacts of that envisioned society.

Aspects of Information Society Research

One way to identify the important issues is to extract them from the body of research developed over the years. Consider the following characteristics so identified: [26]

Information Materialism, or Information as an Economic Commodity. From discussions throughout the book, it is clear that services are gradually increasing their share of the economy and that throughout the economy the role of information is assuming a dominant position. But it is not just improved information processing as a means to increase productivity that is of interest here; rather, it is information as a commodity, as a product in its own right that is of importance. Various scholars have discussed this phenomenon, including Fritz Machlup, Daniel Bell, Marc Porat, and Andrew Oettinger.[27] There exists a problem of definition in this area as information seems to be all-inclusive: information "goods" such as video cassette recorders, personal computers, and television sets; information gathered for one purpose reconfigured for another, for example, motor vehicle records used to identify potential purchasers for upscale products. Furthermore, although bought, sold, borrowed, or stolen, information is neither durable nor intrinsically valuable but its commercial exchange does create a need to treat it as property.

Widely Diffused Information Technology. The development of global communication networks to instantaneously transmit information around the world holds enormous possibilities and is a major theme in any analysis of the information society. From McCluhan's global village to Ellul's technological society, computers and communications may well have eliminated geography as a factor in human society, and perhaps real difference and choice as well.[28] Computers have become pervasive and virtually unchallenged as the leading edge of technological change. It seems almost impossible to think of the information society without the integral role played by computers.

Many Messages and Channels. An enormous number of devices that receive, send, and manipulate information have become ubiquitous in American homes: telephones, telephone answering machines, televisions, radios, VCRs, audio cassette recorders, compact disc players, home computers, modems, printers, and more recently Fax, copiers, and laser printers. In addition, large and growing amounts of paper are flooding homes in the form of mail, newspapers, magazines, and advertisement circulars. They are indicative not only of the vast amounts of information available to Americans but also of the power of the media to shape and influence public opinion.

Interconnectedness. Because of the power and growth of the new information technologies, boundaries and distinctions among institutions have begun to disappear. The facilitation of information flow has created unlimited possibilities for companies to extend their activities beyond their original purpose. Thus, over-lapping financial services are available from an ever-increasing number of companies: banks offer credit cards and credit card companies offer banking services. Many of these possibilities have resulted from the growing number of interconnected channels for carrying information such as cable, satellites, direct broadcasting, personal computers for electronic mail, bulletin boards, and videotex.

A Large Information Workforce. Associated with the growth of information industries is an obvious growth in the associated workforce. Through a variety of approaches, it can be established that the largest percentage of the workforce is clearly involved in the manipulation of information, not in the manufacture of goods. This situation surely has some important implications for the structure of society.

The Special Status of Scientific Knowledge. Scientific knowledge describes the language that scientists employ in discussing their work and communicating ideas. Given the importance of science to the development of technology and hence societal change, science must be supported as a special and privileged domain of inquiry. Thus, scientific knowledge represents in economic terms "intellectual capital," difficult to measure but fundamental to growth and progress. Note that social scientists are included, as their activities underlie the direct relationship between product development and market acceptance.

Information as a Commodity

Of all of the above issues, we wish to focus on the commoditization of information, or perhaps in a more felicitous description, information as a commodity. As mentioned elsewhere, the rapid growth of computers, telecommunications, and software have initiated a transformation in kind rather than degree; that is, it is not just that old things can be done faster but that new possibilities are created, that new markets are opened, and that new uses for old "products" are developed. Thus, information within companies is increasingly being used for purposes that transcend internal needs to external markets. Information as a commodity is not new, but technology has accelerated the pace at which new markets are created, and furthermore, the existence of vast amounts of information in both private and public databases has provided additional motivation. Examination of one so-called information company, Dun & Bradstreet Corporation (D&B), may be instructive.

D&B has been best known for its credit information on businesses in the United States and its credit ratings of debt issuing institutions in the United States and Europe. Its 1988 revenues were nearly $4.3 billion with net income of $500 million. The enormous amounts of information gathered by D&B to perform its primary responsibility have more recently become the means by which it expects to extend its activities into new, profitable enterprises: "We think of the information business like the oil business. In the 1970s and early 1980s, we gathered data, processed it and refined it. Now the critical technology is making it available to customers."[29] Consider the following databases that D&B currently operates and that will provide the information for its next stage of expansion:[30]

D&B Credit Services. Credit information on more than nine million U.S. businesses.

D&B International. Credit information on more than seven million businesses in Europe, Canada and the Pacific.

Donnelley Marketing. Marketing information on more than 83 million U.S. households.

IMS International. Monthly records of 100 million direct and indirect sales transactions from 550 data sources.

Nielsen Marketing Research. Records of sales of more than 600,000 UPC-coded products sold in 50 U.S. markets.

Moody's Investors Service. Ratings of almost the entire taxable corporate debt issued in the United States and Europe. More than half of global short-term borrowings of corporations and financial institutions are covered. More than 28,000 ratings on long-term and short-term debt of municipal issuers, representing the obligations of some 18,000 state and local government units in the United States and Canada.

It can be seen that D&B has built up an enormous database of consumer, corporate, and public information. D&B usually produces complete credit reports for its clients, but it obviously has the resources to refine the data to very specific issues, such as how quickly companies paid their bills, not just that they were paid on time. What D&B would like to do is permit, even encourage, its customers to search the databases for information that they need, thereby saving money by reducing its own staff. To that end, D&B has offered a number of services including DunsNet, which permits electronic interchanges of requests and reports; Worldview, which permits regular stock market updates to be downloaded to the personal computers of market analysts; and DunsVoice, which permits credit reports to be obtained via touch-tone telephones. D&B is being challenged by many other companies, such as the country's largest credit bureau, TRW Inc., in many areas of common interest. One innovative offering that TRW has introduced to its customers, and that D&B cannot because it has not collected personal credit data, is to provide access to its database. Customers with the names and addresses or social security numbers of owners of small businesses can determine the business owners' personal credit ratings.

A long-time critic of the power and influence of the communication and information industries is Herbert Schiller, who has noted, ". . . the information sphere is becoming the pivotal point in the American economy. And, as the uses of information multiply exponentially by virtue of its greatly enhanced refinement and flexibility—through computer processing, storing, retrieving, and transmitting data—*information itself becomes a primary item for sale*."[31] (original emphasis.) The growing commercialization of information has some important effects on the role of public institutions, such as libraries, universities, and the government itself. As long as the costs of gathering, storing, and disseminating information were nonrecoverable, the public was expected to bear the expense, but as soon as it was possible to profit from the information as a product, demands were heard to remove government from the marketplace and to permit business to do its job. Thus, the government is under pressure to privatize its information distributing agencies or at least limit their roles to bulk distribution, permitting private companies to provide customized services, usually electronically.

Global Impact

The information age will provide a stream of benefits to many individuals and to many countries. Productivity will increase, new goods and services will be available, information in greater quantity will be accessible, and—with the increasingly sophisticated use of microelectronics—dangerous and unpleasant jobs will be reduced in number. As noted previously, however, many social problems will accompany this expansive technology. The worldwide impact of information is difficult to gauge, but a study prepared several years ago in Canada, a country likely to be affected by the continuing growth and power of the United States, remains of considerable interest:[32]

Erosion of National Sovereignty. The advanced nations of the world, through their multinational corporations, will greatly expand their control over the international flow of information. As a result, much of the world may become even more heavily dependent on the Western nations and Japan.

Information Blackouts. The analogy to periodic failures of the power system are instructive. Breakdown of large information networks whether by accident or by sabotage could have disastrous consequences for all the countries affected.

Increased Unemployment. Simply put, the future holds reduced employment in the industrial sector because of improved productivity, and the advances in technology in the service area may reduce the rate of growth of jobs as well. Around the world, the instantaneous flow of information means that jobs will be created where labor is cheap and lost where labor is not competitive.

Industrial Dislocations. The current debate about the future of the so-called sunset industries—steel, for example—typifies the rocky road to the information age. Many areas of the advanced industrial countries want to trade their smokestacks for the "clean" factories typical of Silicon valley (although pollution caused by industrial chemicals is a major problem in the Valley). Perhaps the world will be divided in yet another way, namely, between the clean and the dirty, with the West supporting the clean information industries and the rest of the world providing the basic products of dirty technologies.

Economic Reorganization. The combination of computers and communication systems will exert an important influence on new industries, the reorganization of older ones, and the changing role of traditional enterprises.

Threats to National Cultures. The ongoing assault on national cultures will continue, fostered by direct satellite broadcasts and worldwide information distribution networks. International agreements governing information flow, with respect to privacy protection, intellectual property rights, and environmental and job protection, will be necessary.

Risk Management

> Millions of people were unable to make long-distance calls yesterday after the American Telephone and Telegraph Company suffered a major failure in the computer program that operates its new long-distance switching equipment.[33]

The information society is supported by a fragile infrastructure of computers and communication networks, or perhaps more precisely, by complex and fragile software, as hardware breakdowns are rarely the cause of system failure. It is fortunate that the first major software failure to directly affect millions of people occurred in a telephone system, rather than in the air traffic control system, but that is a matter of chance, not foresight. As technology increases in complexity, the possibilities of accidents also increase and the results may be staggering. Witness such serious calamities as Bhopal, Challenger, Chernobyl, and the Exxon Valdez. Information systems underlie most of the present and future technologies at work, home, and play. As the requisite software increases in complexity, it becomes almost impossible to test it sufficiently to guarantee against failures under a rare combination of circumstances. Furthermore, current software, subject to repeated "patches" is itself quite fragile and likely to crash. Systems may fail for a variety of reasons such as human mistakes, both in the design and operation of the system, rare acts of nature, hardware breakdowns, events unforeseen during the design phase, overload, or various combinations of these.

Given that humans are subject to lapses of memory, periods of inattention, and occasional physical disabilities, it is incumbent upon designers to foolproof systems as much as possible and to include clean, error-recovery procedures, because accidents will occur. The problems of developing strategies for risk management and reliability are difficult but obviously of growing importance if technological disasters are not to become a common occurrence. At times this emerging discipline tends to dwell on the unthinkable, namely, placing a monetary value on human life:[34]

> In any applied technology that touches human lives, the decision to accept some level of risk as inevitable calls on subjective judgment about the worth of those lives. The classic, if callous, tradeoff is a cost/benefit analysis of the expense of installing safety systems versus the value of the lives they may save and the political effectiveness of the move.

A Final Note

The information society is not easily characterized but it is eagerly anticipated by technological enthusiasts. Futurologists can hardly wait for the wonders of technology to liberate everyone (read Americans) from work, hunger, and sickness. Inequities will diminish if not disappear. The information society is one of the streams of this bountiful future. The wonders of artificial intelligence, neurocomputers, and parallel processing are hailed as if they have already been realized rather than as technologies with long-term potential. But this is the business of futurologists, to allow their imaginations free reign and to extrapolate as if it were obvious that their vision is inevitable. And usually any negative events are minimized, if they are mentioned at all, and dismissed as minor irritations on the broad road to progress. Surely it is possible to explore the future, cognizant of the past and taking into account the complexity of social, political, economic, and cultural forces which shape the introduction and ultimate impact of technology. The impact of computers on work, both the nature of work and the distribution of jobs, on privacy, on education, on medicine, on the law, indeed on every aspect of life, is associated with a rich network of human values and concerns that must be considered in any study of technology.

SUMMARY

The gathering, processing, storage, and transmission of ever-increasing quantities of information is becoming the major activity of economically advanced societies. The home computer market, after a slump in the mid-1980s, has recently been revitalized by the introduction of new computers by IBM and Apple. It is possible to connect from the home to a wide variety of computer networks that provide services ranging from home banking to stock market quotations. Electronic mail and bulletin boards are gradually becoming more popular beyond their early audience of researchers and computer buffs, for communicating over long distances.

Much acclaimed, but developing at a slower pace than anticipated, especially in North America, videotex—or two-way communication networks—will provide a wide range of information services, including shopping, banking, home security, education, and so forth. In many countries, especially France, but not the United States, government-managed telephone companies have taken an active role in stimulating the growth of videotex. The most successful videotex system in the world is France's Minitel, whose growth is linked to the financial support of the telephone company. There is some concern that videotex will be controlled by a few large corporations and that its potential benefits will thus be compromised. Because the managers of videotex systems will be in possession of vast quantities of information about their customers, it will be necessary to institute regulations to protect their customers' privacy.

The information society has been a topic of study for many years. Concerns have arisen about the power of information and especially those countries that control its flow. Information itself has become a commodity, to be bought and sold, beyond its importance within companies as a means to improve productivity. As systems become larger and society more dependent upon them, the problems of failure become more serious. Whatever the future holds, the role of technology is crucial and the study of its impact must include the associated social effects.

NOTES

1. Peter D. Petre, "Mass-Marketing the Computer," *Fortune,* October 31, 1983, p. 61. Copyright © 1983 Time Inc. All rights reserved.
2. John Markoff, "Looking for Growth in the Domestic Market," *The New York Times,* October 21, 1990, p. F 10.
3. Deidre A. Depke, "Home Computers: Will They Sell This Time?" *Business Week,* September 10, 1990, p. 66.
4. John Markoff, "'Talking' on the Computer Redefines Human Contact," *The New York Times,* May 13, 1990, p. 1. Copyright © 1990 by The New York Times Company. Reprinted by permission.
5. *Ibid.,* p. 16.
6. "C=}>;}))" *The Economist,* October 6, 1990, p. 104.
7. Starr Roxanne Hiltz, *Online Communities: A Case Study of the Office of the Future* (Norwood, New Jersey: Ablex Publishing, 1984), p. 1.
8. Starr Roxanne Hiltz and Murray Turoff, *The Network Nation: Human Communication Via Computers* (Reading, Massachusetts: Addison-Wesley, 1978).
9. J. A. Savage, "Nonprofit Firm Seeks to Create Low-Cost Networks," *Computerworld,* October 8, 1990, p. 60.
10. Felicity Barranger, "Electronic Bulletin Boards Need Editing. No They Don't," *The New York Times,* March 11, 1990, p. E 4.
11. *Ibid.*
12. The formal definition of videotex, adopted by the International Telecommunication Union, International Telegraph and Telephone Consultative Committee in 1984, in *New Telecommunication Services: Videotex Development Strategies,* ICCP, Information, Computer and Communication Policy Series (Paris: OECD, 1988), p. 9.
13. Jean Devèze, "Minitel™ and Its Residential Services," in Felix Van Rijn and Robin Williams (eds.), *Concerning Home Telematics* (New York: North-Holland, 1987), pp. 62–63.
14. James M. Markham, "France's Minitel Seeks a Niche," *The New York Times,* November 8, 1988, p. 29.
15. *New Telecommunication Services,* p. 18.
16. Riccardo Petrella, "Experiences in Home Telematics," in Van Rijn and Williams, *Concerning Home Telematics,* p. 15.
17. Catherine L. Harris, "For Videotex, The Big Time Is Still a Long Way Off," *Business Week,* January 14, 1985, pp. 128, 132–133.
18. *Ibid.,* p. 133.
19. Bill Saporito, "Are IBM and Sears Crazy? Or Canny?" *Fortune,* September 28, 1987, p. 74.
20. Jeffrey Rothfeder and Mark Lewyn, "How Long Will Prodigy Be a Problem Child?" *Business Week,* September 10, 1990, p. 75.
21. In May 1991, Prodigy cancelled its supermarket shopping service, which had permitted users to order goods at participating stores. (*Computerworld,* May 27, 1991, p. 6.)
22. John Markoff, "Betting on a Different Videotex Idea," *The New York Times,* July 12, 1989, p. 27.
23. John Markoff, "Home-Computer Network Criticized for Limiting Users," *The New York Times,* November 27, 1990, p. C 6.
24. Christopher Lindquist, "File Data Upsets Prodigy Users," *Computerworld,* May 6, 1991, p. 4.
25. Herbert I. Schiller, "Paradoxes of the Information Age," an address to a conference on microelectronics,

Santa Cruz, California, May 1983, as quoted in George Gerbner, "The Challenge Before Us," in Jorg Becker, Goran Hedebro, and Leena Paldan (eds.), *Communication and Domination: Essays to Honor Herbert I. Schiller* (Norwood, New Jersey: Ablex Publishing, 1986), p. 233.
26. Jorge Reina Schement and Leah A. Lievrouw (eds.), *Competing Visions, Complex Realities: Social Aspects of the Information Society* (Norwood, New Jersey: Ablex Publishing, 1987), pp. 3–9.
27. Fritz Machlup, *The Production and Distribution of Knowledge in the United States* (Princeton, New Jersey: Princeton University Press, 1962); Daniel Bell, *The Coming of the Post-Industrial Society: A Venture in Social Forecasting* (New York: Basic Books, 1973); Marc U. Porat, *The Information Economy, Volume 1: Definition and Measurement* (Washington, D.C.: U.S. Department of Commerce, 1977); and Anthony Oettinger, "Information Resources: Knowledge and Power in the 21st Century," *Science,* July 4, 1980, pp. 191–209.
28. Marshall McLuhan, *Understanding Media: The Extensions of Man* (New York: McGraw-Hill, 1964); Jacques Ellul, *The Technological Society* (New York: Alfred A. Knopf, 1964).
29. Claudia H. Deutsch, "Dun & Bradstreet's Bid to Stay Ahead," *The New York Times,* February 12, 1989, p. F 1.
30. *Ibid.,* p. F 6. Copyright © 1989 by The New York Times Company. Reprinted by permission.
31. Herbert I. Schiller, *Information and the Crisis Economy* (Norwood, New Jersey: Ablex Publishing, 1984), p. 33.
32. Shirley Serafini and Michael Andrieu, *The Information Revolution and its Implications for Canada,* Department of Communications, Government of Canada (Ottawa, Canada, November, 1980).
33. Calvin Sims, "Computer Breakdown at A.T.&T. Snarls Long Distance Across U.S.," *The New York Times,* January 16, 1990, p. 1. Copyright © 1990 by The New York Times Company. Reprinted by permission. On September 17, 1991, AT&T long distance service in New York failed, resulting in 5 million blocked calls and a paralysis of the air traffic control system. (See Edmund I. Andrews, "AT&T Employees Missed Breakdown," *The New York Times,* September 19, 1991, pp. A1, C18.)
34. Trudy Bell, "Managing Risk in Large Complex Systems," Special Report, *IEEE Spectrum,* June 1990, p. 22.

ADDITIONAL READINGS

Introduction

Dertouzos, Michael and Moses, Joel (eds.). *The Computer Age: A Twenty-Year View.* Cambridge, Massachusetts: MIT Press, 1980.

Forester, Tom (ed.). *Computers in the Human Context,* Cambridge, Massachusetts: MIT Press, 1989.

The Home/Personal Computer

Buell, Barbara, Levine, Jonathan B., and Gross, Neil. "Apple: New Team, New Strategy." *Business Week,* October 15, 1990, pp. 86–89, 92–93, 96.

Chposky, James and Leonsis, Ted. *Blue Magic: The People, Power and Politics Behind the IBM Personal Computer.* New York: Facts On File Publications, 1988.

Friedrich, Otto, Moritz, Michael, Nash, J. Madelain, and Stoler, Peter. "The Computer Moves In." Cover Story: Machine of the Year, *Time,* January 3, 1983, pp. 8–16 (plus pp. 17–25, 27).

Sculley, John. *Odyssey: Pepsi to Apple . . . A Journey of Adventure, Ideas, and the Future.* Toronto, Canada: Fitzhenry & Whiteside, 1987.

Toong, Hoo-Min D. and Gupta, Amar. "The Computer Age Gets Personal." *Technology Review,* January 1983, pp. 26–37.

Electronic Mail and Teleconferencing

Churbuck, David. "Prepare for E-Mail Attack." *Forbes,* January 23, 1989.

Hiltz, Starr Roxanne. "Productivity Enhancement from Computer-Mediated Communication: A Systems Contingency Approach." *Communications of the ACM,* **31**(12), December 1988, pp. 1438–1454.

Rafaeli, Sheizaf. "The Electronic Bulletin Board: A Computer-Driven Mass Medium." *Computers and Social Sciences,* **2**(3), July–September 1986, pp. 123–136.

Videotex

Abramson, Jeffrey B., Arterton, Christopher F., and Orren, Gary R. *The Electronic Commonwealth: The Impact of New Media Technologies on Democratic Policies.* New York: Basic Books, 1988.

Fehida, Sam and Malik, Rex. *Viewdata Revolution.* London: Associated Business, 1981.

Flaherty, David H. *Protecting Privacy in Two-Way Electronic Services.* White Plains, New York: Knowledge Industry Publications, 1985.

Godfrey, David and Chang, Ernest (eds.). *The Telidon Books.* Victoria, Canada: Press Porcepic, 1981.

Hughes, Kathleen A. "IBM-Sears Computer-Services Venture Shows Promise, but a Lot of Kinks Remain." *The Wall Street Journal,* February 8, 1989, pp. B 1, B 2.

Salvaggio, Jerry L. and Bryant, Jennings (eds.). *Media Use in the Information Age: Emerging Patterns of Adoption and Consumer Use.* Hillsdale, New Jersey: Lawrence Erlbaum Associates, 1989.

Sigal, Efram with Roizen, Joseph, McIntyre, Colin, and Wilkinson, Max. *The Future of Videotext.* White Plains, New York: Knowledge Industry Publications, 1983.

Westin, Alan F. "Home Information Systems: The Privacy Debate." *Datamation,* July 1982, pp. 100–101, 103–104, 106, 111–112, 114.

Wilson, Kevin G. *Technologies of Control: The New Interactive Media for the Home.* Madison, Wisconsin: University of Wisconsin, 1988.

Perspective on the Information Society

Broad, William J. "Space Errors Share Pattern: Skipped Tests." *The New York Times,* June 11, 1991, pp. B 5, B 8.

Critical Connections: Communication for the Future. Washington, D.C.: United States Congress, Office of Technology Assessment, OTA-CIT-407, January 1990.

de Sola Pool, Ithiel. *Technologies of Freedom.* Cambridge, Massachusetts: Harvard University Press/Belknap, 1983.

Jacky, Jonathan. "Risks in Medical Electronic Electronics." *Communications of the ACM,* **3**(12), December 1990, p. 138.

Leveson, Nancy G. "Software Safety in Embedded Computer Systems." *Communications of the ACM,* **34**(2), February 1991, pp. 34–46.

Katz, Raul Luciano. *The Information Society: An International Perspective.* New York: Praeger, 1988.

Mosco, Vincent. *Pushbutton Fantasies: Critical Perspectives on Videotex and Information Technology.* Norwood, New Jersey: Ablex Publishing, 1982.

Mosco, Vincent and Wasko, Janet (eds.). *The Political Economy of Information.* Madison, Wisconsin: University of Wisconsin, 1988.

Parnas, David L., van Schowen, A. John, and Kwan, Shu Po. "Evaluation of Safety-Critical Software." *Communications of the ACM,* **33**(6), June 1990, pp. 636–648.

Roszak, Theodore. *The Cult of Information: The Folklore of Computers and the True Art of Thinking.* New York: Pantheon Books, 1986.

14

ETHICS AND PROFESSIONALISM

Now the engineer's professional obligation to protect the well-being of the community, as well as to shun participation in deceptions, conflicts with another obligation: to serve as a faithful agent of his clients.

Excerpt from Stephen Unger, *Controlling Technology: Ethics and the Responsible Engineer.* Copyright © 1982 by Holt, Rinehart and Winston, Inc., reprinted by permission of the publisher.

INTRODUCTION

Throughout this book we have discussed a wide range of issues associated with the use of computers in contemporary society. Many of the examples have pointed to applications that might have detrimental effects on some segment of society. Among these examples are the following:

- The introduction of computers into the office with the immediate result that some employees, usually women, may lose their jobs or discover that their working conditions have changed for the worse: monitoring of their work patterns, reduced social interaction, fear of harmful effects from their terminals, or restricted upward mobility options.
- Computer-aided instruction causes some teachers to feel threatened because they know very little about the subject, have not been properly instructed themselves, and are concerned about the impact on their students.
- A programmer in a criminal investigation unit is ordered to prepare a profile program to predict possible criminal behaviour. The program will be used to monitor a select group of individuals in hope of apprehending them in a criminal act.
- Enormous expenditures on high technology medicine—CAT, PET, and MRI scanners, for example—have limited the amount of money available for preventative medicine, which has a significant impact on poorer people.

• Governments maintain large numbers of databases with information of all kinds about their citizens, and this information may or may not be strictly controlled. Either carelessness or maliciousness may result in the disclosure of personal information damaging to individuals or groups.

• Someone breaks into a computer system via a telephone connection and just "looks around," copies some information into his or her own computer, destroys one or more files immediately, or inserts a program, a virus or worm, to destroy files later in both this system and in others with which it communicates.

• A company purchases a new spreadsheet program and several employees make copies to take home so that they can do some of their work there. Some spouses and children discover this new program and decide it will be useful for their clubs, or other purposes, and also make copies to share with their friends.

• A credit bureau releases information to a reporter on one of the consumers in its database, which causes considerable embarrassment and possible financial loss to that consumer.

• A worker is refused a new job for which she is well-qualified because the prospective employer discovers, via a commercial database to which he subscribes, that she has been involved, in a previous job, with a group attempting to limit daily exposure to video display terminals.

In all of these examples, to a lesser or greater degree, individuals or organizations have had to make decisions that affect the lives of other individuals. How these decisions are made, what the essential ingredients are, and to what principles, if any, appeals are made, form part of the subject of this chapter, namely ethics and professionalism.

In the last few years, the concern with ethical behavior has moved from academia and religious institutions into the public consciousness, propelled by a number of events, some of which have been conditioned by recent technological innovations. Probably no area has had a greater impact, nor received more publicity, than the investment industry and big business in general. The recent spate of insider trading and stock and bond violations have given the impression that honesty and ethical behavior are in short supply when big money is concerned. Consider the following remarks taken from those who either comment on, or who are intimately involved in business:

> • What is this—the business news or the crime report? Turn over one stone and out crawls Boesky's tipster, investment banker Dennis Levine, dirt clinging to his $12.6 million insider-trading profits. Turn over another and there's a wriggling tangle of the same slimy creatures, from minute grubs like the Yuppie Gang to plump grandads like jailed former Deputy Defense Secretary Paul Thayer.[1]
>
> • As the revelations of illegality and excesses in the financial community begin to be exposed, those of us who are part of this community have to face a hard truth: a cancer has been spreading in our industry. . . . The cancer is called greed.[2]
>
> • Not since the reckless 1920s has the business world seen such searing scandals. White-collar scams abound: insider trading, money laundering, greenmail. Greed combined with technology has made stealing more tempting than ever. Result: what began as the decade of the entrepreneur is becoming the age of the pin-striped outlaw.[3]

• The Justice Department is considering almost doubling the office's securities fraud staff . . . there is enough business there to support doubling the current effort.[4]

The public also had some strong feelings about insider trading, the trading of stocks based upon information not available to stockholders or the general public. When given a selection of reasons that some brokers engaged in illegal activities, even though many were legitimately making hundreds of thousands of dollars a year, those surveyed in a *Business Week*/Harris Poll taken during August 1986 answered as follows:[5] pure greed (56%), many others on Wall Street were doing it (21%), they made too much money at too early an age (11%), they were criminal by nature (6%). Most were not surprised by the revelations; when asked how common insider trading was, 64% said very common or somewhat common, 21% only occasionally, and 5% not common at all. Finally, 80% said that the news about insider trading had not made much difference in their opinion about people who work on Wall Street. This last result indicates either a surprising degree of cynicism by the general public or a level of sophistication and realism beyond that revealed by breast-beating market analysts who seem considerably more surprised than warranted, given their supposed expertise.

The other area of growing concern for applied ethics is the impact of recent developments in reproductive medicine, including *in vitro* fertilization, surrogate motherhood, frozen embryos, the use of fetal tissue in the treatment of Parkinson's disease, control of genetic defects by gene insertion, and planned pregnancies in order to obtain compatible bone marrow for older siblings. All of these technologies, as well as those on the horizon, challenge traditional views of parenthood and raise serious ethical issues for prospective parents, physicians, and the judicial system. The courts have already dealt with cases in which the surrogate mother, whose egg was fertilized by the husband of the prospective parents, changed her mind about giving up the infant. More recently, a surrogate mother, whose uterus was, in some sense, rented to carry an externally fertilized egg to term, petitioned for joint parenthood and was denied.

Such cases in medicine and in business, and others in government, law, and science have heightened the concern about ethics and professional conduct and raised such questions as whether there has been a decline in ethical conduct, and if so, what are the contributing factors, how can the situation be improved, and what responsibility do the professional schools bear. In the wake of the insider trading scandals, several major corporations have donated large amounts of money to business schools to endow chairs in applied ethics, presumably to raise the consciousness of future business leaders. Special commissions and panels have been formed by government and professional societies to hold hearings, articulate the relevant issues, and form policies to help professionals deal with difficult problems. Many of the professions have codes of ethics, or codes of professional conduct to provide guidance and to serve as standards against which charges of inappropriate or unethical behavior can be evaluated. Even such a young discipline as computer science has developed codes both for academic practitioners and information processing professionals. The form and purpose of these codes will be examined later in this chapter, as will some of the issues associated with professionalism.

Professionals have a responsibility to their clients or patients, to their profession, to themselves, and to society at large. In some cases these responsibilities clash and it is often difficult to resolve the competing interests. In the public's perception, professional societies tend to protect their members rather than to censure them and bring their actions to the public's attention. On those rare occasions when professionals cannot persuade their superiors that current practices violate ethical or professional standards and feel compelled to "blow the whistle," their societies are not always eager to defend their interests. Such an image has lessened the regard in which many professional societies are held.

How are professionals to acquire knowledge of what constitutes ethical behavior or proper standards of conduct? How can they recognize that they are confronted with an ethical problem and then do the right thing? Are the ethical decisions a professional must make fundamentally different than those facing the ordinary citizen? The questions are numerous and relatively concise but the answers are long, involved, and somewhat ambiguous. There is rarely a situation in which the right thing to do is obvious.

ETHICS

It is not possible to include an introductory course on applied ethics with a special emphasis on computer-related problems in the limited space available, but some important issues can be introduced, discussed, and pointers provided to more detailed and comprehensive treatments. In its most simplistic form, ethics deals with right and wrong. Among the earliest questions considered by philosophers were the following: How should one know what is good? How should one act to achieve it? The task has gotten no easier over the centuries. For the doctor, lawyer, and engineer, the ethical responsibilities of the ordinary citizen are compounded by professional responsibilities. Or are they? A brief overview of approaches to ethical behavior may be helpful.

Approaches to Ethical Behavior

> There can be no question of holding forth on ethics. I have seen people behave badly with great morality and I note every day that integrity has no need of rules.[6]

Most ethical theories are normative in character; that is, they attempt to define, by a variety of methods, what people should or ought to do in given situations. The breadth of such theories is determined by how comprehensive and principled they are. Other approaches are descriptive; that is, they describe what actually happens in the world and are supposed to be evaluated by appeal to the real world. A statement that describes a situation as true or false could be answered presumably by looking for empirical evidence. Throughout this book many examples have been given of how individuals and institutions use computers, accompanied by comments that certain instances may be problematic whereas others seem to be socially useful. In the absence of an ethical framework, all such comments may be seen as gratuitous, as emerging from an unknown author, with questionable consistency.

As Deborah Johnson notes, "ethical theories provide a framework for (1) getting at the underlying rationale of moral arguments, (2) classifying and understanding various arguments, and (3) most importantly, defending a conclusion about what is right and what is wrong."[7] A brief overview of three important ethical approaches follows.

Ethical Relativism

When philosophers wish to disparage an opposing ethical theory they occasionally describe it as ethical relativism. Simply put, this doctrine claims that there are fundamental differences between the ethical principles of individuals, in the sense that even if agreement could be achieved on all the properties of the concepts being defined, there would still be disagreement on the principles. For example, in anthropology, a version of ethical relativism called cultural relativism holds that all disagreements follow cultural lines, although some may also derive from the differing constitutions and personal history of individuals. From this position it follows that there are no universal principles of what is right or wrong, that each individual's behavior must be viewed as relative to his or her own culture. One argument against this approach is that just because people behave in accordance with their culture's normative principles does not automatically mean that they should. For example, suppose at some university called Comp U., it is common practice for computer science students to attempt to gain entry into the files of all the other students and leave behind a message indicating their success. At the end of the year, the student with the maximum number of verifiable coups is given an award. A graduate of Comp U. attends another university, and upon being discovered attempting to enter a student's files, offers the explanation that at Comp U. it is accepted and even encouraged behavior.

Utilitarianism

This term is most often associated with the English philosopher of the late eighteenth and early nineteenth century, Jeremy Bentham. The shorthand version of utilitarianism is that one must always act to achieve the greatest good for the greatest number. Obviously, this definition requires the definition of good, the computation of the greatest good and the greatest number for that good, not an easy task under the best of conditions. Bentham proposed a psychological theory involving pain and pleasure, from which emerged a definition of happiness as the excess of pleasure over pain. Thus, maximizing happiness is equivalent to achieving the greatest good, or in Bentham's own words, the general principle of utility "approves or disapproves of every action whatsoever, according to the tendency which it appears to have to augment or diminish the happiness of the party whose interest is in question." There are problems with the definition of happiness, as well as the calculus to compute overall good, but nevertheless the political consequences of the movement inspired by utilitarianism were positive in bringing about legislative reforms in England. The theory also places public good over private good without justifying this preference.

Deontological Theories

In utilitarianism, it is the consequence of acts, not the acts themselves that are right or wrong. Deontologists, however, take the act itself to be prime and to carry moral weight. Thus, although under a utilitarian approach the happiness of some people may have to be sacrificed to achieve a greater good, for deontologists acts of this sort, as well as others, will have to be rejected. Deontological theories derive in part from the philosophy of Immanuel Kant (1724–1804), whose ethical theory is the most important rival of utilitarianism. His theory is built on three principles: the examination of the facts of moral experience, the analysis of the logic of ethical judgment, and the formulation of the metaphysical principles presupposed by ethical judgments, as distinct from scientific generalizations.[8] What has come to be thought of as most lasting about Kant's theory are his moral or categorical imperatives. A moral, or genuinely categorical imperative is a rule that commands a type of action independently of any desired end, including happiness. Kant's greatest contribution is the criterion of universality, "that is, the logical possibility of requiring universal obedience to a rule of action (logical for 'strict' duties and psychological for 'meritorious' duties). It expresses more precisely and unambiguously the 'golden rule' to be found in all the great religions. . . ."[9] Johnson expresses it as "Never treat another human being merely as a means but always as an end in himself or herself."[10]

The obvious objection to Kant is that surely no one would agree that any one rule should always be followed, without exception. Sissela Bok, in discussing Kant's arguments in support of the maxim "Do what is right though the world should perish," notes that in Kant's time no one took such a maxim literally because no action of any individual could bring the end of the world. Now such an act is a real possibility, which certainly sheds a new light on the absolutist position.[11] Given an order to fire his nuclear missiles, should a submarine commander have second thoughts if he believes that the order is ill-advised under current circumstances? "If we accept the need for exceptions to moral principles in emergency conditions, it becomes necessary to take every precaution to avoid the dangers that Kant rightly stressed—of self-delusion, misunderstanding, lack of moral concern, shortsightedness, and ignorance on the part of government leaders and advisors."[12]

PROFESSIONALISM

The emergence of professionalism—at first through associations, or guilds, of individuals in the clergy, law, and medicine in 11th century Europe—has bestowed special privileges and special duties on their members. In North America the movement towards professionalism seems to be a necessary step to legitimize practitioners of a given skill. Along with doctors, lawyers, dentists, engineers, and others, computer professionals have seen the need to establish standards for membership in their community.

The major distinguishing (and controversial) feature of professionalism is the self-regulatory function of professional societies or organizations. Such societies define a separate group with membership determined by standards they set and expulsion solely determined by them, as well. By maintaining high standards, societies hope to assure the public that all practitioners can be relied upon to serve the public responsibly and competently. For the most part the public *is* well served, and in fact places considerable confidence in most of its professionals—especially doctors, dentists, teachers, and engineers. There is some sense, however, that the major functions of professional societies include the maintenance of high income levels and the protection of members accused of improper actions. Societies attempt to proclaim their responsibility by disciplining wayward members, however infrequently, and by publicizing their stringent membership requirements. Another step taken in recognition of having achieved a professional status is to design a code of ethics or standard of conduct.

The philosopher, James Moor argues for computer ethics as a special branch of applied ethics. He proposes the following definition: "*Computer ethics* is the analysis of the nature and social impact of computer technology and the corresponding formulation and justification of policies for the ethical use of such technology."[13] The term computer technology is meant to be quite comprehensive and includes hardware, software, and communication networks. This definition clearly focuses on the study and analysis of social impact, not overtly on responsibility and ethical behavior, although in his immediately subsequent discussion, Moor does include behavior: "A central task of computer ethics is to determine what we should do in such cases, i.e., to formulate policies to guide our actions." One question that immediately comes to mind concerns the actual need for a special branch of ethics related to computers. Why not automobile ethics, or camera ethics, or telephone ethics? Each of these technologies certainly raises a variety of social concerns and particular ethical problems, but those associated with the computer seem to have a special and far-reaching quality.

Those who are involved in developing the discipline of computer ethics are really attempting to respond to the concerns, within and without the field, about a class of ethical problems that seem to be tightly linked to computers, large and small. Also of prime importance is the process of diffusing the accepted results into the educational system to inform both teachers and students about their power and responsibility.

Professional Codes of Ethics

> An ACM member shall express his professional opinion to his employers or clients regarding any adverse consequences to the public which might result from work proposed to him.[14]

Probably the best known and oldest code governing professional behavior is the Hippocratic oath, for the medical profession, attributed to the Greek physician Hippocrates (460?—370? B.C.) For the computing profession, scarcely 40 years old, a code of ethics may be somewhat premature, as relevant issues are still emerging. Nevertheless, there exist many concerns specifically related to computers—such as the responsibility for gathering, verifying, storing, protecting, and distributing information—that seem to argue for the establishment of a code of ethics. Some applications of computers are sufficiently controversial that an ethics code seems to have intrinsic merit. Motivated by engineering concerns, Stephen Unger has suggested a number of features of such a code, as follows: [15]

- a recognition of the responsibilities of individuals;
- an attempt to create a general recognition and acceptance of ethical behavior;
- the establishment of readily accessible guidelines;
- justification for actions taken in opposition to directives by superiors;
- useful in lawsuits that may follow certain actions; and
- a statement to the public at large that the profession is concerned about the actions of its members.

A major problem in enacting codes is how to restrict them to matters of professional concern, without being influenced by political, economic, or religious opinions. For example, the U.S. Army Corps of Engineers used computer models to formulate economic policy with respect to the construction of large dam projects. The Department of Defense runs computer war simulations as a fundamental part of its planning requirements. Computer Professionals for Social Responsibility (CPSR) has focussed on the role of computers and automated decision-making by the military in determining a rapid response to a possible attack by strategic missiles. CPSR has acted to make their colleagues aware of how their research might be used, to serve as a pressure group to influence public opinion, and to lobby the government. One's response to working on these projects certainly depends on one's political and social beliefs. Thus, drafting a code of ethics requires extreme care, treading a line between professional responsibility and personal belief, among the many issues which must be considered.

Mark Frankel identifies three types of codes of ethics: aspirational, a statement of lofty principles towards which members should aspire; educational, a pedagogical approach to explanation and guidance; and regulatory, with enforceable rules to govern behavior and determine compliance.[16] He also provides a list of eight functions that codes of professional ethics may perform: [17]

1. Enabling document. So that professionals may make informed choices.
2. Source of public evaluation. So that the public knows what to expect of professionals.
3. Professional socialization. To reinforce solidarity and collective purpose.
4. Enhance profession's reputation and public trust.
5. Preserve entrenched professional biases. It may be difficult to introduce innovations.
6. Deterrent to unethical behavior. Code may provide sanctions and monitoring provisions.
7. Support system. Against debatable claims by clients or intrusions by government.
8. Adjudication. To deal with disputes among members or between members and others.

Codes of Ethics for Computer Professionals

Codes of ethics and standards for professional conduct have been adopted by the following major organizations that represent computer professionals:

Association for Computing Machinery (ACM). The oldest association for computer professionals, with considerable representation among academics, has a Code of Professional Conduct for computer scientists.

Institute for Electrical and Electronic Engineers (IEEE). Although it is primarily an organization for engineers, the proportion of the membership involved with computers has increased dramatically in recent years. The IEEE Board of Directors endorsed a simplified Code of Ethics, which includes coverage for computer engineers, in August 1990, which took effect on January 1, 1991. The new Code is shorter, clearer, and more attuned to a worldwide membership, according to a past president of the IEEE, Emerson Pugh, who initiated the revision.

Data Processing Managers Association (DPMA). The DPMA has adopted a Code of Ethics and Standard of Conduct for the managers of computer systems and projects.

Institute for Certification of Computer Professionals (ICCP). The ICCP offers a voluntary certification program for computer professionals and has a Code of Ethics and Codes of Conduct and Good Practice for certified computer professionals.

Canadian Information Processing Society (CIPS). CIPS adopted a brief Code of Ethics in 1975 and a more comprehensive version in 1984.

Other organizations, related to information processing, which either have codes or are in the process of adopting or revising them include International Federation for Information Processing (IFIP), American Society for Information Science (ASIS), and Information Systems Security Association (ISSA).

The ACM code is given in its entirety in Figure 14-1, the new IEEE Code of Ethics in Figure 14-2, the DPMA Code of Ethics in Figure 14-3, and the ICCP Code of Ethics in Figure 14-4. Not included here is the forward to the DPMA code, the associated standards of conduct and the extensive standards of conduct enforcement procedures, or the ICCP codes of conduct and good practice. Martin and Martin identify a number of common themes in these codes,[18] of which the first six appear in all four codes: personal integrity/claim of competence; responsibility to employer/client; responsibility to profession; confidentiality of information/privacy; public safety, health and welfare; increase public knowledge about technology. These four appear in at least two codes: personal accountability for work; conflict of interest; dignity/worth of people; participation in professional societies.

A cautionary note about all these codes is that they lack procedures to deal with emerging issues resulting from technological advances. They vary in their success in integrating ethical behavior into daily activities and this must be an important concern, as computers continue to play a growing role in our lives. Other critics question the effectiveness of ethical codes and even the reasons for adopting them. Among the most prominent is Samuel Florman, engineer and author of the best-selling book, *Blaming Technology.* His opinion is expressed forcefully as follows: [19]

> Engineers must be honorable and competent. Agreed. But engineering ethics cannot solve technical problems or resolve political conflicts. It cannot determine which tradeoffs

PART II.
ACM Code of Professional Conduct (Bylaw 17 of the Constitution of the ACM)

PREAMBLE

Recognition of professional status by the public depends not only on skill and dedication but also on adherence to a recognized code of Professional Conduct. The following Code sets forth the general principles (Canons), professional ideals (Ethical Considerations), and mandatory rules (Disciplinary Rules) applicable to each ACM Member.

The verbs "shall" (imperative) and "should" (encouragement) are used purposefully in the Code. The Canons and Ethical Considerations are not, however, binding rules. Each Disciplinary Rule is binding on each individual Member of ACM. Failure to observe the Disciplinary Rules subjects the Member to admonition, suspension, or expulsion from the Association as provided by the Procedures for the Enforcement of the ACM Code of Professional Conduct, which are specified in the ACM Policy and Procedures Guidelines. The term "member(s)" is used in the Code. The Disciplinary Rules of the Code apply, however, only to the classes of membership specified in Article 3, Section 5, of the Constitution of the ACM.[†]

CANON 1

An ACM member shall act at all times with integrity.

Ethical Considerations

EC1.1. An ACM member shall properly qualify the member's expressed opinion outside the member's areas of competence. A member is encouraged to express an opinion on subjects within the member's area of competence.

EC1.2. An ACM member shall preface any partisan statements about information processing by indicating clearly on whose behalf they are made.

EC1.3. An ACM member shall act faithfully on behalf of the member's employers or clients.

Disciplinary Rules

DR1.1.1. An ACM member shall not intentionally misrepresent the member's qualifications or credentials to present or prospective employers or clients.

DR1.1.2. An ACM member shall not make deliberately false or deceptive statements as to the present or expected state of affairs in any aspect of the capability, delivery, or use of information processing systems.

DR1.2.1. An ACM member shall not intentionally conceal or misrepresent on whose behalf any partisan statements are made.

DR1.3.1. An ACM member acting or employed as a consultant shall, prior to accepting information from a prospective client, inform the client of all factors of which the member is aware which may affect the proper performance of the task.

DR1.3.2. An ACM member shall disclose any interest of which the member is aware which does or may conflict with the member's duty to a present or prospective employer or client.

DR1.3.3. An ACM member shall not use any confidential information from any employer or client, past or present, without prior permission.

CANON 2

An ACM member should strive to increase the member's competence and the competence and prestige of the profession.

Ethical Considerations

EC2.1. An ACM member is encouraged to extend public knowledge, understanding, and appreciation of information processing and to oppose any false or deceptive statements relating to information processing of which the member is aware.

EC2.2. An ACM member shall not use the member's professional credentials to misrepresent the member's competence.

EC2.3. An ACM member shall undertake only those professional assignments and commitments for which the member is qualified.

EC2.4. An ACM member shall strive to design and develop systems that adequately perform the intended functions and that satisfy the member's, employer's or client's operational needs.

EC2.5. An ACM member should maintain and increase the member's competence through a program of continuing education encompassing the techniques, technical standards, and practices in the member's fields of professional activity.

EC2.6. An ACM member should provide opportunity and encouragement for professional development and advancement of both professionals and those aspiring to become professionals.

Disciplinary Rules

DR2.2.1. An ACM member shall not use his professional credentials to misrepresent the member's competence.

FIGURE 14-1 ACM Code of Professional Conduct.*

DR2.3.1. An ACM member shall not undertake professional assignments without adequate preparation in the circumstances.
DR2.3.2. An ACM member shall not undertake professional assignments for which the member knows or should know the member is not competent or cannot become adequately competent without acquiring the assistance of a professional who is competent to perform the assignment.
DR2.4.1. An ACM member shall not represent that a product of the member's work will perform its function adequately and will meet the receiver's operational needs when the member knows or should know that the product is deficient.

CANON 3

An ACM member shall accept responsibility for the member's work.

Ethical Considerations

EC3.1. An ACM member shall accept only those assignments for which there is reasonable expectancy of meeting requirements or specifications, and shall perform his assignments in a professional manner.

Disciplinary Rules

DR3.1.1. An ACM member shall not neglect any professional assignment which has been accepted.
DR3.1.2. An ACM member shall keep the member's employer or client properly informed on the progress of his assignments.
DR3.1.3. An ACM member shall not attempt to exonerate himself from, or to limit his liability to clients for the member's personal malpractice.
DR3.1.4. An ACM member shall indicate to the member's employer or client the consequences to be expected if the member's professional judgment is overruled.

CANON 4

An ACM member shall act with professional responsibility.

Ethical Considerations

EC4.1. An ACM member shall not use the member's membership in ACM improperly for professional advantage or to misrepresent the authority of the member's statements.
EC4.2. An ACM member shall conduct professional activities on a high plane.
EC4.3. An ACM member is encouraged to uphold and improve the professional standards of the Association through participation in their formulation, establishment, and enforcement.

Disciplinary Rules

DR4.1.1. An ACM member shall not speak on behalf of the Association or any of its subgroups without proper authority.
DR4.1.2. An ACM member shall not knowingly misrepresent the policies and views of the Association or any of its subgroups.
DR4.1.3. An ACM member shall preface partisan statements about information processing by indicating clearly on whose behalf they are made.
DR4.2.1. An ACM member shall not maliciously injure the professional reputation of any other person.
DR4.2.2. An ACM member shall not use the services or membership in the Association to gain unfair advantage.
DR4.2.3. An ACM member shall take care that credit for work is given to whom credit is properly due.

CANON 5

An ACM member should use the member's special knowledge and skills for the advancement of human welfare.

Ethical Consideration

EC5.1. An ACM member should consider the health, privacy, and general welfare of the public in the performance of the member's work.
EC5.2. An ACM member, whenever dealing with data concerning individuals, shall always consider the principle of the individual's privacy and seek the following:

—to minimize the data collected,
—to limit authorized access to the data,
—to provide proper security for the data,
—to determine the required retention period of the data, and
—to ensure proper disposal of the data.

Disciplinary Rules

DR5.2.1. An ACM member shall express the member's professional opinion to the member's employers or clients regarding any adverse consequences to the public which might result from work proposed to the member.

* Bylaw 17 of the Constitution of the Association for Computing Machinery. By courtesy of the ACM.
† *Definition*. Hereinafter in the Constitution, the terms "Members" and "Member of the Association" appearing without a qualifier shall exclude members of classes which do not have voting rights.

FIGURE 14-1 *Continued*

We the members of the IEEE, in recognition of the importance of our technologies in affecting the quality of life throughout the world, and in accepting a personal obligation to our profession, its members and the communities we serve, do hereby commit ourselves to the highest ethical and professional conduct and agree:

1. to accept the responsibility in making engineering decisions consistent with the safety, health, and welfare of the public, and to disclose promptly factors that might endanger the public or the environment;
2. to avoid real or perceived conflicts of interest whenever possible, and to disclose them to affected parties when they do exist;
3. to be honest and realistic in stating claims or estimates based on available data;
4. to reject bribery in all its forms;
5. to improve the understanding of technology, its appropriate application, and potential consequences;
6. to maintain and improve our technical competence and to undertake technological tasks for others only if qualified by training or experience, or after full disclosure of pertinent limitations;
7. to seek, accept, and offer honest criticism of technical work, to acknowledge and correct errors, and to credit properly the contribution of others;
8. to treat fairly all persons regardless of such factors as race, religion, gender, disability, age, or national origin;
9. to avoid injuring others, their property, reputation, or employment by false or malicious action;
10. to assist colleagues in their professional development and to support them in following this code of ethics.

* *The Institute, A News Supplement to IEEE Spectrum,* October 1990, p. 2.

FIGURE 14-2 IEEE Code of Ethics.*

I acknowledge:

That I have an obligation to management, therefore, I shall promote the understanding of information processing methods and procedures to management using every resource at my command.

That I have an obligation to my fellow members, therefore, I shall uphold the high ideals of DPMA as outlined in its International Bylaws. Further, I shall cooperate with my fellow members and shall treat them with honesty and respect at all times.

That I have an obligation to society and will participate to the best of my ability in the dissemination of knowledge pertaining to the general development and understanding of information processing. Further, I shall not use knowledge of a confidential nature to further my personal interest, nor shall I violate the privacy and confidentiality of information entrusted to me or to which I may gain access.

That I have an obligation to my employer whose trust I hold, therefore, I shall endeavor to discharge this obligation to the best of my ability, to guard my employer's interests, and to advise him or her wisely and honestly.

That I have an obligation to my country, therefore, in my personal, business, and social contacts, I shall uphold my nation and shall honor the chosen way of life of my fellow citizens.

I accept these obligations as a personal responsibility and as a member of this association. I shall actively discharge these obligations and I dedicate myself to that end.

* *Data Management,* October 1981, p. 58.

FIGURE 14-3 DPMA Code of Ethics.*

Certified computer professionals, consistent with their obligations to the public at large, should promote the understanding of data processing methods and procedures using every resource at their command.

Certified computer professionals have an obligation to their profession to uphold the high ideals and the level of personal knowledge as evidenced by the Certificate held. They should also encourage the dissemination of knowledge pertaining to the development of the computer profession.

Certified computer professionals have an obligation to serve the interests of their employers and clients loyally, diligently and honestly.

Certified computer professionals must not engage in any conduct or commit any act which is discreditable to the reputation or integrity of the data processing profession.

Certified computer professionals must not imply that the Certificates which they hold are their sole claim to professional competence.

* *Your Guide to Certification as a Computer Professional,* Institute for Certification of Computer Professionals, © 1973 ICCP.

FIGURE 14-4 ICCP Code of Ethics.*

should be made between safety or economy or between growth and environmental protection. It cannot provide consistent guidelines for individuals who are troubled by conflicting loyalties. In sum, engineering ethics cannot cover up differences of opinion that are deep and heartfelt. . . . Engineers owe honesty and competence to society. The rest of engineering ethics is a matter of taste—which is to say, political choice.

Case Studies

One method of teaching professional ethical behavior, after an introduction to ethical principles, is to explore a variety of supposed real-life situations, or scenarios, in order to isolate potential ethical dilemmas, then to determine various approaches to deal with them, and finally to select the most appropriate, if possible. If enough different situations are studied in a principled fashion, it is held, students will acquire skills to identify ethical problems, and tools to deal with them. There are no guarantees that a case-based approach will be successful, but then it is virtually impossible to measure success. The general public, as shown above, has no illusions about the ethical standards of Wall Street traders. As calls for improvements in the education of future business leaders have grown in volume, the usual response has been to establish applied ethics courses, a bonanza for philosophy professors. Will they result in a decrease in business crimes, in a reduction in sudden plant closures, in a reduction in privacy violations of employees, in a practical recognition of the worth of employees, in the termination of bribes to foreign governments, in a limitation on significant cost overruns on government contracts, in a reduction in special deals with government agencies, and so on?

In any case, the examination of a few scenarios in engineering and information processing will at the very least highlight some of the ethical problems likely to confront practicing computer professionals.

Case 1[20]

> You are a manufacturing engineer. The product lines in your charge include one turning out a relatively unsophisticated component, but one for which a maximum voltage rating is extremely important. Over the years the yields on this line have been very high. Suddenly a large percentage of the devices are unable to pass the maximum voltage test. Most are barely able to reach 80% of the rating; some even less. An important customer is known to insist on the maximum rating for his particular application.
>
> With only 5 to 10% of the product meeting this test, you decide to screen for this customer. You recommend not informing him that most of the product is not meeting the spec.
>
> This will give you time to find out first whether some customers really need the specified max voltage rating and, second, what's really wrong with the part and fix it.

This is a case involving the withholding of information. Is it justified? Is the engineer behaving ethically? If not, how serious is his or her deviation from ethical behavior? Readers of *IEEE Spectrum* responded to this case in the following way:[21]

- Suppression of information equates to the fabrication of information.
- My mother told me that sins of omission are as bad as sins of commission—but then, my mother was not an engineer.
- I would have told the truth. . . .
- Most condone the screening, provided the other customers who get the culls are notified.
- If possible, many want the culls to be identified by a new product number. . . .
- No deception was involved because the situation did not indicate a need to notify the customer of the yield information.

The dichotomy seems rather clear cut—do the right thing, don't lie, and don't dissemble versus don't jeopardize business, minimize the ethical problem, and lie if necessary. Engineers sympathize with the difficulties of the lone engineer in a corporation trying to accommodate upper management, sales, and marketing, who are not happy about missing deadlines and losing customers. From a utilitarian point of view it might be argued that this engineer's strategy of withholding information and delaying proper notification may ultimately pay off in the greatest good for the customer, the company, and of course the engineer, taking into account that for the other customers there may be some problems. But this argument is tenuous, self-serving, and not very convincing. Doing the wrong thing—lying—is not acceptable in pursuing what may be a worthwhile end, especially in this case when the end seems to be totally in the self-interest of the engineer, however rationalized.

Case 2[22]

> In an effort to keep track of your classmates after graduation, you have developed a database with everyone's name, home address and phone number, job title, work address, work

phone number, and Fax number. You have printed out a directory, which was mailed to everyone listed. In addition to the normal records it keeps, the alumni office also has a copy of this database.

Recently, the alumni office was purchased by a direct marketing firm, which wishes to purchase this database and use it for direct mail campaigns. These campaigns would be for high quality organizations whose products and services are targeted at recent graduates of prestigious universities. For example, people in the directory could receive "two-for-one" coupons for restaurants, discounts on cruises, and other vacation packages.

Should your university sell the database to the direct marketing firm? What responsibility do you have about the uses to which your database is put?

The various agents in this story are you, your classmates, the alumni office, and the university. The direct marketing firm's activities are business as usual and do not fall within the ethical concerns of interest. Your classmates are passive agents and part of the problem is to protect their interests, which include the control of the circulation of personal information, however worthy the supposed benefits. It would be helpful to know how the alumni office acquired the database and under what terms. The people directly affected by one's actions should have an opportunity to be consulted *before* that action takes place. In fact, it is an accepted standard of collecting personal information for databases that information collected for one purpose not be used for another. (Actually this applies for federal government databases that are covered by the 1974 Privacy Act and not private databases that are more or less unregulated; nevertheless, this principle is rooted in common sense and furthermore can easily be subsumed under Kant's categorical imperative.) None of the agents who hold this database, in trust, have a right to sell it to the direct marketing firm without obtaining prior permission from each of the individuals, who may choose to have his or her name removed. You collected the information and built the database; you somehow permitted the alumni office to obtain a copy; you have a special responsibility to your classmates not to permit the sale of the database. The university must have general, well-publicized guidelines on how it treats the various databases that it controls. Students, faculty, and staff should be given the opportunity to request that their names not be included in any commercial arrangements made between the university and interested companies.

Case 3[23]

A computer programmer worked for a business enterprise that was highly dependent on its own computer system. He was the sole author of a computer program he used as an aid in his own programming work. Nobody else used the program, and his manager was only nominally aware of its existence. He had written it and debugged it on a weekend, but had used his employer's materials, facilities, and computer services.

The programmer terminated his employment, giving due notice, and with no malice on his or his manager's part. He immediately went to work for a competitor of his former employer.

> Without his former employer's permission, he took the only copy of the program with him to his new employer and used it in his work. He did not share it with any others. The new employer was not aware of the program or its use, but it enhanced the programmer's performance.

This scenario was presented to a panel, who were asked the following questions: Is there an ethics issue involved? Was the programmer's action unethical or not unethical? What general principles apply? Perhaps you might want to think about this scenario before continuing.

The panel was split, with 13 considering his action unethical, 11 not unethical, and 3 finding no ethics issue. In the comments of the participants the following issues were raised. It was generally agreed that the first employer acquired an interest in the program because it was developed using his resources. The program's value depended solely on its use by the programmer. The analogy of a workman's tools was used to justify the program moving with the programmer even though there is some question about whether the programmer owns the program in the same way the workman owns the tools he or she has purchased. The fact that the program was developed on personal time convinced some that the programmer's act was not unethical but perhaps there was fault in making unauthorized use of company resources. Although the program enhanced the programmer's skills, for the benefit of the company, there were some panelists who did not feel that the programmer was morally required to turn the program over to the company so that other programmers could benefit from its use. Most agreed with the following two statements: The property of one company, a program, was taken and used to benefit a competitor. It is not the case that "as long as the programmer uses his program for his own work and does not sell it, there is nothing wrong with his action."

The general principles identified by the panel are the following:[24]

> Items developed with company resources belong, at least partly, to the company.
>
> A programmer possesses the tools of his trade.
>
> Current use of a product owned in whole or in part by one's employer should not be the sole criterion for determining who has a right to it.

The foregoing discussion has a certain self-serving flavor, as if computer professionals want to ensure that their creative activities are protected from their employers if not explicitly developed as part of the job. Suppose the programmer, realizing how helpful the program could be to others decides to market it after leaving the first employer and does not feel that this employer is owed anything. Is this an ethical act? Surely after having used the employers's facilities without direction permission, the developer owes the employer some share of any profits earned.

What is the difference between this situation and the one described above? Does the answer depend on the fact that in the first instance the program was only used to improve personal productivity whereas in the second it was marketed for personal financial gain? If so, what is the critical difference?

Case 4[25]

> The information security manager in a large company was also the access control administrator of a large electronic mail system operated for company business among its employees. The security manager routinely monitored the contents of electronic correspondence among employees. He discovered that a number of employees were using the system for personal purposes; the correspondence included love letters, disagreements between married partners, plans for homosexual relations, and a football betting pool. The security manager routinely informed the human resources department director and the corporate security officer about these communications and gave them printed listings of them. In some cases, managers punished employees on the basis of the contents of the electronic mail messages. Employees objected to the monitoring of their electronic mail, claiming that they had the same right of privacy as they had using the company's telephone system or internal paper interoffice mail system.

Again this scenario was presented to a panel who were asked the following question, in addition to the first and last questions above: Were the information security manager's, the employees, and the top management's actions unethical or not unethical?

Six ethical situations were identified: the information security manager monitoring the electronic mail of employees (1), informing the management of abuse (2), and not asking for rules on the use of personal E-mail from management (3); employees using E-mail for personal communication (4); and top management for not setting up company rules for E-mail use and informing employees (5), and for punishing some of the employees on the basis of the contents of the collected E-mail (6). There are number of questions to be clarified before these situations can be evaluated, including the nature of E-mail, the prerogatives of management, and the rights of employees. Does E-mail within a company enjoy the same protection that a private telephone conversation does? Because an employer provides the E-mail system, interoffice mail, and interoffice telephone service, does management have the right to examine all such communications, without prior warnings? Do employees surrender their rights as citizens during the eight hours per day they are at work? Worker rights are under assault, as companies employee a variety of tests under the mantle of management exercising its legitimate responsibilities. These include drug tests, psychological tests, and even genetic tests as well as surprise searches. Given this environment, it will be difficult for employees to claim privacy for their communications whether by telephone, mail, or E-mail.

The panel's responses to the situations numbered above are somewhat mixed. For situation (1), a bare majority (14 to 11) found the monitoring itself unethical, while by a 22 to 2 margin, they found the reporting of the actual messages to management (2) unethical. For situation (3), the use by the employees of the E-mail system for private messages, 10 considered it unethical and 11 thought it was not unethical. For (4), 10 members thought there was no ethics issue, 11 agreed that the information security manager's behavior in not asking for rules of use for the E-mail system was unethical, and 3 disagreed. But top management was almost unanimously condemned for its behavior: 20 to 2 for failing to set rules and 23 to 0 for using the messages to punish employees. The root of all the problems seem to be the lack of a clearly stated and well-publicized policy. The lack of such a policy created a moral vacuum, in which management both junior and senior acted irresponsibly and unethically, while employees treated the system as a common resource, similar to the telephone, a rather mild misuse of a company-supported resource. To be sure, in the context of traditional management-employee relations in the United States, the actions taken by management would not seem unusual or particularly subject to criticism, but they are wrong and are indicative of a complete lack of respect for workers as people with feelings and rights.

Blowing the Whistle

> "Whistle-blower" is a recent label for those who . . . make revelations meant to call attention to negligence, abuses, or dangers that threaten the public interest. They sound an alarm based on their experience or inside knowledge, often from within the very organization in which they work. . . . Most know that their alarms pose a threat to anyone who benefits from the ongoing practice and that their own careers and livelihood may be at risk.[26]

One response to a situation involving an ethical dilemma may be the need to appeal to the public at large, because all avenues available internally seem to be blocked and there is no prospect that any change will be forthcoming. It is not an action taken lightly, for a great deal is at risk—personal reputation, career, professional status. Why do some people blow the whistle? Perhaps the situation they find themselves in is so intolerable, so offensive to their ethical standards that they cannot remain silent, they cannot walk away, they must inform the world. As Sissela Bok notes, three factors make whistle blowing a particularly unsettling act, for everyone concerned:[27]

Dissent. By whistleblowing, private dissent becomes public.

Breach of Loyalty. The whistleblower acts against his or her own associates, or team. What about implicit or explicit oaths of loyalty and the sense of betrayal that their violation arouses?

Accusation. It is the charge of impropriety itself that most upsets people. Individuals or groups are singled out as having behaved badly, as having violated the public trust, as having turned their back on responsible behavior.

In spite of the terrible costs involved, whistleblowing is not a rare event. It happens in government bureaucracies, in large companies, and in other institutions. Motives may be political—to expose hidden government policy, as in the case of Daniel Ellsberg and the Pentagon Papers—or because of a perceived violation of accepted professional standards.

Some Thoughts on Ethical Codes for Computer Professionals

The previous discussion suggests a number of features that ethical codes for professionals should contain, with special emphasis on computer-related issues. The following list is illustrative rather than exhaustive, but it does indicate a variety of concerns that an effective code must address:

Readability, Elegance, and Generality. The code should be easily understood or it will not be useful. Elegance is a bonus but generality is a necessity; otherwise, the code will be extremely lengthy and unwieldy. In this regard, the IEEE Code is a model while the ACM code is awkward and obtuse.

"Living" Code. It must be the original intention of the society that the code is written to be used and therefore its use must be regularly monitored and it must be regularly updated.

Responsibility of the Society for the Ethical Behavior of its Members. Enunciating a code is just a first step. The society must respond to questions and problems raised by its members, quickly and effectively. It must use its good offices with employers and act as an ombudsman for its members.

Legal Liability of the Society for the Actions of its Members and for the Enforcement of its Code. Some important issues must be settled with respect to what, if any, legal liability the society has for the actions of its members.

Responsibility of the Society to Educate, Train, and Inform its Members of their Rights and Responsibilities. The society must provide regular training and educational sessions to upgrade the professional qualifications of its members, to assure that they meet minimal standards of performance, and to guarantee that they are fully aware of their rights and responsibilities under the Code of Ethics.

Problems Specific to Computer Professionals Must Be Addressed. There are a number of issues of special interest to computer professionals which should be addressed at the risk of violating the injunctions about elegance and generality. Among these are ethical behavior with respect to intellectual property (when software should be copied), privacy (awareness of issues associated with databases, their development, maintenance and use, electronic mail, and electronic monitoring), computer crime (viruses, worms, and hackers), and computer risks (system security and breakdowns).

FINAL COMMENTS

Hacker Ethics

Hackers were discussed in Chapter 8 with respect to their violations of computer system security and their strong belief in their inalienable right to access information anywhere and any time. Steven Levy, in his book *Hackers,* outlined what he called the "hacker ethic," an approach to computers and information at odds, apparently, with much of the foregoing discussion on ethics. Consider the following statement of this hacker ethic and some of the additional features:[28]

> *The Hacker Ethic.* Access to computers—and anything which might teach you something about the way the world works—should be unlimited and total. Always yield to the Hands-On Imperative!
> *Implications:*
> - All information should be free.
> - Mistrust authority—promote decentralization.
> - Hackers should be judged by their hacking, not bogus criteria such as degrees, age, race, or position.
> - You can create art and beauty on a computer.
> - Computers can change your life for the better.

Adherents of the hacker ethic have increasingly come into conflict with the law and most of the other people associated with computers. Abrogating to themselves the right to enter systems at will and to freely distribute information discovered there places them beyond the pale. As an embattled minority, possessing advanced computer skills, their self-righteousness borders on the hysterical at times. Their facile dismissal of privacy rights and property rights has not won them many friends. Many hackers do not recognize software ownership and believe all software should be freely available. The hacker ethic seems to constitute an "anti-ethic" to most established ethical codes, and hackers themselves are usually viewed as anarchists, if not outlaws. In their concern with the individual against the establishment, hackers do strike a responsive cord among many who feel isolated and occasionally oppressed by the power of large institutions.

Computer Scientists and Society

The most sophisticated and well-meaning of ethical codes will have very little influence on individual behavior if society at large is unsympathetic, nonsupportive, or actually hostile. In the midst of large bureaucracies, individual responsibility can sometimes fade and disappear. History is rich with examples of individuals either standing up for their principles, at great risk, or immersing themselves in the whole and abrogating any sense of personal responsibility. Large computer systems, in their regular use, provide a bureaucratic excuse that can relieve the individual of any reason to accept blame or to provide explanations. Responsibility is diffused and individuals become mere cogs in a great machine. This response is precisely that which Adolf Eichmann's defense argued in his 1961 trial in Jerusalem. Eichmann's responsibility was to ensure that the trains carrying victims to the extermination camps during World War II ran efficiently in the context of the larger transportation system. What happened to the "passengers" was not his concern. Hannah Arendt, the esteemed social critic has noted, "As for the base motives, he was perfectly sure that he was not what he called an *innerer Schweinehund,* a dirty bastard in the depths of his heart; and as for his conscience, he remembered perfectly well that he would have had a bad conscience only if he had not done what he had been ordered to do—to ship millions of men, women, and children to their deaths with great zeal and the most meticulous care."[29]

Langdon Winner, in commenting on the impact of large systems on traditional concepts of ethical behavior, writes, "What is interesting about the new ethical context offered by highly complex systems is that their very architecture constitutes vast webs of extenuating circumstances. Seemingly valid excuses can be manufactured wholesale for anyone situated in the network. Thus the very notion of moral agency begins to dissolve."[30] And this is the great fear, that in large systems of all kinds, no one person either takes or receives responsibility. Unless ethics codes can combat this tendency they will become mere window dressing, if they are not so already. One example of personal integrity may stand as a beacon for computer professionals everywhere.

David Parnas, a distinguished software engineer with a long history of consultation to the U.S. Department of Defense, was asked in 1985 to serve on a $1000/day advisory panel, on Computing in Support of Battle Management, a "Star Wars" project. Two months later he resigned publicly, although he had previously expressed support for any approach which would remove nuclear weapons as a deterrent factor. It is important to note that Parnas believes that people with a strong sense of social responsibility should work on military projects. A statement of his position on professional responsibility follows:[31]

> Some have held that a professional is a 'team player' and should never blow the whistle on his colleagues and employer. I disagree. As the Challenger incident demonstrates, such action is sometimes necessary. One's obligations as a professional precede other obligations. One must not enter into contracts that conflict with one's professional obligations.

The basic question is how did work on this project violate Parnas's sense of his professional obligations. Is there a general principle in force that will be helpful to others in similar circumstances or is this an instance of idiosyncratic behavior? Again Parnas's own words are necessary and instructive:[32]

> . . . I solicited comments from other scientists and found none that disagreed with my technical conclusions. Instead, they told me that the program should be continued, not because it would free us from the fear of nuclear weapons, but because the research money would advance the state of computer science! I disagree with that statement, but I also consider it irrelevant. Taking money allocated for developing a shield against nuclear missiles, while knowing that such a shield was impossible, seemed like fraud to me.
>
> When I observed that the SDIO [Strategic Defense Initiative Organization] was engaged in "damage control," rather than a serious consideration of my arguments, I felt that I should inform the public and its representatives of my own view. I want the public to understand that no trustworthy shield will result from the SDIO-sponsored work. I want them to understand that technology offers no magic that will eliminate the fear of nuclear weapons. I consider this part of my personal professional responsibility as a scientist and educator.

This lengthy statement conveys a strong sense of honesty, responsibility, and commitment, both personal and professional, especially given his past record of involvement in military research and development. Parnas's negative evaluation of the prospects of success of Star Wars have been challenged but for the present purposes, it is his strong action and public statement that are important.

The final words of this section will be given by Joseph Weizenbaum, viewed by some as the conscience of computer science and by others as just a cranky nuisance. Weizenbaum makes clear that he is not arguing against technology itself, which can be used for good or ill, but rather for responsible, informed decision making.[33]

> Today it is virtually certain that every scientific and technical result will, if at all possible, be incorporated in military systems. In these circumstances, scientific and technical workers have a responsibility to inquire about the end uses of their work. They must attempt to know to what ends it will be put. Would they serve these ends directly? Would they personally steer missiles to their targets and watch people die?
>
> Many . . . scientists say that the systems on which they work can help take astronauts to the moon and bring them back as well as guarantee that missiles aimed at a city will actually hit it if fired. How then can they be held responsible for their work's consequences? . . . But the attitude, "If I don't do it, someone else will," a thinly disguised version of this disorder, cannot serve as a basis of moral behavior, or else every crime imaginable is so justifiable.

The Social Costs of Technology

We live in an age of serious contradictions. Technological development is accelerating, and without doubt the benefits to society have been massive and persuasive. To list some of them is to stand in awe of human ingenuity: electrical power, airplanes, space exploration, television, communication networks, microelectronics, genetic engineering, and computers. Surely the improvements in health, food supply, longevity, living standards, safety, working conditions, and so forth are real and largely attributable to discoveries in science and technology. This fact applies to the industrialized countries of the world. Many other countries, to a greater or lesser degree, are facing such basic issues of survival that the relevance of technology as a major force has not yet been established.

Most attempts to describe and analyze the impact of technology on society inevitably give a list of good effects, a shorter list of bad effects, and an assurance that we can ultimately control how the actual technology will be used. Perhaps the choice is ours, but in certain areas control seems elusive at best. Nuclear power is an example, in its domestic and international contexts. Compared to the potential holocaust of nuclear war or serious power-plants accidents, all other issues fade into insignificance. The use of the technology of nuclear weapons could result in the absolute desolation of our planet. Control rests on a delicate balance of mutual threats and assured destruction.

Having created nuclear and thermonuclear weapons, humanity survives under a shadow that affects every person's life. Here is an example of a technology that seems to control us.

A study of the history of the atomic bomb reveals that many of the scientists involved in its original development assumed they would subsequently be consulted about its uses. Such was not the case. Decision making was assumed by the executive branch of the government and the bomb became an instrument of national policy. It is a fact that technological innovators rarely continue to exercise authority over their invention or discovery after it leaves the laboratory. If technology can be controlled for the benefit of society, we must ask, controlled how and by whom?

Even the peaceful uses of nuclear energy have not met the initial optimistic expectations of very low-cost safe power. Plant costs have escalated, and the environmental protection movement has rallied public support to limit the growth of the nuclear industry. Anxiety about the safety of nuclear reactors for power generation has been translated, in North America, into a marked reduction of plant construction. The impact of aroused public opinion has been effective in this area and demonstrates the possibility of an aware populace exercising its political power. Other concerns currently reaching public awareness are acid rain, genetic engineering, and antibiotic supplements for animals. In each of these cases, growing political activity may result in the enactment of controls to protect health and safety.

Meeting the Challenge

It is a formidable undertaking to evaluate the effect of technological change on social, political, and economic institutions. A study of the past is informative and necessary, but predictions of the future have not been particularly accurate, notwithstanding the emergence of a forecasting industry and such powerful tools as large computers and refined simulation techniques.

In a book on computers and culture, J. David Bolter makes the following forceful statement:

> Until recently, however, our technical skills were so feeble in comparison with the natural forces of climate and chemistry that we could not seriously affect our environment for good or ill, except over the millenia. High technology promises to give us a new power over nature, both our own nature and that of our planet, so that the very future of civilization depends upon our intelligent use of high technology.[34]

He further notes that the crucial element in high technology is the computer. Clearly, the attempt to locate the computer in the history of technology, to survey its applications, to probe associated benefits and problems, and to assess the future impact is a worthwhile and in fact necessary exercise.

As with most technological innovations, the choice of when and how to proceed is not usually left up to the individual members of society. Governments and companies, both large and small, multinational and local, have the power and resources to make the important decisions. As ordinary citizens, we live in a world that for the most part is not of our making. Nevertheless, an informed and sufficiently aroused public can make a difference.

In discussing the nature of a liberal democracy, the Canadian political scientist C. B. MacPherson analyzed the opinions of John Dewey as follows:

> He had few illusions about the actual democratic system, or about the democratic quality of a society dominated by motives of individual and corporate gain. The root difficulty lay not in any defects in the machinery of government but in the fact that the democratic public was "still largely inchoate and unorganized," and unable to see what forces of economic and technological organization it was up against. There was no tinkering with the political machinery: the prior problem was "that of discovering the means by which a scattered, mobile, and manifold public may so recognize itself as to define and express its interests." The public's present incompetence to do this was traced to its failure to understand the technological and scientific forces which had made it so helpless.[35]

SUMMARY

Many of the decisions taken by computer professionals have serious social repercussions and affect the well-being of many individuals. The past few years have witnessed serious ethical dilemmas in reproductive biology, including *in vitro* fertilization and surrogate motherhood, and ethical breakdowns in the financial markets, mainly associated with insider trading. All of these issues have awakened an interest in ethical behavior and have stimulated the academic field of applied ethics.

Three major approaches, with of course many subdivisions, have emerged. These are ethical relativism, utilitarianism, and the class of deontological theories. They all attempt to characterize ethical behavior for individuals, but additional questions are raised when the behavior of doctors, lawyers, and other professionals is included. There is some debate about how a professional's responsibility to self, client, and society at large can be reconciled. Four case studies explore a variety of situations that may arise when engineers and information systems specialists encounter ethical problems. These may serve to illustrate the distance between theory and practice. Under some circumstances, it may be necessary for individuals to "go public," however painful that may be, because institutions are unresponsive to genuine misdeeds.

Most professional organizations have adopted codes of ethics or standards of behavior to guide their members and to announce to the public the level of conduct that can be expected of their members. Such codes attempt to resolve the potential conflict between social and professional responsibility.

That group of computer addicts, sometimes called hackers, seem to operate under a set of "principles" at considerable odds with those held by the vast majority of the information processing community. Computer scientists, in general, may be faced with difficult choices about the immediate and long-term impact of computers.

Especially troublesome are military applications; cautionary remarks have been addressed to computer scientists by Joseph Weizenbaum and Langdon Winner, distinguished critics of the technological imperative.

NOTES

1. Myron Magnet, "The Decline & Fall of Business Ethics," *Fortune,* December 8, 1986, p. 65.
2. Felix Rohatyn, "The Blight on Wall Street,"*The New York Review of Books,* March 12, 1987, p. 21.
3. Stephen Koepp, Harry Kelly, and Raji Samghabadi, "Having it All, Then Throwing it All Away," *Time,* May 25, 1987, p. 26.
4. Robert Taylor, "U.S. May Boost New York Office Staff To Pursue Mounting Securities Fraud," *The Wall Street Journal,* January 19, 1988, p. 12.
5. The *Business Week*/Harris Poll, August 1986. *World Opinion Update,* September 1986, p. 108.
6. Albert Camus, *The Myth of Sisyphus* (New York: Knopf, 1957), p. 65.
7. Deborah G. Johnson, *Computer Ethics* (Englewood Cliffs, New Jersey: Prentice-Hall, 1985), p. 6.
8. Raziel Abelson, "History of Ethics." In Paul Edwards (ed.), *The Encyclopedia of Philosophy, Volume Three* (New York: Macmillan, 1967) p. 95.
9. *Ibid.*
10. Johnson, *Computer Ethics,* p. 17.
11. Sissela Bok, "Kant's Arguments in Support of the Maxim 'Do What is Right though the World Should Perish'," in David M. Rosenthal and Fadlou Shehadi (eds.), *Applied Ethics and Ethical Theory* (Salt Lake City: University of Utah Press, 1988), pp. 191–193.
12. *Ibid.,* p. 210.
13. James H. Moor, "What is Computer Ethics?" *Metaphilosophy,* **16**(4), October 1985, p. 266.
14. Disciplinary Rule DR 5.21 of the Association for Computing Machinery Code of Professional Conduct.
15. Stephen H. Unger, *Controlling Technology: Ethics and the Responsible Engineer* (New York: Holt, Rinehart & Winston, 1982), pp. 32–55.
16. Mark S. Frankel, "Professional Codes: Why, How, and with What Impact?" *Journal of Business Ethics,* **8**(2 & 3), February–March 1989, pp. 110–111.
17. *Ibid.,* pp. 111–112.
18. C. Dianne Martin and David H. Martin, "Comparison of Ethics Codes of Computer Professionals," presented at an Ethics Symposium organized by the Special Interest Group on Computers and Society of the Association of Computing Machinery, Washington, D.C., September 1990. An earlier version of this paper appeared in *Social Science Computer Review,* **9**(1), 1990, and *Computers and Society,* **20**(2), June 1990, pp. 18–29. Note that the IEEE Code of Ethics used in this paper has been superseded by the one in Figure 14-2.
19. Samuel C. Florman, "A Skeptic Views Ethics in Engineering," *IEEE Spectrum,* August 1982, p. 57.
20. Case 1 in Donald Christiansen, "Ethical Judgments," *IEEE Spectrum,* February 1989, p. 25. Copyright © 1989 IEEE.
21. Donald Christiansen, "Ethical Dilemmas Revisited," *IEEE Spectrum,* April 1989, p. 21. Copyright © 1989 IEEE.
22. Thanks to Mary Culnan, School of Business Administration, Georgetown University, for the original version.
23. Eric Weiss, "A Self-Assessment Procedure Dealing with Ethics in Computing," *Communications of the ACM,* **25**(3), March 1982, pp. 185–191. The material was edited by Mr. Weiss from Donn Parker, *Ethical Conflicts in Computer Science and Technology* (New York: AFIPS Press, 1981).
24. *Ibid.,* p. 191.
25. Eric Weiss (ed.), "The XXII Self-Assessment: The Ethics of Computing," *Communications of the ACM,* **33**(11), November 1990, pp. 119, 127–130. This material was edited from Donn R. Parker, Susan Swope, and Bruce N. Baker, "Ethical Conflicts in Information and Computer Science, Technology and Business," Final Report, August 1988, SRI International Project 2609.
26. Sissela Bok, *Secrets: On the Ethics of Concealment and Revelation.* Copyright © 1983 Pantheon Books, a Division of Random House, Inc. (Source: Vintage Books paperback, 1984, p. 211.), also by permission of Oxford University Press.

27. *Ibid.*, pp. 214–215.
28. Steven Levy, *Hackers: Heroes of the Computer Revolution.* Copyright © 1984 Doubleday, a division of Bantam, Doubleday, Dell Publishing Group, Inc. (Source: Dell paperback, 1985, pp. 39–49.)
29. Hannah Arendt, *Eichmann in Jerusalem: A Report on the Banality of Evil, Revised and Enlarged* (New York: The Viking Press, 1964), p. 25.
30. Langdon Winner, *Autonomous Technology: Technics-out-of-control as a Theme in Political Thought* (Cambridge, Massachusetts: MIT Press, 1978), pp. 303–304.
31. David Lorge Parnas, "Professional Responsibility to Blow the Whistle on SDI," in M. David Ermann, Mary B. Williams, and Claudio Gutierrez (eds.), *Computers, Ethics & Society* (New York: Oxford University Press, 1990), p. 360. Reprinted with permission from *Abacus* (Springer-Verlag, Heidelberg, Winter 1987), copyright © 1987 David Lorge Parnas.
32. *Ibid.*, pp. 364–365.
33. Joseph Weizenbaum, "Facing Reality: Computer Scientists Aid War Efforts," *Technology Review,* January 1987, pp. 22–23. Reprinted with permission from Technology Review, copyright © 1987.
34. Reprinted from *Turing's Man: Western Culture in the Computer Age,* by J. David Bolter. Copyright © 1984 The University of North Carolina Press, pp. 3–4.
35. C. B. MacPherson, *The Life and Times of Liberal Democracy* (Oxford, England: Oxford University Press, 1980), p. 73. By permission of Oxford University Press.

ADDITIONAL READINGS

Introduction

Ermann, M. David; Williams, Mary B., and Gutierrez, Claudio. *Computers, Ethics & Society.* New York: Oxford University Press, 1990.

Ethics

Bloombecker, J. J. "Computer Ethics: An Antidote to Despair." *Computers & Society,* **16**(4) and **17**(1), Winter–Spring 1987, pp. 3–11.

Edwards, Paul (ed.) *The Encyclopedia of Philosophy, Volume Three.* (New York: Macmillan, 1967, pp. 69–134.

Fitzgerald, Karen. "Whistle-Blowing: Not Always a Losing Game." *IEEE Spectrum,* December 1990, pp. 49–52.

Iannone, A. Pablo (ed.). *Contemporary Moral Controversies in Technology.* New York: Oxford University Press, 1987.

Rosenthal, David M. and Shehadi, Fadlou (eds.). *Applied Ethics and Ethical Theory.* Salt Lake City: University of Utah Press, 1988.

Williams, Oliver F., Reilly, Frank K., and Houck, John W. (eds.). *Ethics and the Investment Industry.* Savage, Maryland: Rowman & Littlefield, 1989).

Professionalism

Andrews, Kenneth R. (ed.). *Ethics in Practice: Managing the Moral Corporation.* Boston, Massachusetts: Harvard Business School Press, 1989.

Benson, George C. S. "Codes of Ethics." *Journal of Business Ethics,* **8**(5), May 1989, pp. 305–319.

Bowman, James S. "Ethics in Government: A National Survey of Public Administrators." *Public Administration Review,* May–June 1990, pp. 345–353.
Hoffman, W. Michael and Moore, Jennifer Mills (eds.). *Business Ethics: Readings and Cases in Corporate Morality, Second Edition.* New York: McGraw-Hill, 1990.
Johnson, Deborah G. and Snapper, John W. (eds.). *Ethical Issues in the Use of Computers.* Belmont, California: Wadsworth Publishing, 1985.
Lewis, Philip V. "Ethical Principles for Decision Makers: A Longitudinal Survey." *Journal of Business Ethics,* 8(4), April 1989, pp. 271–278.
Neumann, Peter G. "Certifying Professionals." *Communications of the ACM* **34**(2), February 1991, p. 130.

Final Remarks

DeMarco, Joseph P. and Fox, Richard M. (eds.). *New Directions in Ethics: The Challenge of Applied Ethics.* New York: Routledge & Kegan Paul, 1986.
Forester, Tom and Morrison, Perry. *Computer Ethics: Cautionary Tales and Ethical Dilemmas.* Cambridge, Massachusetts: MIT Press, 1990.
Lackey, Douglas P. (ed.). *Ethics and Strategic Defense: American Philosophers Debate Star Wars and the Future of Nuclear Deterrence.* Belmont, California: Wadsworth Publishing, 1989.

APPENDIX

MAGAZINES, JOURNALS, AND ASSOCIATIONS

The number of popular magazines devoted to computers is large and growing. Most of these appeal to users of specific home computers such as the IBM PC, the Macintosh, the Amiga, and the Atari. This list includes only magazines of more general interest.

POPULAR MAGAZINES

Computer

Byte — For computer professionals and home users. Reviews of new products and occasional articles on social issues.

Computers & Electronics — The leading computer magazine in sales. For computer professionals and business users.

Computerworld — Tabloid format. For business users. Reviews of major trends, government policies, and occasionally social issues.

Datamation — Sold primarily by subscription. For business professionals. Wide coverage of the industry. Informed articles by data processing professionals and academics. Renowned for its annual list of the top 100 data processing companies.

Personal Computing — Very large circulation, for business users. Regular reviews of new equipment and software.

Technology

Discover — A Time-Life publication with a wide coverage of scientific and technological developments, including a section on computers.

Electronics Week
Excellent survey of developments in electronics with both national and international coverage. Somewhat more technical than a typical newsstand magazine. Regular analyses of production, sales, and applications of electronic components.

New Scientist
A British publication with wide coverage of scientific and technological innovations. Somewhat oriented to British issues.

Scientific American
The most prestigious popular science magazine in the United States. The articles are written by prominent scientists, with excellent graphics. Computers and related technology are treated infrequently but very well.

Technology Review
Published by the Massachusetts Institute of Technology. Well-written and interesting articles on a variety of issues. High level of social concern.

Financial and Business

Business Week
Regular, extensive coverage of technological developments and associated business, labor, and economic issues. Frequent in-depth studies of videotex, electronic funds transfer systems, and the computer industry, especially IBM.

Fortune
Well known for the FORTUNE 500 list of leading U.S. companies. Excellent coverage of technology. Good record of spotting trends and anticipating problems.

Wall Street Journal
Primarily business-oriented but with frequent in depth articles on computers

[illegible]eneral

[illegible], Newsweek
Regular, limited coverage of developments in computers.

[illegible]ew York Times
Excellent treatment of scientific issues in the Tuesday "Science Times" section. Extensive coverage of business and social problems, especially privacy and labor issues.

[illegible]urnals

[illegible]
A publication of the Institute of Electrical and Electronics Engineers. Covers technical issues in papers written by academics. Special issues on such topics as security and CAD/CAM.

Communications of the ACM	A publication of the Association of Computing Machinery. Includes state-of-the-art articles by leading figures in computer science. In depth analysis of many social issues. Overall, a high proportion of theoretical papers.
Science	A publication of the American Association for the Advancement of Science. Most of the articles deal with advanced research topics in biology, chemistry, physics, and so forth. Periodic, serious coverage of technological advances and their social impact.
IEEE Spectrum	Important technical journal that treats serious topics at a nonspecialist level. Special issues on social impact of technology, the Fifth Generation, and education. Highly recommended.
Harvard Business Review	Coverage of important issues associated with computers in business. Regular treatment of management information systems, impact on labor, and Japanese management practices.

ASSOCIATIONS AND SOCIETIES

ACM Special Interest Group on Computers and Society (SIGCAS)

SIGCAS publishes a quarterly newsletter that deals with many issues such as privacy, copyright laws, crime, work, and so forth. It is edited by Richard S. Rosenberg, Department of Computer Science, University of British Columbia, Vancouver, BC, Canada V6T 1Z2. (rosen@cs.ubc.ca)

IEEE Society on Social Implications of Technology (SSIT)

SSIT publishes a magazine with papers on a wide range of technological issues. It also sponsors conferences and workshops. For more information contact Professor Ronald Kline, School of Electrical Engineering, Philips Hall, Cornell University, Ithaca, NY 14850.

Computer Professionals for Social Responsibility (CPSR)

This organization has chapters in Berkeley, Los Angeles, Palo Alto, San Jose, Santa Cruz, Boston, New York, Washington, Madison, and Seattle. It is concerned with more radical issues than the above two organizations. Its newsletter has carried articles on military applications of computers, American computer professionals helping in Nicaragua, and the role of computers in nuclear weapons planning. The CPSR newsletter is published quarterly by Computer Professionals for Social Responsibility, Mark Hall and Daniel Ingalls, eds., P.O. Box 717, Palo Alto, CA 94301.

There are numerous organizations for computer professionals in such areas as the following:

Data Processing	Data Processing Management Association 505 Busse Highway Park Ridge, ILL. 60068 Canadian Information Processing Society (L'Association Canadienne de l'Informatique) 243 College Street, 5th floor Toronto, Ontario, Canada M5T 2Y1
Information Science	The American Society for Information Science 1010 Sixteenth Street, N.W. Second Floor Washington, D.C. 20036
Academic Issues	The Association for Computing Machinery 1133 Avenue of the Americas New York, N.Y. 10036 The Institute of Electrical and Electronics Engineers Computer Society 1109 Spring Street Suite 202 Silver Springs, MD. 20910
Artificial Intelligence	The American Association for Artificial Intelligence 445 Burgess Drive Menlo Park, Calif. 94025 The ACM Special Interest Group on Artificial Intelligence (See ACM address).
Information Retrieval	The ACM Special Interest Group on Information Retrieval (See ACM address).

INDEX

N

O

P

R

S

T

U

V

W

X

Z

ISBN 0-12-597130-3
90018
9 780125 971300